Real Estate Practice
in California

SECOND EDITION

REAL ESTATE PRACTICE IN CALIFORNIA

Edna A. Lundberg

Realtor and Instructor
Pasadena City College

PRENTICE-HALL, INC., Englewood Cliffs, New Jersey

PRENTICE-HALL SERIES IN CALIFORNIA REAL ESTATE

ISBN: 0-13-765222-4

Library of Congress Catalog Card Number: 79-38412

Printed in the United States of America

10 9 8 7 6 5 4 3 2 1

Prentice-Hall International, Inc., London
Prentice-Hall of Australia, Pty. Ltd., Sydney
Prentice-Hall of Canada, Ltd., Toronto
Prentice-Hall of India Private Limited, New Delhi
Prentice-Hall of Japan, Inc., Tokyo

TO SUNNY AND DAVID

Contents

Preface

In 1957, a study of the educational needs of real estate licensees was instituted by the University of California. The research was financed by a portion of the state license fees of brokers and salesmen. As an outgrowth of this analysis, real estate programs were established by the University extension and developed later in the junior and state colleges. Working in close cooperation with the Department of Real Estate and the California Real Estate Association, these institutes provided the best answer to the educational needs of the new licensee. Such professional training supplies him with the confidence needed as he enters a formidably competitive field. In 1971 there were over 36,000 students enrolled in real estate courses being offered in seventy-seven of the ninety-five junior colleges in the state.

Real Estate Practice in California is primarily a text for the student enrolled in these courses and has been written in the language of the layman. Although intended primarily for classroom use, it will also prove valuable to the new salesman by familiarizing him with the expert selling practices of the industry. Ethical operations, honest and reputable merchandising methods, rather than "sure-fire selling gimmicks" are stressed. It is the author's conviction (based on twenty-five years' experience in the field) that the professional approach to real estate selling, with all that it implies, is not only the best but the *only* way to build an enduring business. The broker who can finally state with honest conviction that his clientele looks to him for professional advice concerning real estate problems has his success in the industry assured.

Acknowledgments

The author wishes to acknowledge her indebtedness to the following firms and individuals who have graciously contributed to this revision: The California Real Estate Association; Women's Council of NAREB; Stone and Schulte, realtors of San Jose; Robert C. Westmyer, president of Rex L. Hodges Realty Company, Long Beach; William T. Leonard, executive vice-president of Associated Home Builders of the Greater East Bay, Inc., Berkeley, and the West contra Costa Board of Realtors for permission to duplicate their commercial-property brief; the Department of Real Estate, particularly R. B. (Nick) Nicholls, senior deputy commissioner, Education and Research; Fran McCreery, supervisor Occupational Education, Pasadena Community College; Security First National Bank, Los Angeles; Mrs. Richard Higgins, escrow officer, Arcadia Branch, Bank of America; Title Insurance and Trust Company, Los Angeles; Security Title Insurance Company, Los Angeles; Bank of America National Trust and Savings Association, Los Angeles; Property Research Corporation, Century City, Los Angeles; Hugh L. Gary of Gary Escrow Service, Van Nuys, and the many former students of my real estate practice classes at Pasadena City College, together with many of my fellow realtors throughout the state who have so generously shared with me their knowledge and experiences.

E.A.L.

1

Opportunities in and Potential for California Real Estate

A Brief History of California's Growth

The name *California* first appeared in a popular romance, *Las Serges de Esplandian* (*The Deeds of Esplandian*), which was published in Spain in the year 1510. Its author, Garcia Ordonez de Montalvo, wrote as follows:

> Know ye that at the right hand of the Indes there is an island named California,[1] very close to that part of the Terrestrial Paradise, which was inhabited by black women, without a single man among them, and that they lived in the manner of Amazons. They were robust of body, with strong and passionate hearts and great virtues. The island itself is one of the wildest in the world on account of the bold and craggy rocks. Their weapons were all made of gold. The island everywhere abounds with gold and precious stones, and upon it no other metal was found. They lived in caves, well excavated. They had many ships with which they sailed to other coasts to make forays, and the men whom they took as prisoners they killed. In this island, named California, there are many griffins. In no other part of the world can they be found. And there ruled over that island of California a queen of majestic proportions, more beautiful than all others, and in the very great vigor of her womanhood. She was desirous of accomplishing great deeds. She was valiant and courageous, and ardent, with a brave heart, and had ambitions to execute nobler actions than had been performed by any other rulers. . . . Her name was Calafia.

The first known use of the name *California* by an explorer appears in Cabrillo's diary. This daring Portuguese mariner, sailing in the service of Spain, anchored his two small ships in San Diego Port on September 28, 1542 and found shelter behind the high cliffs of Point Loma. With his landing, history began in California. Spanish occupation of what is now modern California dates, however, from 1769. In that year Spanish soldiers and priests formulated a plan calling for the establishment in the new land of presidios, missions, and pueblos.

The plan was intended to increase the flow of revenues to the royal government and to extend the frontiers of New Spain through the occupation of Alta California. Gaspar de Portola, an experienced Spanish soldier, was made governor of the area. A Franciscan priest, Junipero Serra, a powerful leader and a fervently religious man, was selected to accomplish the spiritual conquest of the new land and later was to prove himself California's greatest hero.

Portola's pioneering march north is a classic of California adventure. His vivid diaries of this journey tell of the land and the Indians and reveal that he failed to recognize the Port of Monterey, traveling on to within sight of the Bay of San Francisco. Though Spain's occupation of Alta California had begun in earnest, the first years were difficult because of the problems of getting supplies. Indian hostility and the clashing viewpoints of military and religious heads also contributed to the critical period. In 1773, Serra made a long trip by land and sea to Mexico City to report on California's needs to the new and dynamic viceroy, Bucareli. The result was regularly scheduled supply ships sailing from San Blas. Additional support was supplied by Juan Bautista de Anza, who at the same time established an overland route from Sonora to Monterey. Exploration was encouraged, and a workable plan of government and administration was formulated.

Before they had finished their task, the Spaniards

[1] Even a century after Cabrillo's visit to southern California, some map makers liked to show California as an island. Edwin Corle, *The Royal Highway* (Indianapolis: The Bobbs-Merrill Co., Inc., 1949), pp. 1–2.

had established four presidios—San Diego, Santa Barbara, Monterey, and San Francisco; three pueblos —San Jose, Los Angeles (and the short-lived Branciforte near Santa Cruz), with a chain of missions that extended from the first one at San Diego to the last one at Sonoma (this built in the Mexican period). With occupation, the title to the land of California became vested in the king of Spain.

Two pueblos that endured were founded by the Spanish—San Jose in 1777 and Los Angeles in 1781. Los Angeles had its inception when eleven families recruited in the Sonora and Sinaloa areas of Mexico were brought to Mission San Gabriel to establish the pueblo. "Founding" consisted probably of tired and dusty people unpacking mules and being assigned house and farm lots under the plans worked out earlier by Governor Neve.

Portola and his party traveled north from San Diego through the coastal plains. As they entered the Orange County area, the two priests with them performed the first baptism of Indians in California.[2] This baptism took place near what is now the city of San Clemente. In the Ventura and Santa Barbara areas, the Portola party passed through many villages of Chumash Indians, who, with their large canoes, plied the waters between the mainland and the Channel Islands.

The late Indian authority, Alice C. Fletcher, in speaking of the Indian concept of the earth as a mother (in her contribution to "Land Tenure," *Smithsonian Institute Bulletin,* No. 30), writes:

> In this primitive and religious sense land was not regarded as property; it was like the air. It was something necessary to the life of the race and therefore not to be appropriated by any individual or group of individuals to the exclusion of all others.

In this sense, *occupancy* was the only tenure recognized by the Indians.

The Missions

Under the tireless direction of Father Serra, a chain of missions was planned and established. The first was founded in the San Diego area on July 16, 1769, followed two years later by the establishment of Mission San Gabriel Archangel on the San Gabriel River and in the following year, on September 1, 1772, by that of the Mission San Luis Obispo. Others followed in the years succeeding, including Mission San Buenaventura, founded in 1782. Bancroft describes Serra as "limping from mission to mission with a lame foot that must never be cured, fasting much and passing sleepless nights, depriving himself of comfortable clothing and nutritious food." By the time he died in 1784 (at his favorite mission of San Carlos de Carmelo), a chain of nine missions had been established.[3]

Established November 1, 1776, Mission San Juan Capistrano, "The Jewel of the Missions," with its arches, gardens, fountained courts, and famous swallows, is a favorite with visitors today. The last of the southern California missions to be founded was Mission Santa Ines in 1784. Its setting in the Santa Ines Valley north of Santa Barbara is one of California's loveliest.

The famous official road, El Camino Real (the Royal Highway), linked the established missions and pueblos. The imaginative traveler today may follow the bells of El Camino Real, reliving, in fantasy, the glorious days of early California.

The Ranchos

The first grants of ranchos were little more than cattle-grazing permits. They date from 1784, when Spanish Governor Pedro Fages granted land concessions to several Spanish army veterans who were planning retirement. In the whole of California, probably not more than thirty grants of ranchos were made during the Spanish period, which ended in 1822, with Mexico's successful revolt against Spain. The rancho movement did not get fully under way until the 1830s. The missions were taken over by the Mexican government, which placed a civil administrator in charge of each establishment and put the missions' vast landholdings at the disposal of the government.

Whereas mission buildings and stock were neglected, a land rush began, and many a rich valley or plain became a privately owned rancho. As in Spanish days, the grants came directly from the governor. Southern California land during the Spanish and Mexican regimes was devoted almost entirely to cattle raising. Flavor to life on the ranchos was provided by fiestas, weddings, rodeos, bullfights, and horse racing.

The Pueblos

The social and trading center for the owners of ranchos in southern California was the pueblo of Los

[2] Some historians have placed California's Indian population previous to the white man at 250,000.

[3] Ultimately there were twenty-one, including the famous Mission Santa Barbara, "The Queen of the Missions," established December 4, 1786.

Angeles (founded September 4, 1781). Los Angeles was a village of one-story adobe homes and shops surrounding a plaza with the church predominating. The village in 1845 attained the distinction of being the actual capital of Alta California.[4] Life in pastoral California was simple, feudal, and, in retrospect, romantic. It is noteworthy, however, that to the end of the Mexican rule in 1846, few owners of ranchos found reading and writing a necessary accomplishment.

In the midst of pastoral activities, gold was discovered in Placeritas Canyon north of Mission San Fernando on March 9, 1842. (This was six years before Marshall's famous discovery at Sutter's Mill.) A gold rush on a minor scale lasted several years, but interest had ended before the great gold rush of 1849.

Pio Pico, the last Mexican governor of California, symbolized in himself the Spanish, Mexican, and American periods. Born at San Gabriel in 1801, he lived nearly a half century in the American regime and at the peak of his power was the owner of many large ranchos. However, at his death at the age of ninety-three, his creditors had stripped him of all his possessions.

The Treaty of Guadalupe Hidalgo in 1848, ending the Mexican War, provided for protection of property rights of Mexicans in California. William Carey Jones, a confidential agent of the U. S. Government, who was sent a year later to investigate land records, compiled a report which has become a landmark in the history of California titles. After receiving the record, Congress appointed a commission and required Californians to prove their titles. The act, passed in 1851, *placed the burden of proof of ownership* on everyone who claimed land in California (this, in spite of a condition to the contrary in the Treaty of Guadalupe Hidalgo). The three-man commission appointed spent five years in California working on land titles. In the event of either confirmation or rejection by the commission of any claim, there was an alternate appeal to the U.S. court for final decision. After confirmation by the courts and an official survey, a patent was issued by the U.S. Government.[5] While the Land Commission and the courts were working to confirm the land titles, immigrants from the east were flocking to California. The rancho grants included "the most usable lands in California." It was inevitable that a conflict would arise between the newcomers and those involved in the process of attempting to prove their claims. Squatting on the land of others was a frequent event, and violent squatter riots occurred. Although land titles in California were never based on squatter claims, California courts were still hearing these cases as late as the 1930s.

When California was admitted to the Union, the state became the owner of all lands lying under navigable streams and lakes and of all land below tidewater and below ordinary watermark. Ownership passed from the United States without the formality of a grant. The government retained as public lands all those not specifically confirmed as Mexican or Spanish grants, tidelands, cities, or towns.

With the great increase in the population of the state, most of the large ranchos have become building lots or small farms. There were no registration or recording laws under the Spanish or Mexican governments, but one of the first acts of the California legislature was to adopt a recording system. The Recording Act of California provides that, after being acknowledged, any instrument or judgment affecting the title to or possession of real property may be recorded.

California's Growth Begins

Southern California drew Indians in prehistoric days and has drawn white men since 1769, but the flow of people to this area has been unabated since California became part of the United States.

> Sometimes the flow has been in the nature of a flood as happened when the Santa Fe Railroad reached Los Angeles in 1885 and engaged in a rate war with the Southern Pacific. It was also true in the early 1920's when the influx to Southern California consisted practically of a mass migration. To a lesser degree it has been true in all the other prosperous periods that have reached climaxes in peak years of real estate activity. These peak years —boom years—have been 1855, 1875, 1887, 1923, and 1946. They have come approximately every 20 years, and, while not peculiar to Southern California, have had a luxuriant flowering in this area.
>
> The role played by climate in persuading people from the earliest times to come to Southern California and to stay here is obvious and has received adequate attention from historians and commentators. Climate explains most things that have happened in this section—agricultural activity, moviemaking, year-round industrialism—but the happy finding of oil is something else.
>
> Southern California's greatest boom was that of the 1880's. Round-trip tickets from the Missouri River to California were sold for as low as fifteen dollars and for a few days at one dollar. Thousands

[4] It had been decreed the capital in 1835, but the people of Monterey resisted the move for a decade.

[5] The average length of time elapsing between presentation of a claim to the Land Commission and the issuance of a patent was seventeen years.

of persons in the East were thus enticed to visit the West Coast. The railroads had land to sell, so their interest in causing the East to move West was very real. The Santa Fe organized the California Excursion Association—with headquarters in Chicago and Los Angeles—to turn the attention of the United States to Southern California and actually to bring the citizens of America to the land of sunshine and subdivisions.

Land prices leaped and shot skyward. The selling of lots and acreage took place everywhere—at the curb, at saloon bars, in restaurants, on the tract, and at all hours of the day and night. New towns sprang up along the railroads—with new hotels and colleges invariable features. To draw crowds there were elephants, human freaks, free lunches, and bands.

The whole of Southern California, and particularly Los Angeles County, was overlaid with a crazyquilt of subdivisions. Never since has there been such a frenzied cutting up of acreage into town, mountain, desert, and beach lots.

Well-known towns and districts had their origin or principal development in the boom of the Eighties, among them Hollywood, Claremont, Fullerton, Arcadia, Burbank, Glendale, Whittier, La Canada, Redlands, Corona, Beaumont, Elsinor, Oceanside, Escondido, La Jolla, and Avalon. Most of the cities and towns born of the period survived the collapse that followed and lived to see new booms and larger populations. Agriculture came into its own in the 1880's, with the citrus, olive, grape, and walnut industries becoming firmly established. Because of this particular boom the United States never forgot that in the southwest corner of the land there was good climate, good soil, and water for development. The people kept coming.[6]

The land fever in southern California began to spread to the central and northern parts of the state. In the 1930s, citrus lands were slowly being replaced by industrial and residential subdivisions, though the big subdivision push really began in the late 1940s following World War II. By 1980 California is expected to reach a total of nearly 23 million people. Through natural increase and the wave of immigration, California gains more than one new resident every two minutes. Governor Edmund G. Brown described the more than 1,000 new people pouring over California's borders each day as "the greatest migration in the history of the world." Almost twice as many new homes as presently exist will be needed to house the burgeoning population in the next eighteen years. (In 1963, Ventura was the state's fastest growing county.)

[6] W. W. Robinson, *Panorama, A Picture History of Southern California* (Los Angeles: Title Insurance and Trust Company, 1953).

"The sharpest advance of people in the state between 1960 and 1970 was in the age group of eighteen to twenty-four (in 1970)." Hopes for job opportunities, favorable climate, and abundant housing all played a part in the migration. Those who settled favored urban or suburban life; the urban fringes (cities of 50,000 or more) showed the highest rate of population expansion, whereas rural areas remained almost static.[7]

California's Industrial Age

California's climate, which is the direct cause of her population increase, has also had a bearing on the development of manufacturing. The population growth has closely paralleled the increase in job opportunities. The pace of industrial expansion in southern California, for example, has greatly exceeded the national average. In 1963, California ranked as one of the leading three manufacturing states of the Union. Manufacturing employment in the southern part was heavily centered in three counties: Los Angeles, Orange, and San Diego, accounting for roughly 90 percent of the area's total manufacturing employment. However, early in 1946 a trend toward employment gains in various nonmanufacturing sectors over those of manufacturing employment evidenced itself. The steady increase in the nonmanufacturing jobs has been slowly taking up the slack in the labor market, with the last few months of 1963 showing the gains in employment coming almost entirely from this group of workers. The largest growth came from government, construction, and the finance-realestate-insurance categories. In other words, California continues to diversify, depending less on any one industry.[8]

Because of the high purchasing power of the state's inhabitants, the greatest market for California goods is California itself. There is an annual need for 150,000 new jobs. This necessitates more homes, schools, and retail establishments. It follows that the demand for new housing coincides with the population increase. Of this new housing, nearly three new units have been built in the suburbs for each one in the central cities.

[7] For a complete study, see the report by Wallace F. Smith, *Housing Market Data from Census Materials, a Study of California and the Bay Area* (Berkeley: University of California, Institute of Business and Research, Real Estate Research Program, Report 21, 1963).

[8] *Monthly Summary of Business Conditions in Southern California,* Vol. 43, No. 3 (Los Angeles: Security First National Bank, March 1, 1963).

Development of Real Estate Controls

As people began to produce crops beyond their capacity to consume at home, some moved to centers and specialized in making products which could be exchanged for food grown by someone else. Cities resulted from this migration and concentration of people, a process we call *urbanization.* Gradually, certain land came to be looked upon as prized, not necessarily for its fertility, but for its location as sites for residential, commercial and industrial uses. Trading in land in turn gave rise to another specialized group of people who traded, improved, bought and sold on their own account or as a service to others on a fee basis. *Thus, the real estate business and the real estate broker, operator, and manager had their beginnings.*

In America, many of the founders of the various colonies were not only pioneers; they were also the first real estate operators. William Penn, James Oglethorpe and others used variations of present day methods to attract people to America and induce them to settle on lands which had been granted to the founders by the Crown. *They were the forerunners* of the present day subdivider....

The person in later history who seems to resemble more nearly our modern broker was known as a *"conveyancer."* He was an attorney who spent most of his time negotiating land transfers and drawing up the necessary legal papers. He was pretty much an abstractor, escrow agent, and broker, all rolled up into one person. Finally the business reached the point where specialization was necessary, and he chose either the legal end or the actual negotiation of the sale of the property. *In the latter capacity he became the prototype of the present day real estate agent or broker.* [Italics the writer's.][9]

Licensing

...As specialists grew up within the field and with the increase in the mobility of people, particularly the western movement, there was a good deal of unorganized and other unscrupulous competition. The real estate people themselves began to feel the need of some controlling organization.... It was not until 1917, however, that a state regulatory body and law was first promulgated. This occurred in California. Now, every state but one has a license law and a regulatory body.[10]

The original California Real Estate Act was adopted in 1919 and upheld by the California Supreme Court in November of that year. The State Real Estate Commission as we know it today was established by legislative act in 1937. It was known as "State Real Estate Board," the name being changed in 1957. The official body consists of the Real Estate Commissioner and eight other members, each appointed by the governor for a four-year term. (Four are appointed from the southern part of the state and four from the northern area.) Two members of the commission are public members, one of which must be qualified as an attorney and one as a public-planning official. Except for the Real Estate Commissioner, members of the commission serve without compensation and are reimbursed only for actual and necessary traveling expenses in the performance of official business.

The main purpose of the Real Estate Law is to regulate those engaged in the real estate business as agents. Practically every activity in connection with a real estate transaction (when the activity is performed for another or others and for a commission or fee or expectation thereof) requires a real estate license. Without a license one cannot legally collect a commission or fee for the performance of any of the above acts. The law provides for severe penalties for the person who acts or purports to act as a real estate broker or salesman without being duly licensed.

The Real Estate Law empowers the Commissioner to issue regulations to aid in the administration and enforcement of the law. *These regulations of the Real Estate Commissioner have the same force and effect as the law itself.*

Steps in Professionalization of the Real Estate Industry

Recognition by the California legislature of a need to provide direction in the development of the real estate business came in 1949. This resulted in a special appropriation of $50,000 for three years from the real estate fund[11] to establish the University of California's Real Estate Research Program. (Much had already been accomplished by the California Real Estate Association, which had pioneered the field in both research and education needs of the industry.) The inadequacies of both quality and quantity of educational opportunity (together with the apparent inefficiency in real estate dealings) had long caused concern among the leaders in the field. The majority of those engaged full time in the real estate business were making somewhat less than the income required to maintain an average standard of living. Surveys had indicated that the real estate salesman was at the bottom of the list when his economic and social status was compared with other

[9] *Reference Book* (Sacramento: California Dept. of Real Estate, 1971), Chap. 1.

[10] *Reference Book.*

[11] Made up of a portion of the license fees.

occupational groups. The needs for development of systematic plans for educational programs could be grouped into three categories: (a) educational opportunities for brokers and salesmen had been inadequate; (b) the strengthening of the examination for renewable licenses had created the need for greater preparation; and (c) the difficulties being experienced by licensees in meeting the conditions of a highly competitive market demonstrated a level of competition that required study and training in addition to experience.

Thus the coordinated program of real estate education in the California institutes of higher learning had its inception. Part of the funds from the 1949 appropriation was used for research; part was used for the establishment of the University extension certificate program. In 1952, a second appropriation of $300,000 for three years was made, followed by a third appropriation in 1955. The ensuing year, a special advisory committee was formed, consisting of representatives from the University of California and the state and community colleges to develop plans for California real estate research and education. Later, representatives from the industry, including the commissioner and the president and secretary of the California Real Estate Association, were added to the committee. The group became known as the Commissioner's Real Estate Educational and Research Advisory Committee (CREERAC), with the ultimate aim of the program "the upgrading of the real estate industry toward professionalization."

From the recommendations of this committee, funds in the amount of $31,000 were appropriated in June, 1957, and a study of real estate education and research needs in California was authorized. Its primary purpose was to analyze the needs of the industry and to propose courses of action to be taken in order that the business might be further developed.

Thus, the concentrated attempt at professionalizing the real estate business through coordinated efforts at the university, state, and community college levels, together with the California Real Estate Association, began in earnest. In addition to the academic courses being offered, professional groups composed of local realty boards, CREA, and the National Association of Real Estate Boards conduct sales conferences, seminars, and workshops in a variety of real estate subjects ranging from listing properties to real estate exchanges and property management. CREA, whose membership in 1971 stood at close to 54,000, conscientiously works for the improvement of the general welfare and professional standing of the real estate business by sponsoring legislation, establishing principles, and cooperating with educational institutions.

Licensing by examination has created a market for "cram" schools and short-cut methods for prospective licensees. Students of these schools are trained primarily to answer examination questions; consequently, licensees trained in this manner do not have the academic prelicensing background to pursue advanced courses. It is the present aim of the industry to provide academic courses in sufficient numbers to satisfy the needs of all prospective licensees. These courses are aimed at furnishing the applicant with a professional background *before* he takes his original state examination. The original recommendation of the advisory committee on real estate education and research was that basic courses be expanded in both scope, content, and duration of study. A two-semester sequence was suggested with the first-semester course in background information serving as a prerequisite to the second-semester course.

> The first semester course would be concerned with real estate economics. Topics considered would be related to the conditions that make for the marketability of real property, sources of funds for financing real property transactions, and services that can or should be provided by realtors. The second semester course would deal primarily with real estate transactions, the nature of contingencies that might affect the quality of a title to real property, and consideration of the kinds of choices that are available to sellers and buyers in real estate.
>
> Upon completion of the two semesters, the student should be equipped to enter the real estate business with (1) knowledge of the economic hazards related to selling property; (2) awareness of the importance of the activities of realtors; and (3) cognizance of the breadth of course content, which must be mastered in order to be prepared to provide clients with real and valuable services.[12]

As an outgrowth of these recommendations seventy-six of the ninety-five community colleges by 1970 had established an eight-course sequence (twenty-four units of credit) as a certificate program and applicable on an associate of arts degree. (In the 1969–70 program there was a total student enrollment of 36,000.)

Real Estate Education, Research, and Recovery Fund

Applicable sections of the real estate law were amended by the state legislature in 1963 to change the name of the special fund previously known as the

[12] *A Study of Real Estate Education and Research Needs in California* (Sacramento: California State Dept. of Education, 1959), p. 72.

Real Estate Education and Research Fund to the Real Estate Education, Research, and Recovery Fund. On January 1, 1964 the fund was, in effect, divided into two subfunds, one portion earmarked for real estate education and research and the other for the purpose of "recovery."

"Recovery" as it applied here refers generally to a special provision in the Real Estate Law. Under this provision an aggrieved person who obtains final judgment in court against any licensed person or persons on grounds of fraud, misrepresentation, or deceit, arising directly out of any transaction occurring on or after July 1, 1964 may file a verified application in court for an order directing payment from the fund of the actual and direct loss in such transaction up to the sum of ten thousand dollars of the amount unpaid upon the judgment.[13]

One-quarter of all real estate license fees collected are diverted to this fund. After excluding from the fund the first ten dollars of each license fee, 80 percent of the moneys is earmarked for real estate education and research purposes and 20 percent goes into the recovery fund.

Blueprint for Professionalization

During a San Francisco real estate education and research conference in September 1968, Commis-

[13] For full text on the "recovery feature," see *Reference Book.*

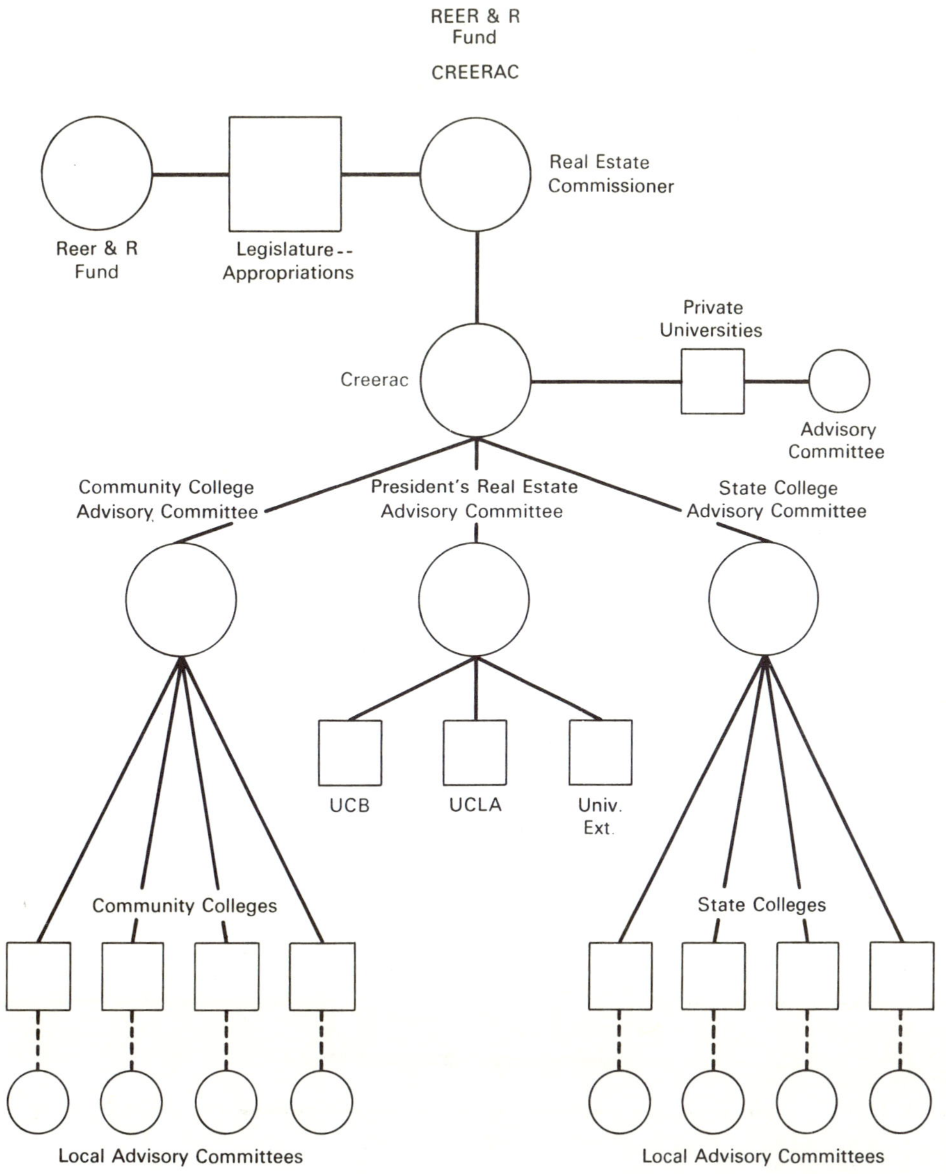

REVISED PROFESSIONALIZATION CHART

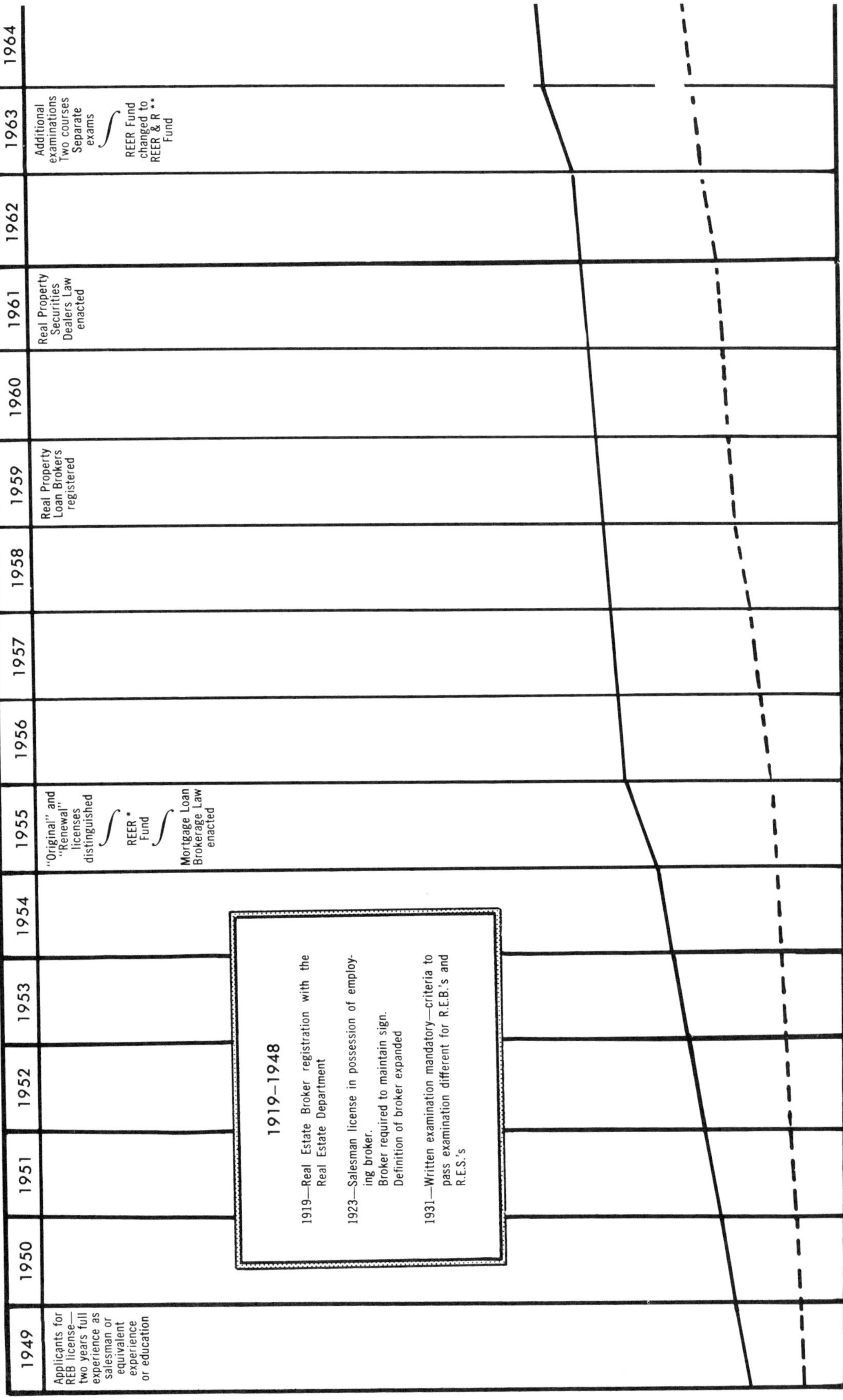

* Real Estate Education and Research

** Real Estate Education, Research and Recovery

*** Mineral, Oil and Gas

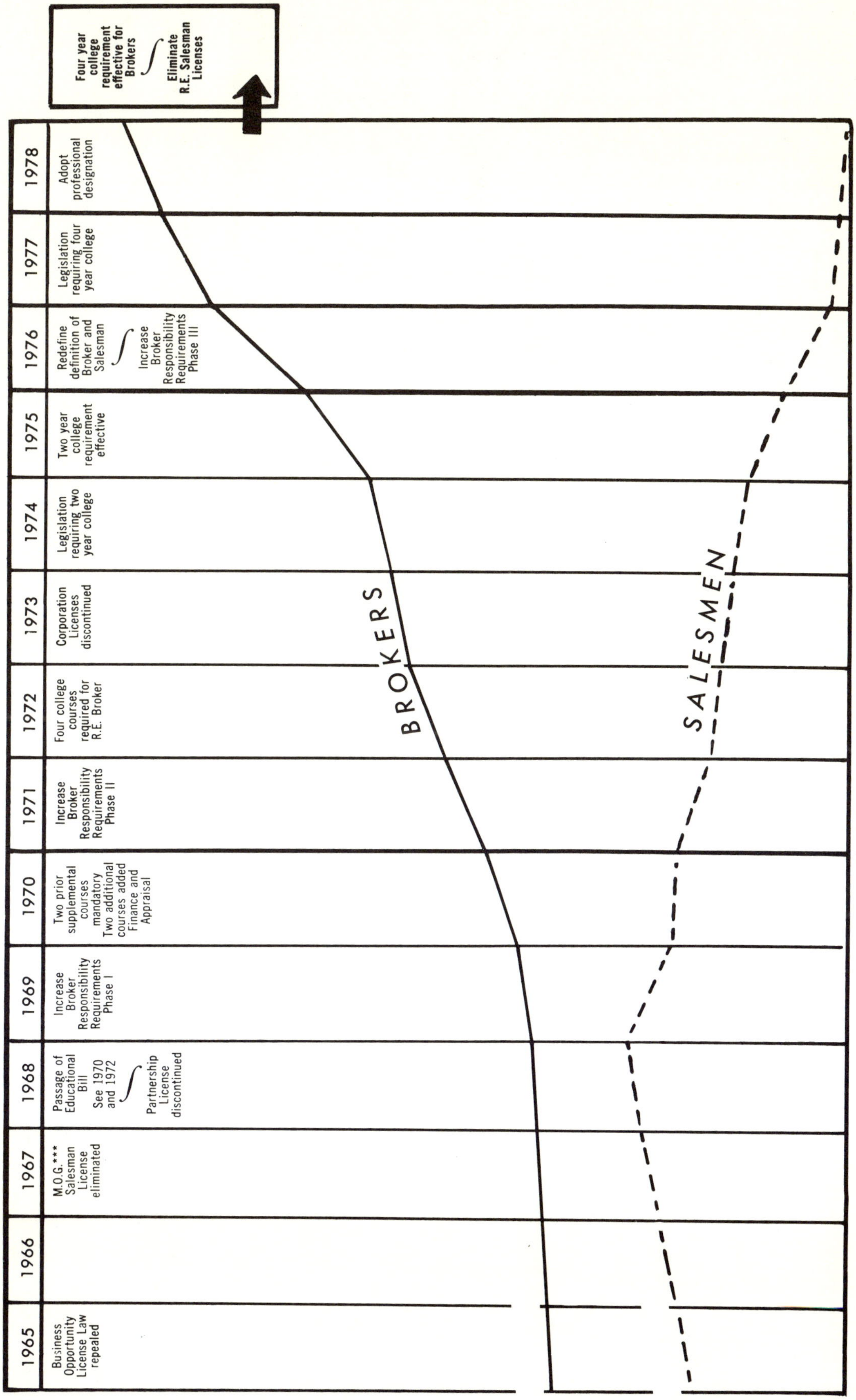
Four year college requirement effective for Brokers
Eliminate R.E. Salesman Licenses
1978
Adopt professional designation
1977
Legislation requiring four year college
1976
Redefine definition of Broker and Salesman
Increase Broker Responsibility Requirements Phase III
1975
Two year college requirement effective
1974
Legislation requiring two year college
1973
Corporation Licenses discontinued
1972
Four college courses required for R.E. Broker
1971
Increase Broker Responsibility Requirements Phase II
1970
Two prior supplemental courses mandatory Two additional courses added Finance and Appraisal
1969
Increase Broker Responsibility Requirements Phase I
1968
Passage of Educational Bill See 1970 and 1972
Partnership License discontinued
1967
M.O.G.*** Salesman License eliminated
1966
1965
Business Opportunity License Law repealed
BROKERS
SALESMEN

sioner Burton E. Smith presented for discussion a blueprint for professionalization[14] (a revision of a previous Blueprint for Professionalization of the Real Estate Business in California printed and distributed by the commissioner's office in 1966). This, Commissioner Smith explained, was merely an outline of a possible plan of action that could lead to a more professional level of service by California real estate brokers and public recognition of the fact that these services can indeed be "professional."

An education bill SB253 was enacted into law in 1968. Briefly the bill provided that in 1970 and 1971 the applicant for a real estate broker license must have completed three-unit college-level courses in legal aspects of real estate and in real estate practice. Special additional tests were required if he had not completed three-unit college-level courses in real estate finance and real estate appraisal. From 1972 on, completion of all four of the named courses is required as a prerequisite for examination for a real estate broker's license.

[14] See p. 8–9.

Intern Program

In the summer of 1970 Commissioner Smith coordinated a pilot intern program with the community colleges throughout the state to test the interest of the career-minded college student in entering the real estate field. It was hoped that the participating students, who served an internship under the tutelage of successful real estate practitioners, would discover that the real estate business is potentially more challenging and remunerative than many other professions.

The intern served in capacities not requiring a license and was paid a minimum wage while earning college credit. Only a limited number of brokers was accepted for this pilot program, results of which had not been evaluated as this text goes to press.

2

Establishing the Real Estate Office

Real estate brokerage today is a complex and competitive business. The salesman planning to move up to the owner-broker status by opening his own office must therefore have specialized knowledge of business administration. Failing this, many a salesman has found himself completely at a loss as to how to proceed as a broker-administrator. Without sufficient funds to see him through the "trial-and-error" years, he may well fail financially in a short time. The successful salesman leaving the selling field for the seemingly greener pastures of the brokerage business may find to his dismay that, although the grass is greener, the water bill is also higher.

What prompts a highly productive real estate salesman to leave the lucrative and satisfying selling field for a more exacting one demanding more of his time and energy, greater skill, and more specialized knowledge? Some leave because they feel that they are being exploited by the boss, that they have superior knowledge of the business, and that they are contributing more than their share of the work without commensurate financial reward. Many feel that their talents are going unrecognized. Probably none of these is the *prime* motivation for the move. The American businessman is noted for his independent spirit, and it is basically this inherent quality that motivates the aggressive salesman to strike out on his own.

The relatively small amount of capital necessary to open a one-man real estate business also holds a certain fascination. Unfortunately, the salesman may be the embodiment of the great American spirit of independence and still lack many or all of the basic qualifications to assure his success as a broker-administrator. Surveys have been made and statistics quoted as to the number of small-business failures in California. Although these figures serve as storm signals, in themselves they are of little value to the man who has failed in business without knowing why. Additional research into the causes of failure and the pitfalls to be avoided can be of real value to the neophyte.

Success in any business is dependent upon investment of *capital and labor.* Too little of either will spell the doom of the undertaking. Certainly the real estate brokerage business has suffered its share of failures, attributable to one or both of these factors. The old trial-and-error approach to the real estate office operation will no longer suffice. Increased sophistication of the business, stricter demands upon the practitioner by the buying and selling public, and stiffer competition in the field are all contributing to the need for tighter management of the brokerage office. Refusal to recognize the importance of these factors, coupled with the imposition of continually increasing overhead costs, eventually may force the small entrepreneur out of the field.

To succeed today the broker opening an office will be required to familiarize himself with cost analyses, market surveys, long-range economic forecasts, and the money market generally (as well as the mortgage money specifically). Added to the foregoing, his clientele will expect of him that he be thoroughly familiar with real estate investments, particularly as they relate to their competition in the general field of financial investments. As the real estate business becomes more professionalized, practitioners will be required to broaden their educational background. As the business becomes more sophisticated, a pursuit of broader and deeper knowledge of the many facets of the real estate field becomes basic to the practitioner's economic survival.

Office-Manager Experience

The broker-salesman aspiring to become an office owner may have had the fortunate experience of serving as office manager for his company. In this capacity he undoubtedly will have encountered and been required to solve managerial problems. In addition to the necessity of increasing his own sales quota, he will have faced the problems of office supervision and cost control. His is now the responsibility of coordinating the many details inherent in office management, personnel selection, and training so that the business will provide an adequate return. Learning how to solve these problems will offer valuable experience available only through actual contact with the day-to-day workings of a business. Without this intermediate step as office manager, the broker is forced to meet the problems of ownership head on. Basically, however, the same qualities that contribute to the success of a salesman apply also to the owner-broker.

Broker Qualifications

Certainly predominant among the qualifications necessary to the success of any real estate salesman is uncompromising integrity. Just as the salesman is the lengthened shadow of the broker, the office is the reflection of the sales force. No organization can succeed that operates under a code of unethical or downright dishonest practices. Aside from the moral issue involved, the business executive has found that his business must be conducted in a dignified, ethical manner if it is to survive and he is to become a leader in his field. This principle applies in an even fuller measure to the real estate industry, where large sums of money, often representing entire-life savings, are involved.

The day of the sharp real estate promoter has passed. A better-informed buying public, together with more stringent licensee regulations, has spelled his demise. Today we find the real estate buyer demanding honest, ethical, professional service from his agent. Those who cannot or will not adhere to this code are soon forced out of business.

Broker–Salesman Relations

When he becomes an office owner and employer, the broker enters into a type of partnership with his salesman in which each party has certain obligations to the other. Now, for the first time, he finds himself on the opposite side of the desk, in the role of counselor and negotiator for his salesman-employee. Now it is he who must be the adviser and not the advised. Does he have the necessary qualifications? Is he one who has kept abreast of the latest local, state, and national legislation affecting his business? Has he taken full advantage of his educational opportunities? In other words, has he equipped himself for this day, when, by the measure of his stature, he will win or lose the respect of those employed by him? As a salesman, he became accustomed to the many demands on his time and energy, involving long, irregular hours and often the relinquishing of weekends with his family. As the office head, he will find these demands increasing rather than diminishing. In addition to the hours devoted to his own sales, he must now make a portion of his time available for his salespeople.

All of the characteristics that contributed to the salesman's proficiency in the field now take on added importance to the broker as he makes the change from salesman–customer to broker–salesman relationship. His success or failure in this area may well provide the key to the *eventual outcome of his entire venture. Management of men is now considered a science,* the basics of which can be learned. Good management and personal relationship do not necessarily mean that the broker is conducting a "popularity contest." Decisions will have to be made from time to time that may prove unpopular with the individual salesman or with the staff as a whole. The good manager will be purposeful, consistent, and frank while at the same time considerate and fair with all concerned. His success as a manager will depend not only on his attitude for managerial work but also on his knowledge of the necessary techniques.

So, to summarize: All the essential qualifications necessary to produce a successful salesman apply also to the broker. To these must be added the requisite of management ability (with all it implies). We may conclude that the financial success of a good brokerage business is limited only by the ingenuity of its owner. The ability to cope with its managerial problems and the fortitude and strength to carry out its goals should bring financial independence and enjoyment of the American free-enterprise system rarely surpassed in any other industry.

Office-Manager Qualifications

To succeed in the formidably competitive world today, business undertakings must be based on sound principles. Basic to these is the employment of expert management. The real estate business is subject to all the vagaries of today's economic scene. The office employing eight or more salesmen will need an office manager, who may be the office owner-broker, and who may double as sales manager. If the owner-broker serves in the capacity of office manager, he will find little time to list and sell property himself. Some experts argue that a sales manager is necessary for the successful operation of an office employing *six or more* salesmen. Most of the problems endemic to the large office will be found in the small office as well. The question is whether it is economically feasible to hire a manager for the smaller office. Obviously the decision will be based upon the amount of remuneration paid the manager for his services, whether the pay is based upon commission overrides, or a guaranteed salary, or both.

What Constitutes a Good Manager? First of all he must be a *leader*. Whether we are discussing the business office manager, the school administrator or the Boy Scout leader, one qualification stands out—*the ability to command respect*. This respect is based primarily upon a sense of fair play. Nothing contributes more to the development of an unhappy or disgruntled employee than the manager's display of favoritism to one or more of the employees. Conversely, good office rapport is engendered by the knowledge that management will administer impartial and uncompromising justice to all. Criticism will usually be accepted graciously if it is known that it is dispensed impartially and intended to be constructive.

The successful manager is a *self-starter*. He is creative, optimistic, and energetic. He displays an enthusiasm born of a love of his work. And he imparts these important qualities to his sales force. *A good manager gets things done through other people*. He is *knowledgeable* in all areas of the business and willing to share his knowledge when called upon. This knowledge covers not only the areas of selling techniques and office budgetary questions, but the problems of the community as well.

Office Overhead

As any other business, the real estate office has certain necessary expenses that must be met regardless of the amount of income. Management's concern is with the company dollar, that is, the amount retained by the company after all expenses (including commissions) have been paid. The cost per desk to the office points up the importance of careful selection, training, and control of sales personnel. Sales volume alone will not necessarily produce a profit. It is only when each desk contributes its share toward the payment of the office expense that the business can continue to grow and show a profit. To arrive at the cost per desk, the net operating cost is divided by the number of salespeople (including part-time workers, if any[1]). What are the principal expenses in a typical real estate office, and how can they be controlled?

Advertising. This constitutes the largest expense item in most offices and is probably the most difficult item to control. Sellers expect that their property will be advertised consistently during the term of the listing. Here is where the control should start. Can an office afford to advertise an overpriced property? Or one whose owner is not well motivated to sell? Salesmen should be trained to evaluate each listing from this angle before accepting it for the office. It is the rare office that will gamble on advertising any other than an exclusive-right type of listing. Promising a seller that his property will be listed in any given media or for any period of time should be predicated on the rating of the listing from a standpoint of salability.

Advertising Media. These should be carefully selected, with the property to be advertised in mind. Such factors as the newspaper circulation, the income level of the reader, the location of the property with respect to school facilities, availability of public transportation, and recreational areas all have a bearing on advertising response. The newspaper with the lowest advertising rates is not necessarily the best bargain. The number of calls generated by the ad are not as important as the number of *qualified* buyers gleaned from those calls. The day of the week, the month of the year, weather conditions, local and national political and economic trends all have a bearing on customer response to properties advertised. These are factors to be kept in mind when analyzing the results of the office advertising program.

Telephones. Telephone expenses need to be tightly controlled if the office is to work within a budget. Although salesmen should certainly be given wide latitude in the use of the telephone for business calls, it should be understood that personal calls, except in cases of emergency, must be held within limits. Long-distance calls should be recorded and the purpose of each call noted. Unnecessarily long telephone conversations not only add to the office expense but tie up lines needed for calls to be made by others of the office sales force.

Signs and Lockboxes. Lost signs and lockboxes mean lost dollars to the office. Salesmen should be

[1] Included in this computation should be the profit figure the office has budgeted, monthly or annually.

held accountable for those checked out to them. Some offices charge the salesperson a nominal fee for any sign not returned to the office after the sale of a property. (Signs should not be permitted to remain on a property any longer than thirty days, or until close of the escrow, whichever is sooner.) Lockboxes, while probably less of a problem, nevertheless are an office expense that cannot be discounted.

Utilities. A small item? How many times are lights left burning unnecessarily? What about heating and air-conditioning units? Pennies saved mean dollars earned. If bonuses awarded salesmen were predicated on net dollars to the office, would there be more concern with the small items of expense? Are stockholders not concerned with economic company operation?

Labor Costs. By this is meant the efficiency of the office personnel. Is management keeping the fifteen-dollar-an-hour salesman busy filling out records that could be performed by the secretary? Does management understand how to delegate duties for the most effective use of time? Are nonproductive salesmen kept on long after their usefulness becomes marginal? And are the productive salesmen achieving their goals? If not, does management review their situation with them periodically to analyze and correct the problem where possible?

Commission Bonus

The Peacock Realty Company, Inc. provides a voluntary commission bonus, in each case payable only if, in the absolute discretion of the company, it is in a prosperous condition, and according to the following plan:

All sales associates licensed with the Peacock Realty Company, Inc. as of December 1st will be eligible to receive a commission bonus on all commissions paid to them in excess of the total amount of $8,400 during the preceding twelve-month period beginning December 1 and ending November 30. The commission bonus payment to be based upon the following schedule:

$ 8,400—$10,000—10 percent
$10,001—$11,000—11 percent
$11,001—$12,000—12 percent
$12,001—$13,000—13 percent
$13,001—$14,000—14 percent
$14,001—$15,000—15 percent
$15,001—$16,000—16 percent
$16,001—$17,000—17 percent
$17,001—$18,000—18 percent
$18,001—$19,000—19 percent
$19,001—$20,000 and over—20 percent

An additional bonus will be paid on the above commission bonus as a reward for length of association with the company, as follows:

0 to 2 years—0 percent
2 to 3 years—½ percent
3 to 4 years—1 percent
4 to 5 years—1½ percent
5 to 6 years—2 percent
6 to 7 years—2½ percent
7 to 8 years—3 percent
8 to 9 years—3½ percent
9 to 10 years—4 percent
10 to 11 years—4½ percent
11 years & over—5 percent

Years of association will be computed on a calendar-year basis, starting January 1, with no proration for part of a year.

Any associate who terminates with the company prior to November 30, and who would otherwise be eligible for commission bonus under the above program, will be paid at the discretion of the company, depending upon the circumstances of termination. He will be paid at the time other bonuses are paid, except that the company may pay earlier. In the event of death prior to payment of commission bonus, the company may, at its discretion, pay either before other bonuses are paid or at the time other bonuses are paid. If name of designated beneficiary is on file with the company, it will pay to designate and if none such, to surviving spouse, and if neither designate nor spouse, to such person or persons as counsel for the company in its discretion believes is entitled thereto.

Commission bonus will be paid after December 1, and prior to December 31 of each year. The above plan became effective as of December 1, 197—.

Example of the Above

$18,000 earnings, plus five years with the company.

$1,600	@	10 percent	=	$160
$1,000	@	11 percent	=	$110
$1,000	@	12 percent	=	$120
$1,000	@	13 percent	=	$130
$1,000	@	14 percent	=	$140
$1,000	@	15 percent	=	$150
$1,000	@	16 percent	=	$160
$1,000	@	17 percent	=	$170
$1,000	@	18 percent	=	$180
$9,600	@	2 percent	=	$192
				$1,512

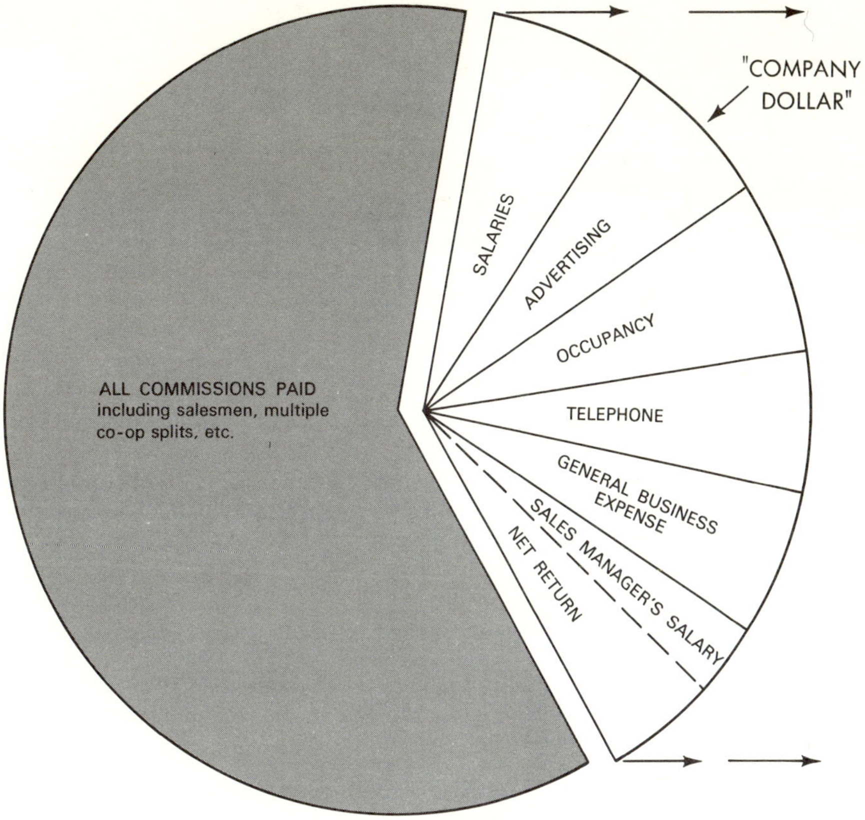
"COMPANY DOLLAR"
ALL COMMISSIONS PAID
including salesmen, multiple co-op splits, etc.
SALARIES
ADVERTISING
OCCUPANCY
TELEPHONE
GENERAL BUSINESS EXPENSE
SALES MANAGER'S SALARY
NET RETURN

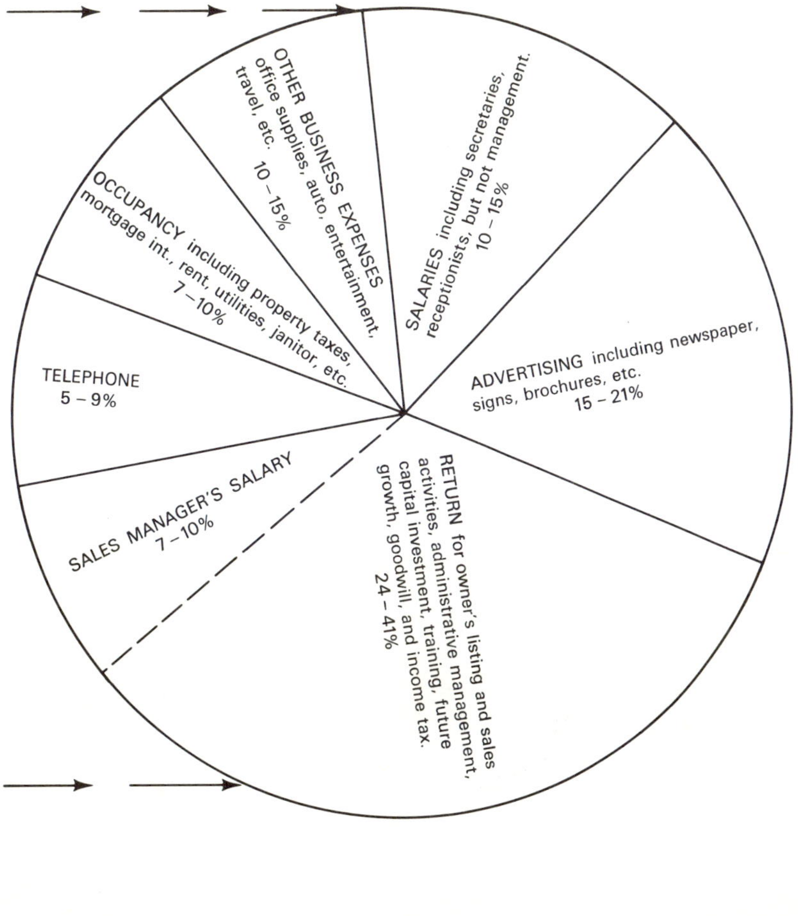
OTHER BUSINESS EXPENSES office supplies, auto, entertainment, travel, etc. 10 – 15%
SALARIES including secretaries, receptionists, but not management. 10 – 15%
OCCUPANCY including property taxes, mortgage int., rent, utilities, janitor, etc. 7 – 10%
ADVERTISING including newspaper, signs, brochures, etc. 15 – 21%
TELEPHONE 5 – 9%
SALES MANAGER'S SALARY 7 – 10%
RETURN for owner's listing and sales activities, administrative management, capital investment, training, future growth, goodwill, and income tax. 24 – 41%

CALIFORNIA REAL ESTATE ASSOCIATION

Code of Practices

The ______________________________

subscribes to the policy that a favorable public attitude for equal opportunity in the acquisition of housing can best be accomplished through leadership, example, education and the mutual cooperation of the real estate industry and the public.

The following is hereby stated as the Code of Practices of this Board:

1. It is the responsibility of a Realtor to offer equal service to all clients without regard to race, color, religion, or national origin in the sale, purchase, exchange, rental, or lease of real property.

   a. A Realtor must stand ready to show property to any member of any racial, creedal, or ethnic group.

   b. A Realtor has a legal and ethical responsibility to receive all offers and to communicate them to the property owner.

   c. A Realtor should exert his best efforts to conclude the transaction.

2. Realtors, individually and collectively, in performing their agency functions have no right or responsibility to determine the racial, creedal, or ethnic composition of any neighborhood or any part thereof.

3. Any attempt by a Realtor to solicit or procure the sale or other disposition in residential areas by conduct intended to implant fears in property owners based upon the actual or anticipated introduction of a minority group into an area shall subject the Realtor to disciplinary action. Any technique that induces panic selling is a violation of ethics and must be strongly condemned.

4. Each Realtor should feel completely free to enter into a broker-client relationship with persons of any race, creed, or ethnic group.

   a. Any conduct inhibiting said relationship is a specific violation of the rules and regulations of this board, and shall subject the violating Realtor to disciplinary action.

California Real Estate Association

520 SOUTH GRAND AVE. • LOS ANGELES, CALIF. 90017 Rev. 10-68

Opening the Office

Having determined to take the decisive step, the broker must now select the type ownership under which he will operate. Three alternatives are open to him: (a) individual ownership, (b) partnership, and (c) corporation. Each has advantages and disadvantages. The broker will want to consider each carefully before making his final decision. It is also advisable for him to consult a competent attorney, preferably one who is also a tax expert.

Individual Ownership

Dr. Frederick Case states, "The real estate business field is primarily one which attracts the independently minded entrepreneur who is willing to risk his own capital and efforts in anticipation of reaping a healthy profit return."[2] Attesting to the popularity of the individual-ownership type of real estate office, a recent California survey showed that the majority of some 100,000 licensees in the state were employed in offices staffed by no more than two or three salespeople. The *advantages* of individual ownership include ease of organization, independence of action, and sole ownership of the profits. It is the ideal arrangement for the broker who has sufficient capital to carry him through the early months without having to seek outside financing.

The *growth* of the business however, is limited to the potential of the owner. Does he have sufficient capital to expand the office to meet business demands, or in lieu of this does he have access to a line of credit with pay-back terms compatible with the business income? Furthermore, competition will demand that he keep abreast of local market conditions and that he continually upgrade his business techniques. Does he have the ability and the desire to do this? With no one to whom he can delegate authority, he may find the business too demanding of his time. Except for the occasional weekend, vacations may have to be forgone. What would happen to the office if the owner would suffer a prolonged illness? Who takes over when his presence is required out of town for personal or business reasons?

2 Frederick E. Case, *Real Estate* (Boston: Allyn & Bacon, Inc., 1962), p. 20.

Partnership

The agreement creating a partnership may be written, oral, or even *implied* from the conduct of the parties. The *intent* of the parties is primarily the basis upon which the courts make their determination as to whether a partnership exists. A partnership is more formally defined as a legal relationship created by voluntary association of two or more persons to carry on as co-owners of a business for profit. The rights and duties of partners toward each other and toward the public are regulated by law.[3]

Under the Uniform Partnership Act, a partner has the following rights in a partnership: (1) rights to specific partnership property; (2) interest in the partnership, and (3) right to participate in the management of the partnership business. A partner is a co-owner of partnership property as a "tenant in partnership" and as such has certain rights including equal right with other partners to possession for partnership purposes. This right is not assignable except with that of the other partners, nor is it subject to attachment except on a claim against the partnership itself. The tenancy is not considered community property and upon the death of a partner the right vests in the surviving partner or partners.

If the business of the partnership is continued after a change of membership due to the retirement or death of one partner or the admission of another partner, creditors of the first or dissolved partnership are also creditors of the new partnership.[4] In other words, the new member is liable for all obligations of the partnership arisen before his admission. However, his liability must be satisfied out of partnership property only. Dissolution takes place whenever any partner ceases to be associated with the business, such dissolution taking place only after the winding up of the partnership affairs. Business may, however, be continued with the new membership if such a contingency has been provided for in the partnership agreement.

3 California Real Estate Law requires that each partner in a real estate firm must hold a real estate broker's license. Since 1968, when the law was changed, the Department of Real Estate no longer issues formal partnership licenses.

4 Unless otherwise provided for in the partnership agreement, the admission of a new member into the partnership or the substitution of a new member for an old one results in the dissolution of the old firm and the creation of a new one.

Partnerships fall into two broad categories, (a) *a general partnership* created normally for a general type of business, and (b) a limited *partnership,* formed usually for a specific or limited purpose, such as a building or subdivision project. Unless otherwise agreed upon, all partners have equal rights in the profits and management of the partnership business. Each partner bears a fiduciary relationship to the partnership and to every other partner. Occasionally partnerships are set up with one party contributing the financing and the other supplying the background of specific know-how. This type of partnership is particularly adaptable to subdivision operations.

All limited partnerships in California must be formed under the Uniform Limited Partnership Act. Under this act a limited partnership is defined as "a partnership formed by two or more persons... having as members one or more general partners and one or more limited partners. The limited partners as such shall not be bound by the obligations of the partnership."[5] The limited partner thus has no liability beyond the contribution made by him, which may consist of property or money, *but may not consist of services.* Under the act, the limited partner is given substantially the same fundamental rights as a shareholder in a corporation. However, within certain limits, he has no right to manage, control, or participate in the daily operation of the partnership business. He thus avoids some of the income-tax disadvantages of corporate ownership but is able to take a passive role as an investor in a development or other project.

Joint Venture. This is an association of two or more persons to carry on a business under a formal or informal agreement to share profits and losses. It is subject to the rules of the Uniform Partnership Act. Joint ventures are often less formal than partnership agreements. Partnerships are normally formed to engage in a continuing business, whereas joint ventures are usually formed for purposes of a single transaction or a series of related transactions. For all practical purposes a joint venture is a partnership and subject to all the general rules of partnership law.

Fictitious Name. If a partnership is operating under a fictitious name, it is required to file a certificate with the clerk of the county in which the principal place of business is located, stating in full the names and places of residence of all members of the partnership. The fictitious-name certificate must be signed by all members of the partnership and published once a week for four weeks in a newspaper of general circulation. The certificate is effective for five years from date of recording.

In a broad sense, the advantages and disadvantages of individual ownership are transposed in the case of a partnership. The advantages of one become the disadvantages of the other. An important *disadvantage* of the partnership is that each partner is considered a co-owner of specific partnership assets of the other. Because of the mutual-agency relationship that exists between the partners (that is, each is the agent of the other insofar as partnership business is concerned), great care should be exercised in the selection of a business partner. A full investigation into his credit standing, his personal habits, and his knowledge and experience in the business is imperative. Over and against this is the valuable *advantage* of a partnership—the partners may pool their ideas, experience, and finances. The partnership form of ownership also relieves each member of constant business supervision. Taxwise it has certain advantages over the corporation, because the tax liabilities in the partnership are limited to the individuals, with the partnership entity being tax-free.

Corporations

Corporate ownership has proved the least-popular form of ownership among real estate brokerage offices in California. The inconvenience and cost of incorporating have discouraged the smaller offices from using this type of ownership, even though there are some advantages. Those offices engaged in large-scale operations have found it practical to incorporate because of certain tax advantages.[6]

A major *advantage* in the corporate type of ownership is that involving personal liability. Holders of fully paid shares in a corporation are not liable for the debts of the corporation, whereas partners (except in the case of a limited partnership) are individually liable for any partnership debts. In addition, some offices have found it advantageous to incorporate and offer shares of stock to certain of their valued executives in order to induce them to remain with the firm.

A definite *disadvantage* is the difficulty of obtain-

[5] Corporations Code 15501.

[6] Corporate tax rates are lower than the individual tax rates of the shareholders. In addition, several corporations may divide the income from one project into several entities in order to spread the tax liability into the lower tax rates of various corporations. (However, the 1969 Tax Reform Act severely curtailed this advantage.)

ing credit. Creditors may not proceed against the stockholders to satisfy a debt beyond the ability of the corporation to pay from its own assets. Because of this, if the firm is acquiring real estate, institutional lenders often require officers of the corporation to execute or guarantee the note evidencing the debt. The double-taxation feature of the corporation (that is, the income of the corporation is taxed in addition to that of the individual shareholder) is a major *disadvantage.*

Syndicates

The syndicate can be a valuable tool for the real estate broker. It is a process whereby two or more individuals agree to pool their investment capital for the purpose of acquiring one or more parcels of real estate while delegating the responsibilities of management to the qualified professional syndicator. Many investors lack the know-how of acquisition, management, development, and disposition of properties. By investing their capital in the syndicate they may take advantage of a good return on their investment without the worry of management problems. The broker may form a syndicate of small investors and thus be in a position to consummate sales that would otherwise have to be passed up because of the large amount of capital required to finance the undertaking. The syndicate may have as few as two or three members, but usually the membership is larger so that sufficient capital may be accumulated to purchase large parcels of land, income properties, or leaseholds. (Syndication will be covered in more detail in Chapter 9.)

It is not the purpose of this text to supply detailed information on any of the various forms of real estate organizations from a tax standpoint. Competent tax attorneys should be consulted whenever the broker is faced with making a decision on the type of organization best suited to his operation.

Area of Specialization

Because the small general-brokerage operation is the most popular, the broker who plans to enter this field must be prepared to meet stiff competition. Also, real estate ventures of this nature are exposed to the same hazards that all small businesses must face. *Lack of capital* and *haphazard planning* contribute most often to their failure. Business experts usually advise against opening an office without sufficient capital for one year's operation. The broker attempting to maintain an office on less than this amount is treading on thin ice. Also, brokers inexperienced or untrained in business administration often fail to project accurately the fixed expenses of an office. Frequently, space selected for the office is inadequate to accommodate the necessary sales force or to provide for expansion of the business. No previous market analysis having been made (much less any goals set), the business is operated on a hit-or-miss basis. Salesmen who might otherwise prove to be top producers soon become discouraged with the unprofessional business attitude of the organization and drift to more productive offices. The operation gradually becomes known as second-rate, and the broker is unable to recruit as salesmen any but the poor producers in the field. The unfortunate eventual outcome is another small-business failure.

But to present an optimistic outlook, we find the more enterprising broker who has prepared carefully for the day when he becomes a businessman in his own right. He may have spent several years as a salesman in a successful brokerage office, possibly being promoted to office manager or department head. Or he may have educated himself in business management through attendance at courses offered in institutions of higher learning. He may have completed both of these experiences. He is now aware of and has prepared for the economic perils involved in opening his own office. He has set goals for himself and for his staff, and he is planning accordingly.

Departmentalizing

Many of the more resolute brokers begin by departmentalizing their operations. Careful selection is made of industry specialists to head up individual departments. The versatility of this type of operation makes for more stability and thus attracts the more career-minded associate. In turn, the high-caliber company representative tends to lend dignity to and inspire confidence in the organization. Strict adherence to these basic principles is the office owner's assurance of business success. As competition becomes keener, more brokers are giving serious consideration to this type of operation. Along with this is the growing trend today toward employment of the carefully selected salesman, with greater emphasis placed on his educational background. Thus, the industry is slowly emerging from the disorganized and aimless business structure of the past. The highly specialized real estate organization is evolving and beginning to take its place alongside the professions.

Areas of specialization related to the average real estate operation include appraising, property management, financing, subdividing, property development, and syndication. Sales of residential, income, industrial, and farm properties also involve specialized knowledge demanding intensified training. The broker handling sales of industrial sites and farmlands, for example, often finds that he requires a background of information equivalent to actual experience in the field. These specialized areas will be discussed more fully in the chapters devoted to them.

Selecting Office Location

Location is all-important when the broker makes plans for his first office. Final selection should be made only after careful neighborhood survey. With the possible exception of the subdivision tract office, the temporary shelters of a few years ago have all but disappeared as real estate places of business. The trend today is toward the well-designed, permanent building, usually owned outright or held under long-term lease by the broker. The office location will be controlled largely by the type of operation in which the broker is specializing. Those handling residential sales usually favor suburban areas centered in their field of operation. Street-level structures are considered superior to "walk-up" offices. Brokers specializing in commercial or industrial sales can locate advantageously in downtown areas with offices either on the ground floor or in upper stories of multistory buildings. In making any selection, plans for expansion must be taken into consideration. Some brokers recognize the value of a main-highway location; others feel that, to obtain maximum sign advantages, a corner lot is essential. Certainly pleasant surroundings are important, and adequate parking facilities are a must. For the residential-sales broker, a dramatic office entrance is sometimes desirable. Some brokers favor an area where they will draw walk-in business and where window displays can be used to full advantage. Offices strategically located in shopping centers are valuable from this standpoint. Imagination and intelligent planning from the beginning will go a long way toward solving working-conditions problems that may arise later. The building architecture should conform to its surroundings and be at the same time tasteful and dignified. Nowhere has originality of design evidenced itself more than in California, with its varied desert, mountain, and seashore climate. Here wide variations of architecture are to be found, blending with the surrounding terrain.

Brokers are free to express their individual tastes in creating the office design best suited to their needs and temperaments. Some offices are impressive structures furnishing space for over 100 employees. Others are neat and compact buildings out of which possibly only two or three salesmen work. Good taste in design and interior layout can be evidenced in the smallest office as well as in the large, imposing building. The adequacy of the location and space for the type of business operation should be the guides to the site selection.

Office Layout

The functional plan of any real estate office should allow for adequate floor area for each employee while providing space for the broker's office, reception room, closing room, and other space requirements. The majority of new offices constructed today allow approximately 125 to 150 square feet *per desk.* In figuring square feet *per person,* estimates run from 50 to 300 square feet per employee. Some brokers feel that, because all salesmen are not in at the same time, the lower figure is adequate. All seem agreed that the closing or conference room is an absolute essential. Larger offices may provide for three or four such rooms. The broker's private office is also considered a basic necessity, regardless of the size of the operation.

Today's brokerage office requires such an abundance of files, maps, records, and supplies that a special room for their storage is provided in any well-organized office. Constant additions to the "historical property files" alone make great demands on space. Good acoustics and proper ventilation, with summer air conditioning and winter heating, are all necessary to top working conditions. Background music (some with high-fidelity equipment) is also provided in many of the new offices.

The importance of the reception room cannot be overemphasized. Here the customer receives his first introduction to the office. The room should be neat, attractive in décor, and comfortably furnished. In larger organizations, the receptionist is seated here to greet customers. In smaller offices, it is the responsibility of the salesman on floor duty to occupy the front desk. Careful selection of office furnishings in keeping with the architecture and décor contributes greatly to pleasant working conditions. Nothing detracts from the professional appearance of a business office more than an array of desks of assorted sizes and finishes. Salesmen's desks should be maintained in a neat and uncluttered condition. Unemptied ashtrays, overflowing wastebaskets, and coats draped over chairs all detract from the businesslike atmosphere.

Trade and Professional Organizations

The "lone wolf" in the real estate industry is gradually fading from the picture. The successful broker today has found that he can best serve his clients and gain the respect of his competitors and the community he serves by membership in his local Board of Realtors. Through his local board he becomes also a member of the California Real Estate Association and the National Association of Real Estate Boards (NAREB).[7] Through his membership in these trade organizations he has access to numerous educational seminars, workshops, and conferences where he is able to keep abreast of the latest information on regulations of the business and modern marketing and financing techniques. Multiple-listing service is available to him through his membership, as well as access to current deed-transfer records and real estate ownership files.

The broker's stature in the community is further enhanced by his membership in the local chamber of commerce, service clubs, and civic organizations. The successful business man in any community is usually found among the leaders in church and youth activities or in any of the many groups working for the betterment of his city. The value of this mingling with his fellow citizens applies particularly to the real estate broker if he wants to keep himself fully informed on local conditions, a very necessary requisite to success in the field.

National Association of Real Estate Boards

In addition to state regulatory measures administered by the Department of Real Estate, trade associations have been formed with rules governing the ethical and professional behavior of their members. Foremost among these is the National Association of Real Estate Boards, formed in Chicago in 1908 and having as its goals, (1) the creation of unity in the real estate field, (2) the compilation of information, (3) the protection and promotion of property ownership, and (4) the establishment of professional standards of practice.

In 1913 the NAREB drafted and adopted the Code of Ethics.[8] In 1916 the term "Realtor" (coined by Charles N. Chadbourne of the Minneapolis Real Estate Board) was registered as a trademark with the U.S. Patent Office. It is the property right of the National Association of Real Estate Boards for the exclusive use of its members. *In California the unauthorized use of the term Realtor is a violation of Real Estate Law.* The NAREB issues a certificate annually to each of its members designating him a Realtor. Display of this certificate is notice to the public that the member is pledged to the NAREB's high standards of business conduct, as evidenced by his pledge to adhere to its Code of Ethics. There have been eighteen court decisions, including one of a federal court,[9] upholding the ownership right of the NAREB and its members to the term Realtor and the NAREB emblem.

The National Association of Real Estate Boards is one of the largest trade organizations in the United States. In 1971 it had a membership of over 95,000, consisting of members in 1,590 Boards of Realtors. It is headed by its executive vice-president, H. Jackson Pontius, formerly executive vice-president of the California Real Estate Association. Among its councils and societies are,

1. National Institute of Farm and Land Brokers
2. Institute of Real Estate Management
3. American Institute of Real Estate Appraisers
4. American Society of Real Estate Counselors
5. National Institute of Real Estate Brokers
6. Society of Industrial Realtors
7. Executive Officers' Council
8. American Chapter, International Real Estate Federation
9. Women's Council[10]

The Graduate Realtors Institute (GRI) program is one developed by NAREB. It confers the GRI designation upon any realtor who has completed 90 hours of attendance at its various educational seminars. Their schedule of courses is offered through the state associations, with eighteen units of credit (108 hours) being required of enrollees to qualify them for the GRI certificate.

California Real Estate Association (CREA)

Formed at Los Angeles in 1905, the California Real Estate Association is a voluntary nonprofit organization made up of the membership in 173 local

[7] If there is no local board, a broker wishing to belong to the state association may join directly as an individual member.

[8] See code of ethics, p. 24 and 25.

[9] *NAREB* v. *Peninsula Real Estate Association,* 1957.

[10] See p. 27.

boards throughout the state.[11] With a membership in 1971 of over 53,900 (made up of both broker and salesmen members) it is the largest state real estate association in the nation. The CREA serves as an adviser, consultant, and coordinator for local-board activities and is the medium for expressing the purposes and objectives of local real estate boards on the state level. As provided in its constitution, CREA has these purposes as well:

1. To enable members to transact their business to better advantage under uniform practices.
2. To promote and maintain high standards of conduct under the terms of the code of ethics.
3. To cooperate with other groups for the civic and economic betterment of California.
4. To advocate legislation beneficial to real estate, its owners, and licensed real estate brokers and salesmen, and to oppose legislation that is detrimental to them.
5. To cooperate in the enforcement of the California Real Estate Act.

The state association recognizes five different types of membership. The local board holds membership in the state association by virtue of its own membership, which may include one or more of these classes of members:

Active. Consists of brokers admitted to local boards as full voting members. Most boards limit active membership to brokers who are principals in the business—either as individuals, partners, or officers of corporations. Active members are realtors.
Associate (salesman). The boards providing an associate membership usually require active members to place in membership associates who are in their employ. In some boards, associates are given fractional voting rights or representation in the board of directors.
Affiliate. Most boards provide affiliate membership for persons and firms engaged in allied businesses, such as banks, title companies, escrow companies, builders, attorneys (not real estate licensees). Some boards maintain strong property-owner divisions and derive considerable supporting revenue from this source.
Individual. This membership does not come through the local board, but is paid to the state association directly by brokers who are located in rural areas not included within the jurisdiction of any organized local board. It is required that the broker also maintain an individual membership in the national association, thus becoming a realtor.

CREA has thirty-one regional vice-presidents, each with jurisdiction over several local real estate boards. In addition, there are approximately one thousand directors appointed by their local boards. These directors have voting rights at the state directors' meetings, held four times a year.

CREA has an education department with director who works with the education committee. Together they provide programs, conducted by CREA members, for training and education. As mentioned on p. 21, the Graduate Realtors Institute is offered by CREA through the national association. (It is known as the Realtors Institute of CREA.)

Among CREA's many committees are:

a. political affairs, established to educate and encourage local boards to seek the election to public office of such persons—regardless of political party—as will reaffirm the American principles of individual freedom and property rights and who will uphold the free-enterprise system;
b. taxation, which considers all legislation concerning taxation of real property, sales tax, and new tax programs and which studies proposals from the legislative committee and submits recommendations;
c. equal rights, which seeks ways of solving the problems of discrimination in housing for reasons of race, religion, or national origin.[12]

Local Boards of Realtors

The local Board of Realtors is a voluntary organization made up of persons engaged in some phase of the real estate business or owners who are directly or indirectly interested in real estate. Affiliate memberships are open to banks, trust companies, escrow officers, and others engaged in fields related to real estate.

The San Diego Realty Board, organized in 1878, pioneered the field, with the San Jose Realty Board following in 1896. Boards were developed out of the need for standardization of real estate brokerage practices, commission rates, and servicing fees. By 1908, there were forty-eight organized boards in the state. Today, most boards are changing over to the standard title of "Board of Realtors." They have as their purpose the uniting of their members to their mutual benefit and to protect their members and the public from irresponsible or dishonest licensees. Their members are required to subscribe to the Code of Ethics of NAREB. Committees on ethics are set up in each board to hear and adjudicate complaints on Code violations.[13]

[11] The local board, however, is an autonomous independent unit. Neither the State Association nor NAREB controls policies or activities of the local board as long as they are consistent with the provisions of the Code of Ethics and the Constitution and Bylaws of both governing bodies.

[12] See California Real Estate Association *Code of Practices,* p. 16.

[13] See copy of the Code of Ethics, pp. 24 and 25.

Most local boards have orientation programs for new applicants for board membership, consisting in some cases of all day Orientation-to-Professionalization courses. The courses, conducted by the board's education committee, are designed to make the candidate aware of board policy and his obligations to the board, his clients, his community, CREA, and NAREB. Successful completion of the courses is a prerequisite to membership in the board.

Where boards are located in districts of community colleges that have a real estate program, members of their education committees serve on the college advisory committee, assisting the college real estate coordinator and advising him on community needs in real estate courses.

CASE STUDY

You are a salesman with the Panorama Realty Company. The company is a member of the local board of realtors and multiple listing. You have been associated with the company for the past six years, engaged principally in sales of single-family residences. Previously you had worked as salesman for a local automobile agency and had been moderately successful. You have a wife and two children; the kids are in elementary school. Your wife has not been employed since your marriage. Education-wise, you have a high-school diploma and an A. A. degree from a community college, where marketing was your major field of study. You own a home valued at $27,000, on which there is an $18,000 mortgage. You are making monthly payments of approximately $116. You have $5,000 in a savings and loan association and a $5,000 life-insurance policy. You do not belong to any service club or the chamber of commerce, nor do you have any particular hobbies, preferring to spend your evenings and weekends at home when you are not working.

You are the top producer in the office of eight salespeople and are averaging $12,000 annually in commissions. Recently there has been considerable friction in the office owing to the hiring of the broker's son as salesman. He is not cooperative and generally not popular with the rest of the sales force.

For some time, your wife has been urging you to open your own office. She has been driving around town and has located a vacant store building on a downtown street with several small specialty shops. The building has a frontage of fifteen feet and a depth of sixty feet with parking area in the rear for four cars. You would be required to sign a five-year lease at $200 per month, with the first and last two months payable in advance. You inspect the property and decide to give it some consideration. You would want to hire at least eight salesmen. Your wife agrees to act as secretary-receptionist, although she has had no previous training for this.

You make a list of the anticipated expenses, including membership in the local board (at an initial cost of $500) and equipping the office with office furniture, telephone service, and files. You plan to deal principally in residential sales but may later add an income-property department.

1. From the above facts, estimate the approximate expenses you would have the first year (including capital outlay).

2. Considering all aspects of the situation, do you believe that the idea of leaving your present position and launching your own business is a good one? Why, or why not? State your reasons fully.

SUGGESTED REFERENCES

AUG, GEORGE, "Figures Don't Lie," *Real Estate Today,* Chicago, Ill. National Institute of Real Estate Brokers of the National Association of Real Estate Boards, January, 1971.

CASE, FREDERICK E., *Real Estate Brokerage.* Englewood Cliffs, N.J.: Prentice-Hall, Inc., 1965.

EISENBERG, LEONARD S., "Brokerage and Management Opportunities through Syndication," *Real Estate Today,* Chicago, Ill. National Institute of Real Estate Brokers of the National Association of Real Estate Boards, January, 1971.

——— *Administration of Real Estate Brokerage Offices.* Los Angeles: California Real Estate Association, 1964.

——— "On Policy and Procedure Manuals," *NIREB's Division Reports,* No. 6, Chicago, Ill. National Institute of Real Estate Brokers of the National Association of Real Estate Boards, May 1969, (Sponsor Lewis Bass).

——— *Successful Real Estate Office Administration Practice.* Los Angeles: California Real Estate Association, 1966.

CODE OF ETHICS

NATIONAL ASSOCIATION OF REAL ESTATE BOARDS

Preamble

UNDER all is the land. Upon its wise utilization and widely allocated ownership depend the survival and growth of free institutions and of our civilization. The Realtor is the instrumentality through which the land resource of the nation reaches its highest use and through which land ownership attains its widest distribution. He is a creator of homes, a builder of cities, a developer of industries and productive farms.

Such functions impose obligations beyond those of ordinary commerce. They impose grave social responsibility and a patriotic duty to which the Realtor should dedicate himself, and for which he should be diligent in preparing himself. The Realtor, therefore, is zealous to maintain and improve the standards of his calling and shares with his fellow-Realtors a common responsibility for its integrity and honor.

In the interpretation of his obligations, he can take no safer guide than that which has been handed down through twenty centuries, embodied in the Golden Rule:

"Whatsoever ye would that men should do to you, do ye even so to them."

Accepting this standard as his own, every Realtor pledges himself to observe its spirit in all his activities and to conduct his business in accordance with the following Code of Ethics:

Part I
Relations to the Public

ARTICLE 1.
The Realtor should keep himself informed as to movements affecting real estate in his community, state, and the nation, so that he may be able to contribute to public thinking on matters of taxation, legislation, land use, city planning, and other questions affecting property interests.

ARTICLE 2.
It is the duty of the Realtor to be well informed on current market conditions in order to be in a position to advise his clients as to the fair market price.

ARTICLE 3.
It is the duty of the Realtor to protect the public against fraud, misrepresentation or unethical practices in the real estate field.

He should endeavor to eliminate in his community any practices which could be damaging to the public or to the dignity and integrity of the real estate profession. The Realtor should assist the board or commission charged with regulating the practices of brokers and salesmen in his state.

ARTICLE 4.
The Realtor should ascertain all pertinent facts concerning every property for which he accepts the agency, so that he may fulfill his obligation to avoid error, exaggeration, misrepresentation, or concealment of pertinent facts.

ARTICLE 5.
The Realtor should not be instrumental in introducing into a neighborhood a character of property or use which will clearly be detrimental to property values in that neighborhood.

ARTICLE 6.
The Realtor should not be a party to the naming of a false consideration in any document, unless it be the naming of an obviously nominal consideration.

ARTICLE 7.
The Realtor should not engage in activities that constitute the practice of law and should recommend that title be examined and legal counsel be obtained when the interest of either party requires it.

ARTICLE 8.
The Realtor should keep in a special bank account, separated from his own funds, monies coming into his possession in trust for other persons, such as escrows, trust funds, client's monies and other like items.

ARTICLE 9.
The Realtor in his advertising should be especially careful to present a true picture and should neither advertise without disclosing his name, nor permit his salesmen to use individual names or telephone numbers, unless the salesman's connection with the Realtor is obvious in the advertisement.

ARTICLE 10.
The Realtor, for the protection of all parties with whom he deals, should see that financial obligations and commitments regarding real estate transactions are in writing, expressing the exact agreement of the parties; and that copies of such agreements, at the time they are executed, are placed in the hands of all parties involved.

Part II
Relations to the Client

ARTICLE 11.
In accepting employment as an agent, the Realtor pledges himself to protect and promote the interests of the client. This obligation of absolute fidelity to the client's interest is primary, but it does not relieve the Realtor from the obligation of dealing fairly with all parties to the transaction.

ARTICLE 12.
In justice to those who place their interests in his care, the Realtor should endeavor always to be in-

formed regarding laws, proposed legislation, governmental orders, and other essential information and public policies which affect those interests.

ARTICLE 13.

Since the Realtor is representing one or another party to a transaction, he should not accept compensation from more than one party without the full knowledge of all parties to the transaction.

ARTICLE 14.

The Realtor should not acquire an interest in or buy for himself, any member of his immediate family, his firm or any member thereof, or any entity in which he has a substantial ownership interest, property listed with him, or his firm, without making the true position known to the listing owner, and in selling property owned by him, or in which he has such interest, the facts should be revealed to the purchaser.

ARTICLE 15.

The exclusive listing of property should be urged and practiced by the Realtor as a means of preventing dissension and misunderstanding and of assuring better service to the owner.

ARTICLE 16.

When acting as agent in the management of property, the Realtor should not accept any commission, rebate or profit on expenditures made for an owner, without the owner's knowledge and consent.

ARTICLE 17.

The Realtor should not undertake to make an appraisal that is outside the field of his experience unless he obtains the assistance of an authority on such types of property, or unless the facts are fully disclosed to the client. In such circumstances the authority so engaged should be so identified and his contribution to the assignment should be clearly set forth.

ARTICLE 18.

When asked to make a formal appraisal of real property, the Realtor should not render an opinion without careful and thorough analysis and interpretation of all factors affecting the value of the property. His counsel constitutes a professional service.

The Realtor should not undertake to make an appraisal or render an opinion of value on any property where he has a present or contemplated interest unless such interest is specifically disclosed in the appraisal report. Under no circumstances should he undertake to make a formal appraisal when his employment or fee is contingent upon the amount of his appraisal.

ARTICLE 19.

The Realtor should not submit or advertise property without authority and in any offering, the price quoted should not be other than that agreed upon with the owners as the offering price.

ARTICLE 20.

In the event that more than one formal written offer on a specific property is made before the owner has accepted an offer, any other formal written offer presented to the Realtor, whether by a prospective purchaser or another broker, should be transmitted to the owner for his decision.

Part III

Relations to His Fellow-Realtor

ARTICLE 21.

The Realtor should seek no unfair advantage over his fellow-Realtors and should willingly share with them the lessons of his experience and study.

ARTICLE 22.

The Realtor should so conduct his business as to avoid controversies with his fellow-Realtors. In the event of a controversy between Realtors who are members of the same local board, such controversy should be arbitrated in accordance with regulations of their board rather than litigated.

ARTICLE 23.

Controversies between Realtors who are not members of the same local board should be submitted to an arbitration board consisting of one arbitrator chosen by each Realtor from the real estate board to which he belongs or chosen in accordance with the regulations of the respective boards. One other member, or a sufficient number of members to make an odd number, should be selected by the arbitrators thus chosen.

ARTICLE 24.

When the Realtor is charged with unethical practice, he should place all pertinent facts before the proper tribunal of the member board of which he is a member, for investigation and judgment.

ARTICLE 25.

The Realtor should not voluntarily disparage the business practice of a competitor, nor volunteer an opinion of a competitor's transaction. If his opinion is sought it should be rendered with strict professional integrity and courtesy.

ARTICLE 26.

The agency of a Realtor who holds an exclusive listing should be respected. A Realtor cooperating with a listing broker should not invite the cooperation of a third broker without the consent of the listing broker.

ARTICLE 27.

The Realtor should cooperate with other brokers on property listed by him exclusively whenever it is in the interest of the client, sharing commissions on a previously agreed basis. Negotiations concerning property listed exclusively with one broker should be carried on with the listing broker, not with the owner, except with the consent of the listing broker.

ARTICLE 28.

The Realtor should not solicit the services of an employee or salesman in the organization of a fellow-Realtor without the knowledge of the employer.

ARTICLE 29.

Signs giving notice of property for sale, rent, lease or exchange should not be placed on any property by more than one Realtor, and then only if authorized by the owner, except as the property is listed with and authorization given to more than one Realtor.

ARTICLE 30.

In the best interest of society, of his associates and of his own business, the Realtor should be loyal to the real estate board of his community and active in its work.

CONCLUSION

The term *Realtor* has come to connote competence, fair dealing and high integrity resulting from adherence to a lofty ideal of moral conduct in business relations. No inducement of profit and no instructions from clients ever can justify departure from this ideal, or from the injunctions of this Code.

The Code of Ethics was adopted in 1913. Amended at the Annual Convention in 1924, 1928, 1950, 1951, 1952, 1955, 1956, 1961, and 1962.

California Real Estate Association
Realtor Week
Call Your Realtor... He Sells America First - Everyday.
A HOME MEANS HAPPINESS
HAPPINESS WITH A HOME Means A REALTOR
NATIONAL ASSOCIATION OF REAL ESTATE BOARDS
REALTORS ARE ACTIVE MEMBERS OF CONSTITUENT BOARDS
NATIONAL ASSOCIATION OF REAL ESTATE BOARDS
REALTORS ARE ACTIVE MEMBERS OF CONSTITUENT BOARDS

NATIONAL INSTITUTE OF REAL ESTATE BROKERS—combines talent and years of experience to equip Realtors and their associates to succeed through specialized techniques. Its annual series of publications include the Real Estate Salesman's Handbook, Real Estate Trader's Handbook, Home Trade-In Handbook and hard cover books on marketing and advertising. The Exchange Division (ITC) emphasizes latest developments in the growing field of property exchanges and trade-ins and awards the CIM designation to its qualified exchange, commercial and investment members. The Commercial and Investment and Residential Divisions render information in specialized areas.

NATIONAL INSTITUTE OF FARM AND LAND BROKERS—carries on an important program of studies in agricultural real estate and land for development.

SOCIETY OF INDUSTRIAL REALTORS—serves the highly specialized industrial real estate field. It publishes a periodic newsletter, a monthly market letter on properties wanted and for sale, pamphlets on different phases of industrial real estate, and an annual directory of members distributed to industry.

AMERICAN INSTITUTE OF REAL ESTATE APPRAISERS—acts as a professional service organization for the Realtor who has a special interest in land economics and the complex field of real estate valuation. Its quarterly Appraisal Journal, textbook material, and case study courses give practical methods and advice.

INSTITUTE OF REAL ESTATE MANAGEMENT—provides aids and promotion pieces for advertising and public relations programs, monthly bulletins and specialized courses. It publishes the quarterly Journal of Property Management and the textbook, Principles of Real Estate Management.

SOCIETY OF REAL ESTATE COUNSELORS—aims to promote real estate counseling as a fee service and to establish high standards of practice and performance through its organization of Realtors qualified to give advice and counsel in real estate matters on a fee, per diem or retainer basis.

AMERICAN CHAPTER OF INTERNATIONAL REAL ESTATE FEDERATION—promotes high professional standards and good relations among individuals engaged in the calling of real estate in all nations and encourages private ownership of real property rights and obligations wherever possible. Its program includes sections on appraisal, consultation, mortgage finance, brokerage, management and the European market. Its quarterly bulletin, printed in English, French and German, is sent directly from the Paris office and contains items about current real estate development in each member's country.

Through business and professional arms of the National Association of Real Estate Boards, the Realtor has the opportunity for continuing his education to professionalism.

Association with Realtors in his own community and State and National organizations provides an exchange of ideas and views which raises and maintains the standards of real estate practice.

THE WOMEN'S COUNCIL is dedicated to the advancement and the recognition of women in the real estate field. It is open to all women Realtors. The Council publishes "What Women Realtors Are Doing," promotes activity in special NAREB projects, and maintains a Speakers' Bureau.

3

Selection and Training of Personnel

Salaried Personnel

Receptionist-Secretary. Basic qualifications for for the real estate office receptionist are no different from those for the receptionist in any other type of business. She is usually the first contact the customer has with the office; therefore, she should be selected for her attractive appearance and friendly attitude and should be a person skilled in meeting people. In most real estate offices, she will probably double as a secretary-typist and as such should meet all of the requisites of that position.[1]

Because much of the business transacted in a real estate office is of a private nature, it is the secretary's responsibility to respect these confidences at all times. She must help to create a setting that will give the impression of efficiency, cleanliness, and general business decorum. In her role as receptionist, she actually assumes the position of office representative in meeting customers. Her professional appearance and attitude can do much to project a favorable impression. She must be rigidly impartial where the salesmen are concerned. Because she will often make the initial contact with "drop-in" customers and those telephoning inquiries on properties advertised, it is her duty promptly to refer each inquiry to the salesman indicated.

A good secretary can be as profitable as a good salesperson. By relieving the sales staff of unnecessary clerical details, she increases their sales potential. Unless she holds a real estate license, she must guard against acting in any capacity where such a license would be required. This could involve such simple matters as giving out addresses, prices, or terms on any advertised property. As secretary, she should endeavor to obtain the names and telephone numbers of all callers, learn the nature of their business, and relay the messages *accurately* to the persons concerned. Included in her duties will be filling out real estate contracts for the salesmen. It is imperative that she become familiar with each of these forms and the necessary industry terminology. Also, because legal contracts are involved, the importance of accuracy cannot be overemphasized.

[1] When a firm employs five or more salespersons in addition to the owner, there should be a secretary.

Janitorial Services

These are a must for each office. Large real estate organizations normally contract for professional janitorial services. In smaller offices, brokers frequently expect the cleaning chores to be part of the salesman's duties. Aside from maintaining his desk area in a neat and orderly fashion, no salesman should be expected to assume the duties of office janitor. A salesman who is a top producer should have his time limited to canvassing the field, contacting customers, showing property, and bringing his records up-to-date. The salesman whose value to his broker is rated no higher than that of a janitor surely can have no sense of pride in his work, nor can he by any stretch of the imagination be considered a professional in his field. For a small cost, cleaning personnel can be hired on a weekly basis. This should be sufficient to maintain an office in a presentable appearance.

Sales Staff

Sales Manager. "The highest and best use of manpower" should be the philosophy of the successful sales manager. Development of this attitude means assessment of the potential of each salesman. The sales manager is, in effect, selling his services as consultant to the employees, who, in turn, sell them to their customers. Thus, the office philosophy, implemented by the office manager and reflected through him to each of the salesmen, is conveyed to the public. The old adage, "A chain is only as strong as its weakest link," aptly applies to the real estate office sales manager. A concept of solid, ethical principles and uncompromising integrity on the part of each salesman reflects the training of the successful sales manager. Quoting from CREA's *Real Estate Office Administration,*

> The range of activities for which a sales manager is responsible is broad indeed. Basic to all of the others, however, is planning. Planning is a process whereby selected facts and assumptions are analyzed and interrelated in order to determine the activities that are considered necessary to achieve desired results. It is axiomatic that planning begins with the formulation of logical accomplishment objectives. But a firm lacks the basis for such objective determination unless it knows realistically where it now stands in relation to its competition. . . .[2]

The man who has been an outstanding salesman does not necessarily make the best sales manager. He may not be fitted for the task of recruiting, training, motivating, and supervising salespeople. The long, tedious hours of office detail are usually distasteful to persons psychologically attuned to selling. For these and many other reasons, the broker searching for a sales manager must use extreme care in selecting just the right personality embodying all these qualifications. Tact, patience, perseverance, understanding, and creative ability would serve as constructive guides with which to evaluate the applicant.

The good manager is *loyal*—to his company and to his employees. In turn he expects and has the right to demand loyalty from them. He may not always be in agreement with company policy, but he acknowledges his responsibility to carry out the policy while it is in effect, or to resign if he cannot conform in good conscience.

Because he is a planner, he inspires good planning on the part of his sales force. By his example he evidences the value of good planning in getting the most out of each day's work. He assists each salesman to set up a goal for himself and to develop a plan to work systematically toward that goal.

Finally, the good manager is appreciative and knows how to express his appreciation. He is generous with praise for a job well done, but sparing of criticism when mistakes are made. The ability to give helpful criticism without offending is the mark of the successful leader. He must have the analytical insight of a psychologist, learning to recognize each individual's good and bad qualities and to deal with each accordingly. Through a combination of understanding, warmth, and empathy the good manager inspires each salesman to *want* to put forth his best effort. In other words *he has the ability to recognize talent in others and to develop it.*

Job Description

Second in importance to planning in the sales manager's duties is competent recruitment and selection of good salesmen. Selection of quality people means less time spent in training. An old axiom in the business world, "you cannot select higher than you recruit" is particularly applicable to the real estate industry where too often recruitment consists of a window card or a classified ad, and selection means hiring any licensee who applies for the position. It is much simpler (and wiser) to turn down the applicant at the outset than to discharge him later, after time and money have been spent on his training. The success of an office will depend upon the quality of its sales force. If the recruitment and selection program has resulted in filling the office with inefficient workers, only a mediocre nonproductive brokerage operation can result. Office overhead today is too high to risk the employment of even one nonproducer.

Screening the applicant should start with having him complete an application form.[3] The sales manager then reviews the completed form, checks on the references given, and obtains a credit report. If he believes the applicant worthy of really serious consideration, he sets up a personal interview with him. Much time can be saved by having the applicant complete the sales questionnaire before he is called in for the initial interview. This constitutes a rough form of screening and should be used even if the applicant is known to the sales manager. His answers to the questions appearing on the form may eliminate him at the outset. The time thus saved can be used for interviewing the desirable applicant. Before a final decision is made, it is good policy to have a second interview to permit the sales manager to explore more fully any doubtful areas that were revealed in the first interview. Psychological tests are

[2] Dr. Taylor W. Meloan and Herold A. Sherman, "Sales Management: Concepts and Strategy," *Real Estate Office Administration* (Los Angeles: California Real Estate Association, 1963), p. 133.

[3] Sample application form appears on pp. 31–34.

SALESMAN APPLICATION

GENERAL INFORMATION

Name ....

Address ....

Date .... Telephone .... Birth date .... Age................

Place of birth (optional) .... Social Security No. ....

U.S. Citizen: Yes................ No................ Length of time in area ....

Reason for applying to this company ....

....

....

Are you applying for full-time ...., part-time .... work? If part-time will you become full-time within six

months? ....

Will you be available to work such nights as necessary? ....

Male ☐ Female ☐ Married ☐ Single ☐ Widow(er) ☐ Divorced ☐

Number of dependent children .... Ages ....

Other dependents (describe) ....

....

Have you ever been arrested? (do not list minor traffic violations)..

....

....

Are you related to anyone in Real Estate? (who and how) ....

....

List churches (optional) clubs, societies, fraternal organizations, etc., to which you belong, including offices you hold ....

....

....

How many hours do you devote to these activities each week? ....

State what special qualifications or talents you have, if any, which you think especially fit you for Real Estate work........................

....

....

FINANCIAL POSITION

Do you own your home? ☐ Rent ☐ Board ☐ Live with parents or relatives? ☐

Do you own your car? .... Make .... Type .... Year..............................

Do you own any real property? .... If so, describe and give location..

....

....

Are you able to finance yourself? .... For how long? ....

Other source of income .... $ ....

....

Describe any debts or financial obligations ....

....

....

Where do you bank? .... How long? ....

Have you ever been refused bond? .... If so, explain fully ....

....

....

HEALTH

Condition of your health ....

List serious illness and operations during past five years ....

....

....

List the names and addresses of physicians you have consulted during the past five years ....

....

....

Do you have any physical limitations? .... If yes, explain ....

....

....

....

Have you ever been absent from work due to a disability of a recurrent or permanent nature? ....

If yes, explain ....

....

....

Have you ever been refused life insurance? .... If so, explain fully ....

....

....

SERVICE RECORD

Have you served in the Armed Forces of the United States? .... If so, what branch? ....

How long? .... Nature of discharge? .... Date? .... Draft status? ....

EMPLOYMENT HISTORY (Last ten years) Begin with your most recent employment:

From	To	Name and Address of Employer	Position	Rate of Pay	Reason for Leaving

Are you employed at present? .... License No. .... Salesman? .... Broker? ....

Name and address of employer ....

....

Spouse employed? .... Type of work? ....

Name and address of employer ....

If you are employed by this firm, would you be willing to attend classes offered by the Realty Board, or other educational courses? ....

What income do you hope to have attained in one year? $ ....

In five years? .... In ten years? ....

If you are employed by this office, when can you report for work? ....

EDUCATIONAL HISTORY

High school .... Highest grade completed ....

Major subjects ....

Graduated? .... When? ....

Vocational school .... Years .... Subjects ....

....

College .... Years .... Degree ....

PERSONAL REFERENCES

Name	Address	Number years known	Occupation

In case of accident notify: Name ....

Address ....

....

I hereby affirm that my answers to the foregoing questions are true and correct, and that I have not knowingly withheld any fact or circumstance that would, if disclosed, affect my application unfavorably.

I authorize you to communicate with references, former employers and any others whom you desire to contact, and agree to hold such persons harmless with respect to any information they may give.

....
Signature of Applicant

CONFIDENTIAL

TELEPHONE CHECKUP

Real Estate Salesman

Applicant's name ______________________ Tel. no. __________

Former employing firm ______________________ Tel. no. __________

Address ______________________ Date contacted __________

Name of person contacted ______________________

Position with the company ______________________

1. Was applicant employed by you? Yes ______ No ______ Dates ______________
2. What types of property did he deal in? ______________________
3. He states that he earned __________ annually while employed by you.

   Is this statement true? Yes ______ No ______ If not, what were his annual earnings? __________
4. What were his reasons for leaving? ______________________
5. Would you rehire him? Yes ______ No ______ If not, why not? ______________
6. As far as you know, did he have any financial troubles? Yes ______ No ______

   Explain ______________________
7. Did he have any domestic troubles that interfered with his work? ______________

   Yes ______ No ______ Explain ______________
8. How were his business ethics? ______________________
9. Did he have any drinking problems of which you were aware?

   Yes ______ No ______ Explain ______________
10. Was he cooperative with others in the office? Yes ______ No ______

    Explain ______________________
11. Did he respond well to direction? Yes ______ No ______ Explain ______________
12. Did he have good rapport with his clients? Yes ______ No ______ Explain ______________

FORM I-A

Confidential

TELEPHONE CHECKUP

Real Estate Sales Person

FOR WOMEN APPLICANTS ONLY (IN ADDITION TO FORM I-A)

1. What is her family situation? Married __________ Single __________ Widowed __________

   Divorced __________
2. Number of children __________ Ages __________
3. Who cares for the children during her working hours? __________
4. What is her husband's position? __________
5. What company is he employed by? __________
6. What is her reason for working? __________
7. How much time has she taken from work because of illness in the past six months? __________

   Explain __________
8. How many other women employees do you have in your office __________
9. How many men employees? __________

being used by an increasing number of the larger firms; it is found that they are more revealing than the ordinary application form.[4]

Checking with Previous Employers. This should be done by a telephone call to the applicant's former employer. (A letter may bring only a form letter in return.) Many employers hesitate to put their true feelings in writing, but tactful and searching questioning on the telephone will usually bring a response with the desired information.[5]

Points to Consider in Salesman Selection

1. *Is the applicant honest?* No office can afford to have on its staff any person of questionable integrity. No amount of other favorable qualifications can compensate for dishonesty. *Is he ethical?* Ethics has become so much a part of good business practice today as to dictate the success or failure of the firm's operation. The salesman who has no regard for the ethics of his profession probably cannot be considered strictly honest in his activities. He soon eliminates himself from the business, but while he is employed, his activities inject a disruptive element into the office and pose a considerable risk to his employing broker.
2. *What is his attitude?* Is he cheerful, optimistic, confident? Is he a good mixer or is he a loner? Would he fit well into the particular office operation? Is he knowledgeable and aware of industry problems? Attitude more than aptitude should be considered in evaluating the salesman.
3. *Does he present a good appearance?* Is he well groomed? Is he conservatively dressed? Does he use good English? Does he radiate self-confidence and enthusiasm?
4. *Can he handle his money?* Does he live beyond his means? Does he have a savings account? Life insurance? Does he meet his obligations on time?
5. *What are his personal habits?* Is he a family man? Is he a gambler? What are his drinking habits?
6. *Is he a "job hopper"?* This could be a danger signal. How many jobs has he had in the past five years? What were his reasons for leaving? Were they for the purpose of improving his position, or did he leave whenever the going got tough?
7. *Will he be loyal to the company?* Tactful questioning during the interview will usually disclose information on which this decision can be based. For example, where does he appear to place the blame for his shortcomings, or for any failure to produce?
8. *Is he well motivated?* Does he really need to work? Is his wife working? Is he retired on a pension? Is he in the field selling as a vocation, or is it his avocation?
9. *Is he declining in achievement?* In other words, is he going up or down? Is he still growing? Or has he reached his peak and is on the downhill?

Successful Selection of Salesmen

A study undertaken by the Real Estate Research Program directed by Dr. Frederick E. Case at the University of California, Los Angeles, disclosed that a majority of real estate brokers in California (58.3 percent) related success to income productivity. The income that denoted success would of necessity be dependent upon the competency of the sales force.

An examination of returned questionnaires showed that certain qualities or characteristics seemed to separate the successful from the average salesman. The survey found that 83.7 percent of the firms used some criteria for selecting sales personnel. However, many of these offices, it was found, used as a basis for hiring such superficialities as looks, neatness of appearance, ability to speak well, age of the applicant, and his automobile. Although brokers showed surprising agreement on the qualities that were responsible for the success of their high producers, they still failed to seek new personnel possessing these same qualities.

A selection-standards checklist indicated nine qualities that characterized successful salesmen:

1. *Perseverance.* Perseverance implies determination to pursue an object until it is gained. . . .
2. *Enthusiasm.* Closely allied to perseverance is enthusiasm. This trait may be defined as a state of intense interest, fervor, zeal, and the like. Briefly, the applicant is not only convinced of the worth of salesmanship, but is sold on real estate ownership, and he conveys this very real interest to his prospect.
3. *Emotional Stability.* Emotional stability [means that the applicant] is certain of his purpose in

[4] Forms available from Marketing Survey and Research Corp. (NIREB Test Division) New York, N.Y.

[5] See p. 35 for telephone check-up form.

life...and has a plan for carrying it out. He has determined the value of his vocation and will stick with it until he is successful....

4. *Confidence.* Confidence is an attitude possessed by the individual who firmly believes that he is capable of relying on his own resources. He is self-assured and certain that his efforts will be rewarded....
5. *Initiative.* Initiative is more than a simple combination of enthusiasm and self-reliance.... [It] is the drive to get ahead, to be successful in whatever is undertaken.
6. *Extroversion.* Extroversion refers to the individual's outlook on society, more particularly, to an interest in society, a sort of gregariousness in which the extrovert prefers being with and working with people.... He is likely to emphasize the service motive before the profit motive as his attraction to selling property.

   Certain other qualities and traits also differentiated low- from high-income salesmen.

7. *Ability to Work Unsupervised.* A vitally important success trait was the individual's ability to work unsupervised. Constant reliance on surveillance to motivate the salesman is not only unnecessary with the successful staff but equally undesirable....
8. *Capacity to Analyze Investment Needs.* Research found that a significantly higher percentage of successful salesmen sold nonresidential properties, that is, they specialized in sales of commercial, industrial, or residential income property. Coincident with sales of this type is the capacity to analyze investment needs rather than mere amenity needs, as one does in residential sales....
9. *Preference for Selling Less Expensive Homes.* Strange as it seems, there apparently was more money to be made in sales of lower-priced residential dwelling units than in more expensive homes. This finding was borne out when researchers compared the average sale price of houses for both groups and found the average price lower for higher-income salesmen.

Their limitations are several.

1. There are numerous variables in attitude and character make-up that are incapable of measurement....
2. The characteristics listed refer to the aggregate sample. No two offices are alike and exigencies of environment, competition, specific location, market make-up, economic activity, and a host of other variables make each office a case for individual consideration....[6]

[6] Lee S. Burns and Frank G. Mittelback, Real Estate Research Program, "Successful Selection of Salesmen," *California Real Estate Magazine,* Vol. 38, No. 4, (February, 1958), 34–35.

The problems that the majority of offices have in selecting personnel are typcially the result of certain practices, as was pointed out by Dr. Frederick E. Case in his pamphlet, *Selecting, Training, and Reducing Turnover of Real Estate Sales Personnel:*

1. Giving a trial to anyone who applies for a sales position.
2. Failing to check the accuracy of statements about previous business experience. Some have found considerable falsification in statements after the person was hired.
3. Failure to secure all information to determine whether applicant was really qualified. After person was on the job they soon failed.
4. Not making a complete record on the applicant so that others in office might also look it over to determine how well person would fit into existing office arrangements.
5. Failure to inform the applicant completely of what was expected so that he soon quit because of unexpected working hours, "unfair" competition, or having to do floor time, etc.
6. Lack of a clear picture of what kind of a person would be most desirable for the job with the result that perhaps only one out of five persons actually hired stayed on the job.
7. Insufficient knowledge of kind of personality, education and experience needed for success in the particular office. The same qualities are definitely *not* required for all offices.[7]

Most offices prefer to hire the neophyte and train him in office policy. Older salesmen coming from other offices may have to be unsold on fixed selling or listing habits that may be at variance with the policy of the new office. Often a senior salesman is assigned to accompany and oversee the new employee for the first few weeks. Many brokers feel that the new man should not be given floor time until he is familiar with the office methods and fully acquainted with all office listings.

Quoting from the summary of the findings of a survey by the NAREB Research Department:

> The plan for salesmen's compensation in most firms provides for income in various proportions from

[7] Dr. Frederick E. Case, *Selecting, Training, and Reducing Turnover of Real Estate Sales Personnel, A Survey of Current Practices in Real Estate Offices in California,* presented by Educational Committee of the California Real Estate Association at 1957 Educational and Sales Conferences, p. 7.

two sources, that is, sales and listings. In addition, incentive payments are used by some brokers, generally in combination with a flat percentage method of calculating compensation from sales.

The gross commission which the salesman receives for his part in a real estate transaction is paid at a flat percentage of the brokerage fee in three-fourths of the firms. In the other fourth, the amount of the salesman's commission is derived from a sliding scale based on one or more factors used to increase the compensation for the usually productive.

Listing Compensation Varies

In addition to income from sales, salesmen in most firms (88%) are compensated for listings. Methods vary from payment for exclusive only to a differential related to whether the listing is open or exclusive. Some seven out of ten firms (69%) pay without regard to the nature of the listing. While 5 per cent pay for exclusive only, 12 per cent relate the percentage of compensation to whether or not the listing is open or an exclusive.

Although the percentage paid for listings ranged from 5 per cent in some firms to 35 per cent in others, the largest group (45.7%) pay 10 per cent. The median compensation for a listing is 15 per cent and represents the practice in about a sixth (16.9%) of the firms. A few brokers reported a system of fees expressed not in percentage but in dollar amounts. Some firms pay a higher than average percentage for sales and a lower one for listings. Others emphasize listings and use a less than average percentage as compensation for sales.

Several Factors Involved

Where a sliding scale is used as the basis of salesman compensation it may relate to—

1. Salesman's earnings in a given period;
2. Salesman's volume of sales;
3. The time lapse between listing and sale;
4. A combination of one or more of the foregoing.[8]

Success in the form of wealth or net profit is the objective of a real estate broker who opens his own office. To maximize this profit, he must attempt to secure a staff of the most productive salesmen available.

[8] Catherine E. Martini, director, and Wray O. Candillis, assistant director, "Salesman Compensation Studied by National Association of Real Estate Boards Research Department," in *California Real Estate Magazine,* Vol. 43, No. 9 (July, 1963), 18–19.

Status of Women in the Real Estate Business

Quoting Grace M. Batavia, of Tucson, Arizona:

> Women's place has always been considered "in the home." It has been established, however, women in business have succeeded and have been instrumental in creating even higher standards of living, which they have passed on to the whole family.
>
> This is particularly true of women in the real estate business. Although this is a profession of many facets, women have succeeded in the home selling field to a very great extent. Many a good woman salesman or broker has been a moving factor in selecting the right type of home for her clients because of her natural insight into the basic needs of most women who are the homemakers of our country. Thus, satisfactory results from her efforts have spurred her on to greater ambition—to become an expert in a particular phase of the real estate business.[9]

Innumerable women enter the real estate field thinking that it is a highly lucrative job filled with glamor and excitement but requiring little effort or skill. In interviewing prospective employees, it is the broker's responsibility to dispel these illusions immediately. The applicants should understand that only concentrated full-time effort can produce maximum results. They should be made to realize also that the hours are often long and many times the transactions are frustrating and require great skill, patience, and superior knowledge.

Women in general, however, are particularly fitted to the selling of homes. They are the homemakers and instinctively appraise a house for the amenities it will provide to the woman buyer. Because it is usually the wife who selects the home, the real estate saleswoman has a natural aptitude for pointing out its appealing features.

It is necessary for the saleswomen to study the real estate business even more thoroughly than men do, because there are many customers (especially among men) who question a woman's competence in the field. Knowledge of the basic construction of a house is highly important and too often is overlooked or underemphasized by real estate saleswomen. Most of the criticism of them is leveled at their lack of knowledge in this area. The value to the professional

[9] Grace M. Batavia, "A Challenge to Women," *What Women Realtors Are Doing,* Vol. 6, No. 10 (October 1963), (Women's Council of the National Association of Real Estate Boards), p. 12.

STONE & SCHULTE INC.

SALESMAN'S AGREEMENT

THIS AGREEMENT is made by and between ______________________ hereinafter referred to as the "SALESMAN", and STONE & SCHULTE, INC., hereinafter referred to as the "BROKER", for and in consideration of their mutual promises and for their mutual benefits.

WITNESSETH:

WHEREAS, the Broker is duly licensed and registered as a real estate broker, and is duly qualified to, and does, produce the listings of real estate for sale, trade, exchange, lease or rental, and all prospective purchasers, lessees, and renters thereof and has and does enjoy the good will of, and a reputation for fair dealing with the public, and

WHEREAS, the Broker has and maintains an office, or offices, properly equipped with furnishings and staffed with employees, suitable to serving the public as a real estate broker, and

WHEREAS, it is deemed to the mutual advantage of broker and salesman to form the association hereinafter agreed to under the terms and conditions hereinafter set out,

THEREFORE:

1. PERFORMANCE BY BROKER

(a) In General:
The Broker agrees to make available to the Salesman all current listings of the office, and all listings received by the office from the Multiple Listing Service of the San Jose Real Estate Board or the Real Estate Board having jurisdiction in the area to which the Salesman is assigned, providing the applicant has qualified for his membership in said Board, and as pertinent to the departments to which the Salesman is actually assigned, and agrees to assist the Salesman in his work by advice, instruction, and full cooperation in every way possible.

(b) Facilities:
The Broker agrees that the salesman may share with other salesmen of Stone & Schulte, Inc., such facilities as the office may be able to furnish in connection with the subject matter of this contract, and to give to the Salesman a key to the office, or offices, to which he is assigned with the full understanding that the Salesman is responsible for said keys and for his conduct in the offices, and that at no time can the keys be given to any other party without the Broker's express permission.

- 1 -

____
Initials

2. PERFORMANCE BY SALESMAN

(a) In General:
The Salesman agrees to work diligently and with his best efforts to sell, lease, trade, exchange or rent any and all real estate listed with the Broker, and otherwise to promote the business of serving the public in real estate transactions, to the end that each of the parties hereto may derive the greatest profit possible.

(b) Conduct:
The Salesman, under duly authorized supervision, as designated by the Broker, agrees to conduct his business and regulate his habits so as to maintain and to increase, rather than diminish, the good will and reputation of the Broker; and the parties hereto agree to conform to and abide by all laws, rules, and regulations, as well as the codes of ethics of the National Association of Real Estate Boards, National Association of Home Builders, and other related organizations with which Stone & Schulte, Inc. is affiliated, that are applicable to real estate brokers and real estate salesmen.

(c) Regulations:

(1) The Salesman shall read and be governed by all the rules and regulations, code of ethics, all of the By-Laws as they may from time to time be amended, as well as the regulations of the Multiple Listing Service of the San Jose Real Es tate Board or the Real Estate Board having jurisdiction in the area to which the salesman is assigned, and the Real Estate Law of the State of California, and any future modifications or additions thereto.

(2) The Salesman witnesseth that he has read and approved all of the policies as set forth in the Stone & Schulte, Inc. Policy Manual together with all additions thereto up to the date of his association and hereafter to be bound by such policies and amendments thereto.

3. DUTIES OF SALESMAN

(a) Membership:
The Salesman agrees, if assigned to the Resale Department, that within one hundred and eighty (180) days of his assignment to become a member of the Real Estate Board in whose jurisdiction the office is located and to maintain his membership in good standing while he is associated with Stone & Schulte, Inc.

(b) License:
The Salesman agrees to remain continuously licensed by the State of California to sell real estate as a salesman during the term of his association with Stone & Schulte, Inc., and to promptly notify the Broker in the event any condition arises which affects the status of his real estate license so that the Broker may take proper action. It is understood that this agreement between Broker and Salesman will be automatically terminated concurrently with the time that the Salesman's license ceases to be effective under California Law, unless moved to another department in the interim.

- 2 -

Initials

(c) Expenses:
The Salesman shall not obligate the Broker for materials or services or contract for anything outside of the execution of the normal real estate listing and selling agreements without the express knowledge and consent of the Broker.

(d) Transportation:
The Salesman agrees to furnish his own automobile and pay all expenses thereof, and to carry liability and property damage insurance satisfactory to the Broker and adequate to meet any liability in regard to the operation of his vehicle. The following limits of liability are considered to be the minimum amounts acceptable: $100,000.00/ $300,000.00.

(e) Meetings:
The Salesman agrees to attend all sales meetings and functions of the Broker except when illness or dire circumstances prevent such attendance, and to lend his loyal support to the team effort of the Broker's organization.

(f) Procedures:
The Salesman shall use only such real estate forms as have been first approved by the Broker, and the Salesman agrees to follow all of the procedures as set forth in the Stone & Schulte, Inc. Policy Manual.

(g) Correspondence:
The Salesman agrees to submit to the Broker for approval, all letters and correspondence written by the Salesman pertaining to the business of the Broker on behalf of the clients and customers for whom the Salesman is performing services, and that these shall be turned over to the Sales Manager, or the appropriate officer of the Broker, to review and file with the appropriate records for future reference.

(h) Sale Transaction:
The Salesman agrees to deliver promptly to the Escrow or Accounting Departments of the Broker all deposit monies, Deposit Receipts, other documents, and property received by the Salesman in connection with any transaction which he executes as a real estate sales agent. All checks must be made payable to Stone & Schulte, Inc. or to the title company handling the sale, unless prior approval of the Broker has been obtained to make it directly payable to other parties.

4. AUTHORITY OF SALESMAN

(a) Decisions:
The Salesman recognizes that all listings and prospects are the sole property of the Broker and all decisions as to their treatment will rest with the Broker. The Salesman agrees to abide by those decisions at all times.

(b) Representations:
(1) The Salesman recognizes and understands that he has no authority from the Broker, either expressly or implied, to represent anything to a prospective purchaser or client unless it is expressly provided for in the listing agreement, sales contract, or unless he receives specific written instructions from the Broker or the client.

- 3 -

Initials

(2) The Salesman recognizes that the Broker reserves the right to reject any exclusive listing agreement that is deemed unsatisfactory for the Broker's representation and complete authority to cancel and return said listing to the owner in the event it does not meet the Broker's standards.

(c) Escrows:
The Salesman acknowledges that all escrows and title searches shall be ordered and handled by the authorized Escrow Officers and Managers of the Broker's offices, and at no time may he open such escrows directly with any Title Company or have recorded any instruments involving his real estate transactions without the advance approval of the Broker.

5. LEGAL LIABILITY

(a) In General:
The Broker shall not be liable to the Salesman for any expense incurred by said salesman or for any of his acts; nor shall the Salesman be liable to the Broker for office help or expenses, and the Salesman shall have no authority to bind the Broker by any promise or representation, unless especially authorized in a particular transaction; but the expenses for the attorney's fees, costs, revenue stamps, abstracts, and title insurance, and the like which must, by reason of necessity, be paid from the commission, or are incurred in the collection of, or the attempt to collect, the commission shall be paid by the parties in the same proportion as provided for in the Stone & Schulte, Inc. Policy Manual.

(b) Legal Actions:

(1) Suits for commissions shall, agreeable to the law, be maintained only in the name of the Broker, and solely at the Broker's discretion, and the Salesman shall be construed to be a sub-agent only with respect to the clients and customers for whom service shall be performed, and shall otherwise be deemed to be an independent contractor and not a servant, employee, joint adventurer, or partner of the Broker.

(2) It is further understood that the Broker reserves the right at any time to take action or not take action, as the case may be, in any specific transaction with which the salesman is involved.

(3) In the event any transaction in which the Salesman is involved results in a dispute, arbitration, litigation, or legal expense, the Salesman shall cooperate fully, and abide by the decision that is acceptable to the Broker. The Salesman recognizes that it is the policy of the Broker to avoid litigation wherever possible and that the Broker reserves the sole right to determine whether or not any litigation or dispute shall be prosecuted, defended, or settled, or whether or not legal expenses shall be incurred. If a dispute or litigation is anticipated on a particular transaction, the Broker reserves the right to defer payment of the commission on said transaction to the Salesman until a settlement satisfactory to the Broker is reached.

Initials

(c) Enforcement of Agreement:
It is further agreed that if the Broker must incur legal expense and attorney's fees in order to obtain the performance of the Salesman on any of the points set forth in this contract, that such expenses and fees will be recoverable from the Salesman.

6. COMPENSATION

(a) In General:
The usual and customary commissions as set forth in the Stone & Schulte, Inc. Policy Manual, shall be charged for any service performed hereunder and the Broker shall advise the Salesman of any special contract relating to any particular transaction which he undertakes to handle, where commissions are other than customary.

(b) Status of Salesman:
Since the Salesman is the sub-contractor, and not an employee, the Broker shall not deduct withholding tax, social security, federal old age benefits, from commissions paid to the Salesman, and the Salesman shall be responsible for his own records and his own payments on any of these items, and is considered an associate of the Broker instead of an employee.

(c) Division of Commissions:

(1) When the Salesman shall perform any service hereunder, whereby a commission is earned, said commission shall, when collected, be divided between the Broker and the Salesman according to the schedule set forth in the Stone & Schulte, Inc. Policy Manual and Commission Schedule and the amendments to said Policy Manual as they shall appear from time to time, at the Broker's discretion. In no case shall the Broker be liable to the Salesman for any commission unless the same shall have been collected from the party for whom the service was performed.

(2) The Salesman acknowledges that any arrangement, other than as approved in the Stone & Schulte, Inc. Policy Manual, for the division of a commission with other Brokers must be expressly approved by the Broker through its authorized personnel. In the event that two or more salesmen with Stone & Schulte, Inc., are involved in a disputed commission settlement, the Salesman agrees to abide by the decision of the Broker as to the final division of such commissions.

(d) Commissions Other Than Cash:

(1) In any transaction where it becomes necessary or desirable to receive all or any part of a commission in property other than cash, the Salesman acknowledges that the express approval of the Broker is mandatory before the Broker is obligated to accept said commission in property other than cash.

(2) The Broker reserves the right to divide such property, if and when taken, between the Salesman and the Broker, in kind, or pay the Salesman his full share of the commission in cash and retain full ownership in the property so received, or retain such property in the name of the Broker and thereafter

____
Initials

dispose of the same at such time and in such manner as the Broker shall deem advisable. Any profit, loss or other expenses with respect to such property shall be shared between the Broker and the Salesman in the same proportion as their respective interests in the commission involved.

(3) The Salesman acknowledges that the Broker is entitled to receive a $2.50 service charge for the bookkeeping and service expenses involved in the maintenance and collection of each note transaction and thereafter the principal and interest are divided proportionate to the interest of all parties named in the notes.

(e) Forfeiture of Deposits:
The Salesman acknowledges that in the event all or any portion of a deposit is forfeited, disbursement of the remaining portion shall be based on the usual commission schedule under which the Salesman is currently working and shall include listings, sales and Broker's portions on their proportionate basis.

7. SUBDIVISION REGULATIONS

If the Broker elects to employ the services of the Salesman on any of the properties or subdivisions which the Broker represents as tracts with model homes and sales office, the Salesman agrees to abide by the following regulations concerning such subdivisions:

(a) Performance:

(1) The Salesman accepts such employment and agrees to perform all of the services specifically required of him as set forth in the Stone & Schulte, Inc. Policy Manual, and as amended from time to time, regarding subdivisions in a diligent and efficient manner.

(2) The Salesman agrees to abide by the Broker's instructions as to processing, staffing of model homes, and maintaining the regular hours, and performing all other services in connection with the sales made on that project.

(b) Prices:
All properties sold by the Salesman pursuant to the terms of the project to which he is assigned shall be sold at prices not less than those fixed by the Broker or by the owners with whom the Broker has negotiated the terms and the contracts.

(c) Compensation:

(1) The Salesman agrees to accept payment for his commissions on the tracts to which he is assigned and recognizes that payment is not due unless the sale has been placed in escrow, a proper application for a loan has been made and approved, if required, all papers of the escrow have been completed and the escrow terminated satisfactorily and the Broker has received his agreed commission from the owner due to the efforts of the Salesman, and then, and then only, shall the Salesman be entitled to a commission for such properties sold.

- 6 -

Initials

(2) It is further agreed that if the Salesman is transferred from one development to another at the Broker's option, or upon mutual request, the Salesman will not be required to forfeit any commissions left to him at the previous development inasmuch as he will in turn be required to service the new development under the terms of this agreement.

(3) However, should the Salesman be requested to or voluntarily transfer to another department or capacity, other than that related to subdivisions, in the various affiliated organizations of Stone & Schulte, Inc., or should the Salesman voluntarily terminate his association with the Broker, or should the Broker find it necessary for any reason to terminate the services of the Salesman, the Broker reserves the right to exercise the forfeiture provisions expressed in this agreement under paragraph 7., (c), (4) below.

(4) Should the Salesman be requested to or voluntarily transfer to another department or capacity in the various affiliated organizations of Stone & Schulte, Inc., or should the Salesman voluntarily terminate his association with the Broker, or should the Broker find it necessary for any reason to terminate the services of the Salesman, the Broker reserves the right to exercise the forfeiture of the 1/3 servicing commission set forth in the Stone & Schulte, Inc. Policy Manual. However, all other commissions earned that are not servicing commissions, namely for procurement and writing of Deposit Receipts, shall not be forfeited as they will be considered the Salesman's earnings during the life of this agreement, providing said escrows close in the normal fashion. If the Broker elects to exercise this forfeiture regarding the 1/3 servicing commission after termination or transfer, a letter will be sent by the Broker to the Salesman at his last known address setting forth this election.

(d) Termination:
In the event that this agreement has been terminated by either party for any reason, and the Salesman has been assigned to a subdivision or tract for which the Broker is responsible during the life of this agreement, the Salesman shall be bound by the competition provisions of this agreement as contained in 8. below.

(e) Competition:
The Salesman further agrees that if after the termination of this agreement he does directly solicit or work for, have connection with or perform services for any of the subdividers, builders or brokers with whom the Broker has contracts during the term of this agreement, the Broker shall have the right to sue for general damages plus the amount of commissions resulting from the Salesman's actions, as well as attorney's fees and court costs.

- 7 -

____
Initials

8. TERMINATION

(a) In General:
The association created by this agreement may be terminated by either party hereto at any time and for any reason upon notice in writing given to the other party; however, such termination of association will in no way void any of the provisions of this agreement created by such association.

(b) Duty of Sales man:
Upon termination of the association, the Salesman shall return to the Broker all property that he has been given by the Broker, including the Stone & Schulte, Inc. Policy Manual, training materials, keys to the offices, etc., and shall transfer to the Broker a list of all clients with whom the Salesman is negotiating and working, and shall assign irrevocably to the Broker all right to listing contracts currently in force at the time of the termination. Further, he agrees to return to the Broker all files, records, listings, names of prospects, and anything else that has been assigned to him during the time of his employment upon the termination of this association.

(c) Effect on Clients and Listings:
Upon termination of this contract, all unsold listings current at the time of said termination and obtained by the Salesman shall become the exclusive property of the Broker as well as the names of all clients with whom the Salesman has been negotiating and working with up to the time of his termination; and these listings and clients shall be considered the exclusive property of the Broker for a period of 180 days from and after the termination of association created by this contract or for 180 days after the expiration of the listing, whichever is later.

(d) Effect on Commissions:

(1) The rights of the parties to any commissions which accrued prior to said notice shall not be divested by the termination of the association created by this contract except as covered under the following aforesaid provisions of this agreement: paragraphs 7., (c), (3) and (4).

(2) The Broker shall not be liable to the Salesman for a commission on any listing procured by the Salesman on the sale of any property unless an offer in writing has been obtained from a bonafide purchaser, accompanied by a Deposit Receipt, and ratified in writing by the seller prior to the termination of the association of the Salesman and the same transaction is later closed in escrow according to its original terms.

(e) Competition Provisions:
The Salesman hereby agrees that at all times, both during his employment and after the termination of his employment, he will hold inviolate and keep secret all knowledge or information as to the listings, clients, files, and business that were made known to him by the Broker or any of its authorized personnel or learned by him while in the Broker's employ and he will not impart or make known any of the same or anything relating to the same to any competitor or other person, firm or corporation, nor use the same to his own advantage or the advantage of any other person or concern except when authorized to do so by writing and signed by the Broker.

Initials

9. TRAINING PROVISIONS

(a) In General:
The Salesman does expressly agree that he needs and desires the real estate training services of the Broker and further agrees to remain as a Trainee during the first twelve (12) months of his association with the Broker.

(b) Training Period:
For purposes of this Agreement, the training period shall be considered completed as of ________________, 19___.

(c) Training Classes and Assignments:
The Salesman agrees to attend all training classes except when prior approval for absence has been obtained from the Broker and, further, to perform all assignments and read all material which the Broker shall designate during the training period.

(d) Trainee Commission and Policies:
The Salesman recognizes the extensive costs involved to the Broker for education and, therefore, agrees to remain on the Trainee Commission Schedule until the completion of the twelve (12) months period and, further, to abide by the Broker's policies and procedures as they apply to the Trainee Classification of personnel.

(e) Promotion to Senior Status:
The Broker agrees that upon the salesman's successful completion of all the stipulated requirements of training and at the conclusion of the 12 months period covered in paragraph 10., (b) above, to promote the Salesman to Senior Status and the Senior Commission Schedule.

(f) Trainee Termination:
In the event of the termination of the association created by this agreement for any reason other than being discharged by the Broker without cause by the Broker within one (1) year from the date of formation, the Salesman agrees that he will not engage as employer, employee, real estate agent, salesman, broker, or otherwise, directly or indirectly, at any time within one (1) year from the date of formation of this agreement in a similar business to that of the Broker in the area serviced by the Broker's offices and should he at any time leave the employ of the Broker, he will not in violation of its terms enter into the employ or service or otherwise act in aid of the business of any rival broker or concern or individual engaged in the same or in similar lines of business; and if he does so in violation hereof, the Broker shall be entitled to an injunction by any competent court of equity enjoining and restraining him and each and every other person concerned thereby from continuance of such employment, services or other act in aid of the business of such rival broker or concern.

(g) In the event the Broker elects to terminate the employment of the Salesman, doing so in writing, then the Broker will waive the restrictions contained in paragraph 10., (f) above.

____
Initials

10. EFFECT OF AGREEMENT

(a) Successors:
This agreement shall be binding upon the Salesman, his heirs, executors, administrators and assigns and shall inure to the benefit of and be enforceable by or against the Broker, its successors and assigns.

(b) This instrument shall represent the entire agreement between the parties hereto, any other or prior understandings, agreements and contracts being hereby cancelled without any further liability whatsoever on either part.

(c) Effective Date:
This agreement is effective upon the execution hereof.

IN WITNESS WHEREOF, the Salesman and the Broker have hereto signed their names this ____________ day of ____________ 19____.

____
SALESMAN

STONE & SCHULTE, INC.

By____________________
General Manager

By____________________
Broker

STATE OF CALIFORNIA)
) SS.
COUNTY OF SANTA CLARA)

On____________________, before me, the undersigned, a Notary Public in and for said County and State, personally appeared ____________________ ____________________, known to me to be the person______ whose name ______subscribed to the within instrument and acknowledged that__________ executed the same. WITNESS my hand and official seal.____________________

(Seal)
Signature____________________

____
Name
Notary Public in and for said County and State

______
Initials

saleswoman of up-to-date information on financing, zoning, and building costs cannot be overstressed.

Women today are said to control 80 percent of the nation's wealth. If these statistics are correct, they will figure prominently as the future real estate investor. Who better to gain their confidence and assist them with their investments than one of their sex who has prepared herself with a background of knowledge in the field?

During 1959 the Standing Committee on Education of the Women's Council of the National Association of Real Estate Boards conducted a national survey to obtain information on the role of women in the real estate business, the basic purpose of which was to learn as much as possible about the present status of women in the profession. Two questionnaires were distributed, from which much valuable information was developed. One set of questions was directed to Women's Council members, and another to 650 real estate firms who were members of NAREB and who were reported to employ women as brokers or salespeople. In answer to a question, "In your opinion, what has been the principal cause or causes of turnover among your saleswomen?" 433 firms replied. Eighteen percent declared that they had no labor turnover, while 23 percent answered that they had "very little turnover." In the latter group, typical answers were, "Our labor turnover is very low, because we choose our women carefully," "Our women leave much less often than our men," and "The only women who have left us are women whose husbands have been transferred out of town."

In the opinion of the vast number of firm executives responding to the questionnaire, lack of technical knowledge is the field in which saleswomen are most in need of more training. Problems relating to financing the sale account for most of the comments regarding training needs. In summing up, the committee making the survey had this to say:

> In the last few years a number of studies of desirable and undesirable traits in salespeople have been made by various independent research groups and universities. These suggest a remarkable similarity between the traits displayed by men and women on the job. Inability to adjust to the situation, personality problems and poor work habits appear to be among the major causes of failure on the job, both among men and women. For example, in a recent survey of 125 selected sales executives by George Washington University, executives, asked to list the greatest weakness of their salesmen, have the following four—listed in the order of their importance:
>
> 1. Inability to get along with the other fellow.
> 2. Not enough time spent in actual selling.
> 3. Poor work habits.
> 4. Insufficient knowledge of the product.[10]

Interviewing Salesmen

The background of a salesman should be most important to the employing broker. As John C. Tyson, of Previews, Inc., puts it, "We believe in putting square pegs in square holes." The type of property being handled by the office will largely determine the type of salesman required. (Ranch properties should be handled by salesmen familiar with the problems of ranching; luxury estates should be entrusted only to salesmen with cultural backgrounds.)

Many thousands of psychological tests have been developed. These include tests for intelligence, aptitude, achievement of performance, personality and temperament, and interest and motivation. In general, what these tests attempt to determine is to what extent the applicant's pattern (of personnel test scores) corresponds to the test patterns of successful persons employed in the field.

At present the problem of selecting real estate salespeople through psychological testing is still in the preliminary stage, and probably no complete scientific studies have been conducted to determine what factors make up a successful real estate salesperson. The prediction and control of employees in any business begin at the hiring stage. Many employers are using aptitude tests that screen out those who are likely to fail and that help to select those who can be successfully developed. These tests are simply measuring devices that determine the differences between people. Corporations estimate that it costs somewhere between \$500 and \$5,000 to train a man for sales work. When an office thinks enough of the quality of people employed to have them tested before hiring, the word soon gets around, and the better applicants apply because they know that they have nothing to fear from the tests.

Personal interviews are probably the principal means used by most offices for selection. In many firms it is the only device used, and the interview is usually conducted in a very casual and disorganized manner.

In order to be effective, the interview should be coordinated. This can be accomplished by means of a form that the interviewer keeps before him during the interview.

[10] Beryl Rogers McClaskey, Ph. D., chairman 1959 Standing Committee on Education, Women's Council of NAREB, *The Status of Women in Real Estate* (Chicago: The Council, 1962), p. 18.

Policy Manual

A productive office-policy manual should contain the policies and procedures of the office, stated concisely and outlined in an easy-to-read manner. It should be explained thoroughly to each trainee as part of his indoctrination. Carefully prepared, the policy manual can double as a training manual and reference book and should be a part of the salesman's kit. Policy manuals will vary according to the size of the organization and the type of properties handled. They should be compiled in a loose leaf binder to allow for deletions, additions, or changes. Major topics to be covered in a manual include:

1. Office procedures
2. Listing and selling policy
3. Financing
4. Advertising
5. Appraising techniques
6. Commission and bonuses[11]

Training

It is the broker's responsibility to guide his salesmen. The first week of the new salesman's employment is probably the most important in his selling career. Too many organizations, after the most careful selection of a salesman, leave him on his own to sink or swim. Before any training program can be set up by an office, the broker must have an objective. That is to say, what does he hope to accomplish by his sales-training program? He will most certainly want to stimulate and motivate his salesman to *want* to sell real estate. This must come before any tools are given him. Only after proper indoctrination in the responsibilities inherent in his license, as well as in the benefits to be derived therefrom, should the salesman be entrusted with the full privileges of acting as agent.

Without constant inspiration, the best salesman can become disinterested, with a resultant drop in his sales record. Surveys that have been made in many selling fields indicate that the monetary return is not usually all that motivates the salesman. Many emotional needs enter into the appraisal of the manager–salesman relationship. As a normal human being, the salesman has a need for recognition of effort expended and praise for a job well done. Inspiration for his best work comes from a sense of belonging, of being "one of the team." Recognition by the sales manager of these needs may be the stimulus needed to lift the salesman from the mediocre field to that of the top producer.

Inspiring his men to greater achievement is a continuing process on the part of the sales manager. Salesmen, even the best of them, will have selling slumps. The dips in their sales charts do not come about by accident, nor are they always the result of the natural trough following the peak. Rather, they may be the direct result of an interruption in the salesman's training program. This usually evidences itself by his lack of enthusiasm for his work, coupled with moods of irritability and depression. He appears to have lost confidence in himself. When his motivation is lacking, the natural consequence is a drop in his sales record.

The salesman's progress should be reviewed each month in his beginning year, and every quarter after that, or whenever the situation appears to call for a reevaluation. This is best accomplished by a conference in the sales manager's private office. The interview is one to be conducted from a helpful rather than from a critical point of view.

When a marked and continuing decline in his sales (from whatever cause) is detected, the salesman should be reevaluated by the manager. Candid discussion of his problems is indicated, and every attempt should be made to uncover the basic causes. Galileo once said, "You cannot teach a man anything; you can only help him to find it within himself." The fact that someone is taking a genuine interest in him is sometimes all that is needed. The individual may feel that his efforts are going unrecognized, even though in his own mind he is convinced that he is doing a good job. Selling is, at best, a lonely business. Each salesman must act on his own, and decisions must often be made by him alone. He succeeds or fails on his own initiative. Like the football player, he must continually be cheered on by his teammates and his coach. The monetary reward alone is rarely sufficient, nor does it provide the strongest motivation if the other more personal incentives are lacking.

Selling His Community

To succeed, the salesman must be confident of his ability to sell, have faith in his company's integrity, and be sold on the worth of his product. Vital also to his success is his faith in his community and the ability to transfer this confidence to his customer. Many tales have been written about the romantic early days of California, about her tremendous population growth, and about the resultant skyrocketing of land values. Although this may be familiar history to California residents, the buyer coming from out-

[11] For sample policy manual, see pp. 39–48.

side the state may not be fully aware of the potential in California real estate.

In conjunction with his formal training, therefore, it is incumbent on the new salesman to review California's history of land ownership, to assemble statistics on its growth possibilities, and to make a study of the trends and factors influencing this growth. Complete knowledge of his immediate community is also essential: of its zoning laws, its business section, its average income, its churches, its schools, and its transportation system. With the assistance of his sales manager, a sales kit of related reference material should be compiled.[12]

Trade-Association Policies

Special attention should be given to the policies of the local Board of Realtors, its bylaws and its regulations. Complete understanding of these procedures, together with NAREB's Code of Ethics, will do much to prevent disputes or friction between offices, often caused by the novice in the field unfamiliar with what is expected of him where his relations with his colleagues are concerned.

In addition, some offices require their salesmen to attend available academic courses. To encourage this participation, offices in increasing numbers are paying the salesman's tuition and other costs in connection with the courses.

Sales Meetings

These are of little value unless a definite program is set up and followed strictly. Meetings should be planned well in advance, and each session should be geared to a specific topic. Techniques of successful listing or selling, current financing policies, changes in legislative rulings, and up-to-date information on zoning or building regulations could be covered. Variety, in the form of guest speakers, panel-type discussions, or films can be used to advantage. Most important is the sharing of experiences and suggestions for solutions of problems in an open-forum-type discussion.

CASE STUDY

The Blue Sky Realty Company has been established for fifteen years in the same location. It has an excellent reputation and does a large volume of repeat business. It employs ten salespeople and a secretary-receptionist. The broker, John Sky, does not compete with his salesmen in selling or listing. He takes only those customers who are specifically referred to him. He spends each weekend with his family at their mountain retreat. Jim Blue is a new salesman with the office. He is a graduate of an eastern college and has a degree in business administration, with real estate his specialization. He has set a goal of $25,000 in annual commissions by the end of his fifth year in the business. The other salespeople have been with the company from ten to twelve years, but none of them is college-educated. They have all been moderately successful, averaging annual incomes of $8,000 from commissions. The company has no bonus plan, preferring instead to reward the entire sales staff with weekend trips to resort areas. There is no sales manager and no formal training program. Jim Blue's commissions the first year amounted to only $6,500, though he worked industriously and built up much good will for the company. He is already getting some referred business from his satisfied customers.

The broker is popular with his sales force, primarily because he never enters into office arbitration problems, preferring to have the salesmen resolve their own disputes. He expects each salesman to write his own advertising, arrange his own financing, draw all documents, and, in general, handle his own transactions from the listing to the closing of the escrow. He believes that too much assistance can destroy the initiative of the salesperson.

1. What, in your opinion, would you consider Jim Blue's opportunities for reaching his goals if he remains with the Blue Sky Realty Company?
2. What do you feel are the attractive features of this office operation?
3. In what areas do you feel improvements could be made?
4. If you were a newly licensed salesman, would you feel that you should apply for a position with the company?

[12] Further details on compiling a sales kit will be included in Chap. 8, "Techniques of Selling."

SUGGESTED REFERENCES

CASE, FREDERICK E., *Real Estate Brokerage.* Englewood Cliffs, N.J.: Prentice-Hall, Inc. 1965.

HAAS, KENNETH B., *How to Develop Successful Salesmen.* New York: McGraw-Hill Book Company, 1957.

Increase Real Estate Office Profits through Effective Administration. Los Angeles: California Real Estate Association, 1965.

Successful Real Estate Office Administration Practice. Los Angeles: California Real Estate Association, 1966.

4

Listings

Types of Listing Contracts

According to the California Department of Real Estate definition, "A listing is an employment contract between principal and agent authorizing the latter to perform services for the principal involving the latter's property. Listing contracts are entered into for the purpose of securing persons to buy, lease, or rent property."

Types of listings in general use in California include:

1. Open Listing. Under this type of listing, only the office which makes the sale receives the commission. *The owner may sell the property without being liable to the broker for commission.* Some owners favor this type of listing under the assumption that circulating the listing through several offices will provide it with a wider market. The more sophisticated seller is coming to recognize the disadvantages of looking to several offices for concentrated sales effort, none of which is inclined to give the open listing preferred attention. The seller who expects this soon discovers that, "Everybody's business is nobody's business." Careful selection of a single competent broker to handle property on an exclusive basis has come to be considered the more professional approach.

From the broker's standpoint, the open listing is very unsatisfactory and is usually accepted only if the subject property is one that will sell readily, and only after all attempts to secure the listing on an exclusive basis have failed. Because of high advertising costs, with no assurance of reimbursement, most offices reject the open-type listing as not good business practice.

2. Exclusive Agency. Under this type of listing also, the owner reserves the right to sell his property without payment of a commission. The listing office, however, collects a commission if another office makes the sale. Although the owner may save the commission, here again he cannot expect concentrated effort on the part of the listing office when it has no certainty of reimbursement for time and money expended. The listing office is, in effect, working in competition to the owner in the sale of a property listed on the *exclusive-agency* basis. If the broker's position in this situation is made clear to the property owner, he can usually be made to understand the impossible situation created when a broker attempts to merchandise a property in competition to his principal (the seller).

3. Exclusive Right. This type of listing is the one most favored by brokers, because the listing office is paid a commission regardless of who sells the property. The office can afford to spend money on advertising and to put forth its best promotional endeavors, because it is certain of a return on its investment (provided the property is sold during the listing period). The listing office also has the added benefit of controlling the actions of cooperating offices. The exclusive-right listing provides the broker with complete protection; hence, he feels free to cooperate with other offices. This also gives a distinct advantage to the seller, an advantage that is often overlooked by him when considering the open listings as against the exclusive right. In many instances, by cooperation between offices, greater coverage is obtained than would be possible under the open listing, where the seller is required to list with a large number of offices to be sure of equal market exposure. (A distinguishing feature of the exclusive-type listing is the termination date required under

Extra Copies 25
Glossy Print yes
To Recip. Board yes
Prepare in triplicate

PASADENA BOARD OF REALTORS
MULTIPLE LISTING SERVICE - RESIDENTIAL LISTING AGREEMENT

This listing expires April 12, 1971

THIS IS AN EXCLUSIVE RIGHT AGREEMENT WITH A MEMBER OF THE MULTIPLE LISTING SERVICE. Area NE Code 3FDr

The Realtor may rely on the accuracy of the following information in presenting the property to prospective buyers, and the undersigned hereby agrees to indemnify and hold the Realtor harmless from all loss, damage, expense or liability incurred by the Realtor, any sub-agent, Pasadena Board of Realtors or the Multiple Listing Service of that Board, should said information prove to be inaccurate. Measurements are approximate. Owner will allow signs to be placed on property. Owner will allow lok-box to be used? Yes ☒ No ☐

ADDRESS 412 South Windsor Drive CITY Pasadena, Ca PRICE $ 29,500
BEDROOMS UP (X) (X) (X) BATHS DOWN $ CTL/CTNL
BEDROOMS DN. 3 (12 X 14) (12 X 16) (10 X 12) BATHS 1 3/4 1ST T. D. $ 19,750 6.6 %
DEN (X) CONV.? LIV. RM. 16 X 19 DIN. RM. 9 X 10 LENDER Grant Federal S & L
FAM. RM. (12 X 19) KITCHEN 8 X 13 BRKFST. 8 X 10 PAYMTS. $ 139.71 MO.
NO. OF ROOMS 6 ENTRY Yes SHOWERS 2 stall 2ND T. D. $ Owner w/c 9 %
AGE 16 yrs. LAUNDRY In serv. pch BASEMENT no PAYMTS. $ One per cent MO.
CONST. Redwood, brick ROOF Cedar shake GARAGE Dbl. attached TAXES $ 485.00
SQ. FT. 1,500 INSUL. Attic PATIO 15 X 20 flagstone BONDS $
LOT 65 X 125 HEAT. Dual Fl. Furn. FIREPLACE LR L/EST $ 172.88 @ 9 % 25 YRS. MO.
ZONE R - 1 FLOORS HW SPRINKLERS Fr. & Rr L/EST $ @ % YRS. MO.
WATER STOCK No SEWERS IN? Yes CONN.? Yes PD.? yes LOK-BOX LOC. Fr. Door
ELEM. SCHOOL Hamilton JR. HIGH McKinley HOW SHOWN Call owner or L. O.
HIGH SCHOOL Pasadena PAROCHIAL St. Rita POSSESSION 2 days after C BUS TOUR YES X NO OPEN HOUSE YES X NO
REMARKS: Well maintained home. New nylon wall to wall carpeting in Living Room and bedrooms. Two amber glass swag lights in living room not included in purchase price. Window [illegible] air conditioner in family room included in purchase price. Extra cupboard space.
OWNER'S NAME (PLEASE PRINT) Albert M. Doolittle et al
OWNER'S ADDRESS 412 South Windsor Drive, Pasadena, Ca PHONE 351-2228

In consideration of services to be performed by the undersigned Realtor, hereinafter called Realtor, for a period terminating at the above expiration date, I do hereby employ said Realtor and any sub-agent working through him as my sole agent, with exclusive and irrevocable right to sell property known as (give address) 412 South Windsor Drive, Pasadena more particularly described as LOT 28 TRACT 11407 as per Map recorded in BOOK 197 PAGE 61 of Maps, Official Records of the County of Los Angeles, State of California, and to accept a deposit thereon. It is understood and agreed that said Realtor will list said property with the Multiple Listing Service of the Pasadena Board of Realtors and that its members act as sub-agents. The contents hereof and the price, terms and conditions of any sale may be reported by the Multiple Listing Service to those authorized by the Multiple Listing Service.

The selling price shall be $ 29,500 payable on the following terms: Minimum of 20 per cent including $1,000 deposit into escrow. Buyer to assume loan of record as listed above. Owner will carry balance back in the form of a second trust deed on above terms. Or sale of all cash

I agree at my own expense to furnish buyer with a good and sufficient deed to said property, policy of title insurance in the amount of purchase price and a report from a licensed structural pest control operator covering termites, dry rot and fungus affecting the living quarters on said premises. If such report discloses active infestation or resultant damage, seller will eliminate such infestation and repair damage at his own expense. Any treatment to be made specifically to guard against future infestation shall be at the option and expense of the buyer. I further agree to pay our share of taxes, insurance premiums, interest payments and rents, prorated to the date of close of escrow.

I agree to pay Realtor a commission of 6 % of the total sales price, if during the term of this agency a purchaser ready, willing and able to purchase said property is produced through said Realtor at the above price and terms, or any other which I may accept, or if said property be sold, transferred or leased during the term of this agency by me, or by another agent or by anyone else. Should sale be made within ninety (90) days after the termination of this agreement to parties with whom said Realtor negotiated during the term or any extension thereof and said Realtor notifies me in writing of such negotiation on or before expiration date, I agree to pay said Realtor the commission agreed upon. Should a deposit be forfeited, one-half thereof may be retained by said Realtor and the balance shall be paid to me. The Realtor's share of any forfeited deposit, however, shall not exceed the commission.

I agree to cooperate in making the property available for inspection by prospective buyers or lenders.

I hereby acknowledge receipt of a copy hereof.

Date January 13, 1971 Signed Dolf Seller
Pasadena, California Signed Nora H. Seller

In consideration of the above employment, the undersigned Realtor agrees to use diligence in procuring a purchaser.

Date January 11, 1971 Realtor James R. Broker
Pasadena, California Salesman
ADDRESS 732 East Wyoming Street BUS. PH. 351-8531 RES. PH. 351-3356

ORIGINAL - REALTOR'S COPY

WHEN RECORDED, PLEASE MAIL THIS INSTRUMENT TO

Escrow No...
Order No...

SPACE ABOVE FOR RECORDER'S USE ONLY

REAL ESTATE OPTION

The undersigned, ,
called Optionor, in consideration of payment of the sum of $,
the receipt of which is acknowledged, grants to
,
called the Optionee, the option at any time on or before , 19 ,
to purchase for the amount and upon the terms hereinafter stated the following property in
County, State of California:

The price which Optionee is to pay for the property is $, and the terms upon which the price shall be paid are as follows:
$ in cash on or before the date stated above; and

In the event this option is exercised, and when the price herein named shall have been paid in the manner and at the times above set forth, then Optionor shall execute and deliver to Optionee a deed to said real property; and shall furnish to Optionee a policy of title insurance, issued by Security Title Insurance Company, insuring therein, in an amount not less than the price of said property, that title to said real property is vested of record in Optionee at the time of the recordation of said deed and subject only to the following encumbrances:

If payment is not made or tendered in accordance with the terms of this option on or before the date above stated, then this option shall be void and of no effect, and the Optionor shall be released from all obligations hereunder. The amount paid for this option does not constitute part of the purchase price of the property.

This option is for the benefit of, and binds the Optionor and Optionee, and any one claiming as a successor to them, in any capacity.

Dated:..19........ ....
Optionor

STATE OF CALIFORNIA
COUNTY OF .... } SS.

On ...., before me, the undersigned, a Notary Public in and for said County and State, personally appeared..
....,
known to me to be the person(s) whose name(s) is (are) subscribed to the within instrument and acknowledged that.............. executed the same.

(Seal) ....
(Notary signature line)

....
("His name (notary's) shall be typed or legibly printed")
(Sec. 8205 - Government Code 1959)

L-53 (G.S.) (Rev. 10-59) 11-2-59 (8 pt.)

California law. Section 10175 (f) states the licensee is subject to disciplinary action for "claiming, demanding or receiving a fee, compensation, or commission under any exclusive agreement authorizing or employing a licensee to sell, buy or exchange real estate for compensation or commission where such agreement does not contain a definite, specified date of final and complete termination").

4. Multiple Listing. This is a listing filed with a multiple-listing service, a real estate marketing system under which the listing offices submit their exclusive listings for processing and distribution to other member offices. Any member may sell the listing and share in the commission. The multiple-listing central office keeps records on the listings taken and the properties sold. For its services as a clearinghouse, it is paid a percentage of the total commission received. (After the service charge is taken off the top, the remainder of the commission is split between the selling office and the listing office.)

Some multiple-listing services require that offices submit all exclusive listings taken. Others operating on a voluntary basis permit offices to reserve certain office exclusives. Critics of the voluntary system point out the tendency of offices to file with a Multiple-Listing service only their "dogs and cats," retaining the more salable listings as office exclusives. Where an MLS has a highly successful operation, brokers have come to recognize its value as a marketing medium, and the more enterprising offices are tending to submit all their exclusive listings to the service, whether it be of the mandatory or voluntary type. Smaller offices especially receive great benefit from the wide exposure of their listings made possible under MLS, providing a service to their clients that is not available elsewhere.

5. Net Listing. In a net listing, the compensation is not definitely determined. The agent is permitted to retain as compensation all the money received in excess of the price set by the seller. Although a net listing is legal certain legal controls have been found necessary to protect the unwary property owner from possible fraudulent practices on the part of the agent. It is imperative that the seller understand clearly that all monies received by the broker above the net price will be retained by him as a commission. The temptation is always present for the agent to accept a listing from an uninformed seller at a price under the true market value, selling it at an inflated price to an unwary buyer, thus enabling the agent to retain a substantial sum as his commission. Legal controls, for this reason, require full disclosure to be made to both parties as to the total amount of monies retained by the broker.

The Option

Although an option cannot be termed a listing in the true sense of the word, brokers occasionally resort to the use of combination listing-and-option forms. Numerous complaints have come to the attention of the Department of Real Estate where licensees have attempted to make large profits from transactions handled by them in endeavoring to act as principals. Full disclosure of the broker's status and of the legal effect of the signed document must be made in order for the broker to act within the law. *American Jurisprudence* summarizes the law as follows:

> If a broker employed to sell property is also given ...an option to purchase the property himself, he occupies the dual status of agent and purchaser and he is not entitled to exercise his option except by divesting himself of his obligation as agent by making a full disclosure of any information in his possession as to the prospect of making a sale to another.[1]

Sources of Listings

An efficient operation for securing and maintaining *salable listings* will do much to insure the success of any real estate office. What are salable listings, and where do you find them? Real estate is the one commodity that touches the lives of all of us. As the preamble to NAREB's code of ethics expresses it, "Under all is the land." Buying and selling of real estate is a common topic of conversation wherever people gather. The most casual discussion, to the observant salesman, can provide a clue to a possible listing.

This does not mean that all listings coming to his attention are salable. In evaluating each listing, careful consideration must be given to: (1) price, (2) location, and (3) terms. Often an adjustment in the price is all that is required to overcome any disadvantage of the other two items. Tactful negotiation with the seller is necessary if an adjustment of the price is called for. Here the new salesman is at a disadvantage in a task calling for experience and diplomacy. Assistance from a senior member of the sales force may be required.

For the salesman starting out fresh, securing good listings can be a major problem. Not yet having an established clientele, he must employ every means available to him to search out salable properties, often in the face of formidable competition. However, to the alert and aggressive salesman, many avenues open up. He soon learns that, unlike the frog in Aesop's fable who sat "waiting for God to send a fly," he

[1] *Reference Book,* California Department of Real Estate.

cannot hope to sit idly by expecting business to gravitate to him. One property carefully listed and taken for a sixty-to-ninety-day period (or longer in a slow market) can, if properly serviced, lead to others. Where, then, is this one good listing to come from, and what are some of the sources to be explored?

Door-to-Door Canvassing

Some offices favor door-to-door canvassing over any other as the best basic way to obtain listings. Others consider it unprofessional and frown on it as an office practice.[2] To canvass or not to canvass becomes a moot question. Again, is it good business practice to place the untrained salesman in the field? Because the well-priced, salable listing is the goal of the successful office, only the most competent office representative should be permitted to negotiate with the seller. Although this method of securing listings may be valuable experience for the neophyte, the bad public relations engendered for the office make it a risky venture for the broker.

Old Listings

Most offices maintain files of unsold, expired listings (including multiple listings). With the rise in California real estate values, properties that were overpriced on last year's market may now become valuable listings. There should be periodic reviews of these properties, including regular contacts with the owners.

Newspapers

Local newspapers contribute a veritable gold mine of information leading to potential listings. Owners advertising their properties for sale, news items of births, deaths, and marriages, legal notices, tax sales, and notices of probate hearings all provide leads to possible listings. Particularly pertinent are news items of local businesses transferring personnel. Personnel managers are always cooperative with offices offering their services in handling the sale of homes for these transferees.

Clubs and Organizations

There is no substitute for seeing people. Particularly is this true of the real estate salesman. Membership in fraternal or civic organizations has long been recognized as one of the best methods of "keeping an ear to the ground." The time and effort expended in community service (Red Cross, Community Chest, Boy and Girl Scouts, or YMCA) pays off richly in increased business.

Classified Advertising

Carefully composed advertisements asking for listings can be most effective, provided that they refer to particular properties. Classified ads reading "Listings wanted" or "We need listings" are a waste of money and do not imply businesslike office procedure. Where the office is attempting to locate a particular property for a customer, the carefully worded inquiry many times produces not only the property solicited but other listings as well. This type of advertising should be used sparingly and with strict honesty (that is, the office actually has a potential buyer for the property solicited).

Signs on Property

It is axiomatic that the salesman who is given floor time in a well-established office will receive his share of calls from property owners who have noted the company signs in the area. "Sold" signs, especially, are productive. The public generally prefers to do business with the successful and enterprising office.

Obtaining the Listing

If he is to survive in today's competitive market, the real estate executive must have a steady flow of listings through his office. These listings constitute the merchandise on his shelves and are as important to his success as is the inventory of any merchant. His degree of success is in direct proportion to the number of *marketable listings* processed through his office. Accordingly, the success of each individual salesman is dependent on the quality of the merchandise he "buys." All his knowledge, training, and experience should be focused on this point. With the realization that good listings earn him commissions virtually "while he sleeps," the salesman soon learns to concentrate his efforts in this direction. He realizes that the more time he spends on intelligent listing, the less time he needs to spend with the buyer.

What, then, is a marketable listing, and what yardstick do we use to measure it?

What is a Marketable Listing?

Basically, it is one where the owner has a strong motive for selling; that is, he is not "trying out the market." When his motive is weak, the seller is usually averse to giving an exclusive listing and is much less inclined to be cooperative during the listing period. The broker normally has difficulty reaching an agreement with him on a fair market price. He

[2] In some areas, this type of solicitation is forbidden by ordinance.

is reluctant to make the necessary improvements required to increase the salability of the property; and, finally, when a buyer is found, he is less receptive to a realistic offer. It is important to determine the seller's real reason for selling and to remember that *this is not always the reason given by him.*

Once the salesman decides that the listing is salable and that it will fit into the office portfolio, he is faced with selling his services and those of his office to the property owner, who must be persuaded of the lister's ability to do a better job of merchandising the property than his competitor can. The seller has a right to inquire into the selling qualifications of the listing office. What is their record of sales? Is their advertising program adequate? Do they have customers for this type of property? And, finally, what is their projected merchandising program for this listing? The property owner may not be interested in the listing broker's marketing problems, his advertising costs, and the time and effort he must expend on the listing. He is interested, however, in whether or not his home will sell readily.

Intelligent answers to the seller's questions should be no problem to the salesman who is prepared with a sales kit containing full information on the practices of his office. Statistics on office sales, samples of advertising, and a review of the educational background and experience of the sales force all make an impressive contribution.

Finally, multiple-listing service and its advantages in expanding the market for the property should be explained.

Signing the Listing Agreement

When a full understanding as to price, terms, and type of listing has been reached, the authorization-to-sell form should be introduced and explained.[3] The implications of the exclusive-right agreement must be thoroughly understood by the seller before he is asked to approve it.

It should be noted here that, because a listing is a definite contract between the broker and the property owner, it must be signed by both parties in order to be valid. If the salesman would avoid possible future embarrassment, he will have both husband and wife sign (if the property is held jointly). Specific performance cannot be enforced where only one signature appears on the listing agreement.

The principles of ethical listing should be carefully adhered to at all times. Article 10 of the National Association of Real Estate Board's code of ethics states: "The Realtor should not submit or advertise property without authority. . . ."[4] This should be carefully pointed out to the seller who may be averse to signing a listing. (The lister is required by law to give a copy of the listing agreement to the seller immediately upon signing.)

Note: Effective January 2, 1970, a ruling of the Real Estate Commissioner further tightened the broker's supervision over his salesmen. This ruling includes all listing agreements, deposit receipts, leases, exchange agreements and other agreements, or amendments to agreements, *prepared or signed by* a salesman. These documents must be *initialed* by the broker within five working days of the execution of the documents or before the close of escrow, whichever occurs first. This initialing becomes evidence of the broker having seen the document, but does not affect its validity. "Working days" do not include Saturdays, Sundays, or holidays. Although the broker may not be relieved of the responsibility of supervision, he may delegate specific authority to review and initial agreements to a licensed real estate broker in his employ. It may also be delegated to a real estate salesman who has at least two years full-time real estate experience during the preceding five-year period. The broker or the salesman must have a written contract with the employing broker relating to the delegation. (The oral listing, as noted above, is not sufficient for the broker to enforce a claim for commission.) Under the *principal–agency* relationship the agent is a *fiduciary,* even though he may be serving his principal without hope or promise of remuneration for his services.

It is also important for the broker to remember that even if he holds an exclusive-right listing, and even though the buyer's offer may meet all the terms of the listing agreement, the broker does not have the right to *bind the owner* to a contract of sale. The owner becomes obligated to sell his property only when he signs the offer to purchase. He may, however, be liable to the broker for payment of commission.

If the grant deed or policy of title insurance is available, the salesman should read it carefully for the correct legal description, as well as for information concerning any easements or encumbrances of record. If neither of these documents is immediately available, arrangements should be made to look them over as soon as possible.

It is assumed that, previous to the contact, the salesman has made a thorough inspection of the

[3] See exclusive-right and multiple-listing forms on pp. 69 and 54.

[4] The complete Code of Ethics appears on pp. 24 and 25.

neighborhood, noting drawbacks as well as advantages, such as proximity to schools or transportation. The property itself should be given close scrutiny, with the salesman noting any touching-up that might be necessary to put the property in top condition. (Awareness of any possible objections to the property gives the salesman a distinct advantage when the same objections are later advanced by the prospect.)

Much can be learned about the property if the salesman will encourage the seller to talk. Why did the home appeal to him? Who lives in the neighborhood? Are the schools adequate? And how near are shopping and transportation facilities? The more the lister can learn about the property at this point, the easier it is for him to find the one buyer whose requirements it will satisfy.

Now is the time for the salesman to formulate his ideas on advertising copy. Before the salesman leaves the premises, the particular sales features should be noted, so that they may be incorporated later in his advertising copy.

The final step in the listing process is placing the "For Sale" sign on the property. If the property is to be listed in a Multiple-Listing Service, a copy of the listing must be filed with them within the period specified in their regulations.

It should be noted here that as it relates to a suit for specific performance, a listing becomes a valid binding and enforceable contract only when it is signed by all parties having a recorded interest in the subject property. (It is assumed that the contract has been properly executed.) Unless the broker has the signatures of all those having a recorded interest, he may produce a buyer "ready, willing, and able," and meeting all the terms of the listing agreement, and then be placed in the unenviable position of having offered for sale a property title to which cannot be delivered. In this case the broker would most certainly be subject to disciplinary action by the commissioner and under certain conditions could be the subject of a suit for damages by the buyer. (The signatories to the listing agreement however, could be liable to the broker for the agreed commission.)

In addition the Realtor could conceivably be found in violation of Article 19 of the Code of Ethics of the National Association of Real Estate Boards, which reads: "The Realtor should not submit or advertise property without authority. . . ."[5]

Confusion occasionally arises as to the status of the broker holding an oral-type listing as against the exclusive-right-to-sell contract. The *broker–principal* relationship requires a *contract of employment* under which the broker is to receive compensation for services performed in procuring a buyer for the property. The *principal–agent* relationship does not require a *written contract,* but it does create a fiduciary relationship between the agent and his principal to which all the laws of agency apply.[6]

When Should a Listing Be Rejected?

The well-established real estate office will have many listings offered without solicitation. All listings should not necessarily be accepted. Certain criteria, as discussed above, should be applied to the listing. In addition, the broker should ask himself,

1. *Is it in the office's area of operation?*
   Accepting listings in areas unfamiliar to the sales force makes appraising difficult and also makes proper servicing a problem.
2. *Is it overpriced?*
   Accepting overpriced listings can only result in a file of expired, unsold listings, an advertising bill, an unhappy seller, and a disgruntled sales force.
3. *Is the seller serious about selling?*
   This has already been discussed.
4. *Is the sales force enthusiastic about the property?*
   This is a valuable test of the acceptability of the listing. If the salesmen are not sold on the property's marketing potential, the office cannot expect constructive selling effort.

In relation to the lister's determining the owner's real reason for selling, it should be mentioned that the broker has a responsibility to the seller to obtain for him the highest price obtainable under the market regardless of his motive for selling.

What Women Realtors Are Doing, the official organ of Women's Council of NAREB, states, "There is a very damaging belief by real estate salesmen that, 'Owner must take less if he must sell.' " Continuing, the publication quotes Frederick J. Bashaw, Realtor, author, and lecturer of West Palm Beach, Florida:

> This is a most unfortunate generalization, carelessly used by salesmen. It can do much to undermine an established reputation of a firm and adversely affect the entire profession.

Summarizing, WWRAD states:

> Of course, it is highly important for a salesman to be familiar with the cause or reason for a Seller's Action—but let us use the reason in the right way and at the right time. Let us remember that an owner's compelling reason to sell does not always mean that his position is weakened. An intelligent, alert salesman knows that it qualifies the client as one who *means business.* It qualifies the client as

[5] The full text of the Code of Ethics appears on pp. 24 and 25.

[6] For example, the broker has a fiduciary responsibility to disclose to his principal any and all offers received by him, whether written or oral.

STONE & SCHULTE

LISTING REPORT FORM - RESALES

(This form to be submitted with every listing for analysis of listing activity)

____
Name of Listing Salesman　　　　　　　　Date Listed

____
Property Address　　　　　　　　　　　　Expires

____
Price and Terms

REASONS FOR SELLING____

____

Are you requesting any financing commitments?____

Is the seller prepared to carry any "Second Paper"?____

____

Are you working with the seller on other property?____

____

Have you put up a "FOR SALE" sign?________ Lock Box?________Type Lock Box ________ SS________

Do you plan on mailing CHOOSE YOUR NEIGHBOR cards?____

How did Stone & Schulte obtain the listing?____

____

CHECK ONE OR MORE OF THE FOLLOWING:

Personal client referral	☐	Owner "For Sale" sign	☐
Phone call to office during floor time	☐	Referral from subdividion	☐
Result of Know Your Neighbor campaign	☐	Trade-in assignment	☐
Result of Stone & Schulte For Sale sign	☐	Result of S&S SOLD sign	☐
Personal door to door canvassing	☐	Friend or relative	☐
Result of "owner ad"	☐	Photo-Facts	☐

Other____

____

____

one worthy of serious effort on our part to consummate a sale.[7]

It has been estimated that 25 percent of all sellers become buyers. If this is true, the salesman who concentrates his time and efforts on securing salable listings has developed a built-in source of customers. Because of the time spent with his sellers, the salesman has a better understanding of their housing problems when the time comes for them to buy. He knows their financial situation, and thus much time can be saved in searching for financing tailored to their needs. If he has given outstanding service to his seller during the term of his listing, the salesman can expect that when the property is sold and his sellers become buyers, he will be the one to whom they will look to locate property suited to their particular needs.

Opinions differ on the number of listings that should make up the salesman's inventory. Some salesmen are able to service as many as ten or twelve listings at a time, while others find that five is the maximum they can handle adequately. A number of factors enter into the salesman's decision in this matter. What are the current market conditions? What is the size of the office staff? Is the office a member of a multiple-listing service? Is there a secretary to handle the details of filing, mailings, answering telephone calls, and drawing contracts? How large is the salesman's territory? How much time is he expected to put in the office?

A daily written work plan is a must for the productive salesman. The plan should be outlined the previous night if at all possible. The importance of each task should dictate the order of precedence. Richard Van Valer, writing in CREA's *Listing Real Estate,* puts it this way:

> A plan is a prerequisite of success, and in planning, approximately seventy-five per cent of the salesman's time should be devoted to securing his inventory. A survey of successful real estate salesmen shows that following a plan faithfully will bring success!
>
> Our daily goal is to:
> a. Have five salable listings at all times.
> b. Show at least one property every day.
> c. See at least seven new listings every day.
> d. Tell every one we meet about our best listing.
> e. Improve our knowledge of real estate every day.[8]

[7] "An Owner's Compelling Reason to Sell," *What Women Realtors Are Doing,* Vol. 8, No. 5 (May 1964), (Chicago, Ill.: Women's Council of the National Association of Real Estate Boards), p. 6.

[8] Richard Van Valer, "Daily Work Plan," Chap. 5, *Listing Real Estate* (Los Angeles: California Real Estate Association, 1969).

Offices are constantly on the lookout for competent listers. There is no such thing as a salesman who is a good closer but a poor lister. *Listing is selling.* The owner is being sold on the ability of the salesman and his office to sell his property. He is listening to representatives from many offices using their best selling methods trying to persuade him that he should list his property with them. It is only when he is finally persuaded that one particular salesman has used the most convincing arguments that the owner agrees to employ him as his agent. Once the salesman recognizes that his inventory of salable listings has every other salesman in the field working for him, he will devote more of his time to securing such listings. But if he is to stay ahead of his competition, he cannot afford to relax. His time must be spent constantly contacting new sellers. When the listing is obtained, he must do a better job of servicing than do any of his competitors. Then and then only will he have earned the referred business that will surely gravitate to him. He has the best type of advertising working for him—word-of-mouth. As a result of his conscientious efforts on his first few listings he will need to spend less and less time in cold canvassing of his territory because of the business being referred to him.

Servicing the Listing

As soon as the completed listing agreement is turned into the office, it should be processed and distributed to the sales force. A file, which serves as a checklist for the salesman, is then set up containing all pertinent data relating to the property. The check list should include:

1. Loan commitments
2. Office inspection (by the sales force)
3. Advertising program
4. Broker's open house
5. Multiple-listing caravan
6. Termite inspection

Also contained in the file should be copies of all newspaper ads and a memorandum of calls, whether originating from these ads or from the sign on the property. (Copies of all ads are sent to the seller.) Notations are made each time the property is shown, together with the results of these showings. By supplying a log of all sales activity, the file becomes a valuable means of checking the office's sales campaign with respect to the particular property (should the question arise with the owner).

After a period of two weeks of concentrated sales effort with no constructive results, it is well to contact the seller and to review with him the activity to date. Results of the advertising program, the salesman's open house, and the cooperative effort of other offices should be discussed and the owner's suggestions solicited. An adjustment in the sales price or the terms may be called for.

Lack of interest on the part of the office after the listing is taken leads to bad customer relations, opening the door for competitors to pick up the listing after it expires unsold. Listing properties at a realistic price and developing a sound program of service during the listing period tends not only to build good will for the office but boosts the morale of the sales force. With concentrated efforts on his listings demanding his full time, a salesman can ill afford to accept any but the best and most salable properties if his time and effort are to prove financially productive.

Properties Offered at Public Sale

Real estate licensees often have the opportunity to negotiate sales on properties offered at public sale. For successful negotiations on these properties special knowledge of the procedures involved is necessary. Sales are often lost to the practitioner who is uninformed on the requirements dictated by statute that govern the handling of these sales. In this chapter we will discuss some of the more common types of properties offered at public sale.

Probate (Estate) Sales

Superior courts in California exercise jurisdiction over probate matters through their "probate courts" (departments of the superior court). Probate proceedings are subject to the statutes governing probate administration and the estates of the decedent are administered either by an executor or an administrator.

> *The executor* (*executrix*) is the one specifically named in a will to carry out the wishes of the decedent.
> *The administrator* is appointed by the court to administer the estate if there is no will, or if no executor has been named in the will.[9]

A *guardian* is court-appointed to administer the estate of a minor or an incompetent. A *conservator* is appointed to administer the estate of those unable to manage their affairs. A bank trust department often serves in this capacity and acts as executor of the estate.

There is very little difference between the authority and powers of an administrator and an executor. Each has certain obligations and each must act under court jurisdiction. During the course of the estate proceedings it may be necessary or advisable to dispose of the property of the estate. It is at this point that a real estate licensee may have an interest in listing the real property and attempting to find a buyer for it. The property may be sold either by private or public sale. Normally a notice of the pending sale is published (Notice of Intended Sale) in a newspaper in the county in which the property is located. It is essential for title-insurance purposes that the sale proceedings comply with the statutory requirements. Such items as a correct legal description in the published notice or the terms of the sale complying exactly with the authorization can be most important in an estate sale.

Listing the Property

Open listings may be given to real estate brokers. The attorney handling the property is usually willing to list the property, in order to expedite a sale by providing a wider market than the notice alone might do. Upon request, bank trust departments will usually mail information on any properties being handled by them to a real estate broker. In addition brokers, alert to the possibilities of increased business through probate sales, usually watch the newspapers for notices of any such properties being advertised. After the first publication of such notices, written bids may be submitted to the estate's representative, or the clerk of the court of the superior court in which the property is located. The amount offered must be at least 90 percent of the inheritence tax appraisal of the property. A deposit of 10 percent of the amount bid should accompany the offer, usually in the form of a certified or cashier's check. If all bids are considered by the representative to be too low, they may be rejected, in which case a new notice of sale must be published and the procedure repeated.

Sale of the Property

On the day of the sale (as recorded in the Notice of Sale) the representative for the estate presents the sealed bids to be opened. The highest *net* bid is the one accepted. The broker's commission, where applicable, is deducted to arrive at a net figure. The accepted bid is now subject to confirmation by the court, such confirmation to be made within ten days after acceptance of the bid. The representative files a statement of sale and petitions the court for confirmation. Provided all the terms of the offer have been met, the court then sets a date for confirmation of the sale.

Raising the Bid in Court

Prior to confirmation of a bid, the judge of the court will ask if there are any higher bids to be presented. These may be submitted by any real estate

[9] An administrator may also be appointed if the executor is unable to serve.

SECURITY PACIFIC NATIONAL BANK

TRUST DEPARTMENT · REAL ESTATE

INVITES OFFERS ON THE FOLLOWING PROPERTY

ACCOUNT NO. 06-1-06902

LOCATION 267 South Community Street, Pasadena, California

LEGAL DESCRIPTION The South 100 ft. of Lot 5 of RANCHO SANTA ANITA, County of Los Angeles, as per map recorded in Book 8 page 147 of Maps in the office of the County Recorder of said County.

LOT SIZE 100 x 200

IMPROVEMENTS A single family residence and detached garage

TAX LEVIES FOR 1971-72 $1685.74 BOND BAL. none PYMTS @ none NEXT PAYMENT

LISTING PRICE $80,000 cash

REMARKS
To inspect, key may be obtained at the San Marino Branch, 2180 Huntington Drive. After inspecting, please lock securely and return key promptly

You are invited to submit offers subject to the following conditions: No signs permitted

Title subject to current taxes, covenants, conditions, reservations, rights, rights of way, easements and assessments of record, if any.

The offeror shall deposit 10% of the purchase price with the offer to purchase. A commission in an amount acceptable to us will be paid only to real estate broker submitting a written offer accepted by us. Any commission is subject to approval by the Probate Court, if confirmation of sale is required. Said commission is payable only upon consummation of sale to purchaser as evidenced by conveyance of the property. No commission will be paid in connection with sale to any tenant of the premises listed above unless otherwise agreed in writing in advance of the sale.

This listing is subject to our ability to convey title acceptable to purchaser, to change in asking price, a prior sale, increased offers, the right to accept or reject any and all offers, mutual release between ourselves and the purchaser prior to actual delivery of deed, termination of our fiduciary capacity prior to sale, to approval of beneficiaries, co-fiduciaries or consultants where deemed by us advisable or necessary and to court approval, if required.

The property is offered for sale in its "as is" condition, without warranty as to the condition or suitability of the soil or of any improvement thereon for construction or occupancy and without termite clearance, termite work or other repair work to be performed by us. No warranty is given as to the zoning of the property nor to the conformance of the improvements located thereon to present day zoning, or building code ordinances.

In acting on this listing, the recipient acknowledges that the Bank holds this property in a fiduciary capacity and agrees that the Bank is not liable hereunder in its individual capacity, and further agrees to look solely to the assets held in such fiduciary capacity for satisfaction of any rights. The above information regarding this property although believed to be correct, is not guaranteed and is subject to errors and omissions. Offers by or on behalf of employees of Security Pacific National Bank not permitted.

THIS IS A PROBATE SALE SUBJECT TO COURT CONFIRMATION

FOR FURTHER INFORMATION CONTACT:

SECURITY PACIFIC NATIONAL BANK
Trust Real Estate Division
312 W. 5th. St. 4th. Flr. Los Angeles

BY ______________________
Timothy Thomas

DATE: February 28, 1971

3898 TR 7589 11-69• P.S.

broker on behalf of his client, or by any other interested person present. The new bid must be in the increased amount of 10 percent of the first $10,000 of the bid under consideration, plus an additional 5 percent of the remainder. Following this, bidding may then proceed on raises of any amount until the court declares a bid to be the best and highest obtainable, and the sale is then confirmed to the highest bidder. He must file a written bid immediately and deposit 10 percent of the amount of his bid with the executor of the estate.

Broker's Commissions

Licensed real estate brokers are entitled to a commission on a sale resulting from a bid which they may have presented on behalf of an interested buyer, provided the petition for confirmation specifically states that a written agreement was entered into between the representative of the estate and the participating broker. If the bid is confirmed by the court, a full commission is usually ordered to be paid out of the proceeds of the sale.[10]

The broker who submits the original bid, which is overbid in open court, is still entitled to one-half of the normal agreed-upon commission, based on the original bid. If a broker submits the final and highest bid in court, the remaining half of the commission based on the original bid, plus all of the normal commission, based on the difference between the original bid and the final bid, is usually awarded.

If the successful *oral bidder* is not produced by a broker, the broker who produced the high *written bid* may be awarded a full commission on the amount of that bid.

Trustee's Sale

When payments on a note secured by a trust deed are made as agreed, there is no problem between the beneficiary, the trustee, and the trustor. But should the trustor (the borrower) not be able to make his payments as agreed, the beneficiary notifies the trustee that a default has occurred. The trustee then obtains from the beneficiary the trust deed and note and any evidence (in the form of receipts) of any advances made by him to protect the security, such as payment of taxes, fire insurance, and so on. A statement showing the date of the original default and the unpaid balance of the obligation is also included.

A notice of default must be recorded in the county where the property is situated before the power of sale may be executed. This notice must be recorded at least three months before notice of sale is given.

[10] Provided the petition for confirmation specifically recites that a written agreement was entered into between the estate representative and the participating broker.

During this three-month period the trustor, his successor in interest, or any junior lienholder may reinstate the obligation by paying all sums due, plus costs and trustee's fees, not exceeding fifty dollars or one-half of 1 percent of the entire unpaid principal sum secured, whichever is greater. This procedure causes the default and stops the sale proceedings.

After the three-month period is ended, the right of reinstatement is gone, and the beneficiary (or his successor in interest) is entitled to payment in full, plus costs and fees. If payment is not made, the property may be sold.

Notice of Sale

The notice of sale is published in a newspaper of general circulation published in the city in which the property is situated. The publication must appear once a week for twenty days. The notice must also be posted for the same period in one public place in the city or judicial district where the sale is to be made and in some conspicuous place on the property. A copy of this notice must be mailed to all persons requesting notice of default.

The Sale

At the time and place specified in the published notice of sale the trustee or his representative begins the proceedings by announcing the reason for the sale and identifies the property to be sold. The bidding is then opened. Only cash bids or their equivalent may be accepted. The beneficiary may, however, bid in the amount due him without putting up any cash. Bidding by those present continues until a closing bid is accepted by the trustee, and a trustee's deed is issued to the purchaser. The former owner has no right of redemption and he must give up possession of the property.

Property owners faced with threat of foreclosure often list their property with a broker, hoping to have a sale effected during the three-month period prior to the foreclosure sale. Licensees handling these properties have an obligation to estimate as nearly as possible any payments that must be made out of funds accruing from the sale, such as delinquent taxes including penalties, mechanic's liens, any bonds of record, in addition to delinquent payments on recorded notes secured by trust deeds. Occasionally it happens that the broker is unable to obtain a price that will cover all outstanding debts and allow for a sales commission.[11]

[11] For more detailed information on trustee's sales, see Arthur G. Bowman, *Real Estate Law in California* 3rd ed. (Englewood Cliffs, N.J.: Prentice-Hall, Inc., 1970).

CASE STUDY

Jim Bone is a new salesman for the Zenith Realty Company; he is also new in the community and has had his license only a month. He is twenty-five years old and has never done sales work before. The company has an extensive four-week training program for its sales staff. After these four weeks of training, each new salesman then serves as an apprentice-trainee for one month under the tutelage of a senior member of the sales force, who accompanies him in the field to list or show property.

The office does not hire any but new licensees in order that they may train them in their particular methods of operation. Jim Bone is very personable and fits in well with the office staff. He is grateful for the opportunity to train under such highly skilled professional, but he chafes at the long period he must wait before being able to prove what he can do on his own. He has already made many contacts in the community including a number of opportunities to hand out his business cards to prospective customers.

At the end of his apprenticeship, he is given floor time. He is excited about finally being "on his own." His first morning on duty, he receives a call from Mrs. Stiles (whose husband was given one of his business cards), asking him to come to the home to take a listing. He checks the historical files in the office but can find no record of the property ever having been for sale previously. He makes an appointment with Mrs. Stiles to see her that afternoon. Taking along his sales kit, which contains office data and sales-promotional materials, he drives directly to the Stiles home and is greeted by Mrs. Stiles, who shows him through the house. He is impressed with her good housekeeping and the charm of the home.

He asks her what price she has placed on the property. Mrs. Stiles replies that she and her husband have been figuring what they have in the property, and they do not want to take a loss. She says that, although they do not have to sell, their children are now grown, and they thought they might like to rent an apartment for a while and do some traveling when Mr. Stiles retires next year. The home has no loan on it, and the Stiles want all cash when it is sold. The home is twenty years old and was bought by them fourteen years ago. They added a swimming pool, wall-to-wall carpeting, and new draperies five years ago. Their lot is 65 by 135 feet, most of which is taken up with the house, patio, and swimming pool. Mrs. Stiles feels that the property has increased in value because the lots across the street have recently been zoned for multiple dwellings. Jim is surprised to hear of the change of zone on the street.

Jim Bone agrees with her that she certainly should not "take a loss." He looks over the figures that the Stiles have come up with, which include the price they paid for the improvements mentioned above. He agrees that the new zoning would increase the value of her home. He says that he would be happy to take the listing at her price (although he feels it is much too high) and states that he anticipates no problem in selling it. He believes he can come back later and get an adjustment in the price. He is very proud of having secured a listing on his first day on duty at the office. He draws up the Exclusive-Right-to-Sell agreement for a ninety-day term, being careful to explain to Mrs. Stiles all the terms contained therein. He tells her of the office's extensive advertising program and, using the material from his sales kit, shows her samples of successful ads they have used in the past. He mentions the office caravan, the open house for brokers, and many of the other services available. Mrs. Stiles is most interested and agrees that the Zenith Realty Company is most aggressive in its sales promotion. After completing the agreement, he asks her to sign, telling her he will leave it with her for her husband's signature that evening. Mrs. Stiles is very surprised that he would ask for a signature. She says she is certain her husband would not approve of her signing a listing, nor does she believe he would be willing to sign either. Jim Bone is disappointed at this turn of events, but he believes Mrs. Stiles is sincere when she says, "If you sell the house, you will get your commission. You have nothing to worry about."

Jim is anxious to put the office sign on the property and to take the the listing back to the office. Although he is concerned about not having the signatures on the listing contract, he agrees to accept the listing anyway, thinking that he can always go back later and persuade the Stiles to sign after he shows them how hard he is working to sell their home. He feels sure Mrs. Stiles will not object to having the sign on the property, so before he returns to the office he puts up the office sign on the front lawn. When he reaches his desk, the office secretary asks him for the copy of the listing to be filed. He realizes then that he has forgotten to leave the seller's copy with Mrs. Stiles.

1. Study the above situation carefully. Would you, in Jim Bone's position, have followed his listing procedure? If not, where would you have deviated? List all the areas where you would have operated differently.
2. What do you feel will be the attitude of the office manager and the sales force regarding this listing? If you were office manager, how would you analyze the present status of the listing? What steps, if any, would you take to change it?

3. In your opinion, has Jim violated the real estate law in any of his listing procedures? The code of ethics? Good business practice?

The Listing Agreement

The listing agreement may be the first real estate contract your seller has ever been called upon to sign. Its correct completion may determine your legal right to collect your fee (in the form of a commission) for the time and money you will expend in your efforts to merchandise his property during the term of the contract. It is imperative that not only must you understand all the implications of the agreement, but that you, as agent, make certain that your seller has a clear understanding of its text before he signs.

So important does the California Department of Real Estate consider the principal–agency relationship that some forty pages are devoted to it in their *Reference Book.* A listing is defined as "a contract by which a principal employs an agent to do certain things for the principal."[12] The text continues ". . . an agent holding a listing, exclusive, nonexclusive, or net, is always bound by the law of agency and has certain obligations to his principal that do not exist between two principals." With the foregoing in mind, let us examine the California Real Estate Association *Exclusive Authorization and Right to Sell Agreement* appearing on page 000. Each section in the agreement is numbered. We shall take them in order and attempt to clarify the intent of each as they relate to the contract as a whole.

1. Right to Sell.

I hereby employ and grant ____________ herein called "Agent," the exclusive and irrevocable right to sell or exchange the real property situated in ____________, County of ____________, California described as follows:

____

Notice that the word "agent" is used throughout. We cannot stress too strongly the principal–agent relationship which exists once an employment contract is signed by the broker.[13] He then becomes subject to all the laws of agency. *He is duty-bound to obey all lawful instruction given him by his principal.* This section of the agreement grants to the agent the "exclusive and irrevocable right to sell or exchange the real property. . . ." Does the seller understand fully the term "exclusive and irrevocable right"? Is he aware that should *anyone,* including himself, sell the property, he is obligated to pay you, as agent, the agreed amount of commission? Does he realize that "irrevocable" means just what it says, i.e., that the contract cannot be revoked except by mutual consent? The inclusion of the word "exchange" broadens the intent of the section and provides a stronger protection for the broker should the seller attempt to subrogate the listing agreement by making an exchange of the property during the listing period, thereby hoping to avoid the payment of a commission to the broker.

Legal Description

In the space reserved for the property address, there is reserved a line for the legal description. This, of course, is necessary where the listing involves unimproved property, but even in the case of improved property it is a much more professional approach to listing if the legal description of the property is included. At the time the listing is taken the seller should be asked to have his deed or policy of title available for your examination. At this time the legal description can be taken down and made a part of the listing agreement. If the description involves a lengthy statement of the metes and bounds, an extra sheet may be stapled or otherwise attached to the listing agreement (in the interest of accuracy, legal description should never be taken off tax bills).

2. Term.

Agent's right to sell shall commence on __________, 19 ____ and expire at midnight on ____________, 19 ____.

Under California law all exclusive listings must have a definite termination date. This section of the agreement makes it very explicit by including the exact hour at which the listing expires. Ambiguity in any contract is the principal cause of misunderstanding between parties. This is particularly true of real estate contracts. These should be no doubt in the mind of any broker or his principal just when the listing expires if in the contract, the *hour* is spelled out.

3. Terms of Sale.

(a) The price for the property shall be the sum of $________, to be paid as follows:

____

____

Because courts of law, when examining contracts, are concerned with the *intent* of the parties, it becomes vitally important that all terms of a listing agreement be spelled out so that there is no mistaking the intent of the seller as to the terms under which he wishes to have his property sold. Not only must the total purchase price be filled in, but the down payment required, and the terms (interest rate, monthly payments, and terms of the note) of any financing

12 Reference Book (Sacramento: State Department of Real Estate).

13 The term "broker" as used here refers also to salesmen.

the seller may be carrying. He may wish, for example, to have the buyer assume the loan of record in order that there will be no prepayment penalty. He may stipulate that the loan of record be paid off, so that he is no longer responsible on the note. He may be willing to carry back the entire first loan, with a reasonable down payment. There must be a clear understanding by the broker of exactly what the *intent* of the seller is regarding the financing of the sale.

(b) The following items of personal property are to be included in the above-stated price:

____

____

Personal Property

The section dealing with the personal property to be included in the purchase price is a most important one. Misunderstandings often arise as to just what personal property the seller intended to include. Note that again we are concerned with *intent.* A little time taken to spell out clearly each item of personal property at the time the listing is being taken may save many embarrassing moments and loss of good will later. Each item should be itemized. (Do draperies include curtains? Does wall-to-wall carpeting mean only the tacked-down carpeting? Are all appliances identified by make and model number? *Which* items of lawn or patio furniture does the owner intend to leave?) To recognize the importance of the careful listing of each item, the broker has only to experience having to buy a refrigerator or the bedroom carpeting for the buyer. It *has* happened. But it could have been avoided if the above procedure had been followed. If the list of personal property is a long one, an itemized list should be typed on a separate sheet and attached to the agreement.

(c) Agent is hereby authorized to accept on my behalf a deposit upon the purchase price in an amount to be not less than $_________.

Amount of Deposit

This is the only clause in the listing contract covering the agent's authority to accept a deposit *on behalf of the owner.* This indicates clearly to the broker that *the deposit never belongs to him. Without authorization the agent has no legal right to accept a deposit from a third party, in connection with the sale of a property.* This authorization also makes the principal (who is bound by the acts of his agent) liable to a third party for any monies paid by him to the agent. The real estate commissioner cautions brokers against promising a buyer that his deposit will be returned to him if he requests it. The broker should have a definite understanding and should make it clear to his buyer that the deposit is not his to return. *It is the property either of the buyer or the seller.* The agent may act only upon instruction of his principal. If the broker has made a promise to the purchaser of the return of the deposit upon certain conditions, then this should be incorporated into the deposit receipt and pointed out to the seller at the time he signs the acceptance of the contract. This subsection provides also for the minimum amount of the deposit to be noted. This is a protection for the seller and the broker, in the event the buyer wishes to enter into a purchase agreement with a minimal deposit.

(d) Evidence of title to the property shall be in the form of a California Land Title Association Standard Coverage Policy of Title Insurance in the amount of the selling price to be paid for by ________.

Title Insurance Policy

Custom varies between southern and northern California as to who pays for the policy of title (buyer or seller). The principal point here is that the space be filled in, to avoid any mistake later as to who is responsible for this item.

(e) I warrant that I am the owner of the property or have the authority to execute this agreement. I hereby agree to permit a FOR SALE sign to be placed on my property by Agent named herein.

For Sale Sign

This section provides a protection clause for the agent. By warranting that he is the owner of the property, or has the authority to execute a listing agreement, the signer assumes all responsibility for having employed the broker as his agent. He also authorizes him to place a sign on the property. Article 29 of the Realtor's Code of Ethics states, "Signs giving notice of property for sale, rent, lease or exchange should not be placed on any property by more than one Realtor, *and then only if authorized by the owner,*[14] except as the property is listed and authorization given to more than one Realtor." From this it is clear than a realtor placing a sign on a property without authorization from the owner is in violation of the code of ethics.

4. Compensation to Agent.

I hereby agree to compensate Agent as follows:

(a) ____% of the selling price if the property is sold during the term hereof, or any extension thereof, by Agent, on the terms herein set forth or any price or terms I may accept, or through any other person, or by me, or ____% of the price as shown in 3(a), if said property is withdrawn from sale,

[14] Author's italics.

transferred, conveyed, leased without the consent of Agent, or made unmarketable by my voluntary act during the term hereof or any extension thereof.

The fee or commission agreement under which the broker will be employed by the seller is specifically spelled out in this section. Terms of the exclusive authorization are indicated, as is the acknowledgment that a commission is due the agent if the listing term is extended. The attention of the seller should be called to that portion of this section referring to the commission due the broker should the property *without consent of* the agent be "withdrawn from sale, transferred, conveyed, leased...*or made unmarketable by my voluntary act during the term hereof or any extension thereof.*" In an attempt to evade payment of a commission, owners have on occasion placed obstacles in the way of the broker attempting to show a listed property (such acts as departing on extended vacations, leaving the broker no way to gain entrance to the property for the purpose of showing it). Protection for the broker against such action on the part of an unscrupulous seller is provided by this clause in the agreement:

(b) the compensation provided for in subparagraph (a) above if property is sold, conveyed or otherwise transferred within 180 days after the termination of this authority or any extension thereof to anyone with whom Agent has had negotiations prior to final termination, provided I have received notice in writing, including the names of the prospective purchasers, before or upon termination of this agreement or any extension thereof. I further agree to register these names and exclude them from any exclusive agency and/or exclusive right to sell listing I may grant to any licensed real estate broker within 180 days of the termination of this authorization or any extension thereof.

Agent's Protection

This is known as a broker's "safety" clause, and simply stated means that should the property be sold during the 180 day period immediately following the expiration of the listing agreement to a party with whom the broker has negotiated during the term of the listing, the owner agrees to pay the broker a full commission. The broker, on his part, has an obligation to the owner, if he would protect his right to a commission. By the wording "...provided I have received notice in writing, including the names of the prospective purchasers, before or upon termination of this agreement or any extension thereof" responsibility is placed squarely on the broker's shoulders. Good business practice would dictate that every effort should be made to protect an investment. A broker who services a listing conscientiously for a reasonable length of time has made an investment of time and money. By the simple expedient of mailing (preferably by registered mail) to the owner of the property in question "prior to or upon termination of the agreement" a list of the prospective buyers with whom he has negotiated, the broker is doing his part in protecting his investment.

Disagreements can arise between brokers after the expiration of an exclusive listing. What happens if, after the expiration of the listing, an exclusive authorization is given on the same property to another broker, and the property is sold to a customer with whom the first broker has negotiated for the purchase of the property? Does the first broker still have a claim on the customer? Who is entitled to the commission? What is the responsibility of the property owner in such a circumstance? Rights and obligations of all parties are spelled out in the last sentence in this section, wherein the owner stipulates that he does "...further agree to register these names and exclude them from any exclusive agency and/or exclusive right to sell listing I may grant to any licensed real estate broker within 180 days of the termination of this authorization or any extension thereof."

5. If action be instituted on this agreement to collect compensation or commissions, I agree to pay such sum as the Court may fix as reasonable attorney's fees.

Attorney's Fees: Involved in Collection of Agent's Fee

Any owner acting in good faith in signing an exclusive authorization with an agent would have no objection to, nor should he require an explanation of this section of the agreement.

6. I authorize the Agent named herein to cooperate with subagents selected by him.

Cooperation with Subagents

This is a particularly important section, as it applies to a listing which is filed with a multiple-listing service, where a number of brokers may be cooperating with the listing broker in their attempts to sell the property. The owner by the intent in this section specifically authorizes the agent to cooperate with subagents. This is a delicate point that could have legal implications should some statement or act of a subagent place the listing broker in jeopardy where a third party is involved.

7. In the event of an exchange, permission is hereby given Agent to represent all parties and collect compensation or commissions from them, provided there is full disclosure to all principals of such agency. Agent is authorized to divide with other agents such compensation or commission in any manner acceptable to them.

Exclusive Authorization and Right to Sell

CALIFORNIA REAL ESTATE ASSOCIATION STANDARD FORM

1. **Right to Sell.** I hereby employ and grant James R. Broker, hereinafter called "Agent", the exclusive and irrevocable right to sell or exchange the real property situated in City of Arcadia, County of Los Angeles, California described as follows:
176 West Peacock Road

2. **Term.** Agent's right to sell shall commence on January 12, 19 71 and expire at midnight on April 11, 19 71.

3. **Terms of Sale.**

(a) The price for the property shall be the sum of $ 32,500.00, to be paid as follows:
Minimum of 20 per cent cash including deposit into escrow. Buyer to assume existing loan of record in the approximate amount of $20,000. Seller to carry balance as set out below.

(b) The following items of personal property are to be included in the above-stated price:
All tacked down carpeting and window coverings throughout the residence. Wrought iron patio table and four matching wrought iron chairs.

(c) Agent is hereby authorized to accept on my behalf a deposit upon the purchase price in an amount to be not less than $1,000.00.

(d) Evidence of title to the property shall be in the form of a California Land Title Association Standard Coverage Policy of Title Insurance in the amount of the selling price to be paid for by seller

(e) I warrant that I am the owner of the property or have the authority to execute this agreement. I hereby agree to permit a FOR SALE sign to be placed on my property by Agent named herein.

4. **Compensation to Agent.** I hereby agree to compensate Agent as follows:

(a) 6 % of the selling price if the property is sold during the term hereof, or any extension thereof, by Agent, on the terms herein set forth or any other price and terms I may accept, or through any other person, or by me, or 6 % of the price shown in 3.-(a), if said property is withdrawn from sale, transferred, conveyed, leased without the consent of Agent, or made unmarketable by my voluntary act during the term hereof or any extension thereof.

(b) the compensation provided for in subparagraph (a) above if property is sold, conveyed or otherwise transferred within 180 days after the termination of this authority or any extension thereof to anyone with whom Agent has had negotiations prior to final termination, provided I have received notice in writing, including the names of the prospective purchasers, before or upon termination of this agreement or any extension thereof. I further agree to register these names and exclude them from any exclusive agency and/or exclusive right to sell listing I may grant to any licensed real estate broker within 180 days of the termination of this authorization or any extension thereof.

5. If action be instituted on this agreement to collect compensation or commissions, I agree to pay such sum as the Court may fix as reasonable attorney's fees.

6. I authorize the Agent named herein to cooperate with sub-agents selected by him.

7. This property is offered without respect to race, creed, color, or national origin.

8. In the event of an exchange, permission is hereby given Agent to represent all parties and collect compensation or commissions from them, provided there is full disclosure to all principals of such agency. Agent is authorized to divide with other agents such compensation or commissions in any manner acceptable to them.

9. I agree to hold Agent harmless from any liability or damages arising from any incorrect information supplied by me or any information I fail to supply.

10. Other provisions: •Balance by buyer executing note secured by second trust deed on subject property in the amount of $3,000.00 payable $62.28 or more per month including 9 per cent interest, and all due and payable five years from date of note.

11. I acknowledge that I have read and understand this Agreement, and that I have received a copy hereof.

Dated January 12, 19 71 Arcadia, California

Nora H. Seller
Owner

Owner

176 West Peacock Road
Address

Arcadia, California 445-3782
City - State - Phone

12. In consideration of the execution of the foregoing, the undersigned Agent agrees to be diligent in endeavoring to obtain a purchaser.

James R. Broker
Agent

516 South Dover Street, Arcadia, California
Address - City

By Samuel Salesman

446-8531
Phone

January 12, 1971
Date

FORM A-11-Rev.

REVISED 1-69 CPS 40M

1. Early American or Garrison House

2. Ranch House or Western

3. California Bungalow

4. Northwestern or Puget Sound

5. Midwestern (Modified Colonial)

4. Cape Cod Colonial

5. Cape Ann Colonial

1. Elizabethan or Half Timber

2. Cotswold (English Cottage)

2. Dutch Colonial

4. French Provincial

5. Regency

1. Bermuda

2. Pueblo or Adobe

1. New England Farmhouse or Georgian or New England Colonial

2. Pennsylvania Dutch (German)

3. Southern Georgian or Southern Colonial

2. Creole or New Orleans or Louisiana

3. Monterey

4. Mediterranean

5. Victorian (Queen Anne)

COMPONENT PARTS OF A HOUSE

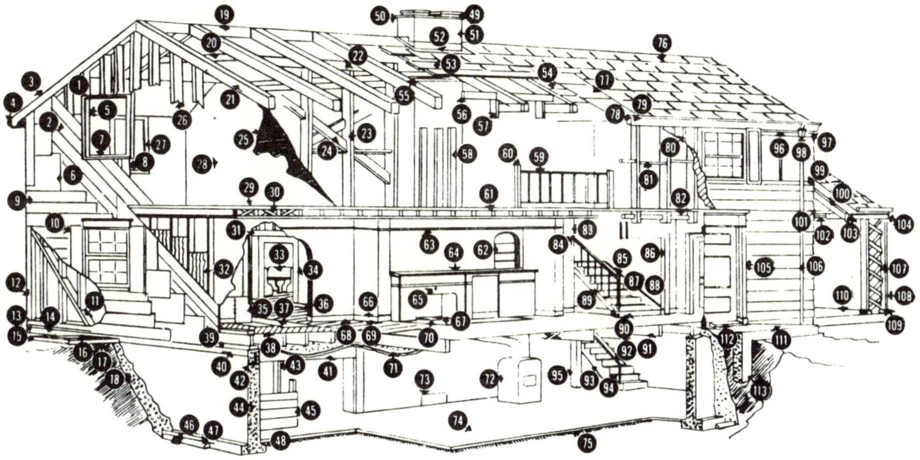

KEY TO CONSTRUCTION DETAILS

1. Window Head Frame
2. Wall Sheathing, Diagonal
3. Verge Board
4. Gutter
5. Window Jamb Trimmer
6. Wall Building Paper
7. Window Sill Frame
8. Cripple Stud
9. Wall Siding
10. Window Shutters
11. Corner Bracing 45
12. Corner Studs, Double
13. Sole Plate
14. Box Sill
15. Basement Areaway
16. Basement Sash
17. Grade Line
18. Gravel Fill
19. Ridge Board
20. Collar Beam
21. Roof Rafters
22. Interior Partition Plates
23. Interior Studs
24. Cross Bracing
25. Plaster Base, Lath
26. Gable Studs
27. Interior Window Trim
28. Plaster Walls
29. Cross Bridging
30. Second Floor Joists
31. Arch Framing
32. Insulation, Batts
33. Dining Nook
34. Interior Door Trim
35. Plaster Base, Rock Lath
36. Finish Floor
37. Floor Lining Felt
38. Sub-Flooring, Diagonally
39. Sill Plate
40. Termite Shield
41. Girder
42. Plate Anchor Bolt
43. Post
44. Foundation Wall
45. Frame Partition
46. Tarred Felt Joint Cover
47. Drain Tile
48. Footing
49. Flue Liner Tops
50. Chimney Cap
51. Brick Chimney
52. Flashing & Counter Flashing
53. Spaced 1" x 4" Sheathing (Wood Shingles)
54. Tight Roof Sheathing (All Other Coverings)
55. Ceiling Joists
56. Exterior Wall Plates
57. Lookouts
58. Furring Strips
59. Stair Rail & Balusters
60. Stair Landing Newel
61. Finish Floor Over Felt Over Sub-flooring on Wood Joists
62. Book Shelves
63. Picture Mould
64. Mantel and Trim
65. Damper Control
66. Base Top Mould
67. Ash Dump
68. Baseboards
69. Shoe Mould
70. Hearth
71. Plaster Ceiling
72. Boiler or Furnace
73. Cleanout Door
74. Basement Concrete Floor
75. Cinder Fill
76. Roof Cover (Shingles)
77. Roofing Felts
78. Soffit or Cornice
79. Facia of Cornice
80. Vert Board & Batten Siding
81. Fire Stops
82. Ribbon Plate
83. Stair Wall Partition
84. Stair Rail or Easing
85. Starting Newel
86. Cased Opening Trim
87. Main Stair Treads & Risers
88. Wall Stair Stringer
89. Face Stringer & Moulds
90. Starting Riser & Tread
91. First Floor Joists
92. Basement Stair Rail & Post
93. Basement Stair Horses
94. Basement Stair Treads & Risers
95. Basement Post
96. Facia Board
97. Cornice Bed Mould
98. Leader Head or Conductor Head
99. Belt Course
100. Porch Rafter
101. Porch Ceiling Joists
102. Porch Ceiling Soffit
103. Porch Roof Beam
104. Porch Beam Facia
105. Entrance Door Trim
106. Leader, Downspout or Conductor
107. Porch Trellis
108. Porch Column
109. Porch Column Base
110. Concrete Porch Floor
111. Concrete Stoop
112. Entrance Door Sill
113. Stoop Foundation

Exchange Permission

Under the Law of Agency, a licensee cannot act for two principals in negotiating with each other unless both have knowledge of and consent to the dual agency. This is a principle with which any licensed real estate broker is familiar, but by the inclusion of the above clause in the agreement pertaining to an excange of properties the owner specifically authorizes the agent to represent all parties and to collect a commission from them, *"provided there is full disclosure to all principals of such agency."* He further provides for authorization of the agent to divide his commission with any other agents with whom he is dealing in the transaction "in any manner acceptable to them." By the use of this terminology, the owner disassociates himself from having to be judge or jury in arbitrating any dispute that might arise over commission splits between or among brokers who are parties to the transaction. The broker, on his part, has his position clearly spelled out should a question arise as to which of the parties the agent is representing in the exchange.

8. I agree to hold Agent harmless from any liability or damages arising from any incorrect information supplied by me or any information I fail to supply.

Liability Protection for Incorrect Information

This section could also be considered a protection clause for the broker. He may have taken considerable care in listing a property, only to find later that the owner has given him misinformation or has concealed pertinent information (whether intentionally or not) concerning his property. Should a third party to the sale charge the broker with giving out misinformation or with having concealed pertinent information, the broker may fall back on the above clause for his protection.

9. Other provisions.

____

Other Provisions

No two listings are ever the same in the extra provisions. Previous listing forms have not provided for space in which to enter these. The seller, for example, may wish to restrict the hours during which the property may be shown. He may wish to reserve certain items of personal property. The special provisions that might be included here would, of course, vary with the particular case. The important point is to make certain that no important provision has been left out.

10. I acknowledge that I have read and understand this Agreement, and I have received a copy hereof. Dated ____________, 19_____. _________, California

______________	______________
Owner	Owner
______________	______________
Address	City-State-Phone

Acknowledgment of Understanding

Most listing agreements contain this clause. It is an important one and may serve at some time to absolve the broker should the seller ever attempt to discredit the broker by alleging that he did not know what the contract involved at the time of the signing. Further, he can never deny having received a copy of the agreement, once he has signed a contract that includes this clause. If the owner is married, it is essential that both signatures be obtained. Although in the event of a sale of the property the broker is entitled to a commission from whichever party signed the agreement, it is not legally possible for the buyer to force a suit for specific performance unless all parties who have an interest in the property have signed the listing agreement. The broker, on his part, may find himself in the embarrassing position of having listed a property that he cannot deliver.

11. In consideration of the execution of the foregoing, the undersigned Agent agrees to be diligent in endeavoring to obtain a purchaser.

______________	______________	
Agent	Address-City	
By______________	______________	
	Phone	Date

Agreement to Be Diligent in Endeavoring to Obtain Purchaser

This is the section that makes the listing agreement a bilateral contract. Thus far in the agreement the owner has committed himself to some ten obligations, but until we arrive at this section of the contract the agent has not been bound by any specific agreement. He now agrees to "be diligent in endeavoring to obtain a purchaser." To return to the dictionary once more, we find that "diligent" means "to be constant in effort." Surely "diligent in effort" then doesn't mean that the listing broker should do nothing more than file the listing with a multiple-listing service in the hope that, with little or no effort on his part, the property will be sold by another member of the MLS. The broker has committed himself over his signature to use every method available to him to obtain a purchaser for the listed property. If the agent has the right to cancel the listing because of bad faith on the part of the seller, surely the seller has the same right under the contract, if the agent is negligent in being "diligent in endeavoring to obtain a purchaser."

Restrictions Contrary to Law

One word of caution to the broker. Sellers, on occasion, have requested that brokers insert into the listing agreement restrictions as to race or religion in the showing of the property. Such restrictions are contrary to law today, and if such are requested by the seller, it is the duty of the broker to point out to him that he is not permitted under the law to take a listing incorporating such restrictions. At this time it is wise for the broker to have a clear understanding with his principal of the broker's responsibility in exercising strict nondiscrimination in giving service to a customer on the basis of race or religion.[15]

SUGGESTED REFERENCES

Advanced Real Estate Sales. Los Angeles: California Real Estate Association, 1968.

HIMMAH, GAEL, *Real Estate Listing Magic.* Englewood Cliffs, N.J.: Prentice-Hall, Inc., 1964.

Listing Real Estate. Los Angeles: California Real Estate Association, 1969.

[15] From "Servicing the Listing," *Listing Real Estate* (Los Angeles: California Real Estate Association, 1969).

5

Valuation of Listings

The appraisal process involves the collection and analysis of pertinent data. How does the new licensee, who is not a professional appraiser, reach his conclusions as to a fair market value of a given property? First of all, what is *"fair market value"*? In law it is defined as "the highest price estimated in terms of money which the land would bring if exposed for sale in the open market, with reasonable time allowed to find a purchaser buying with knowledge of all uses and purposes to which it was adapted, and for which it was capable, the seller not being required to sell or the purchaser to purchase."

Appraising is not an exact science. Rather, it is an opinion based on available facts. From this we may conclude that the better qualified the appraiser is to collect, assemble, and analyze the data, the more accurate will be the appraisal. Value conclusions arrived at by the fee appraiser will have a much higher degree of accuracy than will those of the inexperienced, unqualified salesman, who often arrives at his opinion through a process of "guesstimating."

The real estate executive with an established reputation for careful appraisals and for rejection of overpriced listings has gone far toward achieving professional status. Furthermore, he has (1) placed his office on a sound business footing by stocking salable merchandise only, (2) established good broker–client relationships, and (3) largely eliminated any effective competition.

The *honest* approach to the seller *at the outset* promises a continuing successful and happy broker–client relationship. The broker's obligation to strict honesty involves disclosure of all factors, good or bad, which may affect his appraisal of the property. To list a property too high is as much a breach of good faith as to accept a listing under the market price from an uninformed seller without first apprising him of the fact. The office that consistently accepts overpriced listings will find itself eventually out of business as surely as the merchant who stocks his shelves with shoddy merchandise or who disregards his competitor's offerings.

What about the owner who insists on pricing his property out of the market in spite of the broker's careful evaluation? What is the answer to the seller who attempts to recoup the total cost of all improvements made to the property: the swimming pool, the wall-to-wall carpeting, the draperies, the outdoor barbecue, and the many embellishments installed strictly for his personal enjoyment? How does the lister point out such detriments as neighborhood regression, the evident lack of good housekeeping, deferred maintenance, costly improvements that have resulted in overbuilding the neighborhood, and the many other factors that may have contributed to the depreciation (functional or economic) of the property?

Only when the lister can speak with authority backed by factual information can he hope to convince the serious seller to list his property at market value. (The seller who is not serious about selling has been discussed in the previous chapter.)

Pitfalls of Accepting Overpriced Listings

Although poor listing practice contributes in a large measure to unsuccessful office operation, nothing will spell the doom of an office more than the practice of consistently: (1) accepting listings at the owner's unrealistic price with the hope of bringing the price into line later, or (2) accepting listings at the seller's advertised price *plus the commission.*

(Commission should be considered a *service fee,* and as such should not be added to the sales price.)

The owner who contacts an office for its services obviously does so because of a selling problem. It should be safe to assume that he selected the particular office because (1) it was recommended to him by someone who has had previous experience with the office, or (2) its advertisements or signs have come to the attention of the property owner. In either event, the office in question has doubtless followed a consistently successful course of listing procedure, or neither (1) nor (2) above would have been in evidence to motivate the seller to make the contact.

When the salesman is called in to take a listing, he has the choice of returning to the office with a salable listing, priced competitively with other properties currently on the market, or of refusing the listing unless the owner agrees to a listing price that can be defended to a buyer. If the listing is refused, it should be done tactfully and in a manner that will not close the door to future negotiations. The lister does not *set the price,* but he does make available to the seller factual market data that will assist him in determining the asking price. If the listing is accepted at an unrealistic figure, the office faces (1) an increase in its advertising costs as it attempts to expose the property to potential buyers; (2) wasted time on the part of the salesman servicing the listing; (3) a sales force gradually losing enthusiasm for showing the property, and (4) a risk to the broker's reputation as a good merchandiser.

The effects on the seller who lists his property at a figure too high for the current market can be equally disastrous. The home becomes "shopworn" and even when the price is reduced (usually several weeks later) it is difficult to arouse enthusiastic interest from prospective buyers. The for-sale sign remaining overlong on the property gives the impression that some serious defect has prevented its sale. The listing salesman's enthusiasm for the listing, once it has died, is hard to resurrect.

Although we have discussed the importance of price in listing a property, this factor is not as important as the owner's reason for selling. The office that normally is averse to taking overpriced listings can afford to make an exception if the owner has a compelling reason for selling. With the knowledge that he is negotiating with a highly motivated seller, the lister is assured that eventually the price will be brought into line with the market. The salesman should determine the reason for the sale as soon as possible after his initial contact with the property owner. One of any number of factors may contribute to the urgency of the sale. There may be a job transfer involved. Illness may be forcing the seller to leave the area for a more favorable climate. The birth of a child might require the family to seek larger quarters. There may be a foreclosure pending. The seller may have bought another home and is not in a position to make payments on two loans.

What Is an Appraisal?

The American Institute of Real Estate Appraisers defines an appraisal as a conclusion resulting from an analysis of facts. As mentioned above, the appraisal's accuracy depends upon the competence and integrity of the appraiser, as well as upon the skill with which he processes the available and pertinent data. Real estate brokers may not always qualify as expert appraisers, but they should be familiar with the forces that influence value and the best methods of arriving at these value estimates.

Purpose of the Appraisal

Basically the purpose of an appraisal is to estimate value, usually market value.[1] There are other types of value, depending upon the use to which the appraisal is to be put. There may be a number of diverse reasons for an appraisal, such as:

(1) Transfer of ownership
(2) Financing and credit
(3) Compensation in condemnation proceedings
(4) Basis for taxation

We are concerned in this chapter with an appraisal for the purpose of the transfer of ownership. For this appraisal we will be considering how to:

(a) help prospective buyers decide on offering prices.
(b) help prospective sellers determine acceptable selling prices.
(c) establish a fair basis for exchange of real property.

Information Necessary for an Appraisal

For pricing purposes certain national, regional, and local economic trends must be understood by the broker. Price is predicated on the maximum amount a property will realize on the market. Because the investor in real estate is concerned with the stream of income he may expect from his property—either in monetary return or in terms of the amenities of the property—considerations to be taken into account are, for example, whether the economy is expanding,

[1] See p. 75 for definition of market value.

and if so, how long the trend can be expected to last. What factors are contributing to its expansion? What are the *future growth patterns* of the community? What are the *ecological factors*? (Smog is driving many residents out of the urban areas in search of more favorable climatic conditions. This, today, is having a great impact on property values in certain areas.)

Transportation (freeways, air travel, and to a lesser degree rail traffic) can have either an adverse or a favorable effect on property values. The advent of a freeway through a city changes the entire pattern of land development. Proximity of airports, particularly in the present day of superjets, has had its adverse effect on residential property values while at the same time enhancing industrial sites. The appraiser needs to study the possibilities for *future expansion* of a community. If there are physical barriers, will the city begin a growth of vertical expansion? Or do some of the areas call for a program of urban redevelopment?

The base industries of the community are important to an understanding of the tax structure.[2] It is important to know whether these industries are stable and can be expected to grow. Does the community have a diversified industry, or is it a one-industry city? (Detroit has its ups and downs as the automotive industry moves.)

The real estate practitioner needs to know what raw land is available, and the community's plans for development of this land. *Zoning* is such a basically important factor in land appraisal that the broker who is unfamiliar with his community's master plan for the future development of its land resources cannot be said to have collected and analyzed all pertinent data necessary to his appraisal. The *attitude of the community's governing body* plays a vital role in whether or not the city develops in an orderly manner. The *rating of the school system* has a marked effect on property values as well.

Land Value

This can be determined only through a study and knowledge of land use and current sales in the area. Multiple-listing files are valuable sources for obtaining up-to-the-minute sales information. The lister here is using the market sales comparison approach, which involves comparing recent sales prices of similar parcels of land with the parcel in question, taking into consideration (1) size of the parcel, (2) location, and (3) land use.

"Highest and best use" enters into any evaluation of land. This is defined as that use that is most likely to produce the greatest net return over a given period. "Net return" can take the form of amenities but is usually thought of in terms of money. Land values are based on location, size, shape, and topography. These criteria affect the value according to the land use anticipated. For example, sites for single-family residences may demand a higher price if they are located in hilly terrain, which, by commanding a favorable view, lends an aesthetic value to the area. Level or gently sloping land, on the other hand, would lend more value to commercial or industrial sites. Size and shape are important factors affecting both residential and commercial sites owing to the cost or general feasibility of development. Public and private restrictions both have their effect on land value. Private-deed restrictions affect the value of residential sites primarily. Such items as exposure, drainage, public facilities and services, trees, and soil are also contributing factors.

Approaches to Value

Appraisers for many years have used as value estimates the three approaches of market data, cost, and income capitalization. These are more commonly known today as (1) comparable sales, (2) replacement cost, and (3) capitalization of income. The market-data or comparable-sales approach is the one that we are most concerned with in evaluating single-family residences. This approach is based on comparison of recent sales of *comparable* (and therefore competitive) properties in the area. The cost approach sometimes used to support the market-data analysis is based on reproduction cost less depreciation. The capitalization approach is given little weight in single-family residence appraisal, but it has certain value in correlating all three approaches for a final analysis of available data.

In evaluating any property, all three approaches are used. The weight given to each is dependent on the type of property being considered.

When we speak of "value" it is important that we understand the type of value to which we are referring. In addition to monetary value, we have the following value types:

1. Appraised value
2. Assessed value
3. Book value
4. Cash value

[2] Base industries are those that fabricate goods for shipping beyond the city's boundaries.

5. Depreciated value
6. Economic value
7. Equity value
8. Exchange value
9. Face value
10. Insurance value
11. Leasehold value
12. Liquidation value
13. Market value
14. Mortgage value
15. Nuisance value
16. Potential value
17. Rental value
18. Replacement value
19. Salvage value
20. Tax value

Estimating fair market price is difficult, because it must be based on sales that are never entirely identical. Four major factors requiring adjustment of the value figure enter into the appraisal process: (1) date of sale, (2) real cause of sale, (3) terms of the sale, and (4) length of time that the property was on the market.

Under "information necessary for appraisal" above, we stressed that neighborhood characteristics and their trends must be taken into consideration if the appraiser weighs all aspects of his evaluation.

Generally speaking, a gradual decline takes place in interior locations within a city. Properties lying in the path of city growth usually exhibit good market potential. Good city planning tends to promote continuing desirability of neighborhoods. This is evident in many areas where comparison may be made between neighborhoods laid out in accordance with sound zoning principles (such as harmonious architecture, view protection, lot coverage, light, and air) and other areas suffering from the effects of poor planning embodying all the opposite conditions of good zoning principles.

Evaluating "comparable" properties, the appraiser is confronted with all the above factors affecting his final decision.

Market-Data Approach

Of the three approaches to value, this is the most favored for single-family residences. Alfred A. Ring states, "The greater the number and the more recent the sales of comparable properties, the greater the accuracy and the more convincing the results obtained via the market approach to value."[3]

For the broker in the field, one of the best and most reliable sources of market data is the multiple-listing service. However, in order to make a complete analysis, the sales price alone is insufficient. Time lapse between listing and sale, the reasons for the sale, and the terms under which the sale was made are all requisites of a valid market-data analysis. Some multiple-listing services record all this information, whereas others record sales prices and data only. Where complete records are not available, it is questionable whether that particular reference should be included in the collected data. Also subject to market adjustment are figures based on sales made six months or more previously. Market conditions vary, and all except the most recent sales must be analyzed in the light of current market demand.

The competitive market-analysis form shown on page 79 is a highly effective tool for an office sales force. Its continued use will serve to sharpen the evaluation methods of the office. When the forms are used, data can be organized, analyzed, and a summation made. The completed forms can then be used for the development of the office historical files. The spread between the top market value and the probable sales price should not exceed 5 percent. Using this as a guide, the salesman can readily gauge the accuracy of his appraisals, analyze his errors in judgment, and gradually perfect his appraisal skills. In areas where a great many FHA and VA appraisals are being made, records of these appraisals provide a valuable tool to use in conjunction with the MLS sales records. It is important for the office force to realize that, in order to present a true picture of market conditions, the files must be accurate and current.

Selling the Seller

Using the competitive market-analysis form, the salesman is in a position to organize his presentation to the seller. With the facts before him, he has a clear and accurate picture of (1) what buyers can pay, (2) what buyers will pay, and (3) what buyers will not pay for property in the area. It must be stressed that the form is only as valuable as the accuracy of the information it contains.[4] From the analysis of the information, the seller's marketing position is easily determined. Then, provided that the

[3] Alfred A. Ring, *The Valuation of Real Estate* (Englewood Cliffs, N. J.: Prentice-Hall, Inc., 1963), pp. 163–64.

[4] For an example, see completed form and how to use it, in Don C. Roberts, "How to Take Listings That Sell Fast by Using the Competitive Market Analysis," in *How to List and Sell Real Estate,* Educational and Sales Conference Subcommittee, Donald C. Roberts, Chairman (Los Angeles, Calif.: California Real Estate Association, 1964), pp. 16–17.

Competitive Market Analysis

CALIFORNIA REAL ESTATE ASSOCIATION STANDARD FORM

PROPERTY ADDRESS 1964 Opportunity Street, Your City DATE February 21, 1969

FOR SALE NOW:	BED-RMS.	BATHS	DEN	SQ. FT.	1ST LOAN	LIST PRICE	DAYS ON MARKET	TERMS
2721 Hillside Ave.**	3	2	FK	1300	13,637	20,000	5	1,050 CTL/CTNL or CTNFHAL
1850 Opportunity St.	3	2	FK	1300	13,821	20,300	8	1,100 CTL/CTNL or CTNFHAL
1918 Wentner St.	3	2	FK	1300	13,584	19,950	114	6,466 CTL
2842 Hillside Ave.	3	2	Den	1400	14,153	21,500	136	7,347 CTL or CTNL
1810 Wentner St.	4	2	FK	1450	15,316	21,750	27	2,000 Dn/Balance on 2nd TD
1416 Circle Dr.	4	2	FK	1450	15,496	22,500	94	7,004 TL or CTNL

SOLD PAST 12 MOS.	BED-RMS.	BATHS	DEN	SQ. FT.	1ST LOAN	LIST PRICE	DAYS ON MARKET	DATE SOLD	SALE PRICE	TERMS
1963 Opportunity St.	3	2	FK	1300	13,791	20,000	4	11/16	20,000	2,000 Dn/3,0002nd
2826 Hillside Ave.	3	2	FK	1300	14,166	20,450	34	8/14	20,250	1,050 CTNFHAL
1239 Circle Dr. *	3	2	Den	1400	14,279	20,950	78	3/21	20,500	1,100 CTNFHAL
1948 Opportunity St.	3	2	FK	1300	13,492	20,500	149	10/6	19,500	5;558 CTL
1950 Wentner St.	4	2	FK	1450	15,397	21,950	94	1/6	21,500	1,400 CTNFHAL
2650 Hillside Ave.	4	2	FK	1450	15,276	21,500	18	2/14	21,500	Nothing DN GI

EXPIRED PAST 12 MOS.	BED-RMS.	BATHS	DEN	SQ. FT.	1ST LOAN	LIST PRICE	DAYS ON MARKET	TERMS
1239 Circle Dr. *	3	2	Den	1400	14,428	23,950	120	9,522 CTL
1924 Opportunity St.	3	2	FK	1300	14,236	22,750	90	CTL or Submit/FHA Coming
1910 Wentner St.	3	2	FK	1300	13,984	22,500	90	CTL or CTNL or FHA
2721 Hillside Ave. **	3	2	FK	1300	13,823	22,000	180	CTNL or Submit
1850 Wentner Ave.	4	2	FK	1450	15,458	24,500	30	9,042 CTL
1930 Opportunity St.	4	2	FK	1450	15,263	22,950	60	TL or CTNL

F.H.A. ---- V.A. APPRAISALS

ADDRESS	APPRAISAL	ADDRESS	APPRAISAL
2721 Hillside Ave. **	20,000	1239 Circle Drive *	20,500
1850 Opportunity St.	20,000	1950 Wentner St.	21,500
2836 Hillside Ave.	20,000	1910 Wentner St.	21,500

BUYER APPEAL — **MARKETING POSITION**

(GRADE EACH ITEM 0 TO 20% ON THE BASIS OF DESIRABILITY OR URGENCY)

BUYER APPEAL

1. FINE LOCATION Near Schools and shopping 15 %
2. EXCITING EXTRAS Landscaped to perfection 10 %
3. EXTRA SPECIAL FINANCING No %
4. EXCEPTIONAL APPEAL Neat and clean 5 %
5. UNDER MARKET PRICE YES ____ NO X %

RATING TOTAL 30 %

MARKETING POSITION

1. WHY ARE THEY SELLING Bought new home 10 %
2. HOW SOON MUST THEY SELL 60 days 5 %
3. WILL THEY HELP FINANCE . . . . YES 20% NO ____ %
4. WILL THEY LIST AT COMPETITIVE MARKET VALUE . . YES 20% NO ____ %
5. WILL THEY PAY FOR APPRAISAL . . . . YES 20% NO ____ %

RATING TOTAL 75 %

ASSETS Convenient location - beautiful landscaping

DRAWBACKS Backs up to shopping center parking - neighbors yard untidy

AREA MARKET CONDITIONS Active but extremely competitive. Homes offered within 3% of top C.M.V. are requiring 90 to 120 days to sell.

RECOMMENDED TERMS Adjust list price to FHA or CRV appraisal (est. $20,000) $1,000 down payment to 30 year FHA or nothing down to 30 year V.A. loan

TOP COMPETITIVE MARKET VALUE . . . . $ 20,500.00

PROBABLE FINAL SALES PRICE . . . . $ 20,000.00

SELLING COSTS

BROKERAGE (s/p $20,000)	$ 1200.00
LOAN PAYOFF	$ 15112.00
PREPAYMENT PRIVILEGE	$ 226.00
FHA ---- VA POINTS	$ 380.00
TITLE AND ESCROW FEES: IRS STAMPS, RECONS RECORDING	$ 210.00
TERMITE CLEARANCE	$
MISC. PAYOFFS: 2ND T.D., POOL, PATIO, WTR. SFTNR., FENCE, IMPROVEMENT BOND.	$
	$
	$
TOTAL	$ 17128.00

TOTAL . . . . $ 17,128.00

NET PROCEEDS $ 2,872.00 PLUS OR MINUS $ 200.00

FORM CM 14
REV. 9/64

seller has a valid reason for selling, a competitive market price can be established, the lister's approach is more professional, his work is lessened, and the time spent with the prospective buyer is more productive.

According to the American Institute of Real Estate Appraisers one of the basic principles of appraising is *anticipation,* which is expressed as follows:

1. It affirms the definition of value as the worth of all present and future benefits arising from ownership and use of real property.
2. The value of a property is not established by what it sold for in the past nor the cost to create it.
3. Recent sales prices of comparable properties are indications of the present worth of what informed buyers and investors in the market anticipated the benefit of ownership would yield them.

From this we can appreciate the value of the competitive market-analysis form correctly applied as a marketing tool. First, as is true of any appraisal tool, the form is of no value *unless it is kept current.* It may have to be revised weekly as new sales figures are announced. Second, the figures used in making the comparisons *must be exact.* Square footage or number of bedrooms is not sufficient. Architectural design, construction, cleanliness, neighborhood, proximity to schools and transportation are all factors that should enter into the appraiser's decision to accept or reject a given property for valid competition.

Today more emphasis is given to available financing on properties being appraised. Brokers recognize that the home carrying a low-interest loan that can be assumed, or the one where the seller will finance the sale at an interest rate slightly under that demanded by institutional lenders, will bring a higher price on the market in times of tight money.[5]

The market-comparison approach to evaluating the single-family residence is probably the best and the most widely used not only by brokers but by buyers and sellers of properties, and by fee appraisers. This method of appraising is limited, however, by the amount of sales data available at the time the appraisal is made. The FHA *Underwriting Manual* states, "In selecting the comparative properties *utility* is the initial basis for comparison, *price* is secondary."[6]

We have discussed previously the importance of seller motivation, but equally important in the selection of a comparable property is the motivation of the buyer. For example, he may be overly impressed by the "charm" of the home or its setting and may overlook such vital factors as construction or location. He may be a transferee, whose family is waiting to join him. Time is then a factor in his selection. The home he selects will probably be one where possession can be had relatively fast.

Adjustments in Selections. The appraiser must make certain adjustments in his selection of properties comparable to the one being appraised. This requires a much higher degree of skill than that needed for the selection of the properties. It requires that the appraiser know the current market demand. *Styles in homes* change, just as they do in automobiles or furniture. What is popular today in home design or functional utility may not have been the vogue yesterday. Builders are aware of these trends, and if they are to compete successfully in the new home market, they must study and adhere to current home buyer's demands. As an example, consider the one-bath home with its limited appeal, or the single attached garage. In California the demand for the traditional Spanish-style home appears to be almost a cyclical phenomenon. Four-bedroom homes are growing in popularity, with most buyers insisting upon large rooms and center-hall plans.

In southern California particularly, central air conditioning and a swimming pool are increasing in demand in the more expensive homes. With more leisure time available, boats and campers have become necessary to their way of life for many families. To accommodate these accessories large lots with accessibility to the rear yard are required. Thus *desirability* is an important factor in making adjustments between the properties being used for comparison and the one under appraisal. As to *location,* the properties need not be in the same neighborhood, but the neighborhoods should have the same general social and economic status.

Replacement-Cost Approach

This is sometimes known as the *cost method* and is based "on the assumption that no buyer would pay more for a property than he would for an equally acceptable newly constructed substitute property."[7] A careful distinction must be made between "replacement" and "reproduction" costs.

"Replacement cost" implies replacing the subject property improvements with a structure having exactly the same utilities and amenities; whereas, strictly speaking, "reproduction cost new" is generally accepted as meaning the cost that would be incurred if the improvements were reproduced as an exact

[5] For further information on this subject, see "Favorable Financing Effects on Values of Single-Family Residences," *Appraisal Journal,* July, 1970, p. 398.

[6] My italics.

[7] Dr. F. E. Case, Selecting, Training, and Reducing Turnover of Real Estate Sales Personnel, 1957, p. 159.

replica. Because to do this might involve materials and construction practices long since outmoded, it would be impractical to estimate such costs. Appraisals for insurance purposes, however, are usually made on this basis.[8]

The replacement-cost approach is an estimate of the cost of developing a site. An older structure cannot command the price of a new one, even though it is a duplication with equivalent utilities and amenities.

Three steps are involved in the replacement-cost approach: (1) computing replacement costs, (2) estimating the depreciation, and (3) estimating land costs. This method is used for all types of properties but is particularly suited to special-purpose buildings, where comparable properties are difficult to find or which are rarely sold and which do not yield a measurable dollar return.

To use the replacement-cost method, appraisers and brokers usually arrive at the total cost by the square-foot or cubic-foot method. For example, an estimate is made by comparison with other buildings whose square-foot costs are known. If the two buildings are similar in design and quality, multiplying the square footage of the floor area of the subject property by the known cost of the comparable structure would produce a replacement cost. A unit-in-place cost is sometimes used. This involves valuing all materials and fixtures and adding the cost of installation. (Cost figures are usually obtainable from local building contractors or from trade magazines.) These costs will vary with areas, and even within areas will fluctuate with the efficiency of building methods used.

Building construction costs must be kept up-to-date. A check on labor and material costs should be made at least every six months. Building-cost quotations may be found in national building manuals, where costs in various cities throughout the United States are included.

A further clarification of the three methods of cost approach—(1) quantity-survey method; (2) unit-in-place method; (3) comparative method, or square-foot and cubic-foot factor—follows:

Quantity-Survey Method. This method simply means calculating the quantity and costs of materials, supplies, equipment, and labor involved in building a structure. It requires that the appraiser be completely familiar with current prices of building materials and of labor costs. This method is a detailed and time-consuming procedure, more fitted to the building contractor. Although it supplies the yardstick by which all other methods may be measured for accuracy, it is not practicable for the average appraiser.

Unit-in-Place Method. Under this method, cost factors are developed by the appraiser to represent the cost of a square foot of exterior or interior wall surface, floor, roof, and so on, *in place.* Although not quite as time consuming as the quantity-survey method, the unit-in-place method requires a great deal of time and is considered economically unfeasible for the average appraisal. Its accuracy necessitates knowledge of current material and labor costs. Residential properties lend themselves to the development of unit-in-place factors that can be applied rather quickly with accurate results.

Comparative Market Method. This method is the most widely used for estimating building costs. The applicable unit cost per square or cubic foot of a building is derived by dividing the total building costs of similar structures recently completed by the volume of square or cubic feet contained within the exterior wall dimension of the building's structural surfaces—including attics, basements, and subfloor areas. The unit cost obtained is then multiplied by the total number of square or cubic feet space. To this total is added a percentage for architect's fees and the builder's overhead and profit. The square-foot factor is generally used for the inexpensive residential buildings or industrial buildings. The cubic-foot factor is preferred for the large residential structure, industrial building, office building, apartment house, and so on.[9]

Depreciation

The second step in the replacement-cost approach is that of computing the existing building depreciation in terms of dollars. This figure is then deducted from the replacement cost new to arrive at the present value of all improvements. *Depreciation* is defined as a loss of value in real property from any cause and is classed as curable or incurable. It includes all influences that reduce a property below its replacement cost new.

There are three major types of depreciation: (1) physical deterioration, (2) functional obsolescence, and (3) economic and social obsolescence.

Physical Deterioration. This is sometimes known as physical depreciation. It normally accounts for only a minor part of the total depreciation of a

[8] *Reference Book,* California Department of Real Estate.

[9] A widely used publication in the appraisal industry is the *Residential Cost Handbook* (Los Angeles: Marshall and Stevens Publication Company).

building. As buildings age, their value is decreased by the action upon them by the elements, ordinary use, deferred maintenance (neglect), and damage caused by dry rot or wood-boring insects. The quality of the materials used in the building and the maintenance of the structure affect the degree to which the building suffers depreciation. Deterioration in the poorly constructed building takes place at a more rapid rate than it does in the well-built structure. Physical deterioration is evidenced by leaking roofs, shrinking, warping or rotting lumber, corroded plumbing, or cracked plaster.

Functional Obsolescence. Most properties suffer their greatest loss in value from the effects of obsolescence, which is considered a loss in value from decreased utility, inadequacy, overcapacity, or changes in architectural style. This type of obsolescence is considered "built-in" and is only partly curable. Outmoded kitchens or bathrooms can be modernized and obsolete wiring can be replaced, but faulty room arrangement often is incurable. In general, any items (excluding those considered as deteriorating factors) inherent in the building itself that are responsible for decreased demand are considered to be contributing to functional obsolescence.

Economic or Social Obsolescence. This is a loss in value resulting from conditions *outside the building,* which are usually considered incurable. They are conditions that affect adversely the character and degree of utilization of the structure. Some of the more important factors leading to economic obsolescence are:

1. Population movements which either reduce the total number of persons interested in owning or renting property, or result in the substitution of persons on a low economic level for persons on a higher level as potential buyers.
2. Changes in the consumption habits of the general populace. (Amusement and luxury trades are vulnerable to these changes, which make their production facilities either inadequate or over-adequate; motion picture theaters are a prime example of property subject to such obsolescence.)
3. Growth of industrial and commercial areas that, in the absence of adequate zoning, encroach upon residential areas to the detriment of the residential area to the detriment of the residential properties.
4. Presence of special nuisances and hazards such as excessive noise and danger potentials.
5. Proximity to airfields with their noise and danger potentials.
6. Deterioration in the quality and accessibility of schools, shopping and community facilities.
7. Deterioration or breakdown in public transportation facilities.
8. Excessive level of real estate taxes and assessments.
9. Adverse legislation. (Rent control is a form of "legislative" obsolescence, artificially holding down the rentals and hence the value of controlled properties. A repeal of protective tariffs would adversely affect communities dependent upon protected industries.)[10]

As stated above, economic obsolescence is usually considered incurable because it is not inherent in the property. Correction can sometimes be made by public or private rehabilitation programs.

Estimating accrued depreciation. There are two principal methods of measuring accrued depreciation: (1) the observed-condition method, and (2) the "age–life" method.

The observed-condition method is the most widely used. It consists of determining the total cost of repairs (to correct curable deterioration and functional obsolescence) and adding the loss in value credited to incurable physical deterioration and economic obsolescence. Under *curable physical deterioration* are listed deferred maintenance and repairs necessary to put the building in top condition. Depreciation reserves must also be provided for. Into this reserve would go items of anticipated capital improvements such as roofing, heating, plumbing, wiring, and exterior refinishing. Under the heading of *physical deterioration incurable* is the estimate of accrued loss in dollars due to wear and tear of structural load-bearing parts of the building. *The age–life method* is based on accepted depreciation tables showing age–life experience in depreciation of various types of structures under normal maintenance. Tables are available from the Bureau of Internal Revenue under the titles (a) income-tax depreciation and obsolescence; (b) estimated useful lives, and (c) depreciation rates. The typical economic life of a well-constructed frame building has been estimated at fifty years. Quality of construction, the amount of capital-improvement expenditures that have been made, and the general care and maintenance given the building will add or subtract from the effective age. *The building-residual method* is one used primarily in capitalizing income. The land is valued separately from the improvements, and a fair annual net return on the land is deducted from the net annual return of the entire property.

Book Depreciation

This is a theoretical figure adopted for accounting purposes. There may be considerable variance in the book-depreciation figure and the estimated loss in value as figured by the professional appraiser. Book

[10] Sanders, A. Kahn, et al., *Real Estate Appraisal and Investment* (New York: The Ronald Press Company, 1963), p. 171.

value is normally arrived at by deducting the original cost of the property improvements from the cost of the entire property including the land, and then using the straight-line depreciation on the building itself.[11] After determining the depreciated value of the building, the original cost of the land is added to the depreciated value of the building to arrive at the book value of the property. Depreciation, as defined by the Internal Revenue Code for income-tax purposes, is "a reasonable allowance for the exhaustion, wear and tear, and normal obsolescence of property that is used in trade or business or one held for the production of income."

Appreciation

This occurs when inflation or special supply-and-demand factors are prevalent that concern the subject property. Some areas are affected particularly by supply and demand where social amenities or prestige value influences the market value. In such cases, appreciation may entirely offset the normal drop in value due to depreciation.

Capitalization Method

The capitalization or income approach to appraising is a method of estimating in dollars the current price of future benefits of property that are expected to continue for an estimated number of years. As expressed by the American Institute of Real Estate Appraisers, "The theory of the income approach is this: *Value of a property is the present worth of the net income it will produce during the remainder of its productive life.*"[12]

This approach is used particularly when evaluating income-producing property. In general, it is not used for single-family residences, even though they may have been turned into rental-income properties. It is usually measured by the net income projected into the future. The capitalization approach is complex and should not be used by the inexperienced broker or appraiser. It involves accurate estimates of (1) the gross income and (2) expenses of operation, as well as selection of capitalization method, establishment of the capitalization rate, and determination of the period of time over which the net income is to be capitalized.

The annual net income is derived by subtracting the total expenses from the gross income. (Net income *before* interest and amortization, but *after* deduction of all operating expenses.) Because the capitalization approach deals with *future* net income, future trends in income and expense enter into the picture. Three elements are involved in the gross income: the quantity, the quality, and the durability of the income. By *quantity* of gross income is meant the amount earned or collected in a year. The *quality* of the rent or income is measured by the financial responsibility of the tenant. The durability of the income relates to the *type* of tenancy, such as the terms and provisions of the lease or leases on the property.

Operating expenses to be deducted from the gross income to arrive at the net income are:

(1) Taxes
(2) Insurance
(3) Repairs
(4) Management
(5) Reserve for replacements
(6) Vacancies and collection losses
(7) Maintenance (gardening, painting, and decorating)
(8) Utilities
(9) Depreciation on furniture (where applicable)

Broker's listings often show only the following expenses: taxes and operating permit (or license), utilities, insurance, and management. (Note: attempting to represent this as a *true net* subjects the licensee to disciplinary action under the Business-and-Professions Code. It can also result in the recision of a purchase contract if the buyer has relied upon the broker's figures as an accurate representation of a true net.) Vacancy factors are determined by past experience of the property. Are the vacancies increasing? Would a change of managers correct the situation? Are the rents competitive with those of other comparable spaces and/or with new or more modern buildings under construction? What is the future rental picture for the area?

Selection of the Capitalization Rate

This is a most important step. A variation of 1 percent may mean a substantial difference in the capitalized value of the income. The rate is based upon the return an investor will demand before he is attracted to the investment. Real estate as an investment is constantly in competition to other types of investment, such as government bonds, stocks, trust deeds, and so on. Selection of the capitalization rate must be based on the current money market plus the equity yield that will attract an investor. It must be based upon certain market characteristics including the rate of return demanded by equity investors, the interest rate current in the mortgage market, the number of years in which net income may be expected to continue, and other market characteristics.

[11] See pp. 195 and 196.
[12] *The Appraisal of Real Estate,* 5th ed. (Chicago: American Institute of Real Estate Appraisers), p. 228.

(The income approach to appraising will be further explored in the chapter on income property.)

Gross-Income Multipliers. This is sometimes known as a "gross monthly multiplier" and is based upon the market relationship between rental value and the sales price of a property. As an index of value the gross-income multiplier has gained popularity but must be applied with care. It should not be considered as *part of* the capitalization approach but only *as a check* on the results of more sophisticated methods such as cost, market, and income approaches to value. Multipliers vary from region to region, from community to community, and may even vary from neighborhood to neighborhood. By relating market prices of certain classes of property to the actual gross income of these properties if offered for rent in a competitive market, the multiplier for these properties can be established. Custom has established that the multiplier for single- and two-family homes be applied to the monthly rent, whereas apartment buildings with more than eight units are appraised on the annual-income basis. There appears to be no hard and fast rule for apartment buildings with fewer than eight units; either the annual or the monthly multiplier is used.

Correlating the Value Approaches

Correlating does not mean averaging. The appraiser selects the value approach that best applies to the particular property being appraised, placing the most emphasis on this approach, and using the other two to test the accuracy of the one selected. In other words, each method is carefully considered to arrive at a weighted judgment. It cannot be too highly stressed that appraising is not an exact science. It is at best a subjective estimate or a substantiated opinion of the appraiser who is attempting to evaluate the probable stream of income from a given property. If the appraiser discovers considerable disparity among his three approaches, he must consider the purpose of the appraisal and recheck his results from this angle. For loan purposes, he would give the most weight to the capitalization-of-income approach, but for sale purposes or condemnation he would consider the market-data information most heavily. For insurance purposes the replacement-cost method would carry the most weight.

Legal Factors

Easements, rights of way, covenants, conditions and restrictions of record all affect the value of property. At the time the listing is being taken, the lister should examine the owner's policy of title. From this he may determine any easements of record. Purchasers of property, particularly if they are builders or developers, often make their offers to purchase subject to their approval of the "CC & R's" (covenants, conditions, and restrictions) of record. Land that is crisscrossed with easements probably is not suitable for development. Unless the easements can be removed from the record the land value can be greatly lessened. In land appraisals any easements or restrictions of record must be given considerable weight in the final report if they are of the nature that would restrict the development of the land to its highest and best use.

Zoning

Although it is probably a fallacy to assume that zoning alone *creates* value, we must consider the effects of zoning or rezoning on property values. The zoning change reflects an increase in value only when the demand for such a change is present. By the same token a rezoning if there is no demand for such a change can actually cause a lowering in value of the property affected. Consider a case in point: a new freeway goes through a suburban community. Near an off-ramp is a property zoned R-I (single-family residential) and improved with an older two-story home. The market value is approximately $18,000. With the advent of the freeway off-ramp, the city rezones the property C-I (commercial). A major oil company purchases the property for a service station, paying $75,000 for the land and improvements. An example of the negative effects of rezoning would be a change from a residential zone to one of multiple dwellings before the actual demand was present. The same situation would arise if a residential zone were to be rezoned to M-I (industrial), with city building codes requiring cement-block or brick construction for any additions to existing structures or for any new construction. If the demand for industrial sites was not present, the property owners could suffer a loss in value of their properties as residential sites while the demand for industrial sites was developing.

Financing

We cannot close this chapter without mentioning the effect that favorable or unfavorable financing has on property evaluation. We have already established the fact that the interest rate on a loan of record can influence the selection of the capitalization rate for appraising income property. But today, in estimating the market value of the single-family residence, the effects of financing have a greater impact than ever before. Brokers are well aware of the increased demand for the home carrying a low-

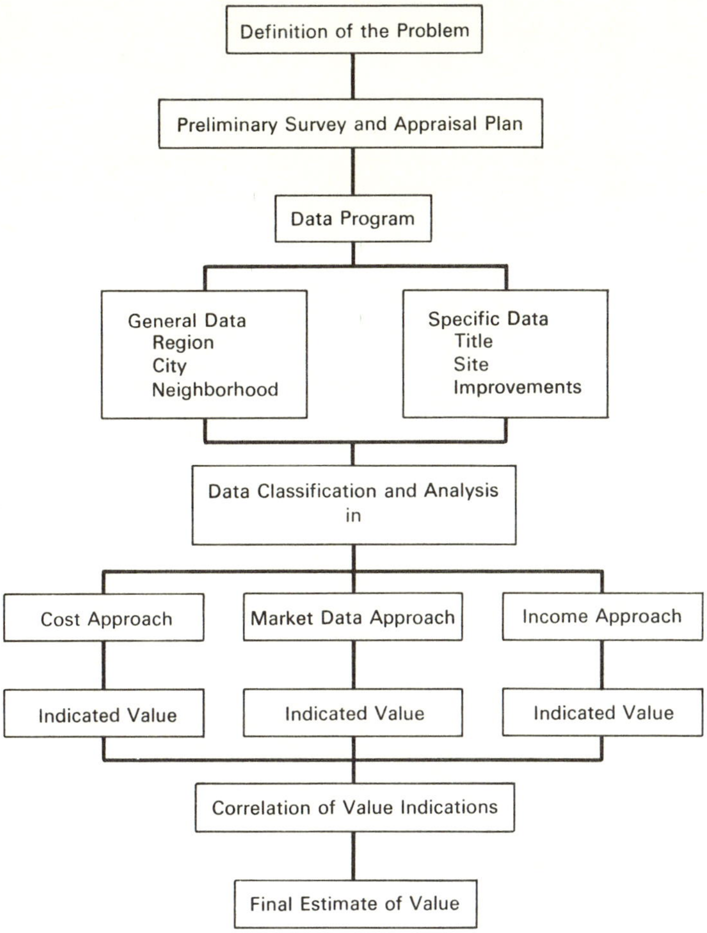

THE APPRAISAL PROCESS (Courtesy of the American Institute of Real Estate Appraisers, Chicago, Illinois.)

interest loan which can be assumed with no increase in the interest rate, or the home whose owner is willing to carry the loan at a favorable interest rate, (sometimes below that being asked by the institutional lenders). In the Competitive Market-Analysis form provision is made for consideration to be given to FHA or VA financing in appraising the subject property. The lister must determine at the time the listing is taken whether the seller has a loan of record that can be transferred to the new buyer at the interest rate designated or the loan must be *renegotiated to the new buyer at a higher interest rate.* Will the owner help with the financing by carrying a second trust deed? Or, if the property is clear, will the seller carry back a first trust deed at a favorable rate of interest? Today there is a growing tendency among appraisers to discount the concept that property should be appraised as though it were free and clear of liens and encumbrances.[13]

We cannot stress too strongly the responsibility of the listing salesman to determine the status of any loan of record on a property to be listed for sale. A raise in interest rate to the new buyer can greatly affect the market value of the property.

CASE STUDY

You are a salesman with the ABC Realty Company. You are on floor duty when a call comes from Mrs. David Conyers to list her home on Tropical Avenue, Arcadia, California. You check the historical files in the office and find that the home has never been on the market but was built by the Conyers two years ago. Mrs. Conyers says that they have been thinking of selling and moving closer to her husband's work (some forty miles distant).

You make an appointment with Mrs. Conyers for later that afternoon. In the meantime, you make a neighborhood survey and check the office files for recent sales in the area. You find that the homes vary in age from eight to twelve years; they are mostly of the three-bedroom or two-bedroom-and-convertible-den type with one and three-quarters baths. The square footage of the homes varies from 1,400 to

[13] For further study on this subject, see James L. Doherty, "Favorable Financing Effects on Values of Single-Family Residences," *The Appraisal Journal,* American Institute of Real Estate Appraisers, July, 1970, p. 398.

1,700. Most of them have dual-floor furnaces. The lots are comparable in size and are all well kept. The neighborhood reflects general pride of ownership. There have been very few recent sales, only four having sold in the past two years. These were cases in which the owners had been transferred to other states. The sales prices of these homes ranged from $27,500 to $32,750. Financing in the area is no problem, lending institutions favoring this neighborhood for top loans.

In comparing the Conyers home with the other properties, you find that it has 1,964 square feet of living area, two and one-half baths, three bedrooms, and an 18 by 24-foot family room. There is a forced-air furnace, thermostatically controlled. The yard has been professionally landscaped, and the Conyers have recently installed all-wool wall-to-wall carpeting throughout. The kitchen has all the modern built-ins, including a dishwasher and refrigerator. The house presents a more modern appearance than any others in the neighborhood; the floor plan is very functional, and the sliding-glass doors from the family room to the large patio make for an attractive area for outdoor living.

During a conference with the Conyers, they tell you that they like Arcadia as a place to live, but Mr. Conyers wishes to cut down on the driving time to his work. They believe that they have built the best house on the street and feel that their property should bring approximately $42,000 on the market. You are convinced, however, that their real reason for calling you in is to "feel out the market." They expect to make a nice profit on their home and continually bring up the point that, because their home is so much better than the other properties on the street, it should bring a much higher price than any of those that have sold. You sense that there is no real need to sell and that the Conyers may prove difficult to deal with. Mrs. Conyers appears to know a great deal about the circumstances of most of the people in her block, although she and her husband admit that they do not socialize with the neighbors too much, preferring their own interests and hobbies—particularly taking motor trips together. They have no children and express annoyance with the neighborhood children and pets "cluttering up the street." You sense that they could also be having some financial difficulties but are bluffing it through.

1. Do you feel that you have the possibility of a good listing here?
2. Would you consider the market-data approach sufficient to evaluate this property? Why, or why not?
3. As a quick-judgment appraisal, would you consider the price the Conyers expect to get for their property too high? Give your reasons.
4. Using the competitive market-analysis form, how would you select the comparable properties for your evaluation?

SUGGESTED REFERENCES

DOHERTY, JAMES L., "Favorable Financing Effects on Values of Single-Family Residences," *The Appraisal Journal,* Vol. 39, No. 4 (July, 1970), 398.

MINAYA, NICHOLAS J., "Consider the Circumstances," *The Appraisal Journal,* Vol. 37, No. 4 (October, 1969), 529.

RING, ALFRED A., *The Valuation of Real Estate.* Englewood Cliffs, N.J.: Prentice-Hall, Inc., 1963, Chaps. 11, 12, and 13.

———, "Valuation and Appraisal," *Reference Book,* Chap. 18. Sacramento: Department of Real Estate, 1971.

SHADE, PHILIP A., "The Income Approach in Appraising Single-Family Dwelling," *The Appraisal Journal,* Vol. 39, No. 4 (July, 1970), 384.

YEAGER, PHILIP J., "Financing Analysis," *Listing Real Estate,* Los Angeles: California Real Estate Association, 1969, p. 69.

6

Advertising

Reasons for Advertising

The basic idea behind advertising in any business is to *interest* a buyer and to *influence* him favorably. Because real estate sales are dependent on the buyer being sold first on the benefits of real estate ownership, advertising in this area is aimed at: (1) arousing public interest in real estate ownership; (2) creating a favorable image of the real estate practitioner; (3) attracting the buyer to a specific sales office; and (4) stimulating the sale of the property offered.

The term *advertising,* used in the broad sense and as it is applied to the real estate industry, embraces more than a classified advertisement in the local or metropolitan newspaper. Development of favorable public relations, for example, resulting in a good reputation for the office, is widely recognized as a productive advertising medium. Thus, the salesman with a reputation for the ethical, honest, and knowledgeable approach to selling is a contributing factor in productive advertising for his firm.

Real estate advertising may be classified as *general* or *specific.* Under the heading of "general advertising" (sometimes called "institutional" or "indirect" advertising) we find, for example, the newspaper or magazine display ad or the billboard and show-card promotion for the industry itself. (These media are also occasionally used by the individual office for its own institutional advertising.)

The National Association of Real Estate Boards utilizes national magazines, where full-page advertisements are used to promote the term *Realtor* or to educate the public on the advantages of home ownership. Promotion by the real estate industry of its role in the protection of individual property rights also receives a large share of this good-will advertising campaign.

Other contributions to general or institutional advertising include the office itself. Distinctive building design, the general attractiveness of the office interior, the professional appearance of the sales force, and the real estate executive's contribution to community activities can all be said to contribute to the public image of the firm.

Specific Advertising

Real estate advertising differs from the popular concept of merchandise promotion. The office listings (merchandise) must actually be *created* by means of direct or indirect advertising. In creating the merchandise to be sold, we might say that the real estate practitioner is dealing primarily in a service and cannot truly be considered a merchandiser of a product. Considered in this sense, institutional advertising is used basically as a means of attracting listings, whereas advertising of a specific nature is employed to arouse the interest of the *buyer.*

The principal medium of specific advertising is the newspaper classified columns. Classified advertisements differ from display advertising in that the reader of the classified column is already in the market and needs only to find the particular item to suit his needs, whereas the display advertisement must attract the buyer by an alluring display advertisement of the product itself.

Types of Advertising

As stated at the beginning of the chapter, the best form of advertising is the good public relations of the office itself. Every salesman is a walking advertisement for the firm (a fact that too often goes unrecognized by the office executive in the selection of his sales force). Because the office name is a continuing form of advertising, it must remain unblemished. The aggressive, high-pressure salesman with little regard for the ethics of the business can do much to defeat the good effect of columns of costly newspaper advertising. The firm that is attempting to build a good public image can ill afford to have it torn down by the actions of even one employee. It follows that the office executive, like Caesar's wife, "must be above reproach."

"For Sale" Signs

These constitute another form of silent and continuing advertising, but for maximum effect they should be properly regulated. Regulation can be established either by the industry itself or by local civil authorities. No more than one sign at a time should be permitted on a property. In areas of single-family residences flags, pennants, and such circus-atmosphere types of promotion are frowned upon as the industry becomes more professional. More than one sign on a property not only detracts from the dignity of the neighborhood but lends an urgent-sale idea to the property. Some communities have sign ordinances forbidding the for-sale sign of any type. Others permit signs in all but single-family residence zones. Such statutes are enacted either at the instigation of the real estate industry or out of civic concern that too many signs tend to indicate a depressed real estate market in the community.

The real estate industry is divided on the benefits of the for-sale sign. It lists among the advantages:

(1) The prospect calling the office in response to a sign on property is already half sold. He is indicating his interest in the neighborhood where he has seen the sign, as well as in the particular property for sale.
(2) The more for-sale and sold signs an office has in the field, the more activity is generated within the office (nothing succeeds like success).
(3) Signs serve as silent salesmen, working around the clock in and out of office hours. Surveys of the effect of real estate signs indicate that the for-sale sign produces more sales per dollar invested than does any other type of advertising.[1]

Arguments advanced for the elimination of signs are:

(1) Too many signs in a neighborhood give the impression that some unfavorable situation exists in the area.
(2) With no signs displayed, buyers are required to contact a broker for their real estate needs.
(3) Signs may serve as an invitation to the buyer to wait out the office exclusive and deal directly with the owner.

To be most effective, signs should be kept simple. To evaluate the effectiveness of a sign,

> ...drive by a property where the sign is on duty. Does it catch your attention? Can you read it from a passing car? Do the color and design stand out? Can you read it from a distance?...
>
> Color helps, too. Experts say these combinations work best, in this order: black on yellow, green on white, red on white, and blue on white. Red and green make a bad team; to the color-blind there's no contrast.
>
> Make your lettering bold. It must stand out from the background while giving the bare facts in simple, direct fashion. Prospects can learn the particulars by calling you. If your sign sells them silently they'll do so soon enough.[2]

Direct Mail

Large offices use direct mail with good results. Some firms use inserts in large metropolitan dailies listing properties for sale, reporting sales made, and publicizing the top producers in the firm. Circularizing a select list of buyers with income-property briefs is a popular and productive form of direct-mail advertising. Farm brokers issue catalogs of their offerings to farmers who may be expanding their operations. This type of advertising is usually considered prohibitive costwise for the smaller offices.

Radio and Television

Large offices have attempted "spot" announcements on radio with varying degrees of success. This is especially true in the promotion of tract housing. The expense involved and the short exposure require a cleverly worded message to hold the listener's interest. Special "giveaway" articles, for which the listener writes or telephones, are occasionally used. Television as an advertising medium for real estate is too new for a value judgment to be made of its benefits to the small firm. Although large housing developments, retirement-home projects, or industrial tracts might profit from this type of promotion, the expense

[1] Richard U. Ratcliff, "Real Estate Research As an Aid to Brokerage Operations," *California Real Estate Magazine,* Vol. 31, No. 2 (December, 1960), 10.

[2] *Real Estate Opportunities* (Englewood Cliffs, N.J.: Prentice-Hall, Inc.) Vol. 6, No. 9 (October 31, 1961), 2.

at present has proved too great for the advertising of individual properties.

Sales-Promotion Items

The use of calendars, ball point pens, key rings, matchbooks, date books, and many other novelties is a generally accepted form of sales promotion and is used regularly in varying degrees by most offices. Results from this type of advertising are difficult to assess, but the widespread and continuing use of the plan attests to its economic soundness.

Press Releases

Real estate executives probably do not use this type of sales promotion to its best advantage. Newspapers are always interested in news that really is news. Editors, on the other hand, are quick to recognize publicity disguised as news. Items that by all rights belong in the classified or display section are not acceptable in the news columns of the paper. Stories of local interest relating to interesting sales or home purchasers, large commercial or industrial sales, office sales-incentive activities, or reports of outstanding individual sales all provide acceptable news. Because such items are usually of interest to the real estate prospect, they furnish valuable office advertising.

Outdoor Advertising

For-sale, sold, or for-rent signs on property have already been discussed. Billboards, except for institutional advertising as a means of directing buyers to large developments, are considered too expensive to be economically feasible for the average office. There is also questionable value in a message that must of necessity be general in nature. Whether the dollar return is commensurate with the money invested is also difficult to evaluate.

Signboards

Fading from the real estate advertising scene is the dilapidated paper sign tacked to the office signboard, often amateurishly printed and constantly a prey to the adversities of the weather. With the trend toward professionalism, less use is being made of this type of advertising; regulation by city ordinance also has played a great part in spelling its demise.

Business Cards and Stationery

Business cards and stationery are important and valuable forms of indirect advertising.

Because the dignified business card and letterhead contribute to the office image, considerable thought should be given to their design and content. (As with the property sign, the cluttered business card defeats its own purpose.) The company trademark in attractive color combinations is a useful means of identification. For best effect, it should be used on business cards, letterheads, and all advertising. For a professional touch the services of an advertising agency should be used. Distinctive slogans ("Holmes for Homes"), used in all advertising, signs, and business cards, are a further means of office identification.

Writing the Advertisement

The well-written classified advertisement remains the most productive means of promoting property sales. Because of its expansive market, it is also the most widely used of all advertising methods in the real estate field. However, one has only to scan the real estate classified pages of any metropolitan or local newspaper to recognize that many times the individual ad constitutes nothing more than the cataloging of statistics concerning the property. Advertising is a form of *communication.* To be effective, it must apply the basic rules for successful communication, foremost of which is: What do you hope to achieve? A definite idea of your *purpose* should precede any attempt at writing the ad. What information are you attempting to convey? Who is your reader? What are his needs? How do you plan to present your message to satisfy these needs? In other words, how do you plan to build the reader's confidence in your ability to help him with his real estate needs? To produce results, there must be an *interesting message aimed at a specific buyer.* The ad that attracts the *qualified* buyer saves the office money, time, and effort. In a sense, the copywriter is attempting to make a sale through favorably influencing the thoughts of the prospective buyer. Considered in this light, advertising constitutes the second step in the selling process (the first being the listing). As Morton J. A. McDonald puts it, "Not advertising *and* selling, but advertising *is* selling."[3]

As was stated previously, institutional advertising is intended to attract the buyer, whereas specific advertising is for the purpose of selling a particular property. At the time the listing is taken, the lister should be making a buyer analysis: Who is the logical buyer for this property? What are the prop-

[3] Morton J. A. McDonald, *Master Guide to Successful Real Estate Advertising* (Englewood Cliffs, N. J.: Prentice-Hall, Inc., 1962), p. 10.

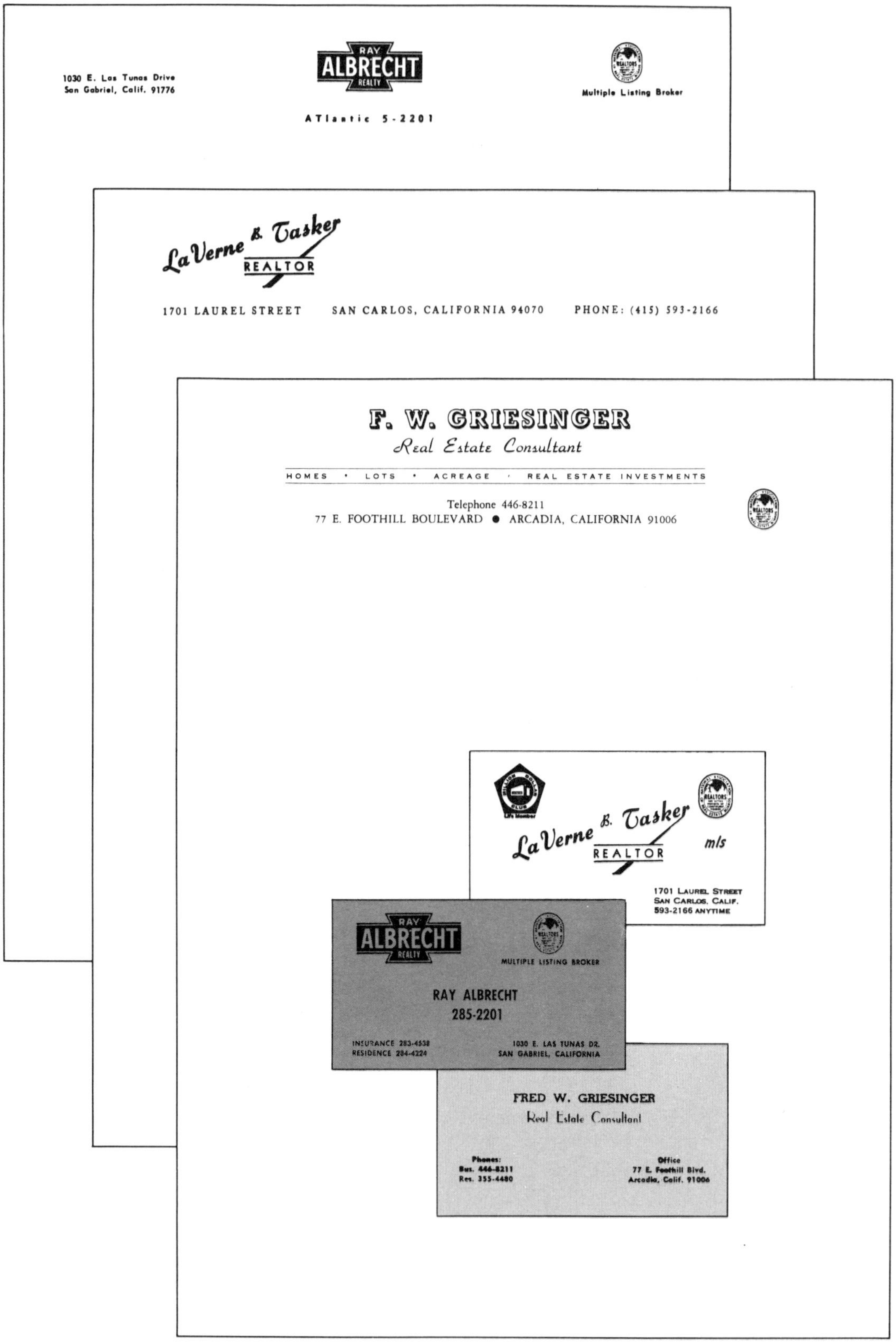
1030 E. Las Tunas Drive
San Gabriel, Calif. 91776
RAY
ALBRECHT
REALTY
Multiple Listing Broker
ATlantic 5-2201
LaVerne B. Tasker
REALTOR
1701 LAUREL STREET
SAN CARLOS, CALIFORNIA 94070
PHONE: (415) 593-2166
F. W. GRIESINGER
Real Estate Consultant
HOMES • LOTS • ACREAGE • REAL ESTATE INVESTMENTS
Telephone 446-8211
77 E. FOOTHILL BOULEVARD ● ARCADIA, CALIFORNIA 91006
LaVerne B. Tasker
REALTOR
m/s
1701 LAUREL STREET
SAN CARLOS, CALIF.
593-2166 ANYTIME
RAY
ALBRECHT
REALTY
MULTIPLE LISTING BROKER
RAY ALBRECHT
285-2201
INSURANCE 283-4538
RESIDENCE 284-4224
1030 E. LAS TUNAS DR.
SAN GABRIEL, CALIFORNIA
FRED W. GRIESINGER
Real Estate Consultant
Phones:
Bus. 446-8211
Res. 355-4480
Office
77 E. Foothill Blvd.
Arcadia, Calif. 91006

erty's most appealing features, and to whom will they appeal? A well-written advertisement is a condensed sales talk. *Property listed right and advertised correctly* can greatly lessen the work of the salesperson by prequalifying the prospect. This is not to say that fitting the right buyer to a property comes about by accident. As a prerequisite to any well-organized sales talk, planning takes time and thought, which leads to reduced time spent in selling. This, combined with savings in advertising costs, increases the net income of the firm.

The A-I-D-A formula is familiar to every advertiser. Spelled out, it embodies the four essentials of a productive ad. The well-written ad is intended:

1. To attract *Attention*
2. To create *Interest*
3. To arouse *Desire*
4. To compel *Action*

Whether he is conscious of it or not, every good copywriter embodies these principles in each ad. To interest the one buyer for a specific property, all four principles must be arranged in logical sequence, closing on the final Action note. *Example:*

INSTANT HOME
Add your furniture and your family. You're Home! Tranquil living room with friendly fireplace. Sunlit room for leisurely dining. Kitchen built-ins—Mother's delight. Den designed for browsing or concentrating. Two bedrooms, spacious and comfortable. Two baths for traffic control. Patio for California outdoor living. Trees! Trees! Trees! Air conditioned? Of course!
PRICED TO SELL AND FINANCED TO BUY

Selecting the Heading

The good copywriter calls the best features of the property to the Attention of the reader through a well-composed heading. What causes a newspaper headline to catch the eye of the reader? Basically, it makes an appeal to his Interest and, by so doing, catches and holds his Attention. *The reader is most interested in news directly affecting him.* A plane crash in faraway Rangoon probably is of only passing interest to him, whereas news of an air tragedy in his immediate area may hit him with great impact. So, *to attract the buyer, the heading must also appeal to his Interest.*

Punch is given to the heading by the use of short, forceful sentences. The short heading also permits the use of larger type, thus increasing its attention-getting value. Unless the attention of the reader is captured at the outset, the time, effort, and money expended on the balance of the ad is wasted.

The more concise, specific, interesting, and colorful the heading, the more effective it will be. At the time the property was listed, the salesman noted its one predominantly appealing feature. Was it the price, the terms, the location, a functional floor plan, an attractive lot? When the selection is made, Attention should be focused on it by the use of one short, well-chosen, descriptive phrase. For example, compare the brief, colorful "Hallmark Quality" with "This House Has Quality throughout"; or "Family-Ready" with "Ready to Move in Today"; or "Kiddies Can Romp" with "Large Home Suitable for Children."

The Body of the Ad

The second principle of advertising is to create Interest and the third, to arouse Desire. To succeed here, the ad writer must convey his ideas clearly. Succinct but descriptive wording in the body of the ad will accomplish this. Although the outstanding features of the property are itemized in the listing form, a mere recital of these would not create interest or arouse desire. There must be a great deal of "window dressing" in the form of colorful descriptions aimed at making an appeal to the reader's emotions or to his intellectual curiosity. After having caught his attention with a compelling heading, the writer has, in a sense, deceived the reader if he fails to follow through in the body of the ad. Because the well-written ad is actually a sales presentation, the selling points must follow in logical sequence. Note the organization of the four basic principles in the following ad:

MR. ED SAYS
"If Wilbur only loved me, he'd buy me this elegant stable with electricity, water and my own phone. He could live in the custom built home. It has three bedrooms and two baths for him and Carol. On lazy Sundays he could sit on the beautiful lanai listening to the birds that nest in those majestic trees surrounding the patio. Shucks, the price has already been reduced to only $31,500."
Do you love horses? Then, you'll love this. Call
Margot McBride
Gladys Blume, Realtor

If the ad is to be effective, the copywriter will observe the following fundamentals: (1) Be *convincing.* If the ad does not convince the reader, obviously it will never sell him on the product, nor probably even hold his interest. Conviction is best accomplished by simple, straightforward writing in the form of a brief message addressed to a specific buyer. For example:

(2) Be *simple.* Extravagant claims or overworked superlatives ("gorgeous," "stupendous," "breathtaking") are best left to the Hollywood press agent. Technical terms of the trade must be avoided. These terms, although common in the industry, only serve to confuse the reader. Use of large, unfamiliar words makes for difficult reading at any time and smacks of artificiality on the part of the copywriter. Care must also be taken when using colorful descriptions. Although they may lend interest to the ad, their overuse tends to destroy confidence in the product advertised.

(3) Be *specific.* Use of generalities weakens the sales talk. Such expressions as "walking distance" instead of "two blocks"; large family room" instead of "25-foot family room," or "extra large lot" in place of "one full acre" are examples of vague terminology typical of the real estate advertising field.

There is no substitute for constant practice to develop the necessary copy-writing skills. However, study of the copy used to promote nationally advertised products is an excellent way to increase proficiency. Magazines of national circulation carry a wealth of these ads. Here the highest-paid professionals in the advertising field pool their knowledge and experience to create eye-catching slogans or to call attention to an attractive display of a product. Short sentences made up of punchy, descriptive phrases are used to develop desire in the reader: "Jet-Smooth Luxury"; "Like Walking on Pillows";" Refreshing as the Land of Sky-Blue Waters."

The Close

Conforming to the A-I-D-A formula, an action-impelling sentence should "close" the ad. Although the closing line follows the body of the ad in logical sequence, it also relates to the subject matter preceding it. Stereotyped phrases should be avoided. An appeal to the tenant-buyer might close with, "Act now. Be your own landlord"; or "You can be your own landlord. Call today. Let us tell you how." For the family needing the larger home, "Make the kids happy. See us today"; or "Bring the family, and your checkbook." The closing line should begin with an action word. This gives the ad the necessary punch while providing the reader with the urge to act on the suggestion.

When to Write the Ad

As was stated in the chapter on listings, the appealing features of the property should be noted at the time of the listing. These items, listed on the office filing card (made up for the purpose), furnish all the information necessary for writing the ad. The time element is important. The ad should be written while the salesman's enthusiasm is at a peak and while the salable features of the property are fresh in his mind. This can sometimes best be done before leaving the property. The homeowner should be asked to discuss any outstanding features of the home that appealed to her at the time the home was purchased. Playing up these features in the ad is an excellent way to attract the same type of buyer. (Some firms require the listing salesman to turn in three different types of ads with the listing.)

Should the drawbacks of a property be mentioned in the advertisement? Opinion differs on this policy, but, on occasion, what would appear to be an objectionable feature can be the property's strongest selling point when aimed at the right buyer. For example, the run-down property might appeal strongly to the speculator. Why not emphasize this feature in the ad and make the appeal to this type of buyer? The large family, needing room to expand, but who cannot afford a new home of the required size, may become interested in the older home where the needed floor space is available for less money. The well-written ad making the correct appeal will reach this buyer. The large yard, which to one buyer might represent only high taxes and a prohibitive amount of yard work, could be made interesting to the family with growing children.

A word of caution should be injected here. The temptation to use the facetious approach in advertising the run-down or out-of-date property should be avoided. The ad of questionable taste is never worth the risk of offending the property owner, nor is it ever used by the professional real estate practitioner.

The Sales Price

Opinion in the industry is sharply divided on the question of including the sales price in the ad. If the ad is written with a particular buyer in mind, it would seem that the price and the terms should be specifically spelled out. The prospect who replies is then fully qualified investment-wise. Stressing a low down payment and easy installments can provide the motivating factor for the tenant-prospect who equates the monthly payments with his rent check.

Truth in Advertising[4]

Care must be taken in the wording of any classified advertising to insure that statements appearing in the advertisement could not be construed to be false rather than to merely glamorize the property amenities. Section 10140 of the Business and Professions Code provides that upon conviction "any officer, agent, or employee of any company and every other person who *knowingly authorizes, directs, or aids* in the publication, advertisement, distribution, or circularization of *any false statement or representation concerning any land or subdivision thereof*. . .offered for sale or lease. . .is guilty of a public offense and shall be punished by a fine not exceeding one thousand dollars ($1,000) or by imprisonment in a county jail not exceeding one year or both. . . ."[5]

The section continues as follows: ". . .and, if a real estate licensee, he shall be held to trial by the commissioner for a suspension or revocation of his license. . . ."

Further, a section of the code that became effective in September 1965—but with which licensees appear not to be as familiar as with other sections pertaining to advertising—reads: "A real estate licensee shall not publish, circulate, distribute, nor cause to be published, circulated, or distributed in any newspaper or periodical, or by mail any matter pertaining to any activity for which a real estate license is required which does not contain a designation disclosing that he is performing acts for which a real estate license is required."[6]

To quote the Department of Real Estate,

> The prudent broker also keeps in mind his duties and responsibilities as a licensee. He avoids extravagant statements and misrepresentations in his advertising. He is aware that untrue statements in advertising can lead to disciplinary action against his license and even to criminal charges.[7]

The U.S. Supreme Court has also stated, "Advertising must not obscure or conceal material facts." In addition, Article 9 of the Realtor's Code of Ethics reads:

> The Realtor in his advertising should be especially careful to present a true picture and should neither advertise without disclosing his name, nor permit his salesmen to use individual names or telephone numbers, unless the salesman's connection with the Realtor is obvious in the advertisement.

Also, Article 19 reads as follows:

> The Realtor should not submit or advertise property without authority, and in any offering the price quoted should not be other than that agreed upon with the owners as the offering price.

The Advertising Dollar

How does the real estate firm budget its advertising dollar? A survey of offices would probably indicate no uniform method. In the past, because of the ease with which a person could enter the real estate field and the relatively small amount of capital required to open an office, many persons with little or no business background flocked to the real estate field, only to become another statistic in business failures. One of the major causes of the inexperienced broker's failure was the uncontrolled amount of advertising used to attract customers to his new office. No advertising budget was set up; the only criterion used to regulate the amount of advertising was the promise made to the property owner in an attempt to build a large portfolio of office listings. Continuance in such a policy doomed the office to financial failure. The executive with no management training often acceded to the demands of the salesmen for sweeping advertising programs as a means of attracting more prospects to the office. Little thought was given to the copy, the medium used, or the salesman's prospect follow-up. Advertising, thus, became the broker's bugaboo. Instead of making an attempt at analyzing the program, the broker reduced his advertising volume in order to minimize expenses. The end result, however, was loss of sales personnel, listings, and customers. What, then, was the answer?

Budgeting Methods

Virtually all offices today have worked out some budgetary method of evaluating advertising costs and results. Some budgets are based on the individual salesman's production. An overall budget of a certain percentage for advertising is set up, with each salesman allowed a share of this total sum. In other words, a percentage of the gross commissions is allowed each salesman based on whether he is the lister or the selling salesman. To offset any deficiency, a reserve sum is set aside from each commission. At the end of the year, an audit is made, and all but a

[4] See p. 96 for truth in lending as it applies to real estate advertising.

[5] See *Reference Book,* Department of Real Estate, for full text.

[6] Section 10140.6

[7] Department of Real Estate, *Real Estate Bulletin,* Fall, 1969.

certain percentage of this amount is returned to the salesman. Under this system, the salesman is made aware of advertising costs and the benefits to him if he budgets his share wisely. He strives to write better ads and to watch the results. He is also aware of the advertising media producing the most for the money expended.

Few offices advertise open listings. Advertising costs make it prohibitive to risk this expense without the certainty of a return on the investment.

Advertising budgets are usually set up for the entire year. They should be reviewed and possibly revised every three months, in the light of changed market conditions. Established offices sometimes budget a percentage of the gross sales of the previous year. Any method devised that points up the cost per unit will present an overall picture of the advertising expense. To build the office prestige, it pays to budget a portion of the cost to institutional advertising. Morton J. A. McDonald puts it, "Advertising is steam, the pressure must be maintained steadily, so spending for advertising must be fuel to insure steam for the upgrades. When competitors are advertising aggressively, you must meet them; when the market is hot, you must make the most of it."[8]

Checking Results

A method employed effectively by some offices involves the use of different telephone numbers on signs or on classified ads inserted in different newspapers. A careful check can then be made on the type of media for advertising that is most productive. By checking the source of the inquiry, the cost per call, and the ratio of calls to sales, a system can be devised to pinpoint the results. A constant reminder to the sales staff or to the secretary is often needed to insure that each call is tabulated. (Some offices note the day of the week and the weather conditions at the time the call was received.) Even state or national crises can affect the number of calls. *The important point is that some sort of scientific study of the results be conducted.* The system used must be kept simple. Any method that proves burdensome will soon be discarded and will too often not be replaced by another of any type. (A simple ring binder is all that is required sometimes to record the calls.) The individual office, probably through trial and error, will usually devise its own method of tabulating and evaluating results.

Best Days to Advertise

Opinions vary widely on the best day in the week to advertise, and surveys taken have developed no conclusive evidence on the subject. A great deal depends on the advertising media. The classified ad in the large metropolitan paper cannot be judged by the same yardstick as that in the local daily or weekly paper. A survey conducted by a large midwestern newspaper revealed that 54 percent of the Sunday advertisers were not satisfied with the results, considering that they paid a higher rate. The same survey showed little difference in results between daily and Sunday advertising.

CASE STUDY

John Hume and his brother, Richard, have recently opened a real estate office in Watertown, a city of some 50,000 population. They have bought a run-down building in the heart of the downtown section. Although they realize that the building's present appearance is against it, they feel that the location is excellent, and they plan gradually to make improvements that in time will give the building a complete face lift; however, this may take several years.

Previous to opening their own office, they had worked for five years for a Realtor in another county; but hearing that the building was for sale, they felt it was too good a buy to pass up. After the purchase of the building, they have very little cash reserve. They begin right away assembling a sales force and what furniture they can purchase for a small outlay of capital. It is important that they get their business launched as soon as possible, so they run an ad in the local paper for salesmen. Two salesmen, Jerry Evans and Donald Douglas, apply immediately. They are employed in an office in the adjoining city of Warner. They have not been too successful in their former office, but they like the idea of working in a new office so well located. Because Watertown's property values are higher than those in Warner where they previously worked, they feel that their commissions will be greater. They tell the Humes that they hope the office intends to do a great deal of advertising, because it has been their experience this is the only way to get prospects.

After a discussion of general advertising policy, including the use of signs and business cards, the Humes decide that, because they are opening a new office, the use of brightly colored signs and cleverly

[8] McDonald, *Master Guide to Advertising,* p. 259.

written ads should be good promotion policy. They think their money would be put to better use here than if it were spent in payment of dues to such civic groups as the chamber of commerce or the merchants' association. Because they were board members previously, they are permitted to join the local board of realtors after the usual preliminaries. They have brightly colored signs made up to read:

> "WE SELL 'EM ALL"
> HUME & HUME, Realtors
> 446–8531 447–2228

Their cards and letterheads carry the same slogan. They have a sign installed on the building reading:

> HUME & HUME, Realtors

with the slogan, "We Sell 'em All" in flashing neon.

Douglas and Evans are instructed to get into the field immediately and to bring in as many listings as possible. There are no special requisites as to the type or price range of property they are to list. There is no mention of listing at market price. The two salesmen decide that they will take a four-block area in the higher-priced residential section and ring doorbells. They select this area because they feel that selling the more expensive properties will bring them greater commissions.

Evans, a middle-aged man who is not too well groomed, drives a small car seven years old that needs new upholstery and possibly a complete paint job. He starts early Monday morning to ring doorbells, handing out a card at each home he visits. He is not successful in listing any of the properties, although he talks with some fifteen homeowners, most of whom say they always transact their real estate business with one of the older, established real estate firms.

Douglas, a very meticulous, likable young man in his early thirties, dislikes ringing doorbells, considering it unprofessional. However, he is persuaded by the Humes that this is the only way for a new office to build its inventory of listings. His approach to the property owner is much more subtle than that of Evans. He feels that his business cards are a little garish and wishes they were more dignified. He wonders if the firm's type of operation will be successful in handling these prestige properties. At one of the homes, Douglas meets a Mr. Watkins, who says that he may be interested in selling his property and invites him in. He shows Douglas around the property, pointing out a small guesthouse near the pool. Douglas is surprised when he is told that the Watkins want $38,000 for the property. He remembers similar homes in a development in the city where he worked previously, none of which sold for over $28,000. However, because the office needs listings, he decides to list at the owner's price. He is able to get only a thirty-day open listing, the owners saying that they are listing with him only because they like his manner and wish to help him get started. They tell him that, if his office will show some real activity, advertise the property, and put up a for-sale sign, they might consider giving him an exclusive listing later.

Douglas is delighted with this and hurries back to the office with the listing. The Humes are pleased to have a property in such a high-priced area and ask Douglas to write a "nice" ad for the metropolitan newspaper the following Sunday. Douglas composes the following ad, which appears in the Sunday paper.

> NICE HOME WITH GUEST HOUSE
> You can live in a prestige area while your tenants make your house payments. Nice three-bedroom home and guesthouse that would bring a guaranteed rental of $100 a month. Good swimming pool. House needs paint and yard is run down, but the owner must sell, so make an offer. House has two baths and a shake roof. This is in a wonderful neighborhood with the best schools and markets. Owner is asking $38,000.
> Call Donald Douglas, Salesman
> 446–8531 447–2228

Computing the cost from the newspaper's rate card, the Humes estimate the ad will cost $30.00. They feel this is well worth it when they consider that there is a $2,280 commission involved. They have never worked out an advertising budget but intend to set one up after they have built up their listing file and have started on a full advertising campaign.

1. Do you approve of the Humes' promotional advertising as it relates to their office and property signs, from the standpoint of (a) professionalism? (b) effectiveness?
2. Discuss the property signs of the Hume brothers. Do you feel that they are adequate? Why, or why not?
3. Do you believe that the type of operation as practiced by the Humes' office will make for good public and customer relations? Discuss.
4. Evaluate salesman Douglas from the standpoint of his contribution to the office image.
5. Do you believe the Humes' general advertising policy to be on a sound fiscal basis? Discuss.

6. Discuss the classified advertisement composed by salesman Douglas from the standpoint of its

   (a) appeal
   (b) honesty
   (c) general effectiveness
   (d) legal aspects

SUGGESTED REFERENCES

BENSON, PHILIP A., NELSON L. NORTH, and ALFRED A. RING, *Real Estate Principles and Practices,* 4th ed. Englewood Cliffs, N.J.: Prentice-Hall, Inc., 1957.

The Broker's Ad Writer, 6th ed. HERBERT T. JACKSON, sponsor. Chicago: National Association of Real Estate Boards, June, 1961.

CASE, FREDERICK E., *Real Estate.* Boston: Allyn & Bacon, Inc., 1962.

Committee on Professional Standards, *Interpretations of the Code of Ethics,* 2nd ed. Chicago: National Association of Real Estate Boards, 1963.

Editors and Contributors to the Prentice-Hall Real Estate Service, The, *Successful Real Estate Ideas.* Englewood Cliffs, N.J.: Prentice-Hall, Inc., 1951.

MCDONALD, MORTON J. A., *Master Guide to Successful Real Estate Advertising.* Englewood Cliffs, N.J.: Prentice-Hall, Inc., 1962.

MCKAY, WILLIAM H., *Real Estate Advertising That Clicks Now.* Los Angeles: Fashion Press, Inc., 1961.

MCMICHAEL, STANLEY L., *Selling Real Estate,* 3rd ed. Englewood Cliffs, N.J.: Prentice-Hall, Inc., 1957.

Pictorial Advertising at Work, L. ALLEN MORRIS, sponsor. Chicago: National Association of Real Estate Boards, December, 1962.

VOGEL, LOIS T., *How to Help Your Real Estate Salesman Produce More Business.* Englewood Cliffs, N.J.: Prentice-Hall, Inc., 1960.

Don't Waste Money on Advertising, STANLEY C. WILEY, sponsor. Chicago: National Institute of Real Estate Brokers of the National Association of Real Estate Boards, November 1969.

"Tests for Classified Ads," *Real Estate Today,* National Institute of Real Estate Brokers of the National Association of Real Estate Boards, July, 1968, p. 55.

Truth in Lending (Federal Reserve Regulation Z)

A federal law pertaining to consumer credit-cost disclosure became effective July 1, 1969. Its purpose is to let borrowers and customers know the cost of credit so that they may compare costs with those of other credit sources and avoid the uninformed use of credit. The *finance charge* and the *annual percentage rate* are the two most important disclosures required by this regulation. (Note: For precise language, see Sec. 226.10 of regulation Z.)

Basically the law does not apply to normal real estate advertising, unless the advertising states any of the following:

(a) The rate of interest on an existing mortgage, or a new mortgage, such as a purchase-money mortgage.
(b) The down payment or lack of down payment.
(c) The amount of each installment payment; the dollar amount of finance charges; the number of installments; the period of payment; or the fact that there is no charge for credit.

For example:

(a) The advertisement states:
"Full price $27,500, with 10 percent down, 5½ percent loan can be assumed."
Nothing more is added. There are two violations.
The advertisement reads:
"Full price $27,500. Low low interest-rate loan can be assumed." There is no violation.
(b) The advertisement states:
"Full price $30,000. 20 percent down. Owner will carry balance at 8 percent interest." No more is added.
There is a violation.
(c) The advertisement reads:
"Asking price $28,500. 15 percent down. Payments of $187 monthly on balance." There are two violations.
(d) The advertisement reads:
"Sales price is $29,500. Owner will finance with acceptable credit." There is no violation.
(e) The advertisement reads:
"Full price $32,500. Excellent financing available." There is no violation.

If the advertisement mentions any one of the terms, the rate, or the amounts of financing, then regulation Z requires that a full disclosure be made of all the financing provisions. This applies basically to the finance-charge and the annual percentage-rate concepts.

Finance charge is the total of *all* costs for originating and carrying credit sale or loan. This is stated in a *dollar amount.*

Annual percentage rate is the division of net credit or loan into the finance charge; it is computed as a yearly *interest percentage.*

Example:
Finance charge $35.00; total amount financed $200; number of monthly payments twenty-four.

Solution:
Step 1—Divide the finance charge by the total amount financed and multiply by $100.

SAMPLE PAGE FROM TABLE FOR COMPUTING ANNUAL PERCENTAGE RATE FOR LEVEL MONTHLY PAYMENT PLANS

EXAMPLE

Finance charge = $35.00; Total amount financed = $200; Number of monthly payments = 24.

SOLUTION

Step 1—Divide the finance charge by the total amount financed and multiply by $100. This gives the finance charge per $100 of amount financed. That is, $35.00 ÷ $200 = .1750 x $100 = $17.50.

Step 2—Follow down the left hand column of the table to the line for 24 months. Follow across this line until you find the nearest number to $17.50. In this example $17.51 is closest to $17.50. Reading up the column of figures shows an annual percentage rate of 16%.

NUMBER OF PAYMENTS	ANNUAL PERCENTAGE RATE															
	14.00%	14.25%	14.50%	14.75%	15.00%	15.25%	15.50%	15.75%	16.00%	16.25%	16.50%	16.75%	17.00%	17.25%	17.50%	17.75%
	(FINANCE CHARGE PER $100 OF AMOUNT FINANCED)															
1	1.17	1.19	1.21	1.23	1.25	1.27	1.29	1.31	1.33	1.35	1.37	1.40	1.42	1.44	1.46	1.48
2	1.75	1.78	1.82	1.85	1.88	1.91	1.94	1.97	2.00	2.04	2.07	2.10	2.13	2.16	2.19	2.22
3	2.34	2.38	2.43	2.47	2.51	2.55	2.59	2.64	2.68	2.72	2.76	2.80	2.85	2.89	2.93	2.97
4	2.93	2.99	3.04	3.09	3.14	3.20	3.25	3.30	3.36	3.41	3.46	3.51	3.57	3.62	3.67	3.73
5	3.53	3.59	3.65	3.72	3.78	3.84	3.91	3.97	4.04	4.10	4.16	4.23	4.29	4.35	4.42	4.48
6	4.12	4.20	4.27	4.35	4.42	4.49	4.57	4.64	4.72	4.79	4.87	4.94	5.02	5.09	5.17	5.24
7	4.72	4.81	4.89	4.98	5.06	5.15	5.23	5.32	5.40	5.49	5.58	5.66	5.75	5.83	5.92	6.00
8	5.32	5.42	5.51	5.61	5.71	5.80	5.90	6.00	6.09	6.19	6.29	6.38	6.48	6.58	6.67	6.77
9	5.92	6.03	6.14	6.25	6.35	6.46	6.57	6.68	6.78	6.89	7.00	7.11	7.22	7.32	7.43	7.54
10	6.53	6.65	6.77	6.88	7.00	7.12	7.24	7.36	7.48	7.60	7.72	7.84	7.96	8.08	8.19	8.31
11	7.14	7.27	7.40	7.53	7.66	7.79	7.92	8.05	8.18	8.31	8.44	8.57	8.70	8.83	8.96	9.09
12	7.74	7.89	8.03	8.17	8.31	8.45	8.59	8.74	8.88	9.02	9.16	9.30	9.45	9.59	9.73	9.87
13	8.36	8.51	8.66	8.81	8.97	9.12	9.27	9.43	9.58	9.73	9.89	10.04	10.20	10.35	10.50	10.66
14	8.97	9.13	9.30	9.46	9.63	9.79	9.96	10.12	10.29	10.45	10.62	10.78	10.95	11.11	11.28	11.45
15	9.59	9.76	9.94	10.11	10.29	10.47	10.64	10.82	11.00	11.17	11.35	11.53	11.71	11.88	12.06	12.24
16	10.20	10.39	10.58	10.77	10.95	11.14	11.33	11.52	11.71	11.90	12.09	12.28	12.46	12.65	12.84	13.03
17	10.82	11.02	11.22	11.42	11.62	11.82	12.02	12.22	12.42	12.62	12.83	13.03	13.23	13.43	13.63	13.83
18	11.45	11.66	11.87	12.08	12.29	12.50	12.72	12.93	13.14	13.35	13.57	13.78	13.99	14.21	14.42	14.64
19	12.07	12.30	12.52	12.74	12.97	13.19	13.41	13.64	13.86	14.09	14.31	14.54	14.76	14.99	15.22	15.44
20	12.70	12.93	13.17	13.41	13.64	13.88	14.11	14.35	14.59	14.82	15.06	15.30	15.54	15.77	16.01	16.25
21	13.33	13.58	13.82	14.07	14.32	14.57	14.82	15.06	15.31	15.56	15.81	16.06	16.31	16.56	16.81	17.07
22	13.96	14.22	14.48	14.74	15.00	15.26	15.52	15.78	16.04	16.30	16.57	16.83	17.09	17.36	17.62	17.88
23	14.59	14.87	15.14	15.41	15.68	15.96	16.23	16.50	16.78	17.05	17.32	17.60	17.88	18.15	18.43	18.70
24	15.23	15.51	15.80	16.08	16.37	16.65	16.94	17.22	17.51	17.80	18.09	18.37	18.66	18.95	19.24	19.53
25	15.87	16.17	16.46	16.76	17.06	17.35	17.65	17.95	18.25	18.55	18.85	19.15	19.45	19.75	20.05	20.36
26	16.51	16.82	17.13	17.44	17.75	18.06	18.37	18.68	18.99	19.30	19.62	19.93	20.24	20.56	20.87	21.19
27	17.15	17.47	17.80	18.12	18.44	18.76	19.09	19.41	19.74	20.06	20.39	20.71	21.04	21.37	21.69	22.02
28	17.80	18.13	18.47	18.80	19.14	19.47	19.81	20.15	20.48	20.82	21.16	21.50	21.84	22.18	22.52	22.86
29	18.45	18.79	19.14	19.49	19.83	20.18	20.53	20.88	21.23	21.58	21.94	22.29	22.64	22.99	23.35	23.70
30	19.10	19.45	19.81	20.17	20.54	20.90	21.26	21.62	21.99	22.35	22.72	23.08	23.45	23.81	24.18	24.55
31	19.75	20.12	20.49	20.87	21.24	21.61	21.99	22.37	22.74	23.12	23.50	23.88	24.26	24.64	25.02	25.40
32	20.40	20.79	21.17	21.56	21.95	22.33	22.72	23.11	23.50	23.89	24.28	24.68	25.07	25.46	25.86	26.25
33	21.06	21.46	21.85	22.25	22.65	23.06	23.46	23.86	24.26	24.67	25.07	25.48	25.88	26.29	26.70	27.11
34	21.72	22.13	22.54	22.95	23.37	23.78	24.19	24.61	25.03	25.44	25.86	26.28	26.70	27.12	27.54	27.97
35	22.38	22.80	23.23	23.65	24.08	24.51	24.94	25.36	25.79	26.23	26.66	27.09	27.52	27.96	28.39	28.83
36	23.04	23.48	23.92	24.35	24.80	25.24	25.68	26.12	26.57	27.01	27.46	27.90	28.35	28.80	29.25	29.70
37	23.70	24.16	24.61	25.06	25.51	25.97	26.42	26.88	27.34	27.80	28.26	28.72	29.18	29.64	30.10	30.57
38	24.37	24.84	25.30	25.77	26.24	26.70	27.17	27.64	28.11	28.59	29.06	29.53	30.01	30.49	30.96	31.44
39	25.04	25.52	26.00	26.48	26.96	27.44	27.92	28.41	28.89	29.38	29.87	30.36	30.85	31.34	31.83	32.32
40	25.71	26.20	26.70	27.19	27.69	28.18	28.68	29.18	29.68	30.18	30.68	31.18	31.68	32.19	32.69	33.20
41	26.39	26.89	27.40	27.91	28.41	28.92	29.44	29.95	30.46	30.97	31.49	32.01	32.52	33.04	33.56	34.08
42	27.06	27.58	28.10	28.62	29.15	29.67	30.19	30.72	31.25	31.78	32.31	32.84	33.37	33.90	34.44	34.97
43	27.74	28.27	28.81	29.34	29.88	30.42	30.96	31.50	32.04	32.58	33.13	33.67	34.22	34.76	35.31	35.86
44	28.42	28.97	29.52	30.07	30.62	31.17	31.72	32.28	32.83	33.39	33.95	34.51	35.07	35.63	36.19	36.76
45	29.11	29.67	30.23	30.79	31.36	31.92	32.49	33.06	33.63	34.20	34.77	35.35	35.92	36.50	37.08	37.66
46	29.79	30.36	30.94	31.52	32.10	32.68	33.26	33.84	34.43	35.01	35.60	36.19	36.78	37.37	37.96	38.56
47	30.48	31.07	31.66	32.25	32.84	33.44	34.03	34.63	35.23	35.83	36.43	37.04	37.64	38.25	38.86	39.46
48	31.17	31.77	32.37	32.98	33.59	34.20	34.81	35.42	36.03	36.65	37.27	37.88	38.50	39.13	39.75	40.37
49	31.86	32.48	33.09	33.71	34.34	34.96	35.59	36.21	36.84	37.47	38.10	38.74	39.37	40.01	40.65	41.29
50	32.55	33.18	33.82	34.45	35.09	35.73	36.37	37.01	37.65	38.30	38.94	39.59	40.24	40.89	41.55	42.20
51	33.25	33.89	34.54	35.19	35.84	36.49	37.15	37.81	38.46	39.12	39.79	40.45	41.11	41.78	42.45	43.12
52	33.95	34.61	35.27	35.93	36.60	37.27	37.94	38.61	39.28	39.96	40.63	41.31	41.99	42.67	43.36	44.04
53	34.65	35.32	36.00	36.68	37.36	38.04	38.72	39.41	40.10	40.79	41.48	42.17	42.87	43.57	44.27	44.97
54	35.35	36.04	36.73	37.42	38.12	38.82	39.52	40.22	40.92	41.63	42.33	43.04	43.75	44.47	45.18	45.90
55	36.05	36.76	37.46	38.17	38.88	39.60	40.31	41.03	41.74	42.47	43.19	43.91	44.64	45.37	46.10	46.83
56	36.76	37.48	38.20	38.92	39.65	40.38	41.11	41.84	42.57	43.31	44.05	44.79	45.53	46.27	47.02	47.77
57	37.47	38.20	38.94	39.68	40.42	41.16	41.91	42.65	43.40	44.15	44.91	45.66	46.42	47.18	47.94	48.71
58	38.18	38.93	39.68	40.43	41.19	41.95	42.71	43.47	44.23	45.00	45.77	46.54	47.32	48.09	48.87	49.65
59	38.89	39.66	40.42	41.19	41.96	42.74	43.51	44.29	45.07	45.85	46.64	47.42	48.21	49.01	49.80	50.60
60	39.61	40.39	41.17	41.95	42.74	43.53	44.32	45.11	45.91	46.71	47.51	48.31	49.12	49.92	50.73	51.55

This gives the finance charge per $100 of amount financed. That is, $35.00 ÷ $200 = .1750 × $100 = $17.50

Step 2—Follow down the left-hand column of the table to the line for twenty-four months. Follow across this line until you find the nearest number to $17.50. In this example $17.51 is closest to $17.50. Reading up the column of figures shows an annual percentage rate of sixteen.[9]
(See table for computing annual percentage rate for level monthly payment plans, p. 97)

To summarize:

If an ad states the rate of a finance charge, that rate must be priced as "annual percentage rate," using exactly that term.

When the cash price is given, no annual percentage-rate term is needed—unless statements such as the following are included in this ad:

Amount of down payment or the fact that no down payment is required.
Amount of any installment payment.
Number of installments.
Period of repayment.
Dollar amount of any finance change.
Credit free of charge.

If any of the statements listed above is used, then the ad must use the following terminology prescribed by the regulation:

The cash price or the amount of the loan, as applicable.
The amount of the down payment, or the fact that no down payment is required.
The number, amount, and due date or period of payments scheduled to repay the indebtedness.
The finance charge expressed as an annual percentage rate—for example, 6 percent add-on charges for thirty-six months equal 11.8 percent.

There is no civil liability under the advertising provisions, but there could be criminal penalties. That means, that although anyone who reads an improper ad may not have the right to sue the advertiser, the enforcement authorities can take action to compel those placing the ad to comply with the advertising provisions or to impose penalties for not complying.

Final responsibility for compliance with the advertising requirements of truth in lending rests on the *advertiser and not on the advertising media.*

[9] The above information was obtained from Bruce Werloff, *Truth in Lending* (Sacramento: Sacramento Building Industry Association), and from *What You Ought to Know about Truth in Lending,* prepared by the Board of Governors of the Federal Reserve System.

7

Securing and Analyzing Prospects

The term *prospecting* can be applied to searching for listings as well as to locating the buyers for those listings. We shall concern ourselves in this chapter with prospecting for buyers. The office in the strongest marketing position is the one that has accumulated an impressive portfolio of salable properties through a consistent policy of listing only at market value and following through with professional service. It has been estimated that the productive salesman spends 80 percent of his working hours securing and servicing his exclusive listings and performing other office duties. This leaves him with only 20 percent of his time to devote to prospecting and selling. Development of the most efficient method for finding the qualified customer thus becomes a necessity if he wants to operate effectively.

The salesman new to the business is faced with two problems; where and how to find listings, and where and how to find buyers. The real estate office is, in effect, a clearing house for sellers and buyers of real estate. The salesman, through his association with the office, has access to these buyers and sellers whom he can then develop into his customers or clients.[1] If the salesman depends entirely upon those persons walking through the door of the office or answering the office advertising to develop a clientele, he will soon discover that the amount of business he generates will not be sufficient to satisfy his needs or the requirements of his office. But the salesman who, using his own ingenuity, generates additional business will soon become a top producer, in demand by any office in the field.

[1] The client is the person who pays the commission, normally the seller. The customer is normally the purchaser.

Source of Prospects

As previously stated, *selling starts with the listing.* A proper analysis of the listing should not only indicate the type of buyer for the property but should also suggest where this buyer is most likely to be found. The method of circularizing the residents in the immediate area with a "Would You Like to Choose Your Neighbor?" type of letter has proved highly successful in selling single-family residences. The letter, written on a personal basis, should be sincere in its approach; to be effective it must be followed up by a telephone call or a personal approach. Names may be secured from reverse telephone directories, city directories, or ownership records. From the salesman's standpoint this is good "prospecting." It also builds good public relations for the office by emphasizing its interest in maintaining harmonious neighborhood relations.[2] A good sales letter conforms to the same basic principles as a good advertisement. It should serve as a good salesman in its appearance, language, dialogue, and personality. Robert E. Moore (*How to Use Successful Letter-Writing Techniques to Increase Your Sales*)[3] suggests that the "Sandwich Outline" be followed in each letter written. This consists of "starting the letter with a paragraph about the reader and his interests. Follow with your proposition. Always end with a paragraph about the reader and his interests."

Prospects are often developed from the listing itself. The seller, under many conditions, is a prospect

[2] See p. 101 for sample "Would You Like to Choose Your Neighbor?" letter.

[3] *Selling Knacks,* National Sales Development Institute, Waterford, Conn. (Englewood Cliffs. N.J.: Prentice-Hall, Inc., August, 1963).

for another home, or at least for another type of real estate investment. The alert lister discovers the owner's reasons for selling and determines the amount of cash he will have available at the close of escrow. If this money is to be invested in another property, the customer is "ready-made" for the lister. Careful and consistent follow-up of this type of prospect should result in a sale.

Advertising and Signs

Probably the major supply of prospects is derived from these two sources. As was stated in the previous chapter, the carefully written ad aimed at a specific buyer should develop a prospect already well qualified for the property in question. The criterion for the "good" ad is no longer the number of calls it produces, but, rather, how soon will it produce a qualified buyer for the advertised property?

Prospects calling on for-sale or sold signs are usually sincere buyers. They are qualified at least as to area and type of property. Telephone inquiries from any source are of no value to the office, however, unless the person taking the call is trained to handle the inquiry in a tactful manner and to gather such necessary information as name, telephone number, and address. He must be adept at arranging an appointment with the prospect to inspect the property.

Open House

This has become an accepted method of merchandising the single-family residence. However, its merits are still open to debate among members of the industry. In many areas, it is felt that the open house virtually constitutes a necessary evil in the industry: certainly it has its drawbacks. To the energetic and imaginative salesman there is little appeal in this type of inactive selling. As Teckemeyer puts it, "This is really expensive baby-sitting. . . ."[4]

Can the hordes of people wandering through open houses on a weekend really be classed as customers? For every sincere prospect there are scores of shoppers, all of whom must be greeted and escorted through the property. It is difficult for the salesman on duty to secure their names and telephone numbers, much less take the time to qualify them. In general, the open house can scarcely be considered a dignified way to sell property. The question arises, can the real estate industry be considered a profession while this type of merchandising is still an accepted practice? On the other side of the coin, however, many offices handling high-priced properties will quote figures attesting to the success of their open houses. Surveys of these offices indicate that sales made from this type of merchandising rank favorably with those resulting from other promotion methods.

Club Affiliations

All club, church, and community affiliations can be grouped under the one heading of contacts. The real estate salesman who discounts the value of constantly seeing people (the loner, as he is known in the trade) does not belong in the selling field. On the other hand, the efficient salesman is the one who circulates, who values his club membership, and who enters wholeheartedly into community activities. His sales are bound to increase in direct proportion to the number of his personal contacts. It is impossible to tell where his next customers are coming from. They are all around him. Attending a luncheon of the chamber of commerce, he may be seated next to a prospective buyer of one of his listings. It has been said of the real estate business, "We are in the people business." Based on this concept, it would appear that the successful salesman is the one who *sees people.*

Former Customers

Keeping in constant touch with former customers provides one of the very best sources of prospects. If the customer is satisfied with the treatment he received from the salesman, he will refer customers to him, knowing that they are in capable hands. Good office practice is to send out letters periodically to former customers, offering the services of the firm for any other real estate needs the customer may have. The basic principle here is not to allow the customer ever to forget the office. This may be done in a variety of ways. Mailing out birthday or anniversary cards and news items concerning him or his family belongs to the successful methods that may be used.

Mailing Lists

Membership lists of country clubs or other organizations are valuable if higher-priced properties are to be presented. Attractively designed brochures on homes for sale and investment real estate briefs provide a dignified sales approach to the business executive or professional man. Personnel managers of local industries provide an excellent source of

[4] Earl B. Teckemeyer, *Teckemeyer on Selling Real Estate* (Englewood Cliffs, N.J.: Prentice-Hall, Inc., 1962), p. 112.

SERVING YOU

Is the Most Important Thing I DO

The Rex L. Hodges Realty Company has a home for sale in your neighborhood. I thought you might appreciate this opportunity to pick your new neighbors. If you know of anyone who might be interested, you would do them a real favor to call me. I would be very pleased to contact them.

If on the other hand you are possibly considering selling your home, please call me. I'm certain we can mutually benefit by becoming better acquainted. Hope to see you soon.

Sincerely,

34 YEARS OF SERVICE — REX L. HODGES REALTY CO. — 14 NEIGHBORHOOD OFFICES

prospects because transfers of personnel are constantly taking place. Company executives are appreciative of the real estate firm which gives reliable and conscientious service, and are glad to refer their employees' real estate problems to them.

Builders, Speculators, and Investors

Builders. Because raw land is the builder's stock stock in trade, he is always in the market for land parcels of any size. Many salesmen derive a good income from specializing in locating building sites for developers. For the salesman with the necessary technical knowledge, this is an enticing and lucrative field, and one that is not highly competitive. The subdivider or developer new in the market must depend upon the services of the experienced real estate practitioner who is conversant with the basic requirements of the builder-developer and his methods of operation, as well as with the local zoning and building requirements.

Speculators. The speculator buys for one reason —to sell at a profit. Once he has developed confidence in the salesman's judgment, he becomes a continuing source of business for him. Contrary to the thinking of many in the industry, he is not a difficult buyer, once his basic requirements are understood. The property must be priced right (based on the current market), and the cost of any improvements or repairs must not be one that will reduce his anticipated margin of profit. *Location* is an all-important factor with the speculator. The saleman who knows market value, current building costs, and the locations most in demand often can make the sale with one telephone call.

Investors. Unlike the speculator, the investor is a person who buys property to hold in anticipation of a fixed return. He is always in the market for an investment that will make him money. The salesman here not only must learn the rate of return demanded by the investor: he must also know the current return on other investments in competition with real estate (stocks, bonds, insurance annuities, and savings accounts). Once the salesman has listed a property, he must be prepared with facts and detailed figures to back up his arguments in favor of the purchaser. Primarily, it is a matter of the salesman gaining the confidence of the investor through evidencing a thorough knowledge of his subject. Investors are usually busy people and have little patience with the salesman who would take up their time with discussion of worthless properties.

Newspaper Items. The successful salesman is constantly alert to fertile fields where prospects may be found. The local newspaper is one such source. For example, on its financial pages will be reported promotions or transfers of business executives, which often indicates a change of residence for them. Most promotions mean an increase in salary, which in turn indicate the executive may be seeking larger and more prestigious living quarters for his family. A personal letter of congratulations sent *immediately* after the news release and followed up by a telephone call may give the salesman entree to a good listing as well as a competitive edge in assisting the prospect to locate another home.

Society pages are rich sources of leads to prospects in the market for larger or smaller homes. Announcements of engagements or marriages are often tip-offs to prospects for homes or apartments. Birth announcements also indicate that the family may be in the market for larger quarters. News of business executives retiring may mean a sale of their present living quarters. These retirees are often good prospects for a condominium or mobile home. Shrinking family sizes as children leave to attend college in distant cities may indicate a change in living standards.

Relocation Services. There are many of these organizations operating on a nationwide basis, most of them as franchises. Salesmen affiliated with offices belonging to such services have access to transferees and an opportunity to contact them *prior* to their move to the local area. Some of these services are computerized, whereas others provide affiliated offices with the service of Wide-Area Telephone Service (WATS) lines. Customers can thus be qualified by the salesman and the properties suited to their needs selected and information conveyed to them before their arrival. Personnel managers of local industries are often alerted to the local broker affiliate in the community with the result that there is a cooperative effort on the part of the broker and the local industry to relocate the transferred employee.

Qualifying the Prospect

A searching analysis of the listing is a basic requisite of the qualifying process, an analysis concerned with (1) who would want the property, (2) who would qualify financially, and (3) whose needs would the property serve? In effect, *the customer's requirements are matched to the property.*

Financial Ability

How can the salesman judge accurately the prospect's ability to purchase the home he has selected? Although the blunt, "How much money do you have?" is not recommended, an approach such as the more tactful, "How much have you budgeted for a down payment?" can be used effectively. The prospect may or may not be familiar with the price range of homes in the area. He may have little or no knowledge of current lending policies. His problem may be the down payment or the monthly payments.

It is the salesman's responsibility to determine whether the buyer's funds are totally inadequate or whether, through the salesman's application of his knowledge of local lending policies, the financing problem can be resolved. This should be done at the outset of the qualifying process. The salesman's responsibility in this field is threefold: (1) to himself—he cannot afford to spin his wheels with the prospect whose finances cannot be adjusted to the property requirements; (2) to the office—the broker has the right to expect of his employees that they expend their efforts in productive use; (3) to the buyer—he should never be encouraged to buy property beyond his ability to finance. With the competent use of suitable yardsticks for measuring this ability, together with full knowledge of real estate financing, the salesman is in a position to present the true picture to his prospect at the outset.

The prospect should be informed of the exact cash outlay required to handle the property. This involves the cost of obtaining the loan and all closing costs, in addition to the down payment. *Note:* The process of qualifying a buyer financially should be done in the closing room of an office. Nobody appreciates the "eavesdropper" when confidential credit information is being discussed.

The Yardstick to Use

What criterion does the salesman use to qualify his prospect financially? FHA has made a valuable contribution in this area by laying down certain guidelines to qualify the borrower. The rating of the mortgagor (borrower) includes an investigation of his credit characteristics, his motivating interest in ownership of the property, the adequacy of his available assets, and the stability of his effective income. It attempts to establish the borrower's ability and intent to carry and repay the loan. Institutional lenders have established regulations along these same lines, so that the informed salesman should have no trouble determining whether his buyer is qualified to purchase the property in question.

FHA does not use or recommend any rule of thumb for qualifying a buyer. However, for a quick estimate of the buyer's ability to qualify for an FHA loan, the following ratio is normally used:

Monthly income less monthly debt payments must be 4½ times the monthly installment payment (including principal, interest, FHA mutual mortgage insurance, hazard insurance, real estate taxes and special assessments or bonds).

If the buyer is making payments on a car, furniture, or has short-term indebtedness with six months or more to run, then the total of his monthly payments is deducted from his *gross* income to determine his *effective* income. "Monthly income" as far as FHA is concerned represents regular monthly income less tax deductions. A borrower's ability to pay normally is based on monthly income less his monthly housing expense (mortgage payments, taxes, insurance, utilities, maintenance, and repairs.)

For example: If you estimate that a buyer's housing expense will be $100, then, in order to qualify, his income should be at least $450 per month, and he should have good prospects for continued employment. It should be remembered that income ratios are only rules of thumb and are secondary in importance to credit standing and job stability.

Family Requirements

Selling the prospect a home that does not meet his family requirements is a breach of good faith equally as serious as that of selling him a home beyond his financial capabilities. The home that is too small, poorly arranged, too far from transportation, located in an undesirable neighborhood, or, in general, the wrong house for the prospect's needs or desires can prove a serious handicap. Each time the buyer is reminded of the property's inadequacy, he is also reminded of the firm that made the sale. Bad customer relations result; and, although a sale has been made, there is no measure of sales lost through careless handling of one transaction.

Thorough knowledge of competitive properties currently on the market is invaluable as a tool for the salesman who would do a successful job of selling. He must be in a position to defend the advantages of his listing over those of other properties being considered by his prospect. This can best be accomplished by complete familiarity with the needs of his prospect. The salesman best equipped with the knowledge necessary to convince the prospect of the superior advantages of his listing *for the prospect's particular needs or desires* will make the sale.

Qualifying the prospect can best be done by the judicious use of questions. The more the salesman can get the prospect to talk, the more he will learn of his needs. What is his work? What is the size of his family? Their hobbies? Their likes and dislikes? Their aspirations? Many times, the answers can be found by a visit to the prospect's home. An informal hour or two with him and his family will tell the salesman much that he could not discover in any other way. Valuable knowledge of the prospect's housing requirements can be obtained by meeting with him and his family where they are most comfortable—in their own home.

Buyer or Shopper

The ability to distinguish the genuine buyer from the shopper is one of the prime requisites of the successful salesman. Unfortunately, there is no magic formula for this. It requires some knowledge of human psychology and years of experience in dealing with people. Prospects must be classified as to intentions: (1) the sincere buyer, in the market to buy *now,* and (2) the shopper, or *future* buyer. Before expanding hours of time and effort, the productive salesman endeavors to distinguish between these two. By careful questioning, it can usually be determined *why* the prospect is in the market and how serious and urgent his needs are. Has he recently sold a home? Is he tired of being a tenant? Has his family increased or decreased recently? Is some neighborhood problem forcing him to move? Has he been transferred into the area? Has a recent promotion placed him in a higher-income bracket? Is he seeking a prestige area? These and many more are legitimate and often pressing reasons for his having contacted the office. Once he has established that the prospect has a bona fide reason for buying, the salesman can justifiably expend his efforts toward locating the suitable property.

Prospecting by Telephone

This requires a special technique, which can be learned and, with consistent practice, developed to a high degree of skill. Once it is mastered, the salesman has access to many prospects that would otherwise be lost—not only to him, but to the office as well. With a salable exclusive listing and good telephone technique, the alert salesman has an open door to investors, home seekers, speculators, or developers, among others.

If the salesman has a listing that will make money or satisfy a need for the prospect, he will find a receptive ear. Actual *selling* over the telephone, however, should not be attempted. The telephone should be used only to set up the appointment with the prospect. Whether it is being used for cold prospecting or to supply information in response to an inquiry, only sufficient facts should be given out over the telephone to create a desire for additional information. His tone of voice and manner of speech are the most important assets the salesman has in prospecting by telephone. They are the only indication to the person at the other end of the wire that the salesman is capable of helping him with his problem.

Some salesmen would appear instinctively to have the "voice with a smile," and seem always to succeed in their telephone contacts, whereas others need the personal interview to bring out the warmth of their personalities. Getting names and telephone numbers is one of the skills to be mastered if the salesman is to work at peak efficiency. The "information swap" technique is frequently used to advantage. This consists of an exchange of information between salesman and prospect. To "XYZ Realty Company, Miss Jones speaking," the caller will often respond

STONE & SCHULTE

PROSPECT FORM

NAME________________________ PHONE______________

ADDRESS________________________ CITY______________

(Note: Be sure to tell them about your "HOME COUNSELING SERVICE" and explain that we have many other similar listings to choose from.)

I. Question: "How many are there in your family?" ______Children______Ages

Bedrooms______Baths______Sq. Ft.______Schools: ☐ Elem. ☐ Jr. Hi___Sr. Hi.

Notes:______________________ ☐ College ☐ Par.___Other

II. Question: "In what area do you prefer to live?"______________

______________City bus______Shopping______

III. Question: "What special features do you desire?"______________

☐ Fm. Rm. ☐ Din. Rm. ☐ Fm. Kit. ☐ Built-ins ☐ Fireplace

☐ Dbl. Gar. ☐ Basement ☐ Ser. Por. ☐ Hdw. Flrs. ☐ F/A Heat

☐ Fenced ☐ Landscaped ☐ Patio ☐ Lot Size ☐

IV. Question: "How soon must you move?" ______Sell first______Trade______Rents

Urgency______________________

Reason for buying______________________

V. Question: "What is the most you feel you want to invest in a home?"

Price______Down______Monthly______Notes______

☐ Cash ☐ G.I. ☐ Cal Vet ☐ FHA ☐ Conv. ☐ Assume

VI. Question: "If new financing is required, we will need to know your approximate monthly or annual earnings..."

Monthly______Annually______Type work______How long______

Where employed______________Wife work?______________

APPOINTMENT RECORD: HOMES SHOWN:

QUALIFYING BUYERS

HOME BUYER'S PROBLEM ANALYSIS

CALIFORNIA REAL ESTATE ASSOCIATION STANDARD FORM

(a check list to aid in determining the Buyer's qualifications and needs)

PERSONNEL DATA:

Name: (husband)__________ Phone (Office)__________

(wife)__________ (home)__________

Address: (home)__________

(work) (husband)__________ (wife)__________

Other Family Data: Boys__________ Cars__________

Girls__________ Boat__________

Relatives__________ Schools__________

Pets__________ Church__________

NEEDS:

Bedrooms__________ Separate Din. Rm.__________

Baths__________ Din. Rm./Fam. Comb.__________

Sq. Ft.__________ Separate Fam. Rm.__________

1 or 2 Story__________ Fam. Rm./Kitch. Comb.__________

Style__________ Fireplace__________

Lot Size__________ Garage Capacity__________

Location__________ Unusual Needs__________

Possession__________ __________

FINANCES:

Capabilities: Down Payment Max.:__________Now

Or from Sale of Own Home__________

Monthly Payment:__________

(Including Taxes, Insurance)__________

(Excluding Taxes, Insurance)__________

Type Loan Needed__________

Other Equities: Amount, Details__________

Location__________

Trade-In Possibility Data:__________

____

EMPLOYMENT NOTES:

Husband: Company__________ Address__________

Position__________ How Long__________ Salary__________

Wife: Company__________ Address__________

Position__________ How Long__________ Salary__________

ADDITIONAL ITEMS:

How Came in Contact:__________

Other Data:__________

____

____

____

For these forms, address California Real Estate Association, 520 So. Grand Ave., Los Angeles 90017.

Form HBP—11

with his name and his reason for calling. "You have a sign at 123 Fourth Street. Would you tell me how many bedrooms are in that home?" The trained salesman can then develop a conversational exchange of information until he has aroused the prospect's interest in the property. Once the prospect is persuaded that no high-pressure selling methods are being used, he is usually willing to provide any requested information. By the time the conversation is terminated (if the interview has been skillfully handled), the salesman should have the name, telephone number, and address of the caller. He should also have set up an appointment to show him property.

The office has an investment in each telephone call, and it is essential that the firm's executive determine how these calls are being serviced. Unless they are handled skillfully, with a maximum number of sales developed from each call, the office stands to suffer a loss not only in income but in customer relations and ultimate prestige. How does the salesman's voice come over the wire? Does it have a sympathetic and helpful tone? Does it convey confidence to the listener? And, finally, is it a voice that puts the caller at ease and that invites further conversation?

The American Telephone and Telegraph Company lists the following five qualities of a good voice: (1) alertness, (2) expressiveness, (3) naturalness, (4) pleasantness, and (5) distinctness.[5] Certainly the salesman who is not alert in his telephone response cannot hope to convey confidence. The same may be said of the dull, monotonous voice. The natural conversational voice tends to evoke a like response from the listener. The pleasant, friendly voice conveys an attitude of helpfulness, suggesting that the salesman may have the answer to the caller's problem. And, finally, his voice must be clear and distinct if he would encourage his caller to do business with him. It is important for the salesman to remember that, to the person at the other end of the line, *he is the company,* and that his company is judged by what is said and how it is said.

Good Telephone Habits

Listed as high on the list of important telephone habits, according to the American Telephone and Telegraph Company, are:

1. Greeting the caller pleasantly.
   This includes being enthusiastic.
2. Using the customer's name.
   This is the most important name in the world to him.
3. Trying to visualize the caller.
   This involves speaking *to* the caller, not *at* the telephone.
4. Being attentive.
   Listening politely and attentively to the person at the other end is only common courtesy.
5. Taking time to be helpful.
   The caller has a problem; otherwise, he would not have called. He expects the salesman to be helpful.
6. Apologizing for errors or delays.
   The caller should never be left on the line for long periods of time while the salesman searches out needed information. He should be asked if he would rather wait or be called later. The salesman on floor duty should have at hand a copy of all ads being run, so that he is prepared with answers to any questions concerning them.
7. Saying "Thank you" and "You're welcome."
   It should hardly be necessary to call this to the attention of the salesman. Courtesy should be the basis of all business dealings.

[5] *Win More Friends by Telephone,* American Telephone and Telegraph Company, 1960.

Prospecting by Mail

Sales promotion by letter has been developed to a high art by the professional advertisers and the communications experts. The well-written business letter and the property brief describing the appealing features of a property require a skill as important as any in the selling processes. The written word has the advantage of a lasting quality in that it can be referred to again and again. A name given over the telephone may be forgotten the next moment, but the signature on a letter presenting information of value to the reader remains as a constant reminder of the person rendering the service.

Letters. The dignity and importance of the office should be reflected in the letterhead itself. The prospect has only this and the text of the letter by which to judge the firm. The well-written and effectively composed sales presentation that indicates an efficient, well-organized office can provide an open sesame to the salesman when making his follow-up call.

Because the letter is actually a sales presentation, the same basic rules of good salesmanship apply, most important of which is "talking in terms of the other man's interests." The letter should be written in short, easily understood sentences. The sales presentation itself must be planned, and should flow along to a logical conclusion, if it is to supply an answer to the reader's problem.

The *A*ttention-*I*nterest-*D*esire-*A*ction formula is

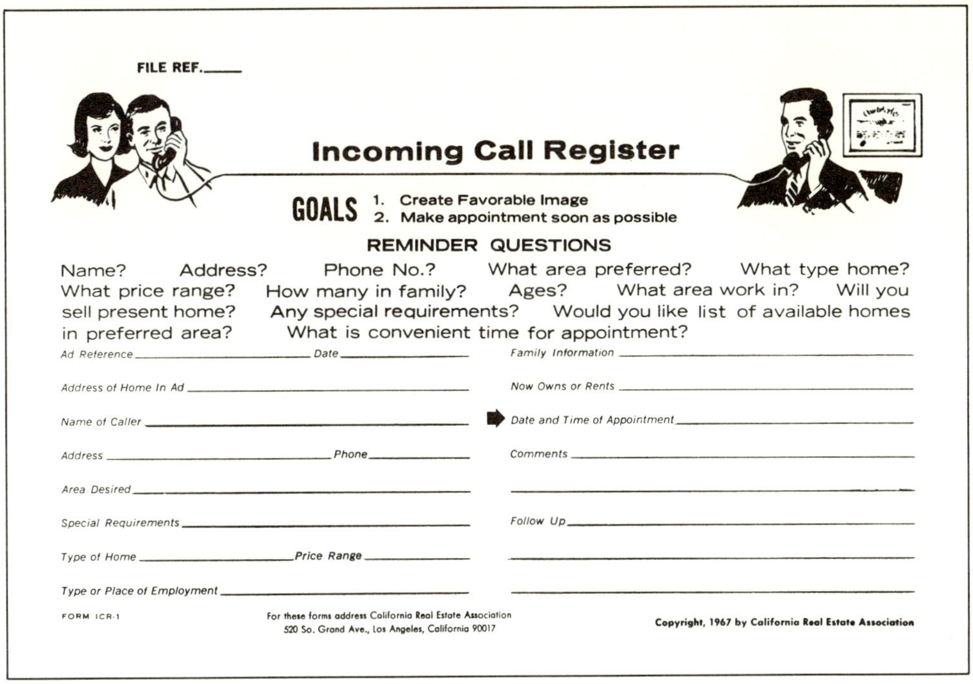

FILE REF.____

Incoming Call Register

GOALS 1. Create Favorable Image
2. Make appointment soon as possible

REMINDER QUESTIONS

Name? Address? Phone No.? What area preferred? What type home? What price range? How many in family? Ages? What area work in? Will you sell present home? Any special requirements? Would you like list of available homes in preferred area? What is convenient time for appointment?

Ad Reference ____ Date ____
Address of Home In Ad ____
Name of Caller ____
Address ____ Phone ____
Area Desired ____
Special Requirements ____
Type of Home ____ Price Range ____
Type or Place of Employment ____

Family Information ____
Now Owns or Rents ____
Date and Time of Appointment ____
Comments ____
____
Follow Up ____
____
____

FORM ICR-1

For these forms address California Real Estate Association
520 So. Grand Ave., Los Angeles, California 90017

Copyright, 1967 by California Real Estate Association

just as effective here as in the oral sales presentation or in the advertisement. Reading the letter aloud before making the final draft will often point up any weaknesses. Finally, the letter should be no longer than is necessary. Good organization and presentation of material could be lost on the reader if he is required to wade through paragraph after paragraph of extraneous material having little or no direct bearing on the subject. Any letter worth the time and effort to compose should be sent by first class mail. Third class or throwaway mailings usually receive the treatment that the name implies.

The Property Brief. In reality, the property brief (or brochure) is pictorial advertising. It is the company's dignified, silent salesman and, properly planned, makes a valuable contribution to the overall sales program. It is the professional way to present residential income, industrial or office buildings, and higher-priced residences. The brochure is also especially adapted to institutional advertising. Designed to sell the firm to the public, it should be persuasive and attractive, and, above all, reflect the prestige of the office. The new as well as the established company can use this type of promotion to advantage. Included in the brochure should be a complete list of the services offered by the company and a list of all organizations of which the firm's executive is a member. Photographs and short biographical sketches of the sales force are effective in serving to acquaint the buying public with the type of firm with whom they may be doing business. Although it may be designed by a professional in the office or turned over to an advertising agency, it is false economy to produce a cheap, poorly planned brochure.

The institutional brochure is usually published on a monthly or bimonthly basis and sent to a regular mailing list. For the property brief promoting specific properties, however, a select list of the most likely prospects is circularized. Depending on the type of properties being offered, this list would normally include builders, developers, professional people and businessmen, or cooperating brokers.

To justify the expense involved in this type of promotion, properties should be listed on a long-term exclusive basis. This should present no problem to owners interested in having their property merchandised in a highly professional and dignified manner.

One of the best examples of this type of promotion is the National Clearing House for Real Estate known as Previews, Inc. With offices in Europe, Canada, and the major cities in the United States, beautifully illustrated brochures of the better properties all over the world are mailed to reliable real estate brokers on request. Established in 1934 and working exclusively through, rather than in competition with brokers, Previews, with its wide coverage and excellent marketing facilities, has established an enviable reputation for moving higher-priced properties.

CASE STUDY

The Garden Realty Company is located in a live section of Garden City, a thriving community of

50,000 population. The office is very modern in design with a good functional layout, and the décor and furnishings are in excellent taste. Donald Rose, realtor and office owner, is a university graduate in business administration and has specialized in real estate subjects. He opened his present office five years ago, after serving as associate broker in another office for three years. He left the latter office because he was dissatisfied with the unbusinesslike manner in which it was being run. He believes that the real estate business should be conducted in a professional manner, and he has hewed closely to this line during the five years that he has been in business for himself.

Rose is concerned with the poor public image of the real estate broker and is determined that his office will be a model of decorum and dignity. He is scrupulously honest in all dealings, adheres religiously to the code of ethics, and demands the same from his staff. He is well thought of in the community and among his competitors. He holds an office in the local board of realtors, is a member of the chamber of commerce, and once ran for city councilman. He has been moderately successful but has had a high turnover of sales personnel. This has been expensive for him and has resulted in the loss of customers as well as of sales. He believes that he has been careful in his hiring practices but in the past he has been disappointed in many of the salesmen selected. They have not always measured up to the rigid specifications he has set for all office personnel. At present, Rose has a sales staff of nine, composed of five men and four women, and he believes that at last he has a good working group. The office morale is high.

The firm deals primarily in residential sales, specializing in the higher-priced homes. Rose believes in "circulating," and he belongs to the country club, where he meets fellow businessmen once a week for a morning of golf, followed by lunch at the club. He also likes to bowl, and he and his wife are avid baseball fans. He buys season tickets for the league games each year.

Sales meetings at the office are held once a week, with the salesmen alternating in leading the discussions. Lately, the discussion has centered on the lack of customers contacting the office. Several of the salesmen blame this situation on what they believe is an inadequate advertising program, although Rose's advertising budget normally runs higher than that of his competitors. Others attribute the lack of customers to the specialized type of properties being handled by the office.

Rose gives the problem considerable thought and decides that he should keep a more careful check on the prospecting being done by the salespeople. He is convinced that the fault does not lie with the office image itself, because he is doing a good job of public relations in the community through his many personnal contacts in civic and recreational activities. He also feels that his advertising program is more than adequate.

Roger Clapp, a retired advertising executive well past middle age, is a meticulous dresser whose cultured and easy social manner makes a good impression on the customers. Rose met him and his wife at a country-club dinner. During the conversation, Rose discovered that Clapp was employed by a competitive firm. He said that he was not satisfied there and inquired of Rose as to whether there was an opening at the Garden Realty Company. He has now been with the company only seven months. Rose is very proud of Clapp and feels that he projects a good office image in the field. His wife is socially prominent in the city and belongs to several women's organizations. In spite of his social assets, Clapp's sales record is not impressive. He is much better at listing than at selling and often complains that he has no "live" customers. He spends a great deal of time in the office, in addition to his floor time, and occasionally he picks up a good customer "filling in" when the floor man is called out. He has held open house when required but does not favor this type of selling; he prefers to spend his weekends at home with his family. Although Rose feels that Clapp is an asset to the office public-relationswise, he is concerned about Clapp's poor sales record. He decides that he should follow Clapp's prospecting and selling methods more closely and possibly discover where his weakness lies.

Clapp has floor duty the following morning. His first call is from a woman who lives in an area close to the office. She asks about an ad on a duplex running currently in the local paper. Clapp gives her the information she asks for and then gives her the address and suggests that she drive by to check the area. He says that he is on duty in the office but will call her later in the day.

About ten o'clock a woman drops in at the office with a newspaper in which one of the office ads appears. It develops that the property advertised is one of Clapp's listings, a $32,500 home in a good neighborhood. It is one of the older homes, with three bedrooms and a formal dining room. There is one full bath in the bedroom area and a half bath off the service porch. The yard is small and has recently been professionally landscaped. The home has always been one of the best kept in the neighborhood, and the owners have insisted that the listed price must remain firm, as they are retiring and moving to a condominium-type apartment. They will need all cash from the sale to invest in their apartment.

Clapp attempts to qualify the prospect through a series of questions, recording her answers on the form provided for this purpose. It develops that her husband is a junior executive in the $15,000-a-year bracket. He has been transferred to Garden City, where he is employed by the Mason Electronics Company, the city's largest industry. They are living at present in a motel until they find a home to suit them. They have four children, two of whom are in primary grades and two are in junior high school. They sold their home in the Midwest for $22,000 but had to carry back a purchase-money second-trust deed for $3,500 in order to make the sale. She is pleased, however, that the note carries 8 percent interest and that it will be paid up in seven years. It is their plan to use these payments to help make those on their new home. Because of a prolonged and expensive illness in the family, they were forced recently to refinance their home in the amount of $12,000, a loan which the new owner has assumed. After paying the brokerage and closing costs, they are disappointed in the amount of cash they had remaining and are rather resentful of the 6 percent commission that the broker collected. They feel that he could have arranged financing on the sale of their home that would have given them all cash. It was their first experience in disposing of a property, and they have found it difficult to buy another home to suit their family needs with the amount of cash they have to use as a down payment. However, she says that she understands that the lending institutions look favorably on Garden City properties, and she is optimistic about qualifying for the necessary loan if they can find the home that suits them. She is anxious to see the home advertised, because she believes, from the way the ad reads, that it should be just what they have been looking for.

Clapp assures her that the home should fit their family needs admirably. He is anxious to sell the home because it has been on the market several weeks and the listing is about to expire. The office has had little response to its ads, and the owner is unhappy with the lack of activity shown. Clapp has not asked for a loan commitment, because he says he is familiar with the lending policy on the homes in the area. The newer homes are being financed in some cases up to 90 percent of the selling price.

At one time Clapp had considered making up an attractive brochure on the property and leaving it with the personnel manager of the Mason Electronics Company. He thinks it is interesting that this prospect should have come from the Mason Company.

Clapp takes his customer in his car to show her the property. The size of the home is a great disappointment to her. She does not consider the small yard adequate; they had hoped to have a yard where they could build a swimming pool later. Also, there is no den or family room where her older children can entertain their friends. She feels that this is important, because they will be going into high school in another year and will need the extra room for their parties. Clapp says that they could build an addition to the home, though he says he will have to consult a builder regarding the cost. He does not have a figure on the exact down payment required but is sure that the prospect has sufficient cash, because the current lending policy in Garden City is very liberal.

Clapp returns to the office with the prospect, who says that she will tell her husband about the property and call Clapp in the morning. He tries to persuade her to wait while he calls the local savings and loan company for a loan commitment. He also plans to contact a builder friend of his regarding the proposed addition to the house. The customer says she must get back to the children, whom she has left with a baby sitter.

Rose questions Clapp when he returns to his desk regarding the outcome of the showing. Clapp hedges, saying only that he is sure he will hear from the prospect in the morning. Under further questioning, he discloses that her name is Mrs. Bridges and that she is staying at the Land's End Motel. He agrees that he should have obtained a loan commitment on the property and would probably have had more prospects for the home if he had made up the brochure as he had originally planned.

He calls the Garden City Savings and Loan, who tells him that they are quite familiar with the property, having made an appraisal for a competitive office, which had held a short-term open listing on the property previous to Clapp's having taken the exclusive listing. They tell Clapp that, owing to the age of the property and its obsolescent floor plan, the maximum that they could lend would be 70 percent of the sales price. This loan would carry an interest rate of 8 percent, with a maximum term of eighteen years.

1. Do you feel, as Rose does, that Clapp is an asset to the office?
2. To what principal factors do you attribute Clapp's poor sales record?

3. Do you think that Rose is attaching too much importance to the office image?
4. Do you think that Clapp did a good job of qualifying Mrs. Bridges? Why, or why not?
5. To what do you attribute the large turnover of salespeople in the office?
6. Would the Bridges qualify financially for the home shown them by Clapp?
7. How would you think Clapp could improve on his prospecting?

SUGGESTED REFERENCES

SCHWARTZ, JACK, *How to Get More Business by Telephone.* Los Angeles: Jack Schwartz Telephone Sales Clinic, 1953.

TECKEMEYER, EARL B., *Teckemeyer on Selling Real Estate.* Englewood Cliffs, N.J.: Prentice-Hall, Inc., 1962.

VOGEL, LOIS T., *How to Help Your Real Estate Salesmen Produce More Business.* Englewood Cliffs, N.J.: Prentice-Hall, Inc., 1957.

WHITING, PERCY H., *The Five Great Rules of Selling,* 1st ed. 1947. New York: McGraw-Hill Book Company.

———, *Real Estate Salesman's Handbook,* 5th ed. Chicago: National Institute of Real Estate Brokers of the National Association of Real Estate Boards.

———, *Marketing Real Estate Successfully.* Chicago: National Institute of Real Estate Brokers of the National Association of Real Estate Boards.

8

Techniques of Selling

The process of selling real estate involves four phases: listing, prospecting, negotiating, and closing. In this chapter we are concerned with negotiating (with the prospect).

Webster defines *negotiating* as "to confer regarding a *basis of agreement,* as, to negotiate for the purchase of a house." The degree of finesse employed by the salesman in his approach to this "basis of agreement" determines his future in the field of real estate selling. Because of the difficulty of bringing buyers and sellers together in the real estate marketplace, the position of the real estate practitioner, whose services facilitate this process, becomes more important than that of the broker or mediator in any other field. The spread between the asking price and the price offered places the salesman in the position of a highly skilled negotiator; thus, to give his best performance, the salesman must have a knowledge of what motivates the buyer. As Husband and Anderson have stated, "Since successful selling means the maximum satisfaction of the buyer's needs, probably the most important task of the salesman is to discover what people want. Specifically, the selling function may best be fulfilled by recognizing the following four needs:

1. The need for confidence.
2. The need for information.
3. The need for advice.
4. The need for financing."[1]

The need for *confidence* in the salesman is the basis of all successful real estate transactions. Recognition of the need is stressed in article 12 of the NAREB Code of Ethics, which reads, "In justice to those who place their interests in his care, the Realtor should endeavor always to be informed regarding laws, proposed legislation, governmental orders, and other essential information and public policies which affect those interests."

Although the broker is the agent of the seller, he is legally and morally bound to "disclose all facts" to the buyer. Any variation from this conduct is a violation of Section 1709 of the Civil Code, which reads: "One who *wilfully deceives* another with the intent to induce him to alter his position to his injury or risk is liable for any damage which he thereby suffers." *Deceit* is defined in the Civil Code as "suppression of a fact by one who is bound to disclose it." (The salesman as an employee of the broker is bound by the same license law as the broker himself.)

The purchaser of property entrusting his funds to the salesman has a natural concern for their safety. To protect the buying public, California Real Estate Law provides that the license of any real estate licensee may be revoked for "commingling with his own money or property the money or property of others which is received and held by him." Section 2830 of the Commissioner's Regulations makes the necessity of the selection and maintenance by the broker of an adequate trust fund a matter of law.

The Need for Information. Recognition of the buyer's need for information would seem too elementary to require exploration, yet most complaints against the licensee stem from the broker's lack of knowledge or his failure to disseminate his knowledge accurately. The industry trade associations have long recognized the responsibility of its members in this area. In addition to article 12, quoted above, article 1 of the NAREB Code of Ethics reads: "The Realtor

[1] William H. Husband and Frank Ray Anderson, *Real Estate,* 3rd ed. (Homewood, Ill.: Richard D. Irwin, Inc., 1960), p. 314.

should keep himself informed as to movements affecting real estate in his community, state, and the nation, so that he may be able to contribute to public thinking on matters of taxation, legislation, land use, city planning, and other questions affecting property interests." Information regarding a property offered for sale that the broker cannot ascertain from the seller at the time of the listing should be sought from other sources. "Ignorance is no excuse under the law" is nowhere more applicable than in the real estate industry, where entire life savings may be in jeopardy because of insufficient, incorrect, or misleading information supplied by the uninformed salesman.

Many problems arise from the failure of the salesman to *disclose* all material facts concerning a property or conditions of the sale. The question arises: What is material? Webster defines *material* as "pertaining to or affecting man's bodily wants, interests, or comforts." The law would appear to be clear on the question of statements made by agents concerning the condition of property being offered for sale:

> Real estate agents, by the very nature of their business, are constantly making statements to prospects concerning the condition of the premises being offered for sale. In addition one or more of the parties involved often has erroneous impressions concerning the property. Such statements and impressions can be generally classified for legal analysis as follows: (1) statements reasonably intended and understood as "predictions" only; (2) statements reasonably intended and understood to be part of the contract (promise) itself; (3) mistakes; (4) statements reasonably intended and understood as representations of fact; (5) nondisclosure of material facts by silence.[2]

Need for Advice. If the salesman is to fulfill his role as the buyer's trusted counselor, he must have familiarized himself with current and accurate data relative to the real estate market, the community, and present or pending legislation affecting the industry. So many complexities are involved today in real estate transactions that the average buyer involved in other fields of endeavor has a great need for advice from his broker. He has a right to expect of the broker that he will be fully informed not only on market conditions but on the legal aspects of property transfers. The real estate practitioner cannot, of course, involve himself in the practice of law, but it is his responsibility to recognize when the situation calls for the advice of an attorney or a tax expert and to so advise his client.

The salesman must also use extreme caution in making promises regarding possible future property values. An opinion expressed is just that, whereas a sale based on a *promise* of future rises in property value could, in some cases, border on fraud.

Need for Financing. Rarely does the purchaser pay all cash for the property. The need for some type of financing therefore becomes an important one. The average sale is in actuality a job of selling financing. Although the law of supply and demand regulates the money market just as it does any other market, the broker who has studied the basic factors that affect the money market is in a position to advise his client who has a financing problem. Financing is the key to success in real estate sales. Consumer credit in the United States has enabled many people to own and enjoy material benefits that would be far beyond their reach if considered on a cash basis. At the same time, it has placed a grave responsibility on the salesman dealing in these commodities. Especially is this true in the real estate industry, where the money invested may represent an entire life's savings.

The professional broker cannot afford to disregard the many financing pitfalls in which his buyer may be trapped. The temptation to do so in the interest of making the sale must be resisted in all cases. Although it is true that lending institutions have established frameworks within which the borrower must be confined, this does not relieve the broker of his responsibility. This will be discussed further in Chapter 9, "Financing the sale."

Types of Buyers

The successful salesman is always cognizant of the *type* of buyer with whom he is dealing. Although human nature is difficult to classify, individuals do fall into certain categories in their buying habits, and each requires a different sales approach. Stanley McMichael, in his *Selling Real Estate,* lists the more general of these as:

The timid.
The silent.
The serious.
The bluffer.
The skeptic.
The curious.
The cautious.
The "kidder."
The practical.
The "know all."
The "smart guy."
The talkative type.
The bargain hunter.
The "too easy" buyer.

[2] Reference Book, Department of Real Estate.

The one easily swayed.
The seasoned "shopper."[3]

Selling Approaches

It has been said that the approach to selling real estate may be made in one of three ways: (1) *have a property* and find a suitable buyer; (2) *have a prospect* and find a suitable property; or (3) *have an idea* and develop it into a sale. (This is also known as creative selling.)

The salesman who has a listing normally tries to attract buyers through some form of advertising or personal prospecting. The state of the market, more than any other aspect, will affect the ease with which the selling job is accomplished. High-pressure selling is no longer countenanced in the better offices. As the industry becomes more professional, buyers tend to seek out the competent, informed broker to solve their real estate problems, just as they would solicit the services of an attorney for legal assistance. Selling real estate is then elevated to the level of professional counseling and involves, among others, the fields of financing, taxation, land usage, and investment.

The selling situation itself is then resolved into one of *buyer conviction* as against one of *sales persuasion.* This does not imply, however, that the buyer will necessarily arrive at this conviction without application of the salesman's skill and knowledge. It is the ability of the broker in this application that determines whether the prospect "buys" or "is sold."

Finding a suitable property begins with the intelligent analysis of the buyer's needs. Then follows the elimination of properties obviously unsuited to the buyer's requirements. To accomplish this, the salesman must have available all pertinent information relating to competitive properties. If the buyer's family and financial requirements have been correctly analyzed, the salesman should have little actual selling work to do. As was mentioned above, the sale resolves itself into a situation of *buyer conviction.*

The "idea" technique is the most exciting and gratifying of the three selling approaches. This type of creative selling has been responsible for the development of our large shopping centers, retirement communities, resort developments, and planned communities. In this field of selling, the imagination and ingenuity of the salesman are brought into full play. Also, this type of skilled entrepreneur is always in demand. As expressed by J. Fred Talley, real estate commissioner for the state of Arizona, "If you are a *creature* of circumstances, people are your *problem.* If you are a *creator* of circumstances, people are your *opportunity.*"[4]

Because the salesman often has neither property nor customer at the outset, more actual labor is involved in the creative type of selling. But, as has been aptly stated, "It is not work, unless you would rather be doing something else." The salesman who has chosen this type of work probably could not be persuaded to "do something else."

Neglected properties, overcrowded areas, and properties in the paths of community development are all of interest to the creative salesman or to the developer. Canvassing the downtown area of his community, the salesman may discover merchants who have outgrown their present quarters. He may locate a parcel of land not being put to its "highest and best use." Many hours of research are usually involved before the salesman is ready to make his first contact, however. This research can be as simple as locating more suitable quarters for the individual or it can involve long-range development plans necessitating highly complex market surveys. With these complexities resolved, usually the broker now has only to convince the buyer or seller that his present position will be improved through the implementation of the creative idea. Because it attracts only the ambitious and imaginative individual, competition in this field is limited. Once the salesman has developed the basic requisites necessary for the informed, skilled negotiator, his success is assured.

Planning the Sale

Intelligent sales planning is probably the most important and yet the most neglected of all requisites for the salesman's success. This planning involves advance organization of (1) time and (2) sales presentation. Organization of time requires severe self-discipline. The good salesman by nature is not methodical. Selling involves creativity and imagination, the very antithesis of plodding orderliness. Yet a certain amount of methodical organization is a must if the best selling results are to be achieved. Organization of time can be as simple as making daily a *list of things to be done* and a *record of things accomplished* but can be as important to the end result as planning a budget and keeping a record of the money spent.

[3] Stanley McMichael, *Selling Real Estate,* 3rd. ed. (Englewood Cliffs, N.J.: Prentice-Hall, Inc., 1957), p. 79.

[4] J. Fred Talley, "Sales Opportunities," in *California Real Estate Magazine,* Vol. 44, No. 7 (May, 1964), 14.

Organization of Time

No organization ever achieved success without establishing definite goals. The real estate salesman who has set no financial goals for himself has no basis for success. Conversely, the successful salesman is one who has demonstrated his ability to organize his work and leisure time intelligently. Recognizing this, some firms require their salesmen to compile daily reports of their activities and to file them with the office each week for analysis and evaluation. There is much merit in this system, because it forces the salesman to plan the day's work in advance and then to adhere strictly to the plan, thus eliminating all time-wasting activities. *Note:* The report form should be a simplified one to prevent its use becoming burdensome to the salesman and thereby defeating its purpose.

Time budgeting is difficult in many real estate offices because there is no schedule requiring salesmen to report in at any given time. Except for the salesman on floor duty, the office personnel often drift in at any time convenient to them. This is not to say that it is productive to have salesmen sitting around the office engaged in nonselling activities. The salesman who succeeds is the one, of course, out in the field listing, seeing customers, or showing property every working hour. However, with the requirement that salesmen report at a specific hour each morning, routine chores can be completed and work schedules set up before the day's interruptions begin. (One method is to divide each day into a morning and afternoon unit but treat each working unit as *one full day.*)

Human beings are creatures of habit. Good work habits established early in the salesman's career and adhered to tenaciously make for the "highest and best use" of his time. Many people who have set goals for themselves fall short of the mark because of poor work habits and lack of self-discipline. One of the most valuable services a broker can render his salesman as part of his training program is that of insisting that good work habits be established and adhered to. This applies particularly to the woman in real estate. Often she has no business training and, as a result, has difficulty adjusting to the tedious routine of listing and selling so necessary to success. Much of the criticism of women in the real estate field is leveled at their unbusinesslike attitude toward their work. An adequate training program and follow-through in the way of supervision should do much to dissipate this attitude on the part of the public as well as of her fellow workers.

To assist the salesman in following out his planned schedule, many of the larger offices, where a secretary is employed, set up "tickler" files. This relieves the salesman of any concern that he may overlook an appointment or neglect an assignment. It is the responsibility of the secretary to check the file each morning and to place a memo reminder on the desk of each salesman covering any item that may concern him.

Reduced to dollar value, every hour spent by the real estate salesman in nonproductive effort costs him money. The following tables, reproduced through the courtesy of the Dictaphone Corporation, dramatically point this up:

WHAT'S YOUR TIME WORTH?[5]

If you earn	*Every hour is worth*	*Every minute is worth*	*In a year one hour a day is worth*
$2,000	$1.02	$.0170	$250
2,500	1.28	.0213	312
3,000	1.54	.0256	375
3,500	1.79	.0300	437
4,000	2.05	.0341	500
5,000	2.56	.0426	625
6,000	3.07	.0513	750
7,000	3.59	.0598	875
7,500	3.84	.0640	937
8,000	4.10	.0683	1000
8,500	4.35	.0726	1063
10,000	5.12	.0852	1250
12,000	6.15	.1025	1500
14,000	7.17	.1195	1750
16,000	8.20	.1366	2000
20,000	10.25	.1708	2500
25,000	12.81	.2135	3125

Organizing the Sale

As is stressed throughout this text, the prime requisite of any sales presentation is knowledge of the product involved. Although "well listed is half sold" is a basic precept of good listing practice, it is not enough. The successful salesman also knows his *prospect* and learns to anticipate his objections before he attempts any organization of the sales presentation. What *type* of buyer is he, and what motivates him to buy? Recognizing the buyer type and analyzing the intelligent selling approach specifically suited to him may involve time and practice, but *it can be learned.* The prospect who is status-conscious can be sold on the *prestige value* of home ownership. The family man will buy the comforts of home and the "togetherness" it can provide him and his family.

[5] *The Career Woman in Real Estate: Lesson No. 4,* Women's Council of NAREB, p. 7.

And the buyer who is money-conscious will buy only if the *value* is there. *The effective salesman learns to take his cue* from his buyer and to pattern the sales presentation along the lines of the particular buyer's needs and desires.

Showing the Property

Much has been written about the correct way to show property. Do you take the scenic route? Should the prospect follow in his car? Arriving at the property, do you park in front, across the street, or down the street? Where do you start your sales talk? What do you say? How many properties do you show? These are all important questions that deserve consideration. However, because home purchases are based primarily on emotion, any effective approach by the salesman must stress the amenities of home ownership. If the prospect can be persuaded that his present position will be enhanced by the purchase, the sale can be developed. Elmer Wheeler's familiar, "Sell the sizzle and not the steak," sums it up very succinctly.

Answering Objections

The salesman, in organizing his sale, will find it helpful to list any features of a property to which his prospect may object. By itemizing these points he is, at the same time, whether consciously or not, formulating his answers to the objections. Sales experts agree, "The selling job begins when the prospect says 'No.' " By this is meant that the prospect who has raised no objections has shown no interest either. Buyers' objections can be classified as general or specific. When the buyer has narrowed his objections to a specific property, it is an indication that he has eliminated all other properties and is now giving careful attention to the one he has selected.

Because of the large sum involved in a home purchase, the most frequently voiced objection relates to *price*. To overcome this type of objection, the salesman must be prepared with accurate information on building costs, land values, and current sales of comparable properties. To be effective, these figures must be specific rather than general. Put another way, price objection can best be answered by selling *quality* and *value;* that is, the buyer must be persuaded that price is always subordinate to inherent value. If the value of the property cannot be justified, the time of the salesman and that of the prospect has been wasted. In addition, the salesman runs a risk of losing his buyer's respect and of jeopardizing his future relations with the buyer as a customer. As a word of warning, price should never be made an issue before it becomes one. ("The asking price is $25,000, but I think it can be had for much less.") Not only is this approach by the salesman a betrayal of his trust as an agent of the seller, but it gives the impression of a property being "hawked" rather than offered for sale on a firm and dignified basis.

Whatever the objection or question raised by the buyer, it deserves a direct, intelligent, and informative reply. The salesman who does not have the answer should never attempt to bluff. No one can be expected to know everything. It is important, however, for the salesman to indicate that, although he does not have the answer at the moment, he will make every effort to get the information as soon as possible.

In a recent study conducted in the San Fernando Valley of southern California[6] to determine whether there was any real difference between the family that purchases a newly built single-family home and the family that purchases an older, used one, it was determined that the basic reasons for seeking a new home may be categorized generally by three groups:

1. Families who need a place to live (those who have newly formed households and the ability to make the down payment) and others who are forced to seek new shelter (fire, demolition, personal disagreements).
2. Individual families whose economic mobility requires a complete change of geographic location and movement to a new area.
3. Families who seek a more suitable home within or close to the same geographic area. This is by far the largest group (about two-thirds). These buyers are motivated by family needs, neighborhood changes, or by a desire to live in a different social climate. (In this latter instance the present home is vacated by choice rather than by economic or physical necessity.)

Home-purchase decisions were based on economic factors and locational factors, with the primary consideration being price. (This was stated by most home purchasers in terms of down payment and/or monthly mortgage payments rather than total cost.) One-third of the families restricted their search to new only or used only homes, with the remaining two-thirds examining both new and used homes.

It was hypothesized that one type of buyer is attracted to new homes, whereas another type is attracted to the used home. The study found that new-home purchasers are more innovative than their

[6] Charles A. Bearchell, Jr., *An Analysis of Factors Influencing Decisions to Purchase New versus Used Single-Family Residences* (Sacramento: Department of Real Estate, 1968).

used-home-buying counterparts. As related to social contacts, the mean amount of social interaction appeared to be slightly higher for the new-home buyers. The median new-home buyer was found to have visited eight homes in the neighborhood versus a median score of five homes for the used-home buyer. However, it was found that the used-home-buying family belonged to an average of 3.4 local groups versus an average of 3.1 for the new-home buyers. Although the study was quick to point out that the conclusions reached would not necessarily apply to all single-family purchasers throughout the country, nevertheless the demonstration of the existence of real differences between psychologically related behavioral characteristics of new- and used-home-purchasing families suggested the need for closer and further analysis of the submarkets themselves and of their interrelationships.

The salesman who is working in an area of used and new homes is often faced with having to assist a customer with a decision as to which of the two types of housing is best suited to his family needs. For this reason an understanding of the type of buyer who is generally interested in either of the two types of housing can be of help.

Basic Appeals in the Sales Process

In a survey by Dr. Clayton C. Curtis, of the University of Florida, for the Florida Association of Realtors, owners interviewed indicated that the most appreciated features in a salesman were: courtesy, patience, and honesty. They resented high-pressure salesmanship and indifference to their needs and expressed dislike at being left in the dark regarding such things as closing costs. They were particularly annoyed at the feeling of being dropped immediately after the sale was made.[7]

The salesman with the well-organized sales presentation speaks in a confident, unhurried, and informal manner, allowing time for the prospect to ask questions and express his views. His success in selling will depend on the degree to which he is able to gain the confidence of the buyer, give him needed advice, and, in general, counsel with him on the unfamiliar details of the sale. This means talking his language and avoiding technical terms of the industry. A certain amount of empathy, with the *buyer's interest* uppermost in mind, is a necessary attribute of any successful salesman.

[7] "Here's How You Can Sell More Homes," *Real Estate Opportunities,* Sec. 1 (Englewood Cliffs, N.J.: Prentice-Hall, Inc., January 23, 1962), p. 3.

Misrepresentation is not only a violation of the law and a breach of ethics but also poor salesmanship. Section 10177.5 of the real estate law reads: "When a final judgment is obtained in a civil action against any real estate licensee upon grounds of fraud, *misrepresentation,* or deceit with reference to any transaction for which a license is required under this division, the commissioner may, after hearing in accordance with the provisions of this part relating to hearings, suspend or revoke the license of such real estate licensee." In addition, Article 3 of the NAREB Code of Ethics reads: "It is the duty of the Realtor to protect the public against fraud, misrepresentation or *unethical practices* in the real estate field. . . ." (Italics the author's.)

Other personal assets important for the salesman to display during the selling process include the ability to concentrate, to incite curiosity, and to hold the interest of the prospect. This involves observing and gauging the customer's reaction. The highly skilled, observant salesman has developed an astute mind capable of interpreting the prospect's readiness to buy. Often, an extra surge of enthusiasm on the part of the salesman will dispel any hesitation or indecision on the part of the buyer; at this point, the actual closing has begun.

The Sales Kit

This can be a brief case, attaché case, or zipper case containing pertinent information assembled from various sources and used as an aid to the salesman making his presentation (whether listing or selling). It is essential that the information be compiled in an orderly, presentable fashion and that it contain all data necessary to answer any sales question that may arise. The sales kit can be as simple or as elaborate as the individual desires. It will vary with the type of property being handled, the community being served, and the type of clientele concerned. To be of any value, it is necessary that all materials be kept current.

Basic items should include real estate forms, tax and assessment figures, escrow and title-company information, loan-amortization tables, tape measure, maps (showing zoning, transportation, and schools), and office promotion materials (including current sales data). Current news items relating to the national, state, and local economy and to real estate in particular can be bound in an attractive folder. The sales kit takes on added importance for the smaller office. Sellers particularly must be sold on the ability of the smaller office to do an adequate job of merchandising. The sales kit as a "silent salesman" can often be an effective persuader in the face of formidable competition from larger offices.

CASE STUDY

Byron Farmer and his wife, Alice, have lived in New Dayton, California for five years. Byron is a pharmacist employed by the local drugstore. They came to California from Chicago, where they were both reared; but, because of Alice's health, they were forced to move to a milder climate. They have one child, a six-year-old girl, enrolled in the first grade in El Cajon elementary school. Alice is expecting her second child in two months.

The Farmers have been living in an apartment since they came to New Dayton. However, with the second child expected, they have decided to buy a home. Byron makes a good salary, and they have been saving for a down payment. They now have approximately $5,000 put aside for this purpose.

They have never purchased property before and have had no dealings with real estate brokers. They watch the papers for ads that seem appealing. They are watching particularly for a three-bedroom home with some type of recreation room. They wish to stay in the El Cajon school district, because their child is very happy and doing well there. On weekends they drive around the area and occasionally stop at open houses, but have not as yet found their "home." One Sunday morning, Alice Farmer sees an ad in the local paper reading:

EL CAJON SCHOOL DISTRICT
Owner moving to Oregon & must sell his 3 BR & den home. Frplc., w/w carpets & drapes. New aluminum siding, large fenced yard. Zoned R-3. Call us to see. $32,500
CANYON REALTY CO.
320 S. Front Street
Phone: 446–8531

It sounds attractive, and they call the Canyon Realty Co. to inquire about the property. Ted Duncan, a salesman, answers the telephone and makes an appointment to show the property to the Farmers. They say that they prefer to meet him after church at the property. Duncan says he will be there at one o'clock. He has been late getting to the office and has been constantly interrupted, so that it is nearly 12:45 when he goes to lunch. It is 1:30 when he arrives at the property. The Farmers are waiting but are growing impatient, because it is a warm day and unusual heat is making Mrs. Farmer very uncomfortable.

They arrive at the front door only to find no one at home. Duncan recalls that, in his rush, he has forgotten to telephone the owners, Mr. and Mrs Morgan. However, Duncan says they will look around the yard anyway and inspect the house from the outside. He says, in answer to their question about the "R-3 Zone" that it means they are permitted to build an apartment house on the lot. They indicate that this is far from their thoughts; they want only a quiet home atmosphere.

The Morgans arrive while Duncan is showing the Farmers around. Mrs. Morgan is perturbed at not having been called for an appointment but agrees to show the property, anyway.

The Farmers are disappointed in the house because, although it is very spacious, it is twenty-eight years old and in need of repair and modernizing. There is only one bath, and the carpeting and draperies are badly worn. They consider that the house is much overpriced when they compare it with some of the newer ones they have seen. However, the broker assures them that the value is there, because R-3 land is selling currently for $1.85 a square foot, and the lot size is 70 by 200 feet. This would leave a value of $6,600 for the house, which he feels is reasonable. He promises them that the land value in the next two years will go at least to $2.75 a square foot, and that, if they spend $4,000 to $5,000 to modernize the house, they can make a nice profit. He suggests they get an FHA loan for the modernization program.

The property is clear, and the Morgans are willing to carry back a purchase-money trust deed at 8½ percent if the Farmers will pay $3,000 down.

Broker Duncan continues to stress the potential profit feature of the property and suggests that they return to the office to talk it over. The Farmers are the "timid"-type buyers. They are intrigued by the possibilities of the property but still feel that it is not the "home" atmosphere they would like for their children, especially because an apartment house which is under construction across the street appears to be of very cheap construction and would rent to low-income groups, all of which would downgrade the area. They are familiar with the work of the builder, a Mr. Ronstan, who has built several such apartment houses in neighboring areas.

Back at the office, they tell Duncan that they are totally ignorant of real estate dealings and must depend upon his judgment.

1. Do you feel that Duncan has answered the four needs of the buyers adequately? Explain.
2. Did he handle their "objections" in a professional manner?

3. Would you say that he has done an adequate job of building customer relations with the seller? With the buyer? Discuss.
4. Discuss Duncan's scheduling of his time.

SUGGESTED REFERENCES

GATEWOOD, EMMETTE T. "Obtaining the Offer," *Successful Real Estate Salesmanship.* Los Angeles: California Real Estate Association, 1966.

GAY, DEAN A. "Positive Approach in Showing Homes and Getting the Buyer to Say Yes," *How to List and Sell Real Estate Property in a Competitive Market,* 1964.

HIMSTREET, WILLIAM "Do Others Understand You?" *Advanced Real Estate Sales.* Los Angeles: California Real Estate Association, 1968.

MCMICHAEL, STANLEY, *Selling Real Estate,* 3rd ed. Englewood Cliffs, N.J.: Prentice-Hall, Inc., 1957.

SIGBAND, NORMAN B. "Communications for Effective Customer Relations," *Advanced Real Estate Sales.* Los Angeles: California Real Estate Association, 1968.

WHITING, PERCY H. *The Five Great Rules of Selling,* 3rd ed. New York: McGraw-Hill Book Company, 1947.

———, *Selling Real Estate.* Los Angeles: California Real Estate Association, 1970.

9

Financing the Sale

Fundamental Aspects

Buyers rarely have sufficient cash to pay the entire purchase price of a property. Even in cases where they have the cash, they may prefer to finance a portion of the total cost. (The business executive may wish to use his cash for business expansion.) Thus, the completion of most real estate sales is dependent on some type of financing. If the broker is to perform his duties as counselor to his clients, he must have a working knowledge of current financing practices. In addition to knowing his buyer and seller, he must know the lenders in his area, their lending policies, and the procedures for obtaining the loan. He must understand the financing instruments in general use. He must also be thoroughly familiar with noninstitutional as well as institutional lenders, and with the government's restrictions on and assistance in mortgage financing.

The constantly changing picture in the financing field requires that the broker keep his information current. This involves an understanding of the money market and the factors that affect it.

The Money Market

The economics of supply and demand affect the money market just as they do that of any other commodity (automobiles, home appliances, oil, or wheat). The center of the money market is in downtown New York, in an area that bounds the location of the head offices of the ten or fifteen banks that provide the major part of the facilities necessary to effect the transfers of money. The *mortgage money market* is only one segment of the general money market. However, for an understanding of the fluctuations of the mortgage money market, there must also be an understanding of the economic factors that affect the general money market. This, in turn, involves a study of the U.S. Treasury Department and the Federal Reserve system. For the purposes of this text, an exploration "in depth" of regulatory bodies is not intended, although real estate practitioners should have an understanding of the function and operation of these as they affect the mortgage money market. The impact of the investment of mortgage funds on the general economy of the country makes this imperative for the broker who would serve as the trusted adviser to his clients.

Qualifying the Buyer

In cases where the seller insists on all cash for the sale of his property, and the buyer does not have or does not wish to pay all cash, the broker in the transaction must be in a position to arrange satisfactory financing. The seller may own a clear property and wish to take back a purchase-money trust deed for one of two reasons: (1) he may be interested from a tax angle if he has owned the property for a considerable time, or (2) he may be interested strictly from an investment standpoint.

In either case, it is necessary to check the borrower's qualifications. His down payment and his credit standing are the two prime considerations. In making a loan, the institutional lender will look to the borrower as well as to the property for security. Since 1934, the borrower has been recognized as a highly important safety factor against risks of loss, though the underlying security is still the property itself. Where government-backed loans, such as those of the VA or FHA, are concerned, the borrower is carefully screened not only as to his income but as to his general reliability. The buyer, especially if he is making his first purchase, probably knows very little about mortgage financing. The broker, however, must know his buyer and his reasons for buying if he is to tailor the financing to his particular needs and prevent his "overbuying."

Although the final screening of the buyer is the function of the lender or the loan broker, a certain amount of preliminary qualifying should be done by the real estate broker. (This is a highly sensitive area, and any questioning must be done in a discreet manner.) Basic information that the broker will require includes: (1) the amount of the down payment available; (2) the buyer's monthly *net* income; (3) the amount of any outstanding debts (automobile or furniture payments, and so forth); (4) other assets (insurance, stocks, bonds, or real estate).

Certain formulas have been established by lending agencies as desirable ratios of expense, such as the ratio of the monthly payment for shelter to monthly income. A ratio of five to one is considered a good ratio for anyone borrowing up to $20,000; that is, interest-and-principal payment for one month, added to one-twelfth of the annual taxes and one-twelfth of the annual insurance premium (the sum of the total monthly payment for shelter) should not be more than one-fifth of the gross monthly income to justify a loan of up to $20,000. For loans from $20,000 to $25,000 the ratio should be six to one, and for any amount over $25,000 the ratio should be seven or eight to one.

By use of the loan amortization payment book it is possible to determine the total amount of the loan for which the borrower will qualify. By adding his down payment to this figure it is a simple matter to arrive at the maximum price of home that he can afford to purchase. It should be remembered that if there is to be secondary financing, the payments on this loan must be included in calculating what his gross income should be.

Overtime Wages. In certain conditions overtime wages will be taken into consideration by the lending institution. If such overtime is a normal condition of the business in which the borrower is occupied, it will probably be considered.

Wife's Income. Certain conditions apply if the lender is to consider a wife's wages in computing the gross income of the borrower. If she is a professional person, or a secretary of long standing, and if she is over thirty-five, most companies will allow her full salary. If she is under thirty-five usually only 50 percent of her salary is allowed. Also if the wife is employed in a nonprofessional capacity, in most cases only 50 percent of her income is allowable. Certain exceptions may be made—if the wife was employed before marriage, has continued working after marriage, and left work for only a short time following the birth of a child, her full salary will probably be allowed.

Cosigners. Occasionally, in order to strengthen the borrower's application, it is necessary to use a cosigner on the note. This situation may exist if the borrower is either very young or elderly. Lenders prefer that the cosigner be a blood relative, and the same information is gathered from him as from the borrower.[1]

Qualifying the Property

Although lenders in the field are varied, only a few will lend on all types of property. Some will make loans only in specified areas that have proved economically sound. Some will lend only on prime residential properties. Because the underlying security for any loan is the property itself, a careful appraisal is required by the lender. His margin of safety is the difference between the loan amount and the appraised value of the property. The same factors apply to a property appraisal for loan purposes as to an appraisal for a sale. Location, age, zoning, architecture, floor plan, and general appearance all have a bearing on the terms of the loan. (The best terms are available when the risk is lowest.) Brokers who are familiar with the lending policies of the various loan companies are able to estimate more or less accurately the maximum amount and the terms of a loan that would be available on a give property. Lending policies are subject to constant change, however, and information must continually be kept current.

Sources of Funds

As was mentioned above, the average buyer is unable or unwilling to pay all cash for a home or a business property. Thus, long-term financing is one of the more important factors in the real estate business. The mortgage money market as applied to real estate is composed of primary and secondary markets. The real estate broker normally is concerned only with the primary market (the market made up of lenders supplying funds directly to the borrower). The principal sources of mortgage funds are: (1)

[1] For further information on qualifying the borrower, see J. W. Pugh and William H. Hippaka, *California Real Estate Finance* (Englewood Cliffs, N.J.: Prentice-Hall, Inc., 1966).

savings and loan associations, (2) insurance companies, (3) mutual savings banks, (4) commercial banks, (5) trust companies, (6) mortgage companies, (7) endowed institutions, (8) pension funds, and (9) individuals. The real estate broker must know which of these lenders are most active in his community and the lending policies of each. The majority of loans are made by a group of lenders known as "institutional lenders," comprised principally of savings and loan associations, insurance companies, mutual savings banks, and commercial banks.

Institutional Lenders

Savings and loan associations (or building and loan associations). These include both federally chartered and state chartered associations. The former are regulated by the Federal Home Loan Bank Board, whereas the latter are supervised by the California savings and loan commissioner. The ownership of all federally chartered associations is vested in their depositors, but state chartered institutions (with few exceptions) are stock companies owned by those holding shares of capital stock. The savings and loan associations function as a depository of savings, which they lend out on amortized first-mortgage loans. These loans are made for the purposes of building, buying, making improvements, and refinancing.

Most savings and loan associations, if qualified, are members of the Federal Savings and Loan Insurance Corporation, whereby owners of accounts are insured up to $20,000 by a permanent instrumentality of the federal government. Savings and loan associations usually pay a dividend rate on savings about 1.5 percent below their prevailing mortgage loan rate. Under Federal Home Loan Bank regulations, federally chartered savings and loan associations may legally make home mortgage loans, other than FHA and VA loans, of up to 95 percent of the lesser of the appraised value or the selling price of the home offered as security, provided that the loan does not exceed $31,500, that the home is owner-occupied, and that no other liens are placed on the property. On loans in excess of 80 percent of appraised value certain limitations apply in addition to those stated above. One of these is the requirement that the monthly payments must include property taxes and hazard insurance in addition to principal and interest.

Interest Rates. Savings and loan association loans generally carry a higher interest rate than those made by insurance companies or by commercial banks. (In late 1971 interest rates on prime single-family homes were ranging from 7¼ to 7½ percent).

Loan Fees. Fees on these loans generally range higher than those made by insurance companies or by commercial banks. They normally run from 1 to 2 percent of the total amount of the loan. This fee is paid by the borrower as a closing cost at the time of escrow closing.

Prepayment Penalties. Unless it is expressly provided for in the terms of the note, or unless the lender gives his consent, the borrower may not prepay a real estate loan before maturity. The lender may specify an amount to be paid by the debtor if he exercises his prepayment right. This amount is usually measured in terms of a percentage of the total amount of the loan. In other words, if no prepayment privilege is provided for in the note, the lender may negotiate the fee he is willing to accept in return for his consent to prepayment of the loan. Normally savings and loan associations permit 20 percent of the loan balance to be paid before the pre-payment penalty is applied. This penalty usually is computed as three to six months' interest.

Appraisal System. Federally chartered associations require that the appraisal report be signed by at least two qualified persons selected by the board of directors. As to state licensed associations, appraisal reports of larger properties must be signed by senior appraisers, designated as grades 3 or 4 by the Department of Savings and Loans. No other person is required to sign the report, provided the grade 3 appraiser does not sign a report on properties he is not authorized to appraise.

Loan Ratio. State licensed associations may lend 80 percent of the first $40,000 of appraised value plus 70 percent of the excess over $40,000 with a term of thirty years. This ratio applies to conventional loans, and the neighborhood and age of the property are given a great deal of weight in the appraisal.

Maximum Terms. On one to four dwelling units the term is thirty years. On five or more dwelling units the term is twenty-five years, and on commercial property the term is twenty years.

Assumption. Alienation (due on sale) clauses are usually included in all savings and loan association notes. This enables them to approve or disapprove of the new borrower, to charge an assumption fee, and to increase the interest rate to that currently prevailing, if desired.

Although the bulk of the loans made by savings and loan associations are conventional loans, they are authorized also to make FHA and VA loans. They are not permitted to make business and consumer loans, as commercial banks are.

Insurance Companies. Insurance companies are governed by the laws of the state in which the company is incorporated, as well as the laws of the state in which they operate. Companies incorporated or doing business in California are restricted on conventional mortgage loans to 75 percent of market value on single-family residences and 75 percent of market value for other types of property. Life-insurance companies hold about one-fifth of the total mortgage debt of the nation; however, by 1969 insurance companies were moving more and more into the very large income-producing properties such as housing developments, shopping centers, and large commercial developments. "Joint ventures" whereby the lender became an equal partner in a property acquisition or development became popular. In these cases the insurance company often furnished up to 100 percent financing. "Loans-with-a-kicker" where the lender shared in either the property's net or gross income, and "equity participation" (whereby the lender received a percentage of the equity ownership in addition to the interest yield) were favored. Many life-insurance companies had their funds committed through 1970, and the balance of funds was earmarked for loans that would provide a hedge against the inflationary increases in the cost of doing business. There are no *legal* limits imposed on the maximum number of years for which the loan may be made, although company *policy* usually limits it to twenty-five years. On residential properties, most companies lend only to a maximum of $25,000, although in some prime property areas, loans may run to $45,000. Interest rates are predicated on the neighborhood, the age of the property, the quality of construction, buyer qualifications, and the amount and term of the loan. They normally favor newer homes in choice locations. The income of the borrower is, of course, an important factor. Recently, some companies have stipulated that the amount of the loan should not be more than one and one-half to two times the amount of the borrower's annual income, and that monthly payments on the loan should not exceed 20 percent of his monthly take-home pay.

Payments on taxes and insurance are included in the monthly payment and, in the case of FHA, the mortgage insurance premium is as well. Appraisal policies of insurance companies are much more liberal than formerly was the case. Such improvements as patios and swimming pools are now given either full or proportionate weight in their appraisal process.

Commercial Banks. These are chartered for the principal purpose of financing business transactions. Because, to meet withdrawal requests of their depositors, they are required to keep their assets on a relatively liquid basis, real estate loans are not a significant part of their lending operations. State-chartered banks are normally permitted to make a proportionately greater number of loans than banks under national charter. Under the Emergency Home Finance Act of 1970, both state and national banks are now permitted to lend 90 percent of their appraised value (or of the sales price, whichever is less) for a term of 30 years. Although the above figures represent a *legal* permission, the actual ratio of loan to appraisal is left to the discretion of the individual bank. The percentage applies to good residential property rated as "A" property, whereas fair or acceptable residential property would justify a loan proportionately less. Bank loans usually have a smaller or no prepayment penalty. Also, the loan fees of banks are generally lower than those of other lending institutions.

Commercial banks, in most instances, will lend up to 80 percent of the appraised value on good, economically operated farm properties. General-purpose commercial buildings are usually acceptable for loans to 80 percent of appraised value and single-purpose or industrial properties to 80 percent. State-chartered banks are permitted to lend on unimproved property.

Both state and national banks are permitted to make an unlimited number of FHA-insured or VA-guaranteed loans, provided that it is feasible and profitable for the bank to do so. On these loans neither bank is legally restricted as they are on their normal mortgage lending, and they are generally considered a prime source of these loans.

Mutual Savings Banks. Located principally in the Northeastern states and chartered under state laws that regulate their operations, these banks are not active in the primary market in California. Depositors are not paid interest but share in the dividends after allowance for reserves and expenses.

Non-institutional Lenders

These include universities, colleges, pension funds, bank trust funds, mortgage investment companies, executors of estates, and individuals. These lenders differ from the institutional lenders in that they are not bound by strict regulations. The noninstitutional lenders are the largest source of second (or junior) mortgage financing.

Mortgage Companies. These are usually organized under state laws but are subject to minimum supervision and have broad mortgage-lending powers. They act principally as loan "originators" and are primarily interested in mortgages that are readily salable in the secondary market. Thus, they are especially active in the government-insured FHA and government-guaranteed VA loans.

Some companies serve only as "temporary" lenders, reselling the loans as soon as they are made. Many of them invest their own funds. Others obtain their funds from commercial banks by arranging for lines of credit. They then make advances against mortgage documents while loans are in the process of being sold to the eventual purchaser. Many mortgage companies act as loan correspondents for insurance companies or mutual savings banks.

One of the functions of mortgage companies is that of servicing loans that they have originated. That is, they collect the payments from the original borrower and forward the payment to the permanent lender (after deduction of a service fee). They also make "construction" loans, then make commitments on "take-out" (or permanent type) loans usually from an insurance company or mutual bank.

Mortgage companies are coming to occupy a significant place in California as an important source of mortgage financing. Real estate practitioners should become acquainted with those companies doing business in their areas. Because they are not restricted in their lending policies as rigidly as are the institutional lenders, they are in a position to act much more quickly, thus possibly saving a sale when there is a time element involved.

Trust Companies. Trust companies and trust departments of banks on occasion have funds of estates or personal trusts available for investment. They are bound only by the rules of discretion and any provisions of the trust agreement. Aware of their responsibilities, trust officers, however, are extremely cautious in their lending practices and usually require a maximum interest rate. Trust funds have been used to finance large office buildings, churches, and shopping centers.

Individuals. These are the largest source of funds for second-mortgage loans. Individuals normally are not interested in making long-term loans except with the possible exception of the purchase-money mortgage. The maximum term of the second mortgage is usually three to seven years. Individuals occasionally obtain mortgage loans through various sources, such as real estate brokers or title companies, mortgage companies, or merely advertising. Because the individual is not regulated by any national or state governmental body, he can take greater risks in his investments. However, because of the risk involved, interest rates run higher than on the conventional loan.

Pension Funds. This type of real estate financing is becoming more of a factor as the large increase in assets causes the administrators of these funds to seek additional investment outlets. Pension plans are constantly receiving new funds from contributions of employers and employees with no outgo except for retirement payments to employees. The problem, then, is to find safe investments with the highest possible return. At present, the largest investment of these funds has been in stocks and bonds. However, there has been a gradual switch to investments in mortgage loans, mostly, at present, in those that are government-backed. "At the end of 1963, according to the Securities and Exchange Commission, pension funds held $2.2 billion in mortgages, vs. $742 million in 1958."[2]

Real Estate Investment Trusts

An *unincorporated* trust or association of investors, managed by one or more trustees the real estate investment trust is the real estate industry's approximation of mutual funds. It provides the small investor a means whereby he may participate in a professionally managed real estate portfolio through freely transferable shares of beneficial interest. Prior to 1960 it would have been taxed as a corporation. Under a 1960 authorization by Congress the trust today is taxed only on retained earnings, as opposed to the prior situation wherein it was held to be taxable at corporate rates on all net income.

Realty trusts may invest in either equities or mortgages, or in a combination of both. Advantages to the investor in the real estate investment trust include:

1. The small investor may pool his funds with others to take advantage of large investment opportunities.
2. The small investor is offered the probability of higher returns from widely diversified investments, as well as added safety for his funds.
3. The best possible legal counsel is available to him.

[2] Arelo Sederberg, "Lenders Awash in the Money Market," *Los Angeles Times,* July 6, 1964, Part 3, pp. 8–9.

4. The trust is directly regulated by state and federal regulatory agencies (the latter applies when shares are sold across state lines). *In California the supervisory power is invested in the corporations commissioner.*

In order to meet the tax-free test under federal law, the following basic requirements must be met:

1. Property must not be held primarily for sale to customers in the ordinary course of business.
2. Property must be beneficially owned by at least 100 investors.
3. No five persons or fewer may hold more than 50 percent of the beneficial interest.
4. This "beneficial interest" must be evidenced by transferable shares or certificates of interest.
5. In California, there is a further limiting proviso that each share or certificate of interest carries with it an equivalent vote in determining trust policy. It is this stricture which has so far controlled the development of trusts in this state.
6. Investments must account for a minimum of 90 percent of the trust's gross income.
7. 75 percent of gross income must come from *real estate* investments.
8. Less than 30 percent of the trust's gross income may result from short-term gains on sales of stock or securities held for less than six months plus sales (but not involuntary conversions) of real estate held less than four years.[3]

For further information on the many technical provisions relating to real estate investment trusts, the student would be well advised to consult the nearest office of the State Department of Corporations.

Government Participation

Federal Housing Administration. Because of the difficulty of obtaining real estate loans in an amount sufficient to permit the average person to purchase a home, individual home ownership was at its lowest ebb when in 1934, by an act of Congress, the Federal Housing Administration (FHA) came into being with the express purpose of encouraging the construction and ownership of homes, principally in the low-price range. This act, known as the National Housing Act, created the greatest change in mortgage lending the nation has ever known. Under Title II of the act, a permanent program of housing insurance was set up. Because of its widespread use, all brokers should familiarize themselves with the program and with its purposes, advantages, and regulations. They should be thoroughly conversant with the procedure for filing and processing an FHA loan, know how to qualify the property and the prospect, and be familiar with current policies of local lending institutions handling such loans (including the current costs of obtaining the loan).

Practically every home buyer in the nation is eligible for an FHA-insured loan, provided he is buying the home for his own occupancy and can meet the loan-to-income ratio requirements of the lender. The *purchaser,* under FHA financing, can take advantage of the lowest interest rates and the longest terms available in the mortgage field. The seller has the advantage of cashing in immediately with no secondary financing involved.[4]

From the standpoint of the real estate broker, there are many advantages to having complete knowledge of the FHA program, including:

1. FHA's low down-payment requirements create a vast new market of potential buyers who otherwise could not be considered as prospects.
2. The availability of an FHA estimate of value will often cause both buyer and seller to be more realistic in their own attitudes toward the value and thereby help the broker to bring them to an agreement.
3. The broker who can offer and discuss FHA financing will enhance his reputation as a *professional* type of broker.
4. The broker will have the satisfaction of knowing he has provided financing the purchaser can live with because FHA's expert underwriters will have determined that the transaction was a sound one.[5]

In its operation, the FHA does not make loans, it insures loans made by supervised financial institutions, such as commercial banks, life-insurance companies, federal and state savings and loan associations, and any institution whose deposits are insured by the Federal Deposit Insurance Corporation, as well as specially approved mortgage companies and pension funds. If the borrower defaults, the lender may foreclose and tender the property to FHA in exchange for debentures or cash, or with prior approval of the FHA the lender may assign the defaulted mortgage prior to foreclosure action. Debentures are guaranteed both as to principal and interest by the U.S. government and are therefore readily marketable. All aggregate net income is credited to the Mutual Mortgage-Insurance Plan. Provision is made for losses to be paid from the reserves built up in the general surplus account under this plan.

[3] *Reference Book,* California Department of Real Estate. See also Phillip G. Faulkner, "Reit's Equity Returns in a Fishbowl," *The Appraisal Journal,* National Association of Real Estate Boards, October, 1970.

[4] Secondary financing (with a single technical exception listed in Section 203K of the National Housing Act) is not permitted on FHA loans.

[5] *Helpful Hints in Preparing FHA Loan Submissions* (Los Angeles, California: The Colwell Company), p. 1.

To reduce the risk factors of this type of lending, a stringent procedure for appraising the risk on the property has been set up, in addition to giving proper weight to the credit rating of the borrower. This includes an investigation of his credit rating, the adequacy of his income ratio to his total obligations, the adequacy of his available assets, and the stability of his effective income.

Procedure for FHA Application. Applications must be made on prescribed FHA forms.[6] Additional exhibits required by FHA that must accompany the loan application include an original or certified copy of the purchase contract (deposit receipt), credit report on the mortgagor, verification of deposit, verification of employment, and, in the case of new construction, the drawings and specifications of the improvements.

The mortgagee first applies for a *conditional commitment.* A firm commitment is requested when the mortgagee asks for a contract with the FHA commissioner to insure the outstanding conditional commitment with a *specified mortgagor* acceptable to the FHA. Limitations and loan-to-value ratios, amortization periods, and interest rates are subject to change by administrative regulations. Real estate practitioners dealing in FHA-financed properties have an obligation to keep abreast of the current interest rates and regulations if they are to serve their clientele in a professional capacity.[7] They should particularly be informed on current provisions of Section 203(b) of Title II of the National Housing Act as amended. They must know how to calculate the maximum FHA-insured loan that might be obtained on a given property.

The main purpose of the FHA program is to meet the housing needs of all citizens. It has the authority to:

(1) Insure loans made to homeowners for the repair, alteration, and improvement of property.
(2) Insure lending institutions against the loss from mortgage loans made to one- to four-family houses and large rental projects.

Certain secondary results have also been accomplished, including:

(1) A comprehensive system of valuing property and rating mortgage risk.
(2) Minimum standards of construction.
(3) Scientific subdivision planning to protect against neighborhood deterioration.
(4) Stimulation of mortgage investment on a nationwide basis.
(5) Long-term mortgage loans with a lower interest rate.[8]

Borrower's Loan Costs

Interest rate. The mortgage may bear interest at any rate agreed upon between the mortgagee and mortgagor but it cannot exceed $8\frac{1}{2}$ percent a year. Interest must be paid in monthly installments on the principal then outstanding.

Mortgage-Insurance Charge. The mortgage may provide for monthly payments by the mortgagor to the mortgagee of an amount equal to one-twelfth of the annual mortgage insurance premium, payable by the mortgagee. The mortgage-insurance premium is $\frac{1}{2}$ percent of the average outstanding principal obligation for the twelve-month period.

What Are "Points"? Point is synonymous with *percent.* It refers to the percent of discount absorbed by the seller in an FHA transaction. FHA mortgages are bought and sold by investors in the secondary market in much the same manner as are stocks or bonds, and the selling price of these mortgages is not always at "par" or 100 percent of their face value. For example, a loan might be purchased from a mortgage company at 97 percent of par value. The mortage company then passes this discount on to some interested party to the transaction. The *buyer* is limited under FHA regulation to paying no more than a 1 percent loan-origination fee. The *seller,* therefore, customarily absorbs the discount. Sellers, usually, will accept the idea of the discount if they are shown the comparison between the cost of discounting an FHA loan and that of a large second-trust deed.[9]

The lender may charge a discount only if the borrower is:

(1) Building a home for his own occupancy.
(2) Refinancing a mortgage on property that he owns.
(3) Constructing houses for sale as a builder who takes the mortgage in his own name.
(4) Purchasing the property from a governmental agency or municipal corporation that is precluded by statute from paying the discount.

Taxes, Special Assessments, Hazard Insurance. The mortgage must provide for such equal monthly

[6] Currently at a cost of $40.

[7] Current facts and figures about various types of FHA-insured mortgages are available from the *"Digest of Insurable Loans,"* published by the Federal Housing Administration (Washington, D.C.: Superintendent of Documents).

[8] See *Guide to FHA and VA Financing* at end of chapter.

[9] See additional information on "points" at end of chapter.

payments by the mortgagor to the mortgagee as will amortize the ground rents, if any, and the estimated amount of all taxes, special assessments, if any, and fire and other hazard insurance premiums.

Other Charges or Costs. In addition the mortgagor may be required to pay to the mortgagee an FHA application fee, an initial service charge (usually 1 percent of the mortgage amount), and the customary recording fees, taxes, credit report, survey, title search, and title insurance.

FHA Requirements for Purchase of Another Home with FHA Financing

Licensees who handle the sale of homes with existing FHA loans that are assumed should advise their principals of the requirements they must meet before they are permitted to purchase another home with FHA financing. If the seller intends to buy another home *within six months,* the following documents must be provided:

1. A credit report on the substitute mortgagor (the purchaser who assumed the loan).
2. A statement as to whether the substitute mortgagor intends to occupy the premises.
3. A statement from the mortgagee as to the current status of the loan.

If the seller intends to buy on FHA terms *after six months, but within two years,* statements from the mortgagee are required as to:

1. The current status of the loan.
2. The payment record of the substitute mortgagor.

If evidence is furnished that the FHA insurance on the property has been terminated, then the above conditions will not be required.

Qualifying the Buyer

The FHA will insure a loan only if the borrower has adequate credit. However, FHA rules on income are not stringent. For instance, a buyer with a smaller income is always seriously considered if his credit and employment record are sound. The income of the wife will be included but will be qualified by consideration of her work, age, and prospects of continuing employment. FHA normally requires that the buyer's base monthly income shall equal four and one-half to five times his *monthly housing expense.* This expense consists of mortgage payments, taxes, insurance, maintenance, and repairs. If the buyer is making payments on a car, furniture, or other short-term indebtedness having six months or more to run, the total of his monthly payments must be deducted from his gross income to arrive at his *effective* income. Job stability and good credit standing of the borrower weigh heavily in the qualifying process.

Once a deposit receipt is signed, it is important that escrow be opened immediately so that processing of the application can begin. Care should be taken to select an escrow officer who is thoroughly familiar with FHA procedure. To expedite the processing, the broker can help materially by making sure that all documents necessary to make up the "package" are in the hands of the escrow office. He may, in some cases, be required to hand-carry papers to the mortgage company or title company if such procedure is necessary to speed up an escrow closing.

Special Types of Mortgages Insured

Three special types of mortgages insured under Section 203(b) of Title II, in addition to the above, include:

(1) Financing the replacement of properties destroyed or extensively damaged by major disasters. [Section 203(h).]

(2) Financing single-family owner-occupied homes in outlying areas and small communities, where it is not practicable to obtain conformity with many of the requirements essential to the insurance of mortgages on housing in built-up urban areas. [Section 203(i).]

(3) Financing alteration, repairs, or major improvements to existing housing. [Section 203 (k).]

Condominiums

The maximum insured mortgage on a condominium is $33,000. If the appraised value of a unit (including common areas and facilities) is no more than $15,000, 97 percent is insurable; if it is from $15,000 to $25,000, 90 percent is insurable; and if it is beyond $25,000, 80 percent is insurable. The mortgage term cannot exceed thirty-five years.

When the borrower is not the occupant of the property, the mortgage cannot exceed 85 percent of the amount available to an owner-occupant.[10]

The interest rate may not exceed the rate specified in FHA regulations.

An investor-sponsor cooperative project may be converted to condominium ownership.

[10] This restriction for the nonoccupant owner applies to all purchases financed under Section 203(b) of Title II.

Lower-Income Home Ownership

Of special interest to brokers whose practice involves them in assisting the lower-income buyer is Section 235 of the National Housing Act. Under this section, low-income buyers of homes, condominium, or co-op units pay 20 percent of the family's monthly income for the following expenses:

(1) Mortgage principal and interest.
(2) Mortgage insurance premium.
(3) Taxes and insurance.

The government pays the lender the difference between this amount and the actual cost, plus a monthly payment to reimburse the lender for the expense of handling the mortgage. Top interest rate is 8½ percent, plus the annual mortgage-insurance premium of ½ of 1 percent on the outstanding principal. The term is generally thirty years, but it may be extended to thirty-five or forty years if this is necessary in order for the borrower to qualify.

The program is limited normally to new or substantially rehabilitated units, involving a single- or two-family dwelling, a family unit in a condominium, or a unit occupied by a member of a cooperative.

The maximum mortgage amounts cannot exceed $18,000 for a single-family dwelling or living unit in a condominium or cooperative. In high-cost areas, a higher mortgage amount may be established, but not to exceed $21,000. An additional allowance of $3,000 may be authorized for large families of five or more persons, requiring four or more bedrooms.[11]

Veterans Administration

Brokers are often called upon to counsel veterans on the purchase of property under the so-called "GI Bill of Rights." It is important that all real estate practitioners familiarize themselves with the requirements and policies of the Veterans Administration, as well as with those of lending institutions in the area which make loans under the act.

The Veterans Administration usually guarantees rather than insures the lender against loss up to certain limits. Note: The difference between a *guaranteed* and an *insured* loan lies in the amount that will be paid the lender in the event of a default. If there is a default on a *guaranteed* loan, the government pays the lender a specified maximum amount. This amount is reduced proportionately as the loan is paid off by the borrower. In the case of an *insured* loan, the VA will pay the net loss of the lender up to the amount of the lender's insurance account. The maximum amount of the loan the VA will guarantee varies with the type of the loan, as follows:

60 percent on homes up to a maximum of $12,500.
50 percent on farms or businesses up to a maximum of $4,000.
50 percent on other than real estate loans, up to a maximum of $2,000.

In the case of a default on an insured loan, the veteran's eligibility is charged with 15 percent of the loan (the amount credited to the lender's insurance account). If there is a default on a guaranteed loan, his eligibility is charged with the amount of the guarantee, and could amount to 60 percent of some loans.

VA home loans are made only in case the borrower is to be the owner-occupant. After living in the home, however, the veteran may move out and rent the property without effect on the loan.

A fee of ½ of 1 percent of the loan amount must be paid to VA in the case of loans for post–Korean veterans and servicemen. This fee is in addition to the allowable closing costs. This loan fee may be added to the loan amount.

What Is the Difference Between VA and FHA Loans?

1. *A service charge* of 1 percent on loans on existing structures are permitted on FHA loans, as well as 2½ percent on buildings to be constructed. Lenders under VA regulations may charge "reasonable" costs. (These "closing" costs usually include the VA appraisal, credit report, survey, title evidence, and recording fees.)
2. *No down payment* for VA loans except as required by the lender.
3. *Guarantee amount.* Although there is a limitation upon the amount of guarantee that may be issued on a VA loan (see above), there is no maximum amount set by government regulation. This loan policy is set by the lender. *FHA prescribes maximum loans.* (See p. 259) Under the VA program, limits on the amount of the guarantee on a loan, as well as the permissable duration of the loan, vary according to the type of security involved. (A GI home or business real estate loan may be made for a term of thirty years, a farm real estate loan for up to forty years, and a non–real estate loan for up to ten years.)
4. *Amortization plan.* VA loans may be amortized

[11] The licensee interested in further exploration of the various types of insurable loans under the FHA program is referred to the *Reference Book* of the California Department of Real Estate, and the FHA's *Digest of Insurable Loans,* available from the Department of Housing and Urban Development, Washington, D.C.

under any generally recognized plan used by established lending institutions. FHA must be amortized on the standard plan of equal payments.

5. *Prepayment of loan.* Under the VA, the debtor may make a full or partial prepayment (if not less than $100 or one installment). Some penalties for prepayments are permitted on loans insured under FHA.
6. *Refinancing of loans.* To avoid imminent default on a VA loan, the loan may be refinanced by the holder of the note under certain limitations. FHA loans are limited to three-fourths of the FHA estimate of the remaining economic life of the building.
7. *Loan appraisals.* The VA appraisal determines "reasonable value" as being a fair price or cost "in the light of prevailing conditions." For home loans, a correlation of all three methods of appraisal (comparative, replacement cost, and income) is employed. No VA loans are authorized in excess of the reasonable value or economic life of the property used as security for the note. *A veteran may pay more than the appraised value, but the excess must be paid in cash at the time of closing.*
8. *Purpose of the loan.* VA loans may also be made for the purpose of purchasing a farm or farm equipment, or for a business loan. The VA will require that the experience of the borrower and the conditions under which he proposes to operate are such that there is a reasonable likelihood of success.

Lending Agencies

Any bank, savings and loan association, insurance company, mortgage company, or other lending agency may make a VA loan. Residential loans must be paid off in full within thirty years; farm property loans within forty years, and non–real estate loans within ten years. There is no limit to the amount of money the veteran may borrow, as far as the VA is concerned, this being a matter between the veteran and the lending agency. In no event will the government guarantee exceed the amounts listed above.

Steps in Securing a VA Loan

1. The first step is for the veteran to find the property.
2. A sales agreement is usually drawn and a deposit paid to bind the agreement. This agreement normally provides for the return of the deposit in case the veteran fails to get the loan.
3. The proposition is presented to a bank or other lending agency. (When the loan is completed, the amount of the guarantee used is stamped on the back of the veteran's discharge papers.)
4. The lender now completes the processing of the loan, automatically committing the VA to a guaranty, without prior approval of the Veterans Administration.
5. The property is then checked by an appraiser qualified by the Veterans Administration, who then issues a Certificate of Reasonable Value (CRV) to the prospective lender. This bank or other lending agency then decides whether or not it will approve and make the loan.

The "package" is submitted to VA through the lender. This consists of the following:

1. Certificate of eligibility.
2. Form 1802 (four copies): application for home-loan guarantee.
3. Certificate of reasonable value (three copies).
4. Verification of deposit (four copies).
5. Verification of employment (four copies).
6. Signed purchase agreement (two copies).
7. VA release letter.

In most cases, these documents are all that will be required. In some instances, where an applicant may recently have gone through bankruptcy, had marital problems, or has some unfavorable items appearing on his credit report, further exhibits may be needed.

In cases where no real estate broker is involved in the sale, the VA will accept escrow instructions as evidence of the transaction, provided the instructions contain a clause reading substantially as follows:

> It is understood and agreed by all parties concerned that these escrow instructions are the only agreement between buyers and sellers, either verbal or written, and if this agreement is amended or altered in any way, then the Veterans Administration is to be made aware of said alteration prior to closing the loan being applied for.

Note: With respect to VA loans, it is especially important that *purchase agreements* and *amendments to purchase agreements* conform to VA requirements.

VA Loan Regulations

1. Lenders under VA regulations may charge "reasonable" costs. In the case of a home loan, they usually include the VA appraisal, credit report, survey, tax service, title evidence (A.T.A. policy), and recording fees. The veteran is not permitted to pay any escrow charges.
2. Under regulations, as of 1964, no down payment was required (except as required by the lender).
3. Prepayment of loan may be made (if not less than $100 or one installment) without penalty.
4. On home loans, the estimate of reasonable value is made after a correlation of the three appraisal approaches, that is, comparative, cost of reproduction, and income.
5. VA loans can also be made for the purchase of a farm or farm equipment or as a business loan, provided that there is reasonable likelihood of success.
6. Loans are made on homes only in case the borrower intends to become an owner-occupant. After living in his home, however, the veteran

may move out and rent it without affecting the loan.[12]

7. Should a veteran who has served in both World War II and the Korean Conflict secure a loan under the World War II Act and later sell his home (provided that the sale is consummated within his period of eligibility, and provided that the old loan at the time of application is not in default), he may take advantage again of full benefits under the Korean Act.
8. Residential loans must be paid off in full within 30 years; farm property loans, within 40 years.
9. The purchase agreement must stipulate that the veteran will not forfeit any portion of his deposit if he fails to qualify for the loan applied for.
10. In areas *where termites are prevalent,* the Veterans Administration requires Certificates of Reasonable Value on existing houses to carry the following clause:

The seller shall furnish the veteran purchaser at no cost to the veteran prior to settlement a written statement (or certification) from a recognized exterminator that there is no evidence of termite or other wood destroying infestation in the existing construction, and, if infestation had existed, it has been corrected and any damage due to infestation has also been corrected.

The lender files this certificate with other closing papers submitted to the Veterans Administration. Prior to closing, it is necessary for the veteran purchaser to submit a signed acknowledgment of receipt of the termite report or certification.[13]

Impounds

Lenders may require the buyer to provide reserves to insure that taxes and insurance may be paid when due. Part of each monthly payment is usually allocated for this purpose. In certain cases, however, the lender may be called upon to pay taxes for a six-month period before the borrower has paid in this amount. As an example, if real estate taxes on a property amounted to $600, with the sale of the property closing on September 1, the buyer would have paid in only two months' taxes (July and August). However, in order to protect the lender and the property the buyer would be required by the lender to provide a reserve of $300 for taxes at the time of closing. In some cases, the lender may require that the full year's taxes be impounded. *Note: See chart on impounds at end of the chapter.*

California Farm- and Home-Purchase Program

This program, created by the state legislature in 1921, permits the State Department of Veterans Affairs to assist qualified California veterans to acquire suitable farms or home property at low financing cost. Loans can be made only to native-born veterans or to those entering the service as California residents.

Funds to finance the program are obtained through the sale of the state's general-obligation bonds. The amount advanced by the state is repaid by the veteran at a low rate of interest through uniform monthly payments over a period of years. The program involves no expense to the taxpayers because the monthly payments made by the veteran cover all costs, including bond issuance, redemption and interest to bondholders, as well as the cost of administering the program.

Eligibility Requirements. To establish his eligibility, the veteran files an application for certificate of eligibility (Form DVA-1). The form, available at any office of the Department of Veterans Affairs, must be accompanied by a large clear photocopy of all discharges, notices of separation, or certificates of service. Any California veteran who served in the armed forces of the United States in time of war is eligible. He must have been born in California or have been a bona fide resident of the state on entry into active service and have served ninety days on active duty, a portion of which must have been in one of the following periods:

World War I ....
April 6, 1917 to November 11, 1918
World War II ....
December 7, 1941 to December 31, 1946
Korean Hostilities ....
June 27, 1950 to January 31, 1955
Army of Occupation of Berlin ....
May 9, 1945 to (still open)
Army of Occupation of Austria ....
May 9, 1945 to July 27, 1955
Navy Occupation of Austria ....
May 9, 1945 to October 25, 1955
Units of the Sixth Fleet (Navy) ....
May 9, 1945 to October 25, 1955
China Service Medal (Extended) ....
September 2, 1945 to April 1, 1957

Armed Forces Expeditionary Medal:

Lebanon ....
July 1, 1958 to November 1, 1958
Vietnam ....
July 1, 1958 to July 3, 1965
Quemoy and Matsu Islands ....
August 23, 1958 to June 1, 1963
Taiwan Straits ....
August 23, 1958 to January 1, 1959
Congo ....
July 14, 1960 to September 1, 1962
Laos ....
April 19, 1961 to October 7, 1962

[12] Permission must be granted by the VA, which is normally given only under special circumstances.

[13] *Real Estate Bulletin,* California Department of Real Estate, June 1964, p. 665.

Berlin . . . . August 14, 1961 to June 1, 1963
Cuba . . . . October 24, 1962 to June 1, 1963
Dominican Republic . . . . April 27, 1965 to (Still open)
Korea . . . . October 1, 1966 to (still open)
Vietnam Service . . . . Prior to August 5, 1964
Any theater after August 5, 1964

Also qualified are California veterans discharged with less than ninety days of service because of a war-service connected disability, and minors who have lived in the state for six months immediately preceding entry into the service in California. Veterans wounded or disabled due to their war service are given preference.

The department may advance on behalf of an eligible veteran up to $20,000 for the purchase of a home or $80,000 for the purchase of a farm. The amount advanced may not, however, exceed 95 percent of the department's appraisal of the property in the case of a home, or 90 percent of its appraisal for farm property. The difference between the sales price and the loan must be paid in cash. (Secondary financing is not permitted.)

What Type of Property is Qualified? Home property must be a *single-family residence* suitably located and must meet the *needs* of the veteran and his family as a residence. Farm property must be shown to be *adequate to provide a living* for the veteran and his family. In all cases the property value must provide sufficient security for the loan to be advanced.

The department will also finance the construction of a residence on a suitable lot in accordance with plans and specifications approved in advance, making progress payments as construction proceeds. The veteran must own the lot acceptable to the department and must agree to deed them this lot without cost. The building contractor must be licensed in California, must furnish an acceptable performance bond, and must agree to build in accordance with plans and specifications approved by the department. These requirements are, generally speaking, equivalent to those of the Federal Housing Administration under Title II, Section 203 (b). Full information regarding these requirements is available at any office of the Department of Veterans' Affairs, Division of Farm and Home Purchases.

The veteran will be required to deposit in escrow the amount needed to cover the difference between the amount authorized for advance by the department and the total cost of the improvements. A Cal-Vet loan cannot be made on a residentially improved property where the market value of the improvements exceeds $35,000.

Interest rate on Cal-Vet loans moves within a ceiling of 5 percent. Interest at 4.25 percent was current as of fall, 1971. However, this rate is subject to periodic redetermination. The contract price, the amount advanced by the department for the purchase, includes certain applicable charges, including fire-insurance premium, title-insurance premium, and in the case of the progress-payment plan, a processing charge. The usual contract period is twenty-three years. A charge of 2 percent of the original loan amount is charged if the contract is paid in full in less than two years from the date of the contract.

The veteran must agree to reside on the property, or agree that a member of his family will reside on the property within sixty days from date of the purchase of the property by the department. He must agree to maintain his residence there, and he may not transfer, assign, encumber, or rent the property without the written consent of the department.

Title is acquired by the Department of Veterans' Affairs and is resold to the veteran under a land-contract plan, with title remaining in the state of California under the DVA. Title is transferred to the veteran upon completion of his purchase contract. Each applicant approved for the purchase of a farm or home is required to apply for life insurance under the department's home-protection plan. Included in the plan are the following benefits:

Term insurance in the amount of the unpaid contract balance plus a 20 percent cash payment, subject to a $4,000 maximum.

Double indemnity for accidental death.

Disability insurance providing the veteran with monthly payments of $120 toward the purchase contract for each month the veteran is unable to work (excluding the first three months of his disability). The insurance coverage terminates at age sixty-five.

Second loans can be made only if the first property purchased is taken by condemnation. Loan balances may be transferred to other properties for reasons of job transfer or health. The time limit for eligibility for all veterans is November 13, 1972 for World War II and Korean veterans or twenty years after discharge from military service, whichever is later (subject to amendment by the state legislature).

Mortgage Discounts

"Points," as mortgage-discount rates are known, were discussed on pages 125 and 144, but further clarification of this very vital but often misunderstood subject might be in order here. By "points" we mean a loan-processing fee paid by the mortgage-borrower to a lender for the use of money. It represents the difference between the principal amount of a mortgage and the amount it sells for (figured on the amount of the loan rather than the sale price). Interest rates on FHA and VA loans are fixed by the federal government. Investors such as insurance companies, savings and loan companies, or commercial banks are interested in the *effective* yield on their investments. When the rates on government insured loans are lower than on other investments, the mortgage must be discounted to attract these investors.

If yields on mortgage loans are lower than on other investments, funds are drawn away from the mortgage market, making the money available for home financing scarcer and more expensive, which causes discount points to fluctuate. The quality of the property and the credit of the borrower also have a bearing on the discount rate.

Discount Point—1/8 percent. Because each discount point adds 1/8 percent to the yield on the mortgage, by charging two points, 2/8 percent (2 × 1/8 percent) is added to the interest rate returned by the loan (or 1/4 percent). With maximum rates (as of fall, 1971) fixed at 7-1/2 percent, by adding two discount points the yield to the lender is raised to 8 percent.

Real Estate Syndicates

The Real Estate Syndicate Act was signed into law and became operative January 2, 1970. Long popular in eastern states, syndication is a comparatively new type of real estate investment in California. The act applies to "noncorporate syndicates formed for the sole purpose of and engaged solely in investment in or gain from interest in real property."[14] The real estate commissioner has jurisdiction over syndicates covered by the act. Excluded from coverage are real estate investment trusts, real estate syndicates for which a registration statement has been filed under the Securities Act of 1933, nonpublic offerings, and syndicate offerings where more than 100 persons are involved. (Other exclusions relate to shares in mutual water companies, participating interests in oil, gas or mining titles or leases, and membership or share interest in a condominium or stock cooperative, and so on.)

The act applies to *offers* as well as to *sales* and an application must be filed and a permit obtained *before* real estate syndicate securities may be advertised, offered for sale, or sold to the public.

[14] *Reference Book.*

There are two basic approaches to organization of the syndicate. The syndicator may "acquire" the property through the use of the option or contract of sale, later syndicating its eventual acquisition. Or he may form the investment syndicate and then find the property for it to acquire. There are certain tax advantages to the syndicator in the first approach, but the valuable advantage of having the machinery set up for rapid acquisition of desirable properties makes the second approach desirable from this aspect.

The formation and operation of a real estate syndicate is so involved and so fraught with tax and legal implications that the real estate broker contemplating entering this field should prepare himself by consulting a competent tax attorney and obtaining applicable materials from the Department of Real Estate in Sacramento.[15]

Instruments of Finance

Mortgages and Deeds of Trust. The basic evidence of the debt or obligation is the *promissory note.* It is a negotiable instrument involving a written *promise* to pay money. There are three kinds of notes in general use with the mortgage and trust deed: (1) the straight note, calling for payment of interest only during the term of the note; (2) the installment note wherein periodic payments are made on the principal, such payments being separate from the interest payments; and (3) the installment note where certain periodic payments of fixed amounts are made, including both principal and interest.

To give the lender specific security for the borrower's obligation, it is customary in real estate financing to use the mortgage or trust deed for the incidental security, with the property itself as the basic pledge.

Mortgage is an all-embracing term used to define any legal financing instrument by which property is pledged *without transfer of title* as security for payment of a debt or obligation. It creates a *lien* on the property used for security. The *trust deed* in a broad sense is also a mortgage, but it has special features that identify it as the trust deed. As the name implies, the deed of trust involves an actual *transfer of a deed* to a trustee to be held for the fulfillment of an obligation. In California, the trust deed is in general use in preference to the mortgage. There are several reasons for this:

1. *Parties. In a mortgage, there are two parties,* a mortgagor (borrower) and a mortgagee (lender). Security for the loan advanced by the mortgagee is in the form of a lien on the property of the mort-

[15] See also the bibliography at the end of this chapter for publications relating to syndicates.

gagor. *In the deed of trust, there are three parties:* the trustor (borrower), the trustee, and the beneficiary (lender). Title to the property is conveyed by the trustor to the trustee as security for an obligation owed to the beneficiary. The title is reconveyed to the trustor when he performs the obligation (pays off the debt). In case the trustor fails to perform, the property may be sold at a public sale for the satisfaction of the obligation or debt.

2. *Title.* As was stated above, the mortgage *creates a lien.* The trust deed *conveys title* to a trustee. (In effect, it is also a lien.) Under the mortgage, an action to foreclose the mortgage is barred when the *statute of limitations* has run on the principal obligation. In the case of the trust deed, the trustee can still sell the property to pay off the debt of the borrower even though the statute of limitations has run on the note.

3. *Remedy.* The only remedy of the mortgagee under the mortgage is foreclosure (except in cases where the mortgage contains a power of sale). This involves securing a decree of foreclosure from the court and then having the property sold by the sheriff under the decree. With the trust deed, the beneficiary has the alternative of the *trustee's sale.*

4. *Redemption.* Under the mortgage foreclosed by court action, the right to redeem exists *for one year* after the sale. With the trust deed (or the mortgage with power of sale), the sale is *absolute;* in other words, there is no right of redemption.

5. *Deficiency Judgment.* This is a judgment given when the security pledge for a loan does not satisfy the debt upon its default. In cases of foreclosure sale, it is the difference between the net proceeds of the sale and the amount of the debt. (This includes interest and costs.)

Purchase-Money Mortgage. In cases where the seller of property carries back all or a portion of the purchase price secured by a mortgage or trust deed, a true purchase-money trust deed or mortgage is created. However, in California any loan made specifically for the purpose of purchasing property is held to be a purchase-money trust deed or mortgage. *In either case, there can be no deficiency judgment.* The purchase-money trust deed or mortgage given at the time of conveyance and recorded before other liens are created has priority over all other liens created by or against the purchaser.

"Subject to" Mortgage. When a grantee takes a title to real property subject to a mortgage, he is not responsible to the holder of the promissory note for the payment of any portion of the amount due. The most that he can lose in the event of a foreclosure is his equity in the property. (See also "Assumption of Mortgage" following.) In neither case is the original maker of the note released from his responsibility.

Assumption of Mortgage. When a grantee takes title to property wherein he assumes liability for payment of an existing note secured by a mortgage or deed of trust against the property, he becomes a coguarantor for the payment of a mortgage or deed-of-trust note. He is said to have "assumed" the note.

Second-Trust Deeds and Mortgages. The function of the second-trust deed or mortgage is to provide supplemental funds necessary to complete a property purchase. The difference between the amount of the first mortgage and the down payment made by the buyer must be provided by some type of "junior financing." This is normally provided by the second-trust deed or mortgage. To facilitate the sale of his property, the owner in many cases provides the financing. This type of junior financing constitutes a *purchase-money* trust deed and is held by the property owner as an investment or sold at a discount.

The second-trust deed or mortgage is also a popular type of financing with builders selling new homes. Another type of participant in the second-trust-deed market is the real estate broker who uses personal funds or invests his commission as an investment or as an incentive to expedite the sale of a property listed with him.

A report issued by the University of California at Los Angeles in 1960, referring to junior-financing activity in Los Angeles County in the years 1958–1959, reads in part:

> ...According to surveys of real-estate brokers and builders, the amount of second trust deeds typically ranged up to 25 percent of sales price; contract interest rates were about 6 to 8 percent exclusive of usually substantial commissions, fees, and other noninterest charges; and maturities clustered around 3 to 5 years. Most of the short-term trust deeds required a sizable "balloon payment" when the loan matures. Discounts in the sale of these instruments varied widely but were often 25 to 30 percent of their face value.[16]

As a result of the 1929 crash and the resultant depression, many property owners today are skeptical of the security of the second-trust deed. The informed real estate broker is in a strong position to advise the property owner of the difference between the types

[16] Leo Grebler and James Gillies, "Junior Mortgage Financing in Los Angeles County, 1958–1959," Research Report No. 2 (Los Angeles, University of California Graduate School of Business Administration), October, 1960, p. 7.

of loans in use prior to 1929 and those in general use today. The major points of variation to be pointed out are: (1) Previously, the loans involved *straight* notes with the entire amount due and payable one to five years from date. These notes could be called on their due date or refinanced at the option of the maker. Today, nearly all loans are of the *amortized* type. (2) Prior to 1929, the holder of the second-trust deed needed to be in position at all times of refinancing the first in order to protect his investment. Today, he may foreclose on his second and need only make the payments on the first during the time of the foreclosure. (Normally, this amounts to less than four monthly payments.)

Certain qualifications can be written into any secondary paper to further protect the holder. It is the responsibility of the real estate broker to alert any client considering this type of financing to all protective devices provided under the law. The holder of the second-trust deed should, for example: (1) stipulate that there be no acceleration clause in the first-trust deed; (2) specify a definite termination date for the note, requiring the property to be refinanced at that time; (3) write into the note before recordation an acceleration clause stipulating that the entire amount becomes due and payable under certain conditions (that is, if the property is sold or further encumbered); (4) record a "request for notice" that requests the trustee, in case of a foreclosure, to give notice to the junior-lien holder that the note is in default and foreclosure steps are being taken.

Subordination. An agreement written into the note providing that such lien will be subordinate in priority to any specific existing or anticipated future lien is known as a "subordination clause." This is used extensively by builders who, in order to secure financing to enter upon a building program, must show that they are the owners of the land but who do not wish to tie up needed capital. In such cases, the landowner may be persuaded to convey the property and carry back a mortgage. To place a construction loan on the land subsequent to the execution of a "purchase-money trust deed," a "subordinate agreement" is entered into. This agreement states that the mortgage given in payment for the land shall be subordinate to a first-trust deed to be placed on the property and shall become a second and subordinate to the first. The second is then paid off at the time the improved property is sold. This type of financing is customary where large residential income developments are being built for resale, as well as in the residential tract developments.

A subordination clause recital may read somewhat as follows:

> The parties hereto, for themselves, their heirs, devisees, successors and assigns, in consideration of the mutual benefits accruing to them and for the protection of the holder or holders of any note or notes secured by a deed of trust or mortgage covering said property, hereafter executed by the owner thereof and complying with the provisions hereinafter set forth, do hereby stipulate and agree as follows: That at all times during the life of the trusts created by this deed of trust, provided said deed of trust is not in default, there may remain and be placed, replaced, renewed, kept and maintained as a lien or charge upon said property, prior and superior to this deed of trust, a deed of trust or mortgage duly recorded, securing a note or notes not exceeding the principal sum of $________ and bearing interest at not more than ________ percent per annum; that any deed of trust or mortgage covering said property and complying with the foregoing provisions shall be deemed to be the deed of trust or mortgage contemplated hereby.

Unconventional Financing Methods

In certain areas and at certain times, FHA or GI financing is not available. To give maximum service to his client, the successful broker is prepared with information on the mechanics and security of many unconventional types of financing.

Contract of Sale. While all contracts providing for the sale of real property can be called contracts of sale, the generally implied meaning of the *land contract, installment sales contract,* or *agreement of sale* relates to a contract entered into between buyer and seller of property that is to be sold on an installment or *deferred-payment* plan. These contracts come under the Civil Code of California, which provides that contracts must be in writing, have parties capable of contracting, their consent, a lawful object, and a sufficient consideration. Specific performance, damages, or both, may be enforced by law. Under the land contract, the buyer becomes the equitable owner. Possession is normally given at once, although the seller retains the title. This type of contract is both an instrument of finance and a sales agreement.

Specifically, the contract provides for the seller to deliver the deed to the buyer under certain conditions, spelled out in the contract terms. Although legality is not so established, all land contracts should be recorded. *Any agreement in the body of the contract whereby the buyer agrees not to record is invalid.* Acknowledgment by the seller is all that is required for recordation. Constructive notice is given by virtue of the buyer taking possession.

Advantages and Disadvantages of the Land Contract. The land contract previously contained a forfeiture clause providing that, in the event the buyer missed a payment, the seller had the right of repossession, forfeiting all payments made by the buyer and eliminating any interests held by him. A recent court decision (*Barkis* v. *Scott*) accorded the defaulting buyer rights of redemption and reinstatement. Thus, the presumed advantage of this type of financing has been largely dissipated.

Disadvantages to the buyer of the land contract include the following:

1. Covenants in restriction of assignment or transfer of the land contract which hamper or prevent the transfer of his interest therein.
2. A prevailing opinion among financial institutions that a land contract is poor collateral because it is subject to a more rapid termination in the event of default.
3. After full performance by the buyer he may receive defective title or no title at all, although normally the contract will require delivery of a policy of title insurance. The buyer may find he has to pay the premium for this.
4. Lack of assurance that the seller has good title at the time the contract is made, coupled with the fact that prior to full performance by the buyer the latter may not rescind the contract on these grounds.
5. If during the interim from the execution of the contract to full performance by the buyer, the seller should be adjudicated a bankrupt, die and title pass to his heirs, be adjudicated an incompetent or have a conservator appointed, the buyer can with reasonable certainty anticipate time consuming, frustrating, and expensive litigation before he obtains his deed and policy of title insurance.[17]

In any real property sales contract entered into on or after January 1, 1969, the buyer is entitled to prepay all or any part of the balance due on the sale of land that has been subdivided into residential lots. This also applies to lots that contain a dwelling with not more than four families. The buyer cannot waive this right. If he agrees to do so by a clause in the contract, that clause, under the law, would be deemed unenforceable and void.

Hypothecation. Simply stated, *hypothecation* means giving something as security without actually giving up possession of it. Relating to real estate, it is a form of financing wherein the buyer signs a note and deed of trust to the seller for the full amount of his debt against the property. The seller then is in a position to borrow from a lending institution, assigning to them the note and deed of trust as security. This type of financing has certain advantages to the seller over more conventional financing: (a) it involves one collection in the place of two, as would be the case if secondary financing were involved (payments can be made to include taxes and insurance as well); (b) a due date could force refinancing at a specific time; and (c) in the event of a sale, the note is usually not discounted.

Real Estate Investment Trusts

A law enacted in September, 1960 authorized the formation of real estate investment trusts to invest in real estate and mortgages. This permits the small investor to become a participant in the purchase of real estate as an investment, much as he does in the "mutual funds" operation in the stock and bond markets. To qualify under the federal act, many rules and restrictions govern the operation of the real estate investment trust: (1) At least 75 percent of the invested capital of the trust must be in real estate (or real estate mortgages), cash, or government securities. (2) The real property must be held for *investment* and not for sale. To qualify for capital gains tax treatment, the property must be held for a minimum of four years. (3) At least 75 percent of the income must be derived from real estate properties, interest on real estate mortgages, or gain on the sale of real estate. (4) At least 90 percent of the net income must be distributed to the shareholders. (5) A trustee may not serve as manager of the trust properties. By adherence to these and other regulations, the real estate investment trust is qualified under the federal act and thus exempt from federal income tax (not, however, from state income tax where applicable).[18]

In California, as in many other states, further restrictive regulations were placed on the REIT by the commissioner of corporations. One of the most restrictive of these prohibits a trustee from selling property to the trust or from making a real estate commission on a sale to or by the trust.

Broker Acting as Loan Agent

Selling real estate is really selling financing. Because it is the rare buyer who pays all cash for a home, some type of financing is always required. Owing to the large volume of loan applications that may originate in an active real estate organization, the broker may wish on occasion to lend his own funds, those of his associates, or those of private investors. For many years it has been a requirement under the law that any person acting for compensation in negotiating a *new loan* or for selling an *exist-*

[17] *Reference Book, op. cit.*

[18] For further study, see *Reference Book,* Chapter 17.

Mortgage Lender Questionnaire and Checklist

CALIFORNIA REAL ESTATE ASSOCIATION

This checklist is designed to determine what charges, conditions and other aspects of a mortgage lender's official policy will apply to a loan committed for a particular property. Its use helps eliminate misunderstandings and uncertainty. Many conditions may be limited to a specific period of time, which should be so noted.

I. Assumption of Existing Loan

Will you permit a new purchaser to assume the outstanding balance of your loan?__________

1. What change in interest will occur?__________
2. Will this change in interest modify the monthly payments?__________
3. Are impounds included in the monthly payments?__________
4. What is the balance of the loan as of the first of the month?__________
5. What is the balance in the impound account as of the first of this month?__________
6. Are the payments current?__________
7. What fee will you charge for allowing this loan to be assumed including forwarding fees, etc?__________
8. What special T.D. terms apply, such as acceleration clause, etc?__________

Will you increase the balance of this loan by an additional advance?__________

1. To what amount?__________
2. At what interest rate?__________
3. Will impounds be required?__________
4. What fees will you charge for this assumption and advance?__________

Will your conditions or transfer be modified if a second trust deed is involved and if so in what manner__________

II. Commitment of a New Loan

Will you commit a loan on this property?__________

1. What amount or percentage of value will you commit?__________
2. What is the interest rate?__________
3. What discount or other charges do you make for this loan, including advance interest?__________
4. Do you require impounds?__________
5. What is the period of amortization?__________
6. What are the privileges of paying off the loan faster than amortized and what charges do you make for this?__________
7. If a second trust deed is involved as part down payment will this change your conditions and if so, how?__________
8. May this loan be transferred in the event of a future sale by the borrower, and if so, under what conditions?__________

III. Acceleration of Loan

Will you permit your loan to remain of record and continue to accept regular monthly payments in the event the status of the borrower is changed by:

1. Divorce__________
2. Death of one of the buyers (i.e. husband or wife)__________
3. Foreclosure by a junior lien holder.__________
4. Selling by Contract of Sale.__________
5. By placing an additional trust deed or security agreement on the property, including an "all inclusive" T.D.?__________

IV. Prepayment Conditions

1. What are the conditions under which this loan may be paid in full?__________
2. What charges or fees do you charge if paid in advance of schedule?__________
3. Are these charges eliminated or modified if the property is refinanced by you to:
   a. The present borrower?__________
   b. A new buyer?__________

V. Late Charges

1. How many days after a payment is due does a late charge become imposed?__________
2. Do you require payment of the late charge with the payment due or add it to the balance of the loan?__________
3. What notice do you send to a borrower notifying him of imposition of a late charge?__________

For these forms, address California Real Estate Association, 520 So. Grand Ave., Los Angeles 90017.

Form MLQ-11

Broker's Loan Statement

CALIFORNIA REAL ESTATE ASSOCIATION STANDARD FORM

(APPROVED BY STATE DIVISION OF REAL ESTATE)

The Peacock Real Estate Company
(Name of Firm)

123 Feather Lane, Arcadia, California
(Address)

Street and address number and/or legal description of property:

28 Winding Lane, Arcadia, California

Statement of all liens against property as disclosed by borrower:

First Deed of Trust	$12,500
	$
	$

1. Description of loan to be secured:

Principal sum of the note .... $ 3,000

Rate of interest per annum .... 8 %

Term of note .... Four years ..... Number of installments 48

Amount of each installment which includes interest and principal . . . $ 73.26

Approximate balance due at maturity . . . . $ None

Terms of prepayment privileges and penalties, if any

1 % of face value

2. Deductions from principal sum of the note:

(a) Maximum costs and expenses estimated by broker:

1. Appraisal fees	$20.00
2. Escrow fees	$35.00
3. Costs of investigating or guaranteeing title	$35.00
4. Notary fees	$none
5. Recording fees	$ 4.00
6. Credit investigation fees	$ 2.00

Give below any other costs and expenses:

7.	$ None
8.	$ None
9.	$ None

Total costs and expenses (1 to 9 inclusive) $96.00

(b) The total of the bonuses, brokerage or commissions contracted for or to be received by any person for negotiating, procuring, or arranging or making such a loan $450.00

(c) Estimated amounts to be paid on order of borrower:

1. Fire insurance premiums	$ None
2. Due on prior liens, including reconveyance, etc., fees	$ None
3. Due other creditors	$ None
4. Assumption, transfer, forwarding and beneficiary statement fees	$ None
5. Any premium or other charges for insurance, other than fire insurance	$ None

Other payments on order of borrower:

6.	$ None
7.	$ None
8.	$ None

Total estimated payments on order of borrower . . . . $ None

TOTAL DEDUCTIONS FROM PRINCIPAL SUM OF NOTE . . . . $ 546.00

For these forms address the California Real Estate Association, 117 W 9th St., Los Angeles 15, Rev. 11-15-63 Form #MS-14

("Principal sum of the Note" carried over from obverse side) . . . . $ 3,000.00

("Total deductions from principal sum of Note" carried over from obverse side) . . . . $ 546.00

3. Estimated balance to be delivered to borrower . . . . $ 2,454.00

(Based upon borrower's representations as to liens and debts)

LIST BELOW SERVICES WHICH MAY BE PERFORMED
BY BROKER UNDER ITEM 2a ABOVE.

Appraisal

Credit investigation

The undersigned broker or representative hereby states that the broker is not the lender and that the above described loan is being made in compliance with the California Real Estate Law.

Broker	License No.	Business Address
Wilbur W. Elliott,	52304,	123 Feather Lane, Arcadia
or Designated Representative	License No.	Business Address

(Note to Borrower: Do Not Sign This Statement in Blank. All Parts of This Form Must Be Filled Out **Before You Sign.**)

The borrower hereby acknowledges receipt of a copy of this statement.

Robert W. Turner (Borrower)

Dated: May 7, 1971 Charlotte D. Turner (Borrower)

ing note secured by real estate must hold a real estate license. In 1955, because of complaints of hidden and often exorbitant charges being made by some brokers, the Real Property Loan Brokerage Law was enacted. Irregularities continued in the bulk trust deed market, requiring more rigid control of what was termed the "ten percenter." AB 1344, passed in 1961 superseding the 1955 enactment, was considered the most comprehensive and stringent mortgage-loan legislation in the history of California.[19] This bill provided as follows: (1) With some additions and changes, most of the provisions of the old law were made a part of the real estate law. (2) A new classification for real estate brokers engaged in the sale of real property securities (real property securities dealers) was created. (3) Controls over their operations were established. Stronger provisions (especially concerning out-of-state sale of subdivisions) were enacted in 1963.

The controls do not apply when the real estate broker negotiates a loan in connection with a property sale or exchange, or the sale or exchange by him of a note in connection with such transaction. It does apply whenever the broker "solicits borrowers or lenders for or negotiates loans or collects payments or performs services for borrowers or lenders or note owners in connection with loans secured directly or collaterally by liens on property" or "sells or offers to sell, buys or offers to buy, or exchanges or offers to exchange a real property sales contract, or a promissory note secured directly or collaterally by a lien on real property and performs services for the holders thereof."

The broker may not legally accept funds in advance from a prospective purchaser or lender with the intention of purchasing notes or real property sales contracts or financing them as they become available. Other regulations that apply are: (1) Money may be accepted only for specified loans or specific sales contracts that the broker has a bona fide authorization to negotiate or to sell, or that he owns in their entirety, or for a specific note or real property sales contract that the broker is obligated to purchase under an unconditional written contract. (2) The broker who collects funds payable according to the terms of a note may not retain them for longer than sixty days without written agreement, in which case no interest may be charged. (3) A written authorization from the borrower is required for the real estate broker to make collections on notes secured by trust deeds or sales contracts. (4) Prohibited are any advertisements that indicate or imply any specific yield or return on any note other than the *interest rate specified* in the note or the discount at which the note is being offered.

Recordation. Every real estate licensee who negotiates a loan secured by a trust deed on real property has the responsibility, under Section 10234 of the Business and Professions Code, to have the trust deed recorded with the county recorder of the county in which the property is located prior to the time that any funds are disbursed, unless the lender has given written authorization for prior release. The trust deed must name as beneficiary the lender or his nominee, who may not be the licensee or his nominee.

If the funds are released on the lender's written authorization, the trust deed must be recorded or delivered to the lender or beneficiary with a written recommendation that it be recorded within *ten* days following the release.

Advertising. False, misleading, or deceptive advertising in connection with making, purchasing, or negotiating loans is strictly prohibited. The advertisement may not indicate or imply any specific yield or return on any note other than the interest rate specified in the note, unless the advertisement sets forth the *actual* interest rate specified in the note and the discount from the outstanding principal at which it is being offered for sale.

Offering of Premiums or Gifts. The licensee is prohibited from offering or giving premiums or gifts as an inducement for making real property loans.

Maximum Commissions and Charges. The broker negotiating "hard money" loans comes under two further regulations: (1) He is restricted as to the amount of commissions and other charges that he may make, and (2) he is required to complete a Broker's Loan Statement.[20]

A table of maximum commission rates follows. These rates do not apply to any bona fide loan secured by a first-trust deed, the principal sum of which is $12,000 or more, or to any bona fide loans secured directly or collaterally by any junior lien, the principal of which is $6,000 or more.[21]

First-trust deeds commission maximums:

5 percent for a loan of less than three years.
10 percent for a loan of three years or more.

Second- or other junior-trust deeds commission maximums:

5 percent for a loan of less than two years.

[19] See "Regulations of Real Property Loan Transaction", *Reference Book.*

[20] See sample broker's loan statement, pp. 136 and 137.

[21] These maximum charges do not apply to FHA loans, bank loans, or savings and loan association loans.

DISCLOSURE STATEMENT OF REAL ESTATE LOAN

(Required and made in compliance with Federal Truth in Lending law)

BROKER/ARRANGER OF CREDIT:

____

(Name)

____

(Address)

Purpose of Loan: ______________________

____

LENDER-CREDITOR: (if not known, insert "the person to be designated as".)

____

(Name)

____

(Address)
beneficiary of Deed of Trust
which secures this credit transaction.

BORROWER

____

(Name)

____

(Address)

Loan of $ ____________ to be secured by Deed of Trust in favor of lender-creditor on property located at ________________________, which (is) (is not) expected to be used as Borrower's principal residence. (If it is, provide Recission Statement.)

Deed of Trust covers after-acquired property and may secure additional advances. The loan may also be secured by an assignment of proceeds from any required insurance protecting this property. **FINANCE CHARGE** accrues from ____.

1. Appraisal fees . . . . $ ____________________
2. Credit Investigation fees . . . . $ ____________________
3. Notary . . . . $ ____________________
4. Recording fees . . . . $ ____________________
5. Cost of guaranteeing title . . . . $ ____________________
6. Escrow fees . . . . $ ____________________
7. Tax service . . . . $ ____________________
8. . . . . $ ____________________
9. . . . . $ ____________________

Total Charges . . . . $ ____________________

Property insurance, if required and written in connection with this loan, may be obtained by borrower through any person of his choice.

II. Other Charges which are part of FINANCE CHARGE:

A. Bonus, brokerage, or commission contracted for or to be received by any person for negotiating, procuring or arranging or making such loan **(PRE-PAID FINANCE CHARGE)** $ ____________

B. Interest for period of loan (at full rate of _______%): $ ____________

Total **FINANCE CHARGE** $ ____________

On prepayment in full, unaccrued interest is cancelled and there is a prepayment charge of ____________

III. **Amount Financed:**

Amount of Note (includes all charges in Item I) $ ____________
Less: Prepaid **FINANCE CHARGE** (Item IIA) $ ____________

Total AMOUNT FINANCED $ ____________

IV. **ANNUAL PERCENTAGE RATE:** ____________ % or ____________ dollars **FINANCE CHARGE** per year per $100 of unpaid balance.

V. **Loan Terms:** ____________ monthly installments of $ ____________ each beginning ____________ 19 ____ and a final/balloon payment of $ ____________ on ____________ 19 ____ .

TOTAL OF PAYMENTS $ ____________

(Any payment which is more than twice the amount of a regular payment must be identified as a "balloon" payment; otherwise mark the word "final".)

VI. **Late Charge:** If a monthly installment is not paid within ____________ days after due date, a charge off ____________ must be paid by borrower.

READ BEFORE SIGNING

I have read and received a completed copy of this statement.

DATE ____________________, 19 ____

____

(Borrower)

____

(Spouse)

____

(Other Person To Whom Disclosure Is Given)

*Important Note: Asterisk denotes an estimate.

10 percent for a loan of between two and three years.
15 percent for a loan of three years or more.

No loan secured directly or collaterally by a lien on real property may provide for payment of interest in excess of 10 percent, as stipulated by the Usury Law of California. No interest may be charged for any period prior to the date that the proceeds of the loan are made available to the borrower or are deposited in escrow.

Maximum Expense Chargeable to the Borrower. The charges (aside from the commissions referred to above) that may be made for any loan subject to the provisions above are as follows:

The maximum amount of all costs and expenses to be paid by the borrower may not exceed 4 percent of the principal amount of the loan or one hundred sixty-five dollars ($165), whichever is greater, but in no event may it exceed two hundred ninety-five dollars ($295). This maximum amount may not exceed actual costs and expenses paid, incurred, or reasonably earned.

Note: Under the law, any loan providing for installment payments, and secured by a lien on real property, which has a term of less than three years, must provide for substantially equal installment payments over the period of the loan, with the final payment not payable until the maturity date of the note. *Exempted from this regulation is the note given back to the seller by the purchaser on account of the purchase price (a purchase-money mortgage).*

Broker's Loan Statement. This form must be completed and signed by the borrower *before* the loan is consummated. The estate licensee who is an authorized representative of such institutional lenders as a bank, savings and loan association, or insurance company, and whose commission rate does not exceed 2 percent is not required to complete the broker's loan statement. (*The broker is required to keep a copy of the statement, as signed by the borrower, for a period of four years.*)

Real Property Securities Dealer

A real property securities dealer is defined as "a person acting as a principal or agent who engages in the business of:

(a) Selling real property securities to the public (securities as defined under Section 10237.1 of the real estate law), or

(b) Offering to accept or accepting funds for continual reinvestment in real property securities or for placement in an account, plan, or program where the dealer implies that a return will be derived from a specific real property sales contract or promissory note secured directly or collaterally by a lien on real property which is not specifically stated to be based upon the contractual payments thereon."

"Sale to the public" is interpreted as excluding sales to corporations, to pension, retirement, or similar trust funds, to institutional lending agencies, or to real estate brokers, attorneys, or licensed general building contractors.

Real Property Securities. These are defined as deeds of trust sold under an investment contract where the dealer guarantees the deed of trust in any-one of several ways, or makes advances to or on behalf of the investor. Also included is the sale of one of a series of "promotional notes" or sales contracts.

Real Property Securities Permit. A permit must be obtained from the real estate commissioner before selling real property securities to the public.

Advertising. All advertising material to be used must be filed with the commissioner ten days prior to its use. No dealer may use such material after receiving notice in writing that the material contains statements that are false or misleading or fails to include information necessary to make the statements complete and accurate.[22]

Consumer Credit Act (Truth-in-Lending Law—Regulation Z)

A law designed to tell the customer how much he is paying for credit and the relative cost of credit expressed in percentage terms became effective July 1, 1969. Known as the truth-in-lending law, it applies to all real estate loans for personal, family, household, or agricultural purposes. Business loans are exempted.

Advertising. The law does not apply to normal real estate advertising *unless* the advertising refers to any of the following:

(a) The *rate* of interest on an existing mortgage, or a new mortgage, such as a purchase-money mortgage.
(b) The *down payment* or lack of down payment.
(c) The *amount* of installment payment, the *dollar amount of finance charges,* the *number of installments,* the *period of payment,* or the absence of a charge for credit.

Example:

If the advertisement states:

"Sales price $28,500 with 10 percent down,

[22] Further information on real property securities, including a schedule of fees for permit applications may be obtained from the office of the real estate commissioner of the state of California in Sacramento.

FHA 7 percent loan available,"
and no more information is given, there are *two* violations of the law.

If the advertisement reads:

"Sales price is $28,500. Good financing available," there is *no* violation.

If the advertisement reads:

"Sales price $28,500 with twenty years to pay," there *is* a violation unless the full law is complied with.

If the advertisement reads:

"Sales price $28,500. Payments only $187 per month,"
there *is* a violation.

If the advertisement reads:

"Sales price $28,500, with owner financing,"
there is *no* violation.

The legal requirement is that if you mention in the advertisement any one of the rates or terms or amounts of financing, you must disclose *all* of the financing provisions. These disclosures in advertising rules are basically applications of the finance-charge and annual percentage-rate concepts.

Finance charge is the sum total of *all* costs of originating and carrying credit sales or loans. This is stated in a *dollar amount.*

Annual percentage rate is the division of the net credit or loan into the finance charge, computed as a yearly *interest percentage.*

If the advertisement includes any of the following:

(a) $500 down.
(b) Nothing down.
(c) $300 per month.
(d) Only $280 finance charges.
(e) Pay balance over sixty months.
(f) Balance over fifteen years.
(g) No charge for financing.

Then the advertisement must include *all* of the following:

(1) Cash price or loan amount.
(2) Whatever down payment is required.
(3) The number of payments required to pay off the loan.
(4) The amount of each payment.
(5) The due date of each payment.
(6) The total amount of finance charges expressed in the annual percentage rate.
(7) Except in the case of a home purchase-money mortgage or first-trust deed on a dwelling, the total deferred payment price or the total sum of all payments must be stated.

Example: A lot sale, where the owner carries 90 percent of the financing at 8 percent, with monthly payments extending over ten years. The buyer will then know that whereas the loan may be $6,000, he is paying an additional $4,800 over the ten-year period, and this is a finance charge stated in a dollar amount. The exception is if this is a purchase mortgage first-trust deed for a dwelling.

Note: Advertising means publication in newspaper, magazine, leaflet, catalog, radio, television, public-address system, billboard, office advertising signs, or display cards. A letter written to a customer is not considered an advertisement. Neither is a contract, escrow instructions, or other documents not published for consumption.

Right of Recision

The truth-in-lending law gives the owner or buyer of a dwelling the right to rescind a contract of finance, credit, or extension of services within three days after the disclosure notice has been given him.[23]

The law applies only to credit involving the actual and existing or anticipated dwelling of the borrower or customer. It does *not* apply to open credit transactions given agricultural borrowers, whether or not they live on the farm. This section does *not* apply to a purchase-money mortgage, purchase of home contract or any first-trust deed used to purchase or build the dwelling of the borrower or creditor. The section does apply to any credit transaction that would be a non-purchase-money first- or second-trust deed or other security interest in the dwelling property of the borrower of customer.

Penalties

Penalties can be threefold:

(a) Criminal liability
(b) Civil liability
(c) Loss by rescision.

Criminal. For criminal liability to apply, one must knowingly, willfully, and intentionally disclose false information, use the wrong interest tables, fail to disclose or give notice of the right to rescind, or violate the advertising provisions. The fine can be as high as $5,000. Jail can be as long as one year. *Both can be imposed.* The prosecution would be handled by the U.S. attorney general.

Civil Liability. For failure to disclose to the consumer the creditor can be sued for: (a) twice the amount of the finance charge, but no less than $100 nor more than $1,000; (b) court costs and attorney fees. The statute of limitations limits the civil liability to one year after date of the occurrence of the violation. There is no liability to a medium in or through which an improper or illegal advertisement appears or is broadcast. The Federal Trade Commission is

[23] For copy of the notice-of-right-to-cancel form see p. 142.

(Creditor)

(Office)

(City)

NOTICE OF RIGHT TO CANCEL

Name(s) of Customer(s)________________

Type of Loan________________

Amount of Loan________________ **$**________

Notice To Customer Required By Federal Law:

You have entered into a transaction on ________________, 19____ which may result in a lien, mortgage, or other security interest on your home. You have a legal right under federal law to cancel this transaction, if you desire to do so, without any penalty or obligation within three business days from the above date or any later date on which all material disclosures required under the Truth in Lending Act have been given to you. If you so cancel the transaction, any lien, mortgage, or other security interest on your home arising from this transaction is automatically void. You are also entitled to receive a refund of any down payment or other consideration if you cancel.

If you decide to cancel this transaction you may do so by notifying:

(Name of Creditor)

at ________________

(Address of Creditor's Place of Business)

by mail or telegram sent not later than midnight of ____________, 19____.

(Date 3 business days after date of receipt of this notice.)

You may also use any other form of written notice identifying the transaction if it is delivered to the above address not later than that time. This notice may be used for that purpose by dating and signing below.

I hereby cancel this transaction.

________________, 19____ (Date)

________________ (Customer's signature)

____

ACKNOWLEDGMENT OF RECEIPT

I hereby acknowledge receipt of TWO copies of the foregoing Notice of Right to Cancel.

________________, 19____ (Date)

________________ (Customer's Signature)

________________ (All joint owners must sign)

See reverse side for important information about your right of rescission.

Form RZ 226.9

For these forms address California Real Estate Association,
520 So. Grand Ave., Los Angeles 90017

EFFECT OF RESCISSION

When a customer exercises his right to rescind, he is not liable for any finance or other charge, and any security interest becomes void upon such a rescission. Within 10 days after receipt of a notice of rescission, the creditor shall return to the customer any money or property given as earnest money, down payment, or otherwise, and shall take any action necessary or appropriate to reflect the termination of any security interest created under the transaction. If the creditor has delivered any property to the customer, the customer may retain possession of it. Upon the performance of the creditor's obligations under this section, the customer shall tender the property to the creditor, except that if return of the property in kind would be impracticable or inequitable, the customer shall tender its reasonable value. Tender shall be made at the location of the property or at the residence of the customer, at the option of the customer. If the creditor does not take possession of the property within 10 days after tender by the customer, ownership of the property vests in the customer without obligation on his part to pay for it.

NOTICE OF INTENT TO PROCEED

I hereby certify that I have elected not to cancel or rescind the transaction referred to on the reverse side and that I have not delivered, mailed or filed for transmission by telegram to the Creditor any notice of cancellation or rescission of that transaction.

_______________________, 19_______
(Date and mail or deliver no sooner than 3 business days after date of receipt)

____
(Customer's Signature)

____
(All joint owners must sign)

ESTIMATING BUYERS CHARGES FOR TAX IMPOUNDS

WHERE LENDER PAYS ½ TAXES WHEN DUE

Date of Escrow Closing	1st Payment Will Be	Months Impounded	Months Prorated	Total Adjustment
1-31	3-1	0	5	5
2-28	4-1	1	4	5
3-31	5-1	2	3	5
4-30	6-1	3	2	5
5-30	7-1	4	1	5
6-30	8-1	5	0	5
7-31	9-1	6	(1)CR	5
8-31	10-1	7	(2)CR	5

WHERE LENDER PAYS FULL TAXES WHEN DUE

1-31	3-1	4	5	9
2-28	4-1	5	4	9
3-31	5-1	6	3	9
4-30	6-1	7	2	9
5-30	7-1	8	1	9
6-30	8-1	9	0	9
7-31	9-1	10	(1)CR	9
8-31	10-1	11	(2)CR	9

To determine monthly impounded amount take actual taxes after disallowing any exemptions plus 10% for future increases and divide by 12.

Should escrow close prior to date on chart pro-rations will increase for that portion of the month due to or from seller to buyer. For example: closing on 1-15 total adjustments = 5½ mo.

Hazard insurance will be ½ of annual or 1/36 of 3 year premium as monthly amount with 2months due on closing.

Mutual Mortgage Insurance will be 1/12 of ½ of 1% of average principal balance with 2 months due on closing.

CLOSING GUIDELINES

POINTS

Whether called POINTS, DISCOUNTS, LOAN BROKERAGE FEE, or NEW LOAN FEE–they're all the same. POINTS provide the MAGIC behind over half the home sales in this area. Without Points, most new loans and sales with low down payments would not be possible. So, since POINTS are a very vital part of today's home selling picture, an understanding of them is important.

1. What are POINTS? Thru the use of POINTS, money is paid to lending institutions (Banks, Savings & Loans, Mortgage Co's., etc.) so lenders will be able to make loans on property under the existing money market conditions. POINTS result in INCREASING THE YIELD or RATE OF RETURN to lenders.

2. How are POINTS figured? Very easy – One POINT is just one percent of the new loan amount. So if the current market is "5 POINTS," it means that the POINTS on a $15,000 loan would be 5% x $15,000 or $750. Note that the POINTS are figured on the amount of the new loan, NOT the selling price of the property.

3. Why are POINTS necessary on New FHA and GI Loans? In order to allow more people to buy their own home, the U.S. government establishes the maximum interest rate borrowers may be charged on any Government Insured loans, which are either FHA or GI loans. It is important to realize that the Government does not loan the money, but insures its repayment to the lender. The most important factor is that THE INTEREST RATE FIXED BY THE GOVERNMENT IS NOT ENOUGH TO ATTRACT TODAY'S LENDING INSTITUTION. There are many places where money can be invested, such as stocks, bonds, conventional loans, – where the rate of return to a lender may exceed that obtainable from FHA or GI loans. To make FHA GI loans sufficiently attractive in order to compete with other types of investments, the idea of paying POINTS was developed. POINTS make the difference – and enable lenders to make FHA and GI loans.

4. Why do POINTS vary? The "cost" of borrowing money goes up and down, depending on the demand for money and the supply available. It is perhaps similar to the stock market – the price of any stock will rise or fall depending on its demand. Heavy demands on the available money supply thru business expansion, requirements of a military effort or Government anti-inflation policies, all have a MAJOR effect on the availability of money.

THE RESULT IS THAT MONEY FOR THE HOME MORTGAGE MARKET BECOMES MORE SCARCE AND MORE EXPENSIVE THUS ACCOUNTING FOR THE VARIATION IN POINTS ON GOVERNMENT FIXED RATE FHA AND GI MORTGAGES.

5. Why must the Seller pay the POINTS? Government regulations on FHA and GI loans DO NOT ALLOW THE BUYER TO PAY POINTS. Actually, the Buyer does pay a "Loan Origination Fee" to the lender in the amount of 1% of the new loan.

6. Why should the Seller pay POINTS? By paying the necessary POINTS, the Seller makes it possible for his property to be sold thru FHA or GI financing. In lower priced and medium priced homes, the overwhelming majority of home buyers obtain FHA or GI loans. The low-down payment, low interest rate, and long term loans result in reduced monthly payments which enable many people to buy homes who otherwise could not afford one. To obtain a Non-Government insured loan, or what is normally referred to as a Conventional Loan, a Buyer must pay a much larger amount down (usually a minimum of 20-25% of the purchase price), a higher interest rate, and oftentimes for a shorter term resulting in higher payments. Therefore, it can be seen that these FHA and GI loans bring many, many more buyers in to the market and, as a result, greatly improve the opportunity for a property owner to make a sale. Because a new loan can be placed on an existing home, a Seller can effectively compete with the Builder of new homes by also being able to offer a minimum down FHA or GI loan. (The Builder must pay POINTS, too.)

7. How about just adding the POINTS to the Selling Price? On FHA or GI loans, the property must be appraised by a Government appraiser. The Buyer may pay any amount he agrees to – even more than the appraised amount – BUT that additional amount MUST be all in cash. Although there are exceptions in some areas, generally a Buyer will not be willing to pay more than the value placed on the property by the Government appraiser. So if adding the POINTS to the overall selling price makes the new selling price greater than the appraised value – the result is that the property is over priced and much less likely to sell.

SUMMATION: To sell the majority of property today we not only need a Buyer ready, willing, and able to buy – we also need to obtain financing. The very excellent Government-regulated FHA and GI programs allow most people to become Buyers with a small cash outlay. We can obtain the financing because of POINTS. Thru the use of this tool, Lenders are able to invest their money in FHA and GI Loans and still realize a rate of return comparable to other investment opportunities. Thus it can be said that POINTS ARE INDEED THE MAGIC INGREDIENT BEHIND A LARGE PORTION OF ACTIVITY IN THE WORLD OF REAL ESTATE.

California Real Estate Association
Closing Guidelines
1971

charged with enforcement of the law as it applies to real estate brokers.[24]

CASE STUDY

Paul Atkins and his wife Cynthia, a young newly married couple come to broker Kaupp's real estate office stating they are in the market for a home. Kaupp takes them into his private office to discuss the listings the firm is offering that might suit their needs. Atkins tells Kaupp he is employed as credit manager at the local building-supply company.

After having Atkins complete a brief home buyer's problem-analysis form,[25] Kaupp reviews their answers. He learns that Paul Atkins has an annual salary of $15,000. His wife is employed as a dental assistant, and their combined take-home pay is $18,000. They are presently renting an unfurnished apartment, for which they pay $200 a month rent. They are buying their furniture on contract, with monthly payments of $130. There are fourteen months remaining on the contract. They own a late-model automobile, with an approximate contract balance due of $2,500, on which they are making monthly payments of $92. The contract runs for two more years.

On the credit side, the Atkinses have a $4,000 savings account in the local savings and loan company. Paul Atkins carries a $10,000 life-insurance policy naming his wife as beneficiary. The policy has a cash value of $1,800. They also have ten shares of General Motors stock with a current total market value of $800.00.

After analyzing their financial standing and taking into account Mr. Atkins's position with the lumber company, Mr. Kaupp suggests that they would probably like to buy in one of the executive areas of the city. He believes they should be looking at homes in the $30,000 to $32,000 class. Among the homes he shows them is a ranch-style newer home in top condition in a well-kept attractive neighborhood. The home is priced at $32,000 and the owner says the price is firm. There is an existing loan balance of approximately $20,000 on the property, payable $131.20 a month, including principal and annual interest of 6-1/2 percent. The owners have indicated they might be willing to carry back a small purchase-money second-trust deed, but they will want 8 percent interest and amortization of the note in three years from date. The taxes on the home are $620.00.

Broker Kaupp has obtained a conditional loan commitment from the local savings and loan association for 80 percent of the purchase price with interest at 7.2 percent for a twenty-five year term. There will be a 1 percent loan cost. No secondary financing is permitted, and the lender requires that taxes and insurance premiums be placed in an impound account.

The Atkinses like the home but are hesitant about going into debt any further at the present time. They feel they should leave a minimum of $1,000 in their savings account for emergencies. They return to the office with broker Kaupp, who after some calculations is persuaded that the Atkinses can handle the purchase and upkeep of the property without undue burden on their finances.

1. Estimate the total monthly payments that the Atkinses can safely make on the home.
2. Would it be better for them to apply for a new loan on the property? What problems might arise in this case?
3. Do you believe that they would qualify for the 80 percent loan that is available?
4. Would you suggest that they try to assume the loan of record and accept the owner's offer to carry back a purchase-money second-trust deed: Why, or why not?
5. In the final analysis, would you consider the Atkinses a good credit risk for this particular home purchase?

SUGGESTED REFERENCES

GARVEY, GEORGE, and MARTIN R. BLYN, *The Velocity of Money.* New York: Federal Reserve Board, 1970.

HIRSCH, FRED, *Money International, Economics and Politics of World Money.* Garden City, N.Y.: Doubleday & Company, Inc., 1970.

KLARREICH, HAROLD, "Land Contracts; an Aid to Selling Homes," *Real Estate Today.* Chicago: National Institute of Real Estate Brokers of the National Association of Real Estate Boards, October, 1970.

PUGH, J. W., and WILLIAM H. HIPPAKA, *California Real Estate Finance.* Englewood Cliffs, N.J.: Prentice-Hall, Inc., 1966.

SMITH, BURT, "Real Estate Syndicates," *Real Estate Investment Property.* Los Angeles: California Real Estate Association, 1964.

STEIN, CHARLES, "The Creative Use of Secondary Financing in Today's Tight Money Market," *Real Estate Today.* Chicago: National Institute of Real Estate Brokers of the National Association of Real Estate Boards, October, 1970.

YEAGER, PHILIP J., "Financing the Home," *Selling Real Estate.* Los Angeles: California Association of Real Estate Boards, 1970.

——— *Real Estate Syndication Workbook.* Los Angeles: California Real Estate Association, 1970.

[24] For further information on the truth-in-lending law (Regulation Z) it is recommended that the student write to Truth-in-Lending, Federal Trade Commission, Box 36005, San Francisco, Calif. 94102.
Portions of the above are taken from the booklet *Truth in Lending* published by the Sacramento Building Industry Association, Inc., 2 Sacramento Inn Plaza, Sacramento, Calif. (available by writing to the publishers at the above address).

[25] For copy of this form see p. 105.

10

Closing the Sale

Before any sale can be closed, there must be a realistic seller and a realistic buyer. Careful groundwork must be laid at the inception of the selling process to assure that only property seriously for sale will be listed. The *Attention* of the buyer is attracted to a well-listed property. He goes then from *Attention* to *Interest* to *Desire,* leaving only the last step (*Action*) to be completed.

The salesman who attempts to put Action before any of the other three steps in violating the basic precepts of successful selling; that is, the steps must follow in logical sequence. Reversal or omission of anyone of the steps results in disorganization of the entire selling process. Conversely, where there is a single-mindedness of purpose and no digression from a carefully charted course, the procedure leads to a successful conclusion of the sale. The basic difference between the top producer and the mediocre salesman (or the complete failure) is his ability to *close.* The inexperienced salesman demonstrates his ineptness when he assumes that there is a magic formula for closing a sale. The *professional* salesman recognizes that: (1) There is no precise, perfect, psychological time to close; (2) Closing is an integrated part of the entire sales process; (3) Closing of the sale has its inception at the time listing; and (4) With the right property and a qualified buyer, the sale falls together naturally.

Four important steps are involved, however, in the carefully organized *closing* process:

(1) Getting step-by-step agreements from the buyer.
(2) Pointing out the buyer benefits of each step.
(3) Using the "which" rather than the "what" approach.
(4) Asking for the deposit.

Getting step-by-step agreement from the buyer (closing on a minor point) is an established principle of selling. The effective salesman must be part psychologist. He studies his buyer, learns his motives, and attempts to satisfy his needs. By granting concessions on minor points, the buyer is led to an eventual complete acceptance.

If, through *intelligent sales arguments,* the buyer is persuaded that the property is right for him, the sale has been made. Although the buyer is interested in the *benefits* accruing to him through ownership of the property, without the help of the salesman he may not recognize these benefits, whether acknowledged or not. The buyer's hesitation usually stems from a sense of fear, particularly if he is buying for the first time. The prospect may sincerely want to be *convinced,* but many salesmen fail in their selling job by not closing at this point. Once having uncovered the reasons for his fear, the salesman must gain the confidence of the buyer through tactful persistence bolstered by informative arguments.

Financing fears, probably more than any other, plague the average buyer. These can be dispelled by the salesman who is conversant with the current sources and types of financing that are available, and who is qualified to tailor the financing to meet the buyer's needs.

This requires careful appraisal of the buyer's financial situation. Given a choice of several types of financing, he may study each one and determine for himself the one best suited to his particular situation.

Buyer Fears

Among other fears evidenced by the prospect in the form of objections is the familiar: "I think I'll wait until prices come down." With the trend in property values in the state consistently up, the salesman has only to quote available facts and figures (obviously he must take the trouble to search them out). Bearing this out, stories are legion of buyers who have become wealthy through wise investments in California real estate. Just as numerous also are tales of those who have missed golden opportunities through not recognizing and so not taking advantage of properties presented to them.

"I want to think it over." This is typical of the timid prospect or the buyer who has still to be convinced. He has fears that have not been resolved and questions that are still unanswered. His fears may revolve around uprooting his family from familiar environs to take up life in new surroundings where new social and business contacts must be made. He wants most of all to be told that he is making a wise choice. This type of buyer, more than any other, requires the confident, firm, businesslike approach from the salesman who is sensitive to the buyer's needs. This can only be developed through experience; but once the salesman has demonstrated that he has the courage to meet the situation, he often finds a grateful buyer who becomes his best source of referred business.

Getting the Offer

When the prospect has made his final selection of the properties shown him, there is the offer to be considered. Much has been written about asking the prospect to buy, asking for the check or employing other methods to motivate action on the part of the buyer indicating his readiness to buy. Each is an individual situation and the salesman normally has to "play it by ear." Once the prospect has indicated his satisfaction with the property, there should be no reason for delaying the drawing of the purchase contract. Rarely does the buyer offer the full asking price of the property. Often this is the fault of the salesman, who has become accustomed to receiving low offers and expects to play the role of negotiator between buyer and seller.

If the property has been carefully evaluated at the time of the listing and if there has been a professional presentation to the buyer, the margin between the listed price and the buyer's offer should not vary more than 5 percent on the average-priced home. As an agent of the seller, the licensee has an obligation to obtain the highest price possible in the market. Too often this is forgotten in the salesman's haste to "write up a deal" or to "get an offer" (regardless of how ridiculous the offer may be).

It is at this point that the salesman maintains or loses the respect of the buyer, depending upon how professionally he handles the closing of the transaction. The salesman who takes a firm stand (backed by his knowledge of property values) can usually raise the low offer to a more equitable one. The buyer normally wants only to know that he is getting full value for his money. Use of the competitive market analysis (discussed in Chapter 5) is one of the strongest arguments the salesman can employ to support his valuation of the property selected. In addition to the responsibility that the salesman bears as an agent of the seller, there are important other reasons why he should obtain the highest possible offer at the outset. Often the buyer is willing to pay more for the property than his first offer would indicate. (1) If the salesman can persuade him to make his highest offer at the inception, it obviates the necessity of continued negotiations, during which time the property may be sold. (2) The seller is more responsive when he knows that the buyer is making his highest offer, and so he is more amenable to acceptance of any contingencies in the deposit receipt.

Writing the Contract

Once the offer has been made, it must be reduced to writing, in the form of a *purchase contract and receipt for deposit.*[1] The purpose of this document is twofold. It serves as a receipt for all monies received and, properly drawn and signed by buyer and seller, it constitutes a legal, binding sales agreement. The buyer may wish to include in the contract one or more sale contingencies (or *subject to's*) relating to: possession date, financing terms, approval of title report, personal property, or zone change, among others. Because of the complexities of a real estate transaction, if an offer is to be considered bona fide, it must be in writing. The verbal offer binds no one and should never be presented to a seller. The prospect who discounts the necessity of a written and signed sales contract cannot be considered a legitimate buyer.

Asking for the Deposit

A substantial deposit (preferably not less than 5 percent of the amount of the offer) is necessary to lend stature to any offer. It is often the size of the deposit by which the seller evaluates the sincerity of

[1] See pp. 153–155 for completed real estate purchase contract and receipt for deposit.

the purchaser, and incidentally the skill of the agent as well in his ability to secure a bona fide purchaser for his property. The inexperienced or timid salesman may fail at this point to ask for a substantial deposit. A simple "I will need your check for $500 as earnest money to accompany your offer," will suffice. This may take courage on the part of the neophyte until his confidence in the direct approach has been developed. Loss of control at this stage of the negotiations can mean the loss of a sale.

Real Estate Purchase Contract and Receipt for Deposit

There are many forms of purchase contracts and deposit receipts in use throughout the state. Larger offices have developed their own forms applying particularly to their area and type of operation. In general use, (where multiple-listing service forms are not employed) is the California Real Estate Association form, which appears on pp. 153–155. Constructive suggestions from legal advisers, title-insurance executives and realtors have been pooled to produce this form, under the auspices of the Standard Forms Committee of CREA. Regardless of the form used, it should be reviewed by the buyer before it is completed and any unfamiliar language or terms clarified by the salesman before the buyer is asked to sign.

Arguments are advanced that the time to write the contract is when the prospect is ready to buy, even though it means "writing up the deal" on the fender of a car. Although there may be merit in the premise that the prospect not be allowed to "cool off," it would appear that if the sale has been handled intelligently and the buyer is convinced of the value of the property, there should be no need for haste in securing his approval of the purchase contract. If the sale is to be conducted in a dignified manner, the contract should be drawn in the office closing room under conditions of minimum distraction.

As we have mentioned above, the purchase contract should be introduced early in the interview and explained fully to the buyer. Any questions he may have as to trade terms or legal terminology can be cleared up at this time. It is important that he understand that the contract is not just a receipt for his deposit but also a legal document, and that once it has been approved and signed by all parties it becomes a binding contract enforceable in a court of law—assuming, of course, that it has been properly drawn. He should understand clearly the disposition of his deposit in the event of a forfeiture on his part. His responsibilities under the contract as well as those of the seller should be made clear to him before he has affixed his signature thereto.

As a party to the contract, the salesman has a responsibility to draw the agreement so that it has a legal and binding effect on all parties once it is signed by them. Contingencies in the contract have a weakening effect and should be discouraged as much as possible at the inception. The buyer should understand that the contract has no effect until each contingency has been accepted by the seller or removed by mutual agreement. If a contingency should appear in the agreement, however, the method by which it is to be removed and the time limit should be noted. In part, the test of the legality of a contract lies in the degree of specification of the *intent* of the parties. Such items as date of possession, escrow period, personal property to be included, and terms of financing of the purchase are among those that might appear in a purchase contract. In cases where highly technical terms are dictated by the buyer to be included in the sales agreement, the services of an attorney should be employed.

The buyer may be assuming the loan or loans of record, or he may be taking the property "subject to" these loans. In either case it is important that he understand the implications of each, and that the contract spell out under which of these conditions he is buying the property, or that he is arranging other financing. If covenants, conditions, and rights of way of record (CC and R's) are to be approved or disapproved by the buyer, the contract should reflect this, along with a recitation as to the method by which he is to perform and the time limit agreed upon. If under the terms of the contract the buyer is to deposit sums into escrow in addition to his original deposit, a notation of this fact and the time limit under which he is to perform should be spelled out (that is, after the escrow instructions have been signed by all parties, any contingencies have been removed, and the preliminary title report has been received).

The licensee is to be particularly aware of Sections 2900, 2901, and 2902 of the regulations of the real estate commissioner, which read as follows:

> 2900. *Blank Spaces not to Be Filled in after Signature Obtained.*
> No licensee shall solicit, accept, or execute any contract, writing, or other document relating to a real estate transaction or escrow in connection therewith, which shall contain any blank to be filled in after signing or initialing such contract, writing, or other document.
> 2901. *Conditions for Additions, Deletions, or Alterations.*

No licensee shall make or permit any other person to make any addition to, deletion from, or alteration of any contract, writing, or other document unless such addition, deletion, or alteration is signed or initialed by all persons who have signed or initialed such contract, writing, or other document, prior to such addition, deletion, or alteration.
2902. *True Copies of All Instruments.*
A true copy of the original or corrected contract, writing, or other document referred to in the previous Sections 2900 and 2901 shall be given to the person signing or altering any such contract, writing, or other document at the time of signing or initialing such original or correction.

Termite Report

Other than legal and financing problems, probably no single item is of as much concern to the broker, the seller, or the buyer in the transfer of property as the so-called termite clearance. Many sellers are under the mistaken impression that an inspection of the premises for termite infestation is *required under law* and that elimination of any infestation is an expense to be borne by them. In California, climatic conditions favor the existence and growth of these wood-boring insects, and buyers from other areas are often unfamiliar with them or the damage they can inflict on a property. Prevalence of the termite in California and efforts to control its damage are explained in part by Earl E. Bowe, former executive secretary of the Termite Investigation Committee and author of *Termites and Termite Control*:

It must be remembered that as our population increased, we took over land that was orchard, forest, or pasture. Tree growth was removed, often only to the extent that stumps were not even taken out to ground level. Orchards changed to housing developments, but no tree root was removed.

The effect was that the forces of nature which return to the soil the decaying and insect-infested woody growth continued, but because of lack of natural woody growth, man-made structures were attacked where conditions were suitable.

Beginning in the 1920's the Uniform Building Code of the Pacific Coast Building Officials' Conference was adopted by cities and counties, and strict enforcement of building codes followed. However, in spite of building codes with requirement for continuous concrete foundation, houses went up which did not have sealed-off porches, with the result that scraps of lumber and shaving thrown into the porch fill became food for fungi and termites.

Soon the problem of correcting this was apparent, but not before a termite operator industry sprang up. The cooperative efforts of industry, state, utilities, cities, and the University of California resulted in the formation of the Termite Investigations Committee. From the Committee's five-year study, further building construction practices came about. In the mid 1930's, the FHA made its appearance, and with their strict requirements and on-the-job compliance inspections, we improved our building construction practices tremendously.

Today we have building codes with requirements for reinforced concrete foundations and brick chimneys, elimination of cripple studs, minimum clearance, minimum ventilation in the sub-structure, minimum height above finish grade for foundations, moisture-proofing of shower stall and shower over tub, kitchen sinks, etc. No longer do subdivisions arise where orchards once were, without a thorough removal of tree roots and aeration of the soil when the bull-dozer grades the land. . . .[2]

At the time a home is sold, the expense of an inspection by a licensed pest-control operator and that of eliminating any infestation is normally borne by the seller, although this is purely a matter of agreement. Section 2903 of the regulations of the real estate commissioner reads:

A licensee shall disclose to any and all purchasers, or prospective purchasers, and to any and all sellers, or prospective sellers, or parties to an exchange, any and all knowledge he may have, as soon as it may be practicable for him so to do, of any infestation of wood destroying organisms or any structural defect caused by wood destroying organisms in any improvement on premises, sale, purchase, or exchange of which is negotiated by him.

In addition, under Section 8614 of the Business and Professions Code, the parties to a contract may request and, upon payment of the required fee, obtain a certified copy of all inspection reports and completion notices prepared and filed by any structural pest-control operator during the preceding two years.

Following is a typical clause to be inserted in a deposit receipt:

Seller agrees to furnish a current termite report by a licensed structural pest-control operator covering ________ located at ________ showing property free from visible evidence of wood-destroying pests or organisms. If any infestation is found, seller agrees to have all damage caused by said infestation repaired at his expense and furnish an operator's certificate of completion. Other recommended work is to be done at the buyer's option and expense.

It is generally conceded that the seller should not be responsible for preventive work to protect against

[2] Earl E. Bowe, "State Structural Pest Control Act Needs Revision, Appraiser Says," *California Real Estate Magazine,* Vol. 43, No. 9 (July, 1963), 14.

future infestations. Normally, the termite company inspects only the house and garage. Care must be used in the wording. If *improvements* is used, this could be interpreted to include a wooden fence, toolshed, or any other structure on the premises. By designating specific buildings, this pitfall can be avoided.

Presenting the Offer

The overworked term *offer* has come to imply to the homeowner, the buyer, and the real estate practitioner that a listed price is never synonymous with the price the buyer is willing to pay. Negotiating a real estate sale too often takes on the air of a Middle East bazaar, with buyer and seller haggling over prices until an agreement is reached. The salesman's hasty, "Let's make them an offer," as soon as interest is evidenced by the buyer suggests that the property is on the auction block and bids are being taken. As the industry becomes more professional, however, with its members attaining higher appraisal skills, improvement in this situation can be noted and sales are being made nearer the listed price.

In 1963, a research into the real estate market behavior in Los Angeles dealing specifically with multiple-listing system data was instituted by the University of California at Los Angeles under the direction of Dr. Frederick E. Case. The following interesting data relating to cuts from the listing price speak for themselves:

> The percentage of cut from listing price averaged 4.3 percent for all MLSS in the period between 1953 and 1960 (...). Over-all the San Fernando MLS showed the lowest average cut, 3.7 percent, and the Glendale MLS with 5.5 percent and the Pasadena MLS, with 5.4 percent, showed the highest averages. The other MLSS were between these two extremes, with the Burbank MLS averaging 4.1 percent, Long Beach 4.8 percent and Southeast 4.0 percent. This universality of price cutting in the seven MLSS confirms the belief that this practice is common in the sale of residential properties in Los Angees County and presumably elsewhere in Southern California.[3]

The more dignified, "Let's go back to the office and draw up a sales agreement," is a businesslike approach. The salesman who has defended the listed price of the property, justifying the value through quoted loan commitments, comparable sales, and replacement-cost figures, is placed in a position of "losing face," if not of having made actual misrepresentation, when he suggests that an offer much lower than the asking price is acceptable. Also, having persuaded the seller to list at a realistic figure, he is in a poor bargaining position when he presents a low offer (sometimes ridiculous not only in price but in the terms and "extras" requested). By holding firm to the listed price, the salesman gains the respect of both buyer and seller.

In spite of a good selling job and attempts at "holding the line," the salesman occasionally must accept an offer considerably below the listed price. If the buyer insists on such an offer, it should be reduced to writing, with all details of the purchase clearly spelled out. The offer, regardless of its terms, must be presented to the seller. If it is too low or its terms too rigid, it may be met with outright hostility on the part of the seller, directed not only at the buyer but at the salesman as well.

Offers should never be presented over the telephone. Appointments should be set up (preferably by the secretary, where one is employed) at a time when husband and wife can both be present in a relaxed atmosphere, preferably after dinner in the evening.

Presentation of an offer requires extreme tact and patience. Too much conversation at this point can be fatal. The seller requires time to analyze the situation. His thinking, which has been geared to the listed price, must now be readjusted in the light of the buyer's offer.

In cases of cooperative sales (where one office sells the listing of another), the salesman negotiating the sale is the agent of the buyer and takes on another role than if he represents both buyer and seller. In the first situation, he is bargaining for his buyer. The offer is presented to the seller, in most cases, in the presence of a representative of the listing office. The situation then evolves into one where the buyer's representative presses for the best price and terms, while the seller's agent endeavors to negotiate a transaction that best serves the interests of his client.

In presenting the offer, correct procedure calls for clarification of all contingencies to the contract at the outset. Once these are disposed of, the seller is more inclined to give careful consideration to the offer as a whole. As a professional, the salesman presents the offer in a dignified, unhurried manner. Finesse and skill are requisites to maintaining the confidence of the seller. The use of high-pressure methods designed to persuade the seller to accept a low offer is the mark of the "operator."

[3] Frederick E. Case, *Real Estate Market Behavior in Los Angeles—A Study of Multiple Listing System Data* (Los Angeles: University of California, Graduate School of Business Administration, 1963), p. 19.

The seller should be kept informed of all activity that the listing office has experienced during the term of the listing and of the results thereof. If the salesman sincerely believes that no higher offer will be forthcoming, he has the responsibility to inform the seller accordingly. He has the dual responsibility of trying to understand the position of the buyer and that of the seller if he is representing both in the negotiations. (The seller wants to sell, the buyer to buy.) The *principle* involved, however, must be right for all parties concerned.

The seller usually is not familiar with market trends. He has not had the experience of talking to a variety of buyers, as has the salesman. In addition, often the seller who has appeared the most anxious during the listing period, demanding the most service from the listing office, can suddenly became very disinterested in selling when the offer is presented.

Counteroffers

Counteroffers should be encouraged when all attempts to secure an acceptance of the original offer have failed. On the reverse side of the purchase agreement, the salesman draws a counteroffer, reading, in effect:

> All conditions of this purchase agreement as stipulated on the reverse side are acceptable to me as seller with the following exceptions:

These exceptions may include, among others, such items as (1) purchase price, (2) possession, (3) financing terms, (4) personal property to be included, (5) escrow period, and (6) possession date. The counteroffer is then signed by all legal owners of the property and dated.[4]

Nonperformance

The buyer's remedies under the marketing contract include:

1. *Damages.* The buyer's compensatory damages in the event the seller fails to perform under the contract depend upon whether *bad faith* on the seller's part has been proved. In the absence of bad faith, the buyer is entitled only to the amount actually paid by him to the seller, plus any normal expenses incurred in title searches, preparation of papers, and interest. In the event bad faith has been proved, the buyer may recover any difference between the contract price and the fair market price at the time of the breach of the contract.[5]
2. *Specific performance.* Because no two parcels of land are exactly alike, the law takes the position that money damages alone cannot recompense a buyer adequately. Therefore a buyer may sue for specific performance if a seller breaches his purchase contract.

If the buyer fails to perform, the seller may take any of the following measures:

1. *Declare the contract at an end* and return the deposit.
2. *Sue for damages.* He can recover the excess, if any, of the contract price over the value of the property to him.[6]
3. *Declare the contract forfeit* and keep the buyer's deposit. (See Clause 7 in CREA's real estate purchase contract and receipt for deposit.)
4. Ask that the buyer be required to perform or, in some areas, he may offer the deed and sue for the purchase price.

CASE STUDY

Alfred Lance is a salesman with the Sacramento Realty Company. He has a home, listed for $25,000, which he has shown to Mr. and Mrs. Homer Brown. They tell him they like it better than any of the other properties he has shown them, but they are hesitant about paying that much for a home. Mr. Brown is employed as a truck driver for a local bakery at a salary of $10,000 a year. They have two children in elementary school. They have managed to save $4,000 and are at present living in an apartment for which they pay $110 a month rent, but they feel that they should own their own home so that their children may have a yard and a place to bring their friends.

Lance has obtained a loan commitment on the property for 80 percent of the sales price at 7¾ percent interest on a thirty-year term. The taxes on the property are $328 annually.

Lance tells Brown that, although the property is listed for $25,000, he is positive he can deliver it for $23,000. Brown agrees to make the offer in this amount. He gives Lance a check for $1,000 and signs a purchase agreement on the following conditions: Purchase price—$23,000; down payment—$3,500; loan to be secured by Brown—$18,400, balance of the purchase price to be in the form of a purchase-

[4] California real estate law requires that copies of all real estate documents be handed to the signators *at the time* the signatures are obtained.

[5] See also Clause 7 in real estate purchase contract and receipt for deposit (p. 154).

[6] Value of the property being determined by the fair market value at the time of the breach.

CALIFORNIA REAL ESTATE ASSOCIATION STANDARD FORM

Real Estate Purchase Contract and Receipt for Deposit

THIS IS MORE THAN A RECEIPT FOR MONEY. IT MAY BE A LEGALLY BINDING CONTRACT. READ IT CAREFULLY.

Pasadena, California, November 19, 1970

Received from Walter R. Buying and Mary R. Buying, Husband and Wife (herein called Buyer), the sum of One Thousand and 00/100 Dollars ($1,000-00/100) evidenced by cash ☐, personal check ☒, cashier's check ☐, or as deposit on account of purchase price of Twenty Seven Thousand and 00/100 Dollars ($27,000-00/100) for the purchase of property, situated in City of Arcadia, County of Los Angeles, California, described as follows: Lot 57, Tract 12527, City of Arcadia, recorded in Arcadia Records Book 234 of Maps, at Page 7 also known and designated as 165 West Forest Avenue, Arcadia, California

Buyer will deposit in escrow with Uptown Escrow Company the balance of purchase price as follows: $6,700 cash (including above deposit of $1,000), $1,700 at opening of escrow and $4,000 upon demand before close of escrow; contingent upon the buyer's ability to assume the first deed of trust of approximately $18,000, payable $135.32 per month including interest of 6% per annum; seller to carry balance of approximately $2,300 represented by a note secured by a second deed of trust payable * (continued below)

1. Title is to be free of liens, encumbrances, easements, restrictions, rights and conditions of record or known to Seller, other than the following: (1) A lien for 1967/68 property taxes of approximately $801.45 (2) first deed of trust of approximately $18,000 (3) street improvement bond in the approximate amount of $600 (4) public utility easements on map referred to above and (5) tract covenants of record.

Seller shall furnish to Buyer at Seller's expense a standard California Land Title Association policy insuring title in Buyer subject only to liens, encumbrances, easements, restrictions, rights and conditions of record as set forth above. If Seller fails to deliver title as herein provided, Buyer at his option may terminate this agreement and any deposit shall thereupon be returned to him.

2. Property taxes, premiums on insurance acceptable to Buyer, rents, interest, ~~and~~ xx utilities (Insert in blank any other items of income or expense to be prorated) shall be prorated as of (1) the date of recordation of deed or (2) X X X X X X X X X X X X X X X X X X X X (Strike (1) if (2) is used). The amount of any bond or assessment which is a lien shall be ~~paid~~ assumed (Strike one) by Buyer. Seller shall pay cost of revenue stamps on deed.

3. Possession shall be delivered to Buyer (Strike inapplicable alternatives) (a) on close of escrow, or (b) not later than fifteen days after closing escrow, or (c) Seller shall pay buyer $30.00 per diem for any such holding over as seller in possession

4. Escrow instructions signed by Buyer and Seller shall be delivered to the escrow holder within 10 days from the Seller's acceptance hereof and shall provide for closing within 45 days from the opening of escrow, subject to written extensions signed by Buyer and Seller.

5. Unless otherwise designated in the escrow instructions of Buyer, title shall vest as follows: Walter R. Buying and Mary R. Buying, husband and wife, as joint tenants

(Continued on next page)

* $23.00 or more per month, including interest at 7% per annum, all due and payable in five (5) years.

112

Real Estate Purchase Contract and Receipt for Deposit -- Continued

(THE MANNER OF TAKING TITLE MAY HAVE SIGNIFICANT LEGAL AND TAX CONSEQUENCES. THEREFORE, GIVE THIS MATTER SERIOUS CONSIDERATION.)

6. If the improvements on the property are destroyed or materially damaged prior to close of escrow, then, on demand by Buyer, any deposit made by Buyer shall be returned to him and this contract thereupon shall terminate.

7. If Buyer fails to complete said purchase as herein provided by reason of any default of Buyer, Seller shall be released from his obligation to sell the property to Buyer and may proceed against Buyer upon any claim or remedy which he may have in law or equity; provided, however, that by placing their initials here (   ) Buyer (   ) Seller Buyer and Seller agree that it would be impractical or extremely difficult to fix actual damages in case of Buyer's default, that the amount of the deposit is a reasonable estimate of the damages, and that Seller shall retain the deposit as his sole right to damages.

8. Buyer's signature hereon constitutes an offer to Seller to purchase the real estate described above. Unless acceptance hereof is signed by Seller and the signed copy delivered to Buyer, either in person or by mail to the address shown below, within five days hereof, this offer shall be deemed revoked and the deposit shall be returned to Buyer.

9. Other terms and conditions: (Set forth any terms and conditions of a factual nature applicable to this sale, such as financing, prior sale of other property, the matter of structural pest control inspection, repairs and personal property to be included in sale.)

(1) This offer is contingent upon buyer completing sale through close of escrow of his present home at 1630 Mockingbird Lane, Monrovia, California within 45 days from date of acceptance of this offer. Buyer agrees to use diligence in effecting the sale of the present home

(2) Furthermore, the seller shall provide at the sellers expense, a termite report by a licensed structural pest control operator showing property free from visible evidence of * (con't)

10. Time is of the essence of this contract.

Real Estate Broker George F. Baker   By

Address 243 N. San Rafael, Pasadena, Calif.   Telephone 795-8790

The undersigned Buyer offers and agrees to buy the above described property on the terms and conditions above stated and acknowledges receipt of a copy hereof.

Dated: November 19, 1970

Address 1630 Mockingbird Lane, Monrovia, Calif.

Telephone --   Buyer

ACCEPTANCE

The undersigned Seller accepts the foregoing offer and agrees to sell the property described thereon on the terms and conditions therein set forth.

The undersigned Seller has employed the Broker above named and for Broker's services agrees to pay Broker, as a commission, the sum of One Thousand Six Hundred Twenty and 00/100 Dollars ($1,620.00) payable as follows: (a) On recordation of the deed or other evidence of title, or (b) if completion of sale is prevented by default of Seller, upon Seller's default, or (c) if completion of sale is prevented by default of Buyer, only if and when Seller collects the damages from Buyer, by suit or otherwise, and then in an amount not to exceed one half that portion of the damages collected after first deducting title and escrow expenses and the expenses of collection, if any.

The undersigned acknowledges receipt of a copy hereof and authorizes Broker to deliver a signed copy of it to Buyer.

Dated:

Address: 165 West Forest Avenue, Arcadia, Calif.

Telephone: Seller

Broker consents to the foregoing.

Dated: Broker

A REAL ESTATE BROKER IS THE PERSON QUALIFIED TO ADVISE ON REAL ESTATE. IF YOU DESIRE LEGAL ADVICE CONSULT YOUR ATTORNEY.

THIS STANDARDIZED DOCUMENT FOR USE IN SIMPLE TRANSACTIONS HAS BEEN APPROVED BY THE CALIFORNIA REAL ESTATE ASSOCIATION AND THE STATE BAR OF CALIFORNIA IN FORM ONLY. NO REPRESENTATION IS MADE AS TO THE LEGAL VALIDITY OF ANY PROVISION OR THE ADEQUACY OF ANY PROVISION IN ANY SPECIFIC TRANSACTION. IT SHOULD NOT BE USED IN COMPLEX TRANSACTIONS OR WITH EXTENSIVE RIDERS OR ADDITIONS.

* wood destroying pests or organisms. If any infestation is found, seller agrees to have all damage caused by said infestation repaired at his expense and furnish an operator's certificate of completion. Other recommended work is to be done at the buyer's option and expense.

See Attached Counter Offer

112-A

Counter Offer

This offer is rejected as presented, however, the following counter offer is made:

All original terms are accepted with the following exception,

Purchase price is to be twenty eight thousand dollars (28,000), buyer to obtain his own financing. Seller to carry back a second deed of trust payable $43.57 per month including interest at 7% per annum, all due and payable in five years. Upon transfer or further encumbrances of the subject property, all remaining sums become due and payable.

ACCEPTANCE
(Buyer)

Date ____________________

Address 1630 Mockingbird Lane
Monrovia California

____

Buyer

(Seller)
ACCEPTANCE

The undersigned Seller accepts the foregoing offer and agrees to sell the property described thereon on the terms and conditions therein set forth. The undersigned Seller has employed the Broker above named and for Broker's services agrees to pay Broker, as a commission, the sume of One thousand six hundred eighty and oo/100 dollars ($1,680.00) payable as follows: (a) On recordation of the deed or other evidence of title, or (b) if completion of sale is prevented by default of Seller, upon Seller's default, or (c) if completion of sale is prevented by default of Buyer, only if and when Seller collects the damages from Buyer, by suit or otherwise, and then in an amount not to exceed one half that portion of the damages collected after first deducting title and escrow expenses and the expenses of collection, if any.

The undersigned acknowledges receipt of a copy hereof and authorizes Broker to deliver a signed copy of it to Buyer.

Dated: ____________________ ____________________

Address: 165 West Forest Avenue, Arcadia, Ca.

Telephone ____________________ Seller ____________________

Broker consents to the foregoing.

Dated: ____________________ Broker ____________________

money trust deed for a term of three years at 9 percent interest.

Lance takes the offer to the seller and spends considerable time urging him to accept it.

Assume now that the owner makes a counteroffer of $24,000 and says he must have all cash.

1. Do you believe that Lance represented the seller in a professional manner in the transaction?
2. In your opinion, will Brown qualify for the required loan? (Assume that Brown has no other assets.)
3. What steps should Lance now take to firm up the transaction?
4. Where might he obtain the necessary secondary financing to supply the extra funds for the purchase?

SUGGESTED REFERENCES

ALLEN, JOHN B., "Completing the Deposit Receipt," *Selling Real Estate.* Los Angeles: California Real Estate Association, 1970.

CASE, FREDERICK E., *Real Estate.* Boston: Allyn & Bacon, Inc., 1962.

FRANZ, LYDIA, "The Art of Negotiating," *Real Estate Today.* Chicago: National Institute of Real Estate Brokers of the National Association of Real Estate Boards, April, 1970.

STONE, DAVID, "Presenting the Offer," *Selling Real Estate.* Los Angeles: California Real Estate Association, 1970.

11

Escrow Procedure

Escrow Defined

The purchase agreement having been signed by all parties, together with any counteroffers, it is the broker's responsibility to open an escrow. Section 1057 of the Civil Code defines an escrow as follows:

> A grant may be deposited by the grantor with a third person, to be delivered on the performance of a condition, and, on delivery by the depository, it will take effect. While in the possession of the third person, and subject to condition, it is called an escrow.

Section 17003 of the California Financial Code gives the following definition of an escrow:

> Escrow means any transaction wherein one person for the purpose of effecting the sale, transfer, encumbering, or leasing of real or personal property to another person, delivers any written instrument, money, evidence of title to real or personal property or any other thing of value to a third person, to be held by such third person until the happening of a specified event or the performance of a prescribed condition, when it is then to be delivered by such third person to a grantee, grantor, promisee, promissor, obligee, obligor, bailee, bailor, or any agent or employee of any of the latter.

The law requires that any deposit received by the broker must be given to his principal, placed into escrow or into the broker's trust account. Section 2830 of the regulations of the real estate commissioner reads:

> Every person, partnership or corporation holding a broker license under provisions of the real estate law who does not immediately place all funds entrusted to him by his principal or others in a neutral escrow depository or in the hands of principals, shall maintain a trust fund account with some bank or recognized depository and place all such entrusted funds therein upon receipt.
>
> Such trust fund account shall designate him as trustee, and all such trust fund accounts must provide for withdrawal of the funds without previous notice.

Trust-Fund Records

In addition, Section 2831 of the regulations provides that:

> Every broker shall keep a record of all trust funds received by him, including uncashed checks held pursuant to instructions of his principal. Said records shall set forth in columnar form:
>
> 1. date funds received;
> 2. from whom received;
> 3. amount received;
> 4. with respect to funds deposited to trust bank account, date of said deposit;
> 5. with respect to funds previously deposited to trust bank account, check number or date of related disbursement;
> 6. with respect to funds not deposited in a trust bank account, nature of other depository and date funds were forwarded;
> 7. daily balance of trust bank account.
>
> Each broker who maintains a formal trust cash receipts journal and a formal cash disbursement journal or other similar records, in accordance with sound accounting principles, shall be deemed to have complied with the above.
>
> *All records and funds shall be subject to inspection by the commissioner or his deputies.*

Section 2831.1 of the regulations stipulates:

> Each broker shall keep a separate record for each beneficiary or transaction, accounting for all funds therein which have been deposited to the broker's trust bank account. These separate records shall set forth information sufficient to identify the transac-

tion and the parties thereto. Each such record shall set forth in columnar forms:

1. date funds deposited;
2. the date of each related disbursement;
3. the check number of each related disbursement;
4. the amount of each related disbursement.

Each broker who maintains a formal trust ledger or similar record, in accordance with sound accounting principles, shall be deemed to have complied with the above.

Commingling. Commingling, where the broker mixes the funds of his principal with his own moneys, is a violation of California real estate law and subjects the licensee to disciplinary action by the commissioner. Commingling as related to the real estate licensee is defined as:

> Failure to deposit or place trust funds received (1) into a neutral escrow depository or (2) in the hands of principals or (3) in a trust fund account in accordance with Section 2830 above *by the next business day following their receipt.* However, it shall not constitute commingling to hold an uncashed check until acceptance of an offer *when directed to do so by the buyer or offeror, and it shall not constitute commingling to hold an uncashed check after acceptance of an offer when directed to do so by the seller or offeree. The fact that a check is being held in an uncashed form must be specifically disclosed to the seller or offeree before he accepts the offer.*[1]

What Constitutes a True Trust Account? Strictly speaking, it is one that is not only labeled a trust account but that names the broker as a trustee and that contains only funds of clients. To cover any contingency, such as a service charge by a bank, the broker is permitted to have *not more than $100* of his personal funds in a trust-fund account. Also, from time to time brokers may have earned commissions in their trust accounts. Although brokers are urged to transfer any earned commissions to their general accounts as soon as possible, occasionally it is not practical to do so. For this reason, the law permits earned commissions to remain in a trust account for a period *not to exceed thirty days.*

Is a Trust Fund Mandatory? General real estate brokerage is covered by a legal requirement that *the broker who does not immediately place all funds entrusted to him by his principal or others in a neutral escrow depository or in the hands of his principal must maintain a trust fund account with some bank or other recognized depository and place all such entrusted funds therein upon receipt.* Therefore, according to real estate law *it is not mandatory for a broker to maintain a trust fund* (except in certain special circumstances, relating to real property securities dealers or sales agents in a subdivision where impound accounts are handled).

To those licensees who are members of NAREB, however, it might be pointed out that Article 8 of the Realtors' Code of Ethics reads:

> The Realtor should keep in a special bank account, separated from his own funds, moneys coming into his possession in trust for other persons, such as escrow, trust funds, clients' moneys *and other like items.*

Regulations of the real estate commissioner also specify the conditions under which withdrawals may be made from a trust-fund account:

1. The real estate licensee must be designated as the trustee of the account.
2. All trust fund accounts must provide for withdrawal of the funds without previous notice.
3. Withdrawals may not be made excepting on the signature of the broker or upon the signature of at least one or more of the following persons when authorized by the broker:
   a. A salesman in the broker's employ.
   b. Any corporate officer of a corporation licensed as a broker.
   c. Any unlicensed employee, provided such employee is covered by a fiduciary bond indemnifying the broker against loss of money or property by act of the employee in an amount sufficient to cover the funds or property held in trust.

Although the broker may delegate the authority to withdraw trust funds or by other methods handle trust funds, *he cannot delegate his accountability under the law.*

Reasons for a Trust-Fund Account. Basically the trust-fund account is intended for the broker to separate the money in his general account from any trust moneys so that there will be no commingling of funds. However, there are at least two other legal reasons why a trust fund is important, both having to do with protection of the client:

1. Should a broker's general account be tied up because of legal action taken against him, and even though the broker might have a separate trust account, the money of his clients could be tied up as well, unless it is in fact *a true trust-fund account* (that is, meeting the requirements set out above). If the broker should die or become incapacitated, his clients' funds could also be tied up during probate.
2. The FDIC has ruled that funds of various owners

[1] See trust-account records pp. 159–161 and in Appendix.

RECORD OF ALL TRUST FUNDS RECEIVED – NOT PLACED IN BROKER'S TRUST ACCOUNT

TRUST FUNDS INCLUDING UNCASHED CHECKS RECEIVED			Description Property or Identification	Disposition of Uncashed Checks or Other Funds Forwarded to Escrow or Principal	Date Forwarded
Date Received	Received From	Amount			
(1)	(2)	(3)		(6)	(6)

2831. RECORDS TO BE MAINTAINED. SUBJECT TO INSPECTION BY COMMISSIONER OR HIS DEPUTIES. Every broker shall keep a record of all trust funds received by him including uncashed checks held pursuant to instructions of his principal.
Said record shall set forth in columnar form:

- (1) date funds received;
- (2) from whom received;
- (3) amount received;
- * (4) with respect to funds deposited to trust bank account, date of said deposit;
- * (5) with respect to funds previously deposited to trust bank account, check number or date of related disbursement;
- (6) with respect to funds not deposited in trust bank account, nature of other depository and date funds were forwarded;
- * (7) daily balance of trust bank account.

Each broker who maintains a formal trust cash receipt journal and a formal cash disbursement journal or other similar records, in accordance with sound accounting principles, shall be deemed to have complied with the above.

All records and funds shall be subject to inspection by the commissioner or his deputies.

* For compliance with (4), (5), and (7) see form entitled, "Use For All Trust Funds Which Go Into Trust Account."

placed in a custodial deposit will be recognized for insurance purposes to the same extent as if their names and interests were disclosed on the records of the bank, provided

a. the account is specifically designated as a custodial account, and
b. the name and interest of each owner in the deposit is disclosed on the depositors' record.[2]

Opening the Escrow

If the real estate purchase contract has been properly drawn, it will incorporate all the terms of the sales agreement in such a manner that based thereon *escrow instructions* can be drawn.

[2] Portions of the above are taken from the *Reference Book* (Sacramento: Department of Real Estate).

The broker going into escrow should be prepared with the following documents:

1. *Correct legal description:* The grant deed should be brought if possible. Legal descriptions obtained from tax statements are not acceptable.
2. *Full* names of parties to the transaction (these should conform to those on the deed).
3. Statements of *how buyers are to take title* and the names in which title is to be taken.
4. Names and addresses of all holders of mortgages or trust deeds. The loan number should also be submitted.
5. Terms of any *new encumbrances.*
6. All insurance policies. If these are held by a mortgagee, then the seller's certificate of insurance should be submitted.
7. Current tax bills.
8. In the case of income property, a complete list of tenants, as well as the rental statement for

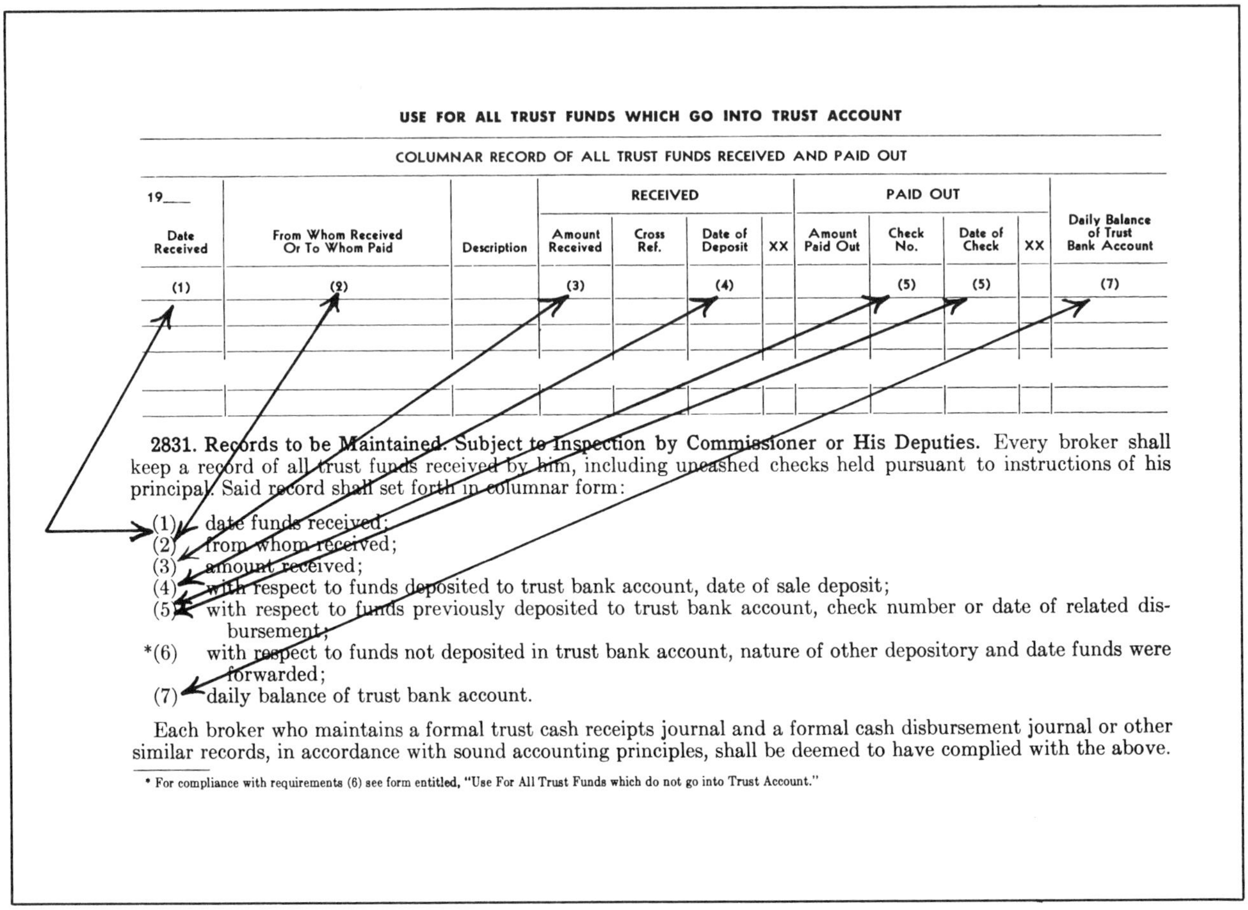

USE FOR ALL TRUST FUNDS WHICH GO INTO TRUST ACCOUNT

COLUMNAR RECORD OF ALL TRUST FUNDS RECEIVED AND PAID OUT

19___			RECEIVED				PAID OUT				
Date Received	From Whom Received Or To Whom Paid	Description	Amount Received	Cross Ref.	Date of Deposit	XX	Amount Paid Out	Check No.	Date of Check	XX	Daily Balance of Trust Bank Account
(1)	(2)		(3)		(4)			(5)	(5)		(7)

2831. Records to be Maintained: Subject to Inspection by Commissioner or His Deputies. Every broker shall keep a record of all trust funds received by him, including uncashed checks held pursuant to instructions of his principal. Said record shall set forth in columnar form:

(1) date funds received;
(2) from whom received;
(3) amount received;
(4) with respect to funds deposited to trust bank account, date of sale deposit;
(5) with respect to funds previously deposited to trust bank account, check number or date of related disbursement;
*(6) with respect to funds not deposited in trust bank account, nature of other depository and date funds were forwarded;
(7) daily balance of trust bank account.

Each broker who maintains a formal trust cash receipts journal and a formal cash disbursement journal or other similar records, in accordance with sound accounting principles, shall be deemed to have complied with the above.

* For compliance with requirements (6) see form entitled, "Use For All Trust Funds which do not go into Trust Account."

each, indicating the rental amount and date of payment. (If rents are paid in advance this must be indicated for proration purposes.)

9. If there are two or more brokers involved in the transaction, a statement of how the commission is to be divided. Also, if a multiple-listing service fee is involved, the amount of this fee.

"Going into escrow" means depositing money and documents with the escrow agent[3] to be used *only as set forth in the written instructions* of the parties. The escrow officer must be able to reduce the intentions of the parties to writing in plain, concise language. All escrows by their nature must be confidential. Only the principals to the transaction are permitted to see the escrow instructions, and then only as they apply to and dovetail with each other's instructions. The escrow officer must at all times maintain a neutral position. He must not attempt to give advice but is to follow *specific* instructions of the parties. It is his duty to act as trust officer during the term of the escrow. Although it is his duty to safeguard the rights of all parties, he is not permitted to give legal advice any more than is the broker to the transaction.

Taking the Escrow

The escrow officer will need to have certain information in order to "take an escrow." He will need to know:

1. What type of transaction is it to be?
2. If it is a sale, who is the seller?

[3] An individual cannot be licensed as an escrow holder. The license must be held in a corporation duly organized for the purpose of conducting an escrow business. Applicants for escrow licenses under the Escrow Act must be financially solvent, must furnish a surety bond in the amount of $5,000, and must arrange for the bonding of responsible employees. All money deposited in escrow must be placed in a trust account that is exempt from execution or attachment for any claim against the escrow agent.

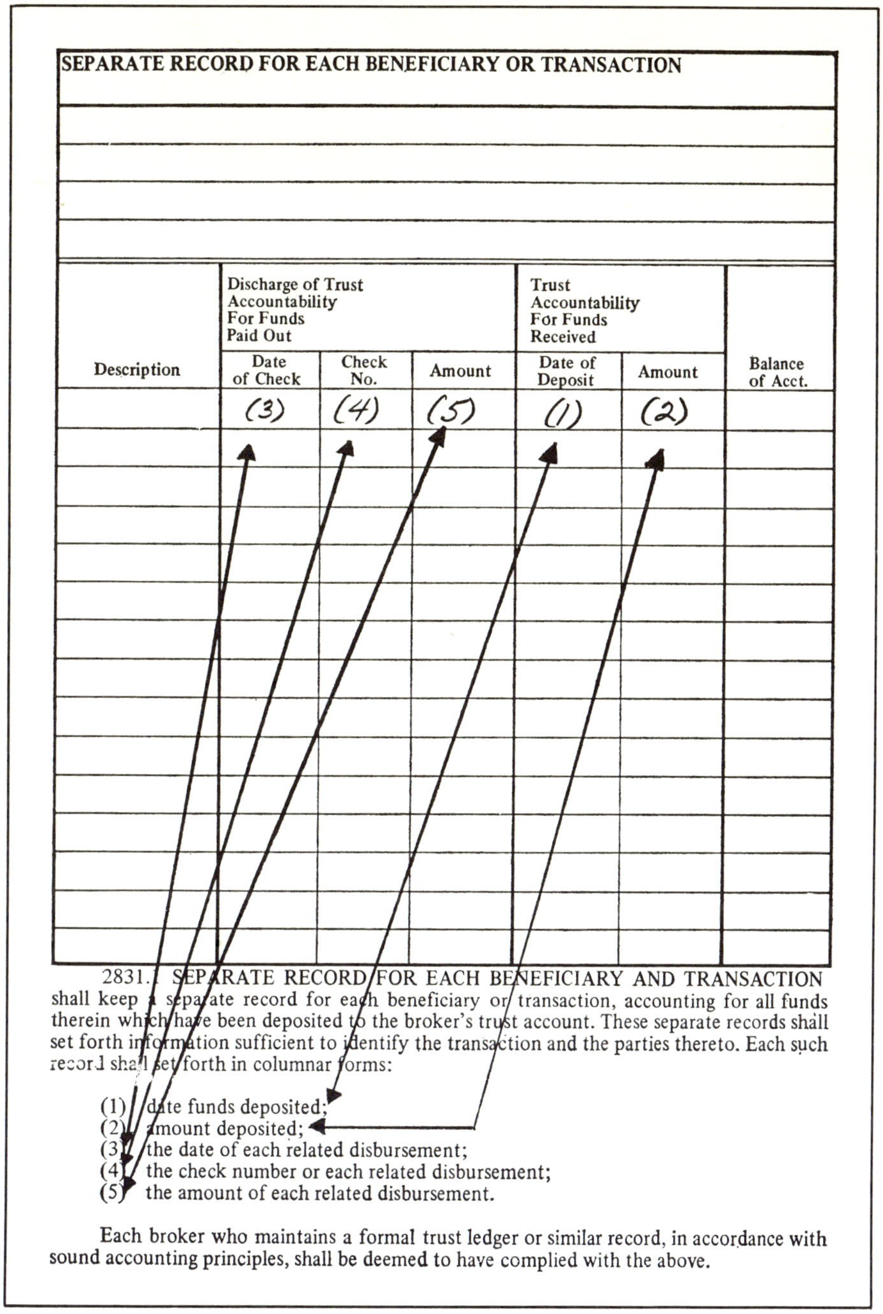

SEPARATE RECORD FOR EACH BENEFICIARY OR TRANSACTION

Description	Discharge of Trust Accountability For Funds Paid Out			Trust Accountability For Funds Received		Balance of Acct.
	Date of Check	Check No.	Amount	Date of Deposit	Amount	
	(3)	(4)	(5)	(1)	(2)	

2831. SEPARATE RECORD FOR EACH BENEFICIARY AND TRANSACTION shall keep a separate record for each beneficiary or transaction, accounting for all funds therein which have been deposited to the broker's trust account. These separate records shall set forth information sufficient to identify the transaction and the parties thereto. Each such record shall set forth in columnar forms:

(1) date funds deposited;
(2) amount deposited;
(3) the date of each related disbursement;
(4) the check number or each related disbursement;
(5) the amount of each related disbursement.

Each broker who maintains a formal trust ledger or similar record, in accordance with sound accounting principles, shall be deemed to have complied with the above.

3. What is his name, and is he married?
4. Who is the buyer, and how does he wish to take title?
5. What is the total purchase price?
6. How is it to be paid?
7. Has any money been paid out of escrow?
8. Have the parties agreed on how much money is to be deposited at the inception of the escrow?
9. What is the escrow period?
10. When should funds be in?
11. Is the buyer's money to be obtained through a new loan, or is he taking title subject to an existing loan?

In selling farmlands or other acreage, there may be water stock involved. The escrow officer will need to know if he is to write the secretary of the corporation regarding any unpaid assessments that might interfere with the stock transfer. Escrow instructions must state clearly if the water stock is to be transferred to the grantee at the close of the escrow.

The instructions govern the use and delivery of the money and documents that are held in escrow until all conditions of the instructions have been satisfied.

Commission. The escrow officer must inquire if there is a broker involved in the escrow and provide the instructions for a commission to be paid to him (or to others as well, if more than one broker is involved).

Execution of Documents. Any documents drawn by the escrow officer may be acknowledged in his office, provided that the escrow officer knows the parties personally.

Deposits. Deposits are required from the parties obligated to pay escrow charges.

Preliminary Report. After escrow instructions have been signed by all parties, the search of the title is begun, the beneficiary is notified of the amount of any demand to be paid off through escrow or is asked for a beneficiary's statement in the event the loan is to remain on the property. Everything possible should be done at the inception to have all necessary documents in hand by the time the title search is completed in order that escrow closing will not be unnecessarily delayed. Where the instructions read that the buyer is to approve the conditions and restrictions, this should be done at the beginning of the escrow as soon as they can be obtained. Any further changes that may require the buyer's approval can be taken care of through supplemental instructions.

Complete Escrow. A complete escrow is one that contains all of the necessary instructions that show a complete meeting of the minds in all the essential requirements of the transaction; that is, a "complete" escrow is where all the terms of the instructions have been met. Once the designated conditions of an escrow have been met and performed, the escrow agent is generally released from all liability.

Termination. Escrows may be terminated in one of two ways: (1) by full performance and closing by the parties, or (2) by mutual consent and cancellation. All performances required by the escrow instructions must be performed within the time limit set forth. The escrow agent has no authority to enforce or accept the performance after the time limit provided in the instructions.

Revocation by one of the parties to the escrow may occur if he should not meet any one or more of the conditions previously agreed upon. In case this results in the termination of the escrow and if legal action follows the escrow holder will take no action, pending a court decision.

Note: It is important that it be understood that once there is a binding and enforceable contract between the parties to an escrow, supported by adequate consideration, neither party may withdraw his documents or money before the escrow conditions have been met.

Division of Escrow Charges

The *seller* is generally responsible for the following:

1. The broker's commission.
2. Documentary stamps for the deed transfer.
3. The policy of title insurance.[4]
4. Notarial fee on instruments in favor of the buyer.
5. Drawing of instruments in favor of the buyer.

The *buyer* normally pays for the following:

1. Drawing instruments in favor of the seller or lender.
2. Recording the deed.
3. Recording the trust deed in favor of the lender.
4. Notarial fee on instruments in favor of the seller or lender.

In southern California the escrow work is normally performed by escrow departments of banks, lending institutions, or private escrow companies. In northern California the escrow function is usually performed by the title company, in which case the buyer pays one fee, which covers both the escrow fee and the policy title fee. Escrow fees in southern California are usually split evently between buyer and seller. Any deviation from the customary practice can of course be agreed upon by the parties to the transaction.

Closing the Escrow

After all documents have been deposited, all approvals have been obtained, and all necessary funds have cleared, the escrow officer is in a position to close the escrow. Prior to recordation, he must make a complete recapitulation, including prorations, advances, and payments so that he may be certain he has sufficient funds to meet all requirements at closing. After all documents have been recorded, disbursement of funds is made. Checks are drawn by the escrow agent to the sellers, to any principals making written demands on the escrow, and to the

[4] This practice varies between northern and southern California. In northern California it is customary for the *buyer* to pay for the title-insurance policy.

broker, if applicable. Section 10138 of the Business and Professions Code provides that:

> It is a misdemeanor, punishable by a fine of not exceeding fifty dollars for each offense, for any person, whether obligor, escrow holder or otherwise, to pay or deliver to any one a compensation for performing any of the acts within the scope of this chapter, who is not known to be or who does not present evidence to such payor that he is a regularly licensed real estate broker at the time such compensation is earned.

If the broker is not known personally to the escrow office, he will require that the broker show his real estate broker's card, which bears his license number. An escrow officer may not pay a commission to a salesman unless specifically authorized in writing by the employing broker.

Real Estate Brokers Holding Escrows. Real estate brokers may not hold escrows except in connection with some transaction wherein they acted as a real estate broker, and they may not hold escrows for compensation in connection with those made by other brokers.

Prorations. Prorating is the dividing or proportioning among the parties to the escrow of certain items that have accrued to date of proration, or that have been paid to a date in advance of proration. Items with which the escrow officer is primarily concerned are:

1. *Taxes.* Because taxes are paid on the basis of a ficsal year, July 1 to June 30, they must be prorated on that basis.
2. *Fire insurance.* Fire insurance is usually purchased on a three-year basis. If the insurance is paid three years in advance, and the property is sold before the expiration of the three years, the seller is entitled to a refund of the unused portion of the premium.
3. *Interest.* Interest payments on any loan or loans on a property are prorated. They are adjusted in favor of the purchaser from the last interest payment to the close of escrow (date of recording).
4. *Rents.* Where rents are collected in advance, they are adjusted in favor of the seller from the date of close of escrow.

Although most prorations are made as of close of escrow, they must be made in accordance with the instructions. Most escrow forms provide that prorations are to be made on a thirty-day basis. If the provision is not made in the printed form, an actual day basis is used.

Documentary Stamps. Effective January 2, 1968, a state enabling act permits a county to adopt a documentary transfer tax that applies on all real property transfers within the county.

The tax applies when the consideration (exclusive of the value of any lien or encumbrance attaching to the property *at the time of sale and not removed or replaced upon consummation of the sale*) exceeds $100. The tax is computed at the rate of fifty-five cents for each $500 of consideration or fraction thereof. If a portion of the total price paid for the property is exempt because a lien or encumbrance remains on the property, this fact must be stated on the deed or on a separate paper filed with the deed.

The law further requires that "The declaration (of the amount of tax due) shall include a statement that the consideration or value on which the tax due was computed was, or that it was not, exclusive of the value of the lien of encumbrance remaining on the interest or property conveyed at the time of sale."

A city within a county that has adopted the transfer tax may also adopt its own transfer tax ordinance with the tax amount fixed at one-half the rate chargeable by the county. In this event the county collects the total tax but does not keep it all for county use; half the amount collected is turned over to the city.[5]

Closing Statements. The total sales price and the amount of the broker's commission must be clearly spelled out in the closing statement. Section 10176(g) of the California Real Estate Law requires the licensee to reveal to his employer (usually the seller) the full amount of his commission "prior to or coincident with the signing of an agreement evidencing the meeting of the minds of the contracting parties, regardless of the form of such agreement whether evidenced by documents in an escrow or by any other or different procedure."

The closing statement shows receipts and disbursements of the buyer and seller, who must be shown in written form the cash requirements, the proceeds, and the charges and prorations.

It is the responsibility of the broker to familiarize himself with the charges and proration methods of escrow so that he may explain them to all parties at the time the settlement sheet is received.

The salesman's duties to his buyer and seller do not end when the transaction is placed in escrow. He is required to "stay on top of the deal." It is his duty to keep in close touch with the escrow officer in order to ascertain when all conditions of the escrow have been complied with. It is not considered good policy to have buyer and seller both present in the

[5] From information contained in the *Reference Book.*

ESCROW CHECK LIST

Complete names of all persons involved in transaction:

SELLER ______________________________ PHONE ____________

Address ______________________________ City ____________

BUYER ______________________________ PHONE ____________

Address ______________________________ City ____________

LENDER ______________________________ PHONE ____________

BROKER ______________________________ PHONE ____________

Address of Property ______________________________ City ____________

✓	OBTAIN FROM SELLER	OBTAIN FROM BUYER	✓
	1. Legal description of property and present vesting. *SOURCE: Grant deed, title policy.*	8. Exact name(s) and manner in which title is to be held. *SOURCE: Purchaser, deposit receipt.*	
	2. Name, address, loan number of holder of existing loan and unpaid balance. *SOURCE: Payment book.*	9. Name, address and telephone number of proposed lender, if any. *SOURCE: Purchaser.*	
	3. Fire insurance policies. *SOURCE: Actual policies or name and address of lender holding policies.*	10. Financial terms of the transaction and special instructions to be set forth in escrow. *SOURCE: All parties.*	
	4. If income property, complete list of tenants, rentals, including advance payments; vacancy list; leases, if any. *SOURCE: Owner or manager.*	11. Name, address, telephone number and license number of broker, or brokers involved and amount of commissions.	
	5. Real estate tax and improvement bond information. *SOURCE: Current tax bill; bond payment notice.*	FOR FASTER ESCROW SERVICE Furnish your escrow agent with all essential details of the sale when the escrow is opened.	
	6. If personal property is included in sale, an inventory, and if possible, completed bill of sale. *SOURCE: Owner.*	Always refer to the escrow number in correspondence or telephone calls to your escrow agent.	
	7. Name of title company to issue title policy and type of title insurance to be secured. *SOURCE: Owner.*	Use this checklist on every sale. Just ask for additional copies whenever you need them.	

Los Angeles Land Title Company

DOCUMENTARY STAMPS

VALUE OR CONSIDERATION			TAX	VALUE OR CONSIDERATION			TAX
$ 101	to	$ 500	$ 0.55	$25,001	to	$25,500	$28.05
501	to	1,000	1.10	25,501	to	26,000	28.60
1,001	to	1,500	1.65	26,001	to	26,500	29.15
1,501	to	2,000	2.20	26,501	to	27,000	29.70
2,001	**to**	**2,500**	**2.75**	**27,001**	**to**	**27,500**	**30.25**
2,501	to	3,000	3.30	27,501	to	28,000	30.80
3,001	to	3,500	3.85	28,001	to	28,500	31.35
3,501	to	4,000	4.40	28,501	to	29,000	31.90
4,001	to	4,500	4.95	29,001	to	29,500	32.45
4,501	**to**	**5,000**	**5.50**	**29,501**	**to**	**30,000**	**33.00**
5,001	to	5,500	6.05	30,001	to	30,500	33.55
5,501	to	6,000	6.60	30,501	to	31,000	34.10
6,001	to	6,500	7.15	31,001	to	31,500	34.65
6,501	to	7,000	7.70	31,501	to	32,000	35.20
7,001	**to**	**7,500**	**8.25**	**32,001**	**to**	**32,500**	**35.75**
7,501	to	8,000	8.80	32,501	to	33,000	36.30
8,001	to	8,500	9.35	33,001	to	33,500	36.85
8,501	to	9,000	9.90	33,501	to	34,000	37.40
9,001	to	9,500	10.45	34,001	to	34,500	37.95
9,501	**to**	**10,000**	**11.00**	**34,501**	**to**	**35,000**	**38.50**
10,001	to	10,500	11.55	35,001	to	35,500	39.05
10,501	to	11,000	12.10	35,501	to	36,000	39.60
11,001	to	11,500	12.65	36,001	to	36,500	40.15
11,501	to	12,000	13.20	36,501	to	37,000	40.70
12,001	**to**	**12,500**	**13.75**	**37,001**	**to**	**37,500**	**41.25**
12,501	to	13,000	14.30	37,501	to	38,000	41.80
13,001	to	13,500	14.85	38,001	to	38,500	42.35
13,501	to	14,000	15.40	38,501	to	39,000	42.90
14,001	to	14,500	15.95	39,001	to	39,500	43.45
14,501	**to**	**15,000**	**16.50**	**39,501**	**to**	**40,000**	**44.00**
15,001	to	15,500	17.05	40,001	to	40,500	44.55
15,501	to	16,000	17.60	40,501	to	41,000	45.10
16,001	to	16,500	18.15	41,001	to	41,500	45.65
16,501	to	17,000	18.70	41,501	to	42,000	46.20
17,001	**to**	**17,500**	**19.25**	**42,001**	**to**	**42,500**	**46.75**
17,501	to	18,000	19.80	42,501	to	43,000	47.30
18,001	to	18,500	20.35	43,001	to	43,500	47.85
18,501	to	19,000	20.90	43,501	to	44,000	48.40
19,001	to	19,500	21.45	44,001	to	44,500	48.95
19,501	**to**	**20,000**	**22.00**	**44,501**	**to**	**45,000**	**49.50**
20,001	to	20,500	22.55	45,001	to	45,500	50.05
20,501	to	21,000	23.10	45,501	to	46,000	50.60
21,001	to	21,500	23.65	46,001	to	46,500	51.15
21,501	to	22,000	24.20	46,501	to	47,000	51.70
22,001	**to**	**22,500**	**24.75**	**47,001**	**to**	**47,500**	**52.25**
22,501	to	23,000	25.30	47,501	to	48,000	52.80
23,001	to	23,500	25.85	48,001	to	48,500	53.35
23,501	to	24,000	26.40	48.501	to	49,000	53.90
24,001	to	24,500	26.95	49,001	to	49,500	54.45
24,501	**to**	**25,000**	**27.50**	**49,501**	**to**	**50,000**	**55.00**

escrow at the same time. The efficient salesman has a deposit receipt so drawn that all terms of the transaction are spelled out, and the escrow instructions are drawn from it. The papers, when completed, should be taken to the buyer and seller for their signatures. Having the parties come in to the escrow office for the signing is not good practice. It is not the responsibility of the escrow officer to interpret the instructions to the parties. Documents that must be notarized may be signed later at the escrow office, or, if the broker is a notary, he may often take care of the notarizing. In cases where it is necessary to expedite the closing of the escrow, the salesman must be prepared to hand-deliver loan papers or to handle other details in connection with the closing.

Title Insurance

The term *title* has been defined as the means whereby an owner has the just possession of his property, or as the method by which his right to property is established or evidenced, or as the evidence of ownership.

It is in this sense that the term *record title* is used, or *examining the title* as examining the instruments and acts of record that evidence the ownership of real property. In short, "title" means simply ownership.

Title may be acquired by several methods: (1) by private grant; (2) by intestate succession; (3) by will or devise; (4) by adverse possession; (5) by accretion; (6) by right of eminent domain; (7) by dedication; (8) by involuntary transfer; (9) by escheat; and (10) by estoppel.

When Title Passes. It has been broadly stated that an instrument in the form of a deed deposited in escrow becomes effective to pass title as soon as the conditions of the escrow are so far performed that the grantee is entitled to possession of the deed, although it is not then actually delivered to him. The moment at which the conditions of the escrow are performed and the title passes is controlled in any given case *by the provisions of the particular escrow instructions.*

The escrow instructions may provide that the conditions of the escrow are performed when the escrow holder has received funds and an instrument "by the use" or "delivery" of which title will vest in a stated manner, in which case title has been held to pass when the escrow holder holds the funds and the instrument, although the instrument is neither manually delivered nor recorded and clerical functions (such as adjustments of taxes, insurance, and interest) are yet to be performed.

In other instances, the instructions may authorize the use of funds when the escrow holder can obtain or secure a policy of title insurance showing title vested in the grantee, in which case it has been held that title does not pass until a deed has been recorded, which will enable the title company to issue its policy.

Still other instructions leave no doubt as to the event of closing; they may expressly authorize use of the funds when a deed or other instrument has been "filed for record," enabling a title company to issue a policy showing title in the grantee. The courts have held that if an escrow holder does not comply with an instruction, the injured party may sue for breach of contract.[6]

Even the government, whether city, county, state, or federal, must know about ownership of the land it buys, condemns, or takes over and, in California, is in the habit of depending on the title company to segregate and interpret the public records and to insure the correctness of its findings.

A policy of title insurance is an insured statement of condition of the "title," that is, the ownership of a particular piece of land. The policy shows who owns the land, according to the public records, and what is against it in the way of taxes, mortgages, and other liens or encumbrances of record.

Public records may be incomplete or erroneous. They may not necessarily disclose shortcomings arising from forgery, incompetency, or failures to comply with legal requirements. Title insurance is a protection against not only most of the risks that are a matter of public record, but also against those that lie outside the public records. The beneficiary of title insurance is usually the purchaser of a property or the lender who has loaned money with the property as security, but it may be a governmental agency or any person with some special interest in the property.

Standard-Coverage Policies. The standard policy of title insurance insures single or multiple estates and interests in land. In addition to risks of record, it also protects against forgery, impersonation, and lack of capacity of the party to any transaction involving title to the land. It is the "owner's policy" if the owner only is insured, a "loan policy" if a lender only is insured, and a "joint-protection policy" when both owner and lender are insured. The standard policy *does not* protect the policyholder against (1)

[6] From a paper, "Title, Possession, and Performance of Conditions," by Hugh L. Gary, owner and manager of Gary Escrow Service, Van Nuys, California, delivered before the California Escrow Association, September 28, 1963.

Bank of America
NATIONAL TRUST AND SAVINGS ASSOCIATION

Arcadia Branch   Date January 13, 1971

Statement of Richard B. Buyer and   **ESCROW STATEMENT**   Escrow No. 88-3808

Mary R. Buying

Purchase of 765 North Arcadia Street, Arcadia

ITEMS	DEBITS		CREDITS	
Consideration: Sale	30,750	00		
Loan Republic First National ($30,750)			30,207	75
Outside of Escrow				
Purchase Money Trust Deed				
Balance of Mortgage or Trust Deed of Record				
Interest Adjustment				
Tax Pro Rata 1-1-7- to 1-13-71			30	36
Insurance Pro Rata				
Rent Pro Rata				
Current Mut. Mtg. Ins. Pro Rata				
Loan Trust Funds				
Deposited (Towne Realty)			500	00
Deposited: Buyer			654	18
Title Policy ALTA	43	95		
Internal Revenue Stamps				
Reconveyance Fee				
Taxes - second installment	454	94		
Assessments or Bonds				
Tax Service Contract				
Recording: ´ deed and deed of trust	6	40		
Payment Mortgage or Trust Deed				
Int. on $ @ % from to				
Payment Mortgage or Trust Deed				
Int. on $ @ % from to				
Commission				
Termite Report				
Escrow Fee				
Completing Forms Home Insurance Co. on year premium	137	00		
Notary Fees				
Real Estate Loan Fees				
Check to Balance	31,392	29	31,392	29
TOTALS				

THIS FORM SHOULD BE RETAINED FOR INCOME TAX PURPOSES

TRU-902 5-63

Bank of America
NATIONAL TRUST AND SAVINGS ASSOCIATION

Arcadia Branch Date January 13, 1971

Statement of Donald E. Seller and
Anita S. Seller

ESCROW STATEMENT

Escrow No. 88-3808

ITEMS	DEBITS		CREDITS	
Consideration: Sale			30,750	00
Loan				
Outside of Escrow				
Purchase Money Trust Deed				
Balance of Mortgage or Trust Deed of Record				
Interest Adjustment				
Tax Pro Rata 1-1-71 to 1-13-71	30	36		
Insurance Pro Rata				
Rent Pro Rata				
Current Mut. Mtg. Ins. Pro Rata				
Loan Trust Funds				
Deposited:				
Title Policy	192	25		
~~Internal Revenue Stamps~~ Documentary transfer tax	33	55		
Reconveyance Fee	15	00		
Taxes				
Assessments or Bonds				
Tax Service Contract				
Recording: two reconveyances	4	00		
Payment Mortgage or Trust Deed First Western Bank	3,685	15		
Int. on $ @ % from 12-1-70 to 1-14-71	20	27		
forwarding fee	15	00		
Payment Mortgage or Trust Deed Harris	7,708	34		
Int. on $ @ % from 8-20-70 to 1-14-71	327	59		
Commission	1,781	50		
Termite Report Brown Bug Termite Company	85	00		
Escrow Fee	181	00		
Completing Forms				
Notary Fees				
Real Estate Loan Fees for buyer's new loan, including inspection fee, title endorsement and document fee	672	50		
Home Furance Company	47	00		
Safeway Roofing Company	612	00		
Check to Balance	15,339	49		
TOTALS	30,750	00	30,750	00

THIS FORM SHOULD BE RETAINED FOR INCOME TAX PURPOSES

TRU-902 5-63

defects in the title known to him to exist at the date of the policy and not previously disclosed to the insurance company; (2) easements and liens not shown by public records; (3) rights or claims of persons in physical possession of the land and not shown on the public records; (4) rights or claims not shown by public records but that could be ascertained by physical inspection of the property or by a survey; (5) mining claims, reservations in patents, or water rights; and (6) zoning ordinances.

Extended-Coverage Policies. The *general* exceptions contained in standard-coverage policies are eliminated in the extended-coverage policies, at an increased premium.

The ALTA Policy. The full name for this type of policy is "American Land Title Association Loan Policy—additional coverage." It is an extended coverage for the benefit of *lenders* and is used primarily in connection with loans made on recently completed structures. Insurance is given that the lender has a valid and enforceable lien, subject only to the exclusions from the coverage and such defects, liens, and encumbrances on the title as are shown therein. The policy also expressly includes priority insurance to cover mechanics' liens and street-improvement assessments. The cost of an ALTA Policy is based on the amount of the loan. A survey may be required in issuing the policy but is often waived.

California Land Title Association. This is the trade organization of the title companies of the state. Their standardized forms are used generally by the title companies in the state for their policies of title.[7]

CASE STUDY

John Baldwin is a real estate salesman employed by Michael Bush, realtor, of Corona, California. He is new in the real estate business and has had only two sales since joining the Bush office. His broker has always had an office policy of taking all transactions to escrow himself. He maintains that, because he is responsible for any errors or omissions, he wishes to dictate the instructions himself to avoid any mistakes.

On August 16, 1971, Baldwin sells a home to Mr. and Mrs. James Potter, who are new arrivals from the East Coast. They offer $20,000 for a home in the city, which is accepted. They indicate that they will pay all cash for the property, which is at present encumbered with an 8 percent loan in the amount of $12,000, held by the local savings and loan company. The loan was placed on the property the previous year when the sellers needed the cash to make a down payment on a four-unit apartment house they were purchasing.

The home that the Potters are purchasing was listed originally for $24,000, but there has been little activity, so, after much persuasion on the part of Baldwin, the owners decide to accept the offer of $20,000. Potter is unfamiliar with real estate sales procedures in California and has never experienced an escrow sale. Baldwin asks him for a check for earnest money, but Potter remembers that he was "warned" before he left the East about the "slick" real estate operators in California. He hesitates to write a check; but, on Baldwin's insistence that he will require a token amount to "bind the deal," Potter gives him a personal check on his bank in the East for $100. He says that, if his offer is accepted, he will make a deposit in escrow at opening, although he is still concerned about not having an attorney present to handle the details of the sale. He is anxious to have quick possession of the property, because his two children by a previous marriage are waiting to fly out from the East to enter school at the beginning of the fall semester.

The day following the acceptance of Potter's offer, realtor Bush is called out of town because of the serious illness of his mother. The length of his absence appears to be indefinite, so it becomes necessary for Baldwin to take his sale to escrow himself. He is a little nervous about his first escrow, but, because it is to be an all-cash sale, he feels he should have no problems. However, he decides to make an appointment with an escrow officer whom he has met socially. He calls his buyers and sellers and arranges for them to meet him in escrow that afternoon.

Before the principals arrive, Baldwin confides to Miss King, the escrow officer, that this is his first escrow and asks her if she will assist him with any details that may be unfamiliar to him. He introduces his buyers and sellers when they arrive and waits for Miss King to proceed. She asks the usual questions as to the total consideration, the names of buyers and sellers, and the financing. Baldwin remembers that in his nervousness over his first transaction in escrow, he has forgotten to ask the sellers to bring their documents with them. He has also left the purchase agreement at the office, but he does remember that the Potters have indicated they would want to take out a new loan because the current interest rates are lower than the 8 percent carried by the loan of

[7] For further information on title services, see *Title Services of Title Insurance and Trust Company* (Los Angeles: Title Insurance and Trust Company).

POLICY FEES
Effective Jan. 6, 1970

Amount of Insurance	C.L.T.A. Owners, Joint Protection, or A.L.T.A. Lenders: Basic Rate	C.L.T.A. Owners, Joint Protection, or A.L.T.A. Lenders: Short Term Rate	C.L.T.A. Lenders Standard Coverage: Basic Loan Rate	C.L.T.A. Lenders Standard Coverage: Short Term Rate
$ 1,000	$ 40.00	$ 32.00	$ 32.00	$ 25.60
1,500	43.00	34.40	34.40	27.52
2,000	46.00	36.80	36.80	29.44
2,500	49.00	39.20	39.20	31.36
3,000	52.00	41.60	41.60	33.28
3,500	55.00	44.00	44.00	35.20
4,000	58.00	46.40	46.40	37.12
4,500	61.00	48.80	48.80	39.04
5,000	64.00	51.20	51.20	40.96
5,500	67.00	53.60	53.60	42.88
6,000	70.00	56.00	56.00	44.80
6,500	73.00	58.40	58.40	46.72
7,000	76.00	60.80	60.80	48.64
7,500	79.00	63.20	63.20	50.56
8,000	82.00	65.60	65.60	52.48
8,500	85.00	68.00	68.00	54.40
9,000	88.00	70.40	70.40	56.32
9,500	91.00	72.80	72.80	58.24
10,000	94.00	75.20	75.20	60.16
11,000	98.25	78.60	78.60	62.88
12,000	102.50	82.00	82.00	65.60
13,000	106.75	85.40	85.40	68.32
14,000	111.00	88.80	88.80	71.04
15,000	115.25	92.20	92.20	73.76
16,000	119.50	95.60	95.60	76.48
17,000	123.75	99.00	99.00	79.20
18,000	128.00	102.40	102.40	81.92
19,000	132.25	105.80	105.80	84.64
20,000	136.50	109.20	109.20	87.36
21,000	140.75	112.60	112.60	90.08
22,000	145.00	116.00	116.00	92.80
23,000	149.25	119.40	119.40	95.52
24,000	153.50	122.80	122.80	98.24
25,000	157.75	126.20	126.20	100.96
26,000	162.00	129.60	129.60	103.68
27,000	166.25	133.00	133.00	106.40
28,000	170.50	136.40	136.40	109.12
29,000	174.75	139.80	139.80	111.84
30,000	179.00	143.20	143.20	114.56
31,000	182.25	145.80	145.80	116.64
32,000	185.50	148.40	148.40	118.72
33,000	188.75	151.00	151.00	120.80
34,000	192.00	153.60	153.60	122.88
35,000	195.25	156.20	156.20	124.96
36,000	198.50	158.80	158.80	127.04
37,000	201.75	161.40	161.40	129.12
38,000	205.00	164.00	164.00	131.20
39,000	208.25	166.60	166.60	133.28
40,000	211.50	169.20	169.20	135.36
41,000	214.75	171.80	171.80	137.44
42,000	218.00	174.40	174.40	139.52
43,000	221.25	177.00	177.00	141.60
44,000	224.50	179.60	179.60	143.68
45,000	227.75	182.20	182.20	145.76
46,000	231.00	184.80	184.80	147.84
47,000	234.25	187.40	187.40	149.92
48,000	237.50	190.00	190.00	152.00
49,000	240.75	192.60	192.60	154.08
50,000	244.00	195.20	195.20	156.16

Amount of Insurance	Basic Rate	Short Term Rate	Basic Loan Rate	Short Term Rate
$ 51,000	$247.25	$197.80	$197.80	$158.24
52,000	250.50	200.40	200.40	160.32
53,000	253.75	203.00	203.00	162.40
54,000	257.00	205.60	205.60	164.48
55,000	260.25	208.20	208.20	166.56
56,000	263.50	210.80	210.80	168.64
57,000	266.75	213.40	213.40	170.72
58,000	270.00	216.00	216.00	172.80
59,000	273.25	218.60	218.60	174.88
60,000	276.50	221.20	221.20	176.96
61,000	279.50	223.60	223.60	178.88
62,000	282.50	226.00	226.00	180.80
63,000	285.50	228.40	228.40	182.72
64,000	288.50	230.80	230.80	184.64
65,000	291.50	233.20	233.20	186.56
66,000	294.50	235.60	235.60	188.48
67,000	297.50	238.00	238.00	190.40
68,000	300.50	240.40	240.40	192.32
69,000	303.50	242.80	242.80	194.24
70,000	306.50	245.20	245.20	196.16
71,000	309.50	247.60	247.60	198.08
72,000	312.50	250.00	250.00	200.00
73,000	315.50	252.40	252.40	201.92
74,000	318.50	254.80	254.80	203.84
75,000	321.50	257.20	257.20	205.76
76,000	324.50	259.60	259.60	207.68
77,000	327.50	262.00	262.00	209.60
78,000	330.50	264.40	264.40	211.52
79,000	333.50	266.80	266.80	213.44
80,000	336.50	269.20	269.20	215.36
81,000	339.50	271.60	271.60	217.28
82,000	342.50	274.00	274.00	219.20
83,000	345.50	276.40	276.40	221.12
84,000	348.50	278.80	278.80	223.04
85,000	351.50	281.20	281.20	224.96
86,000	354.50	283.60	283.60	226.88
87,000	357.50	286.00	286.00	228.80
88,000	360.50	288.40	288.40	230.72
89,000	363.50	290.80	290.80	232.64
90,000	366.50	293.20	293.20	234.56
91,000	369.50	295.60	295.60	236.48
92,000	372.50	298.00	298.00	238.40
93,000	375.50	300.40	300.40	240.32
94,000	378.50	302.80	302.80	242.24
95,000	381.50	305.20	305.20	244.16
96,000	384.50	307.60	307.60	246.08
97,000	387.50	310.00	310.00	248.00
98,000	390.50	312.40	312.40	249.92
99,000	393.50	314.80	314.80	251.84
100,000	396.50	317.20	317.20	253.76
Each Additional $1,000				
Up to $ 300,000 Add	2.50	2.00	2.00	1.60
Up to $ 1,000,000 Add	2.00	1.60	1.60	1.28
Up to $ 5,000,000 Add	1.75	1.40	1.40	1.12
Up to $10,000,000 Add	1.50	1.20	1.20	.96
Over $10,000,000 Add	1.25	1.00	1.00	.80

SHORT TERM RATES apply to an insured owner only, depending on the date of a prior C.L.T.A. or A.L.T.A. form of policy as follows:

80% of Basic Rate or Basic Loan Rate if within 24 months.

Basic Rate or Basic Loan Rate after 24 Months.

A.L.T.A. LENDERS POLICY ISSUED CONCURRENTLY WITH A C.L.T.A. JOINT PROTECTION POLICY FOR FULL VALUE

Amount of Insurance	Additional Rate	Amount of Insurance	Additional Rate
$ 1,000	$15.50	$ 46,000	$53.70
1,500	16.10	47,000	54.35
2,000	16.70	48,000	55.00
2,500	17.30	49,000	55.65
3,000	17.90	50,000	56.30
3,500	18.50	51,000	56.95
4,000	19.10	52,000	57.60
4,500	19.70	53,000	58.25
5,000	20.30	54,000	58.90
5,500	20.90	55,000	59.55
6,000	21.50	56,000	60.20
6,500	22.10	57,000	60.85
7,000	22.70	58,000	61.50
7,500	23.30	59,000	62.15
8,000	23.90	60,000	62.80
8,500	24.50	61,000	63.40
9,000	25.10	62,000	64.00
9,500	25.70	63,000	64.60
10,000	26.30	64,000	65.20
11,000	27.15	65,000	65.80
12,000	28.00	66,000	66.40
13,000	28.85	67,000	67.00
14,000	29.70	68,000	67.60
15,000	30.55	69,000	68.20
16,000	31.40	70,000	68.80
17,000	32.25	71,000	69.40
18,000	33.10	72,000	70.00
19,000	33.95	73,000	70.60
20,000	34.80	74,000	71.20
21,000	35.65	75,000	71.80
22,000	36.50	76,000	72.40
23,000	37.35	77,000	73.00
24,000	38.20	78,000	73.60
25,000	39.05	79,000	74.20
26,000	39.90	80,000	74.80
27,000	40.75	81,000	75.40
28,000	41.60	82,000	76.00
29,000	42.45	83,000	76.60
30,000	43.30	84,000	77.20
31,000	43.95	85,000	77.80
32,000	44.60	86,000	78.40
33,000	45.25	87,000	79.00
34,000	45.90	88,000	79.60
35,000	46.55	89,000	80.20
36,000	47.20	90,000	80.80
37,000	47.85	91,000	81.40
38,000	48.50	92,000	82.00
39,000	49.15	93,000	82.60
40,000	49.80	94,000	83.20
41,000	50.45	95,000	83.80
42,000	51.10	96,000	84.40
43,000	51.75	97,000	85.00
44,000	52.40	98,000	85.60
45,000	53.05	99,000	86.20
		100,000	86.80

Each Additional $1,000		Up to $ 5,000,000 Add	.35
Up to $ 300,000 Add	.50	Up to $10,000,000 Add	.30
Up to $ 1,000,000 Add	.40	Over $10,000,000 Add	.25

record on the property. Miss King mentions there will probably be a prepayment penalty on the existing loan if it is paid off. The sellers are surprised at the mention of a "penalty" and when a figure of possibly $480 is mentioned, they become most indignant. Miss King asks the Potters how they wish to take title. They indicate that they are unfamiliar with California law and ask her for her suggestion in the matter. Her answer is that taking title as "husband and wife in joint tenancy" is customary. She explains the survivorship benefits of a joint-tenancy vesting. The Potters agree that this might be the best way to have the recital in the deed, and Baldwin and Miss King concur.

Baldwin gives Potter's $100 check to Miss King and says that Mr. Potter will give her additional funds when the papers are drawn. Miss King inquires about a termite report, which causes Potter to inquire as to its meaning. Baldwin attempts to explain, but Potter is very upset that he should be buying a house where there might be "insects eating away at the foundation." Baldwin assures him that there will be an inspection made by a licensed operator, and that any repairs necessary will be made at no expense to him. The seller counters with, "There was no mention of a termite report in the deposit receipt. Mr. Potter is not taking out a new loan, so why should a termite report be required?" He implies that, because he is being put to the expense of prepaying the existing loan on the property, and has accepted a low offer anyway, he does not want to incur any further expense. Potter is adamant and insists that the "deal is off" unless a complete "clearance" is given on the property.

A call from his office comes for Baldwin, and the secretary tells him that an out-of-town customer is waiting to see him. He has forgotten the appointment he had made with them, so he excuses himself and asks Miss King if she will complete the paper and have the principals sign them and call him later if she needs any more information.

1. Discuss the office policy of Bush in taking all transactions to escrow himself.
2. In your opinion, should Baldwin have insisted on a larger check as earnest money?
3. Do you see anything wrong with Baldwin's having buyer and seller in escrow together? Why, or why not?
4. Do you feel that Miss King was an efficient escrow officer? Why, or why not?

SUGGESTED REFERENCES

Reference Book. Sacramento: California Department of Real Estate.

SMITH, BURTON E. "Trust Fund Requirements and Records," *Advanced Real Estate Sales.* Los Angeles: California Real Estate Association, 1968.

12

Taxes and Real Estate Transactions

Principles of Taxation

The two broad principles of taxation that are widely recognized base taxes either on the *ability to pay* or on *the benefits received.* It has been argued that these two concepts overlap because the ability to pay is a consequence of the benefits received. Under the benefits-received concept, taxes are levied in proportion to the benefits received from governmental services. But what of the less-fortunate members of society who are most dependent on government benefits? Are they in a position to meet their share of government expenses? Because of the tenuous nature of the ability-to-pay or benefits-received philosophy of taxation, the ad valorem (according to value) tax system, applicable particularly to real and personal property at the city and county levels, has come into widespread use.

Real Property Taxes

Because of the effect on real estate (whether direct or indirect) of most forms of taxation, there is a need for understanding of the basic taxation principles involved. Real property (as opposed to businesses) is subject, as we have said, to an ad valorem tax, which must be paid whether or not the real estate is revenue producing. Although income and capital-gains tax have an indirect influence on real property, the ad valorem tax has a direct effect on it. This tax is protected by lien rights and must be paid regardless of local, state, or national economic conditions or the financial status of the property owner.

The assumption that taxes should be assessed on the basis of a man's ability to pay is not a new concept. Agricultural lands in England were used an indication of the individual's wealth over 600 years ago. The landowner was taxed on the basis of his holdings. *It has been said that as applied to property values, the power to tax is the power to destroy.* In the sense that taxation raised to a confiscatory level destroys the incentive to purchase or own property, the concept is correct. (As an example, the property tax is a heavily weighted item in the total fixed expenses of income property.) Taxes raised to a high level will depress the real estate market in a given area. On the other side of the coin, real estate taxes provide an important source of government revenue, particularly at the local level, and are considered necessary to provide the protection and enforcement of the property owner's rights.

Assessing Procedure. By the first day in July of each year, all county property must have been assessed. The assessment rolls are then turned in to the county board of supervisors, who, in turn, give them to the county auditor. The auditor lists the total number of acres of land and the value of all real estate, personal property, improvements, and moneys. Thus, he arrives at the entire value of county property. The board of supervisors then determines the total expenses for the coming year. With the information on the total value of all county property, the tax rate is fixed.

Personal property taxes (both county and city) become a lien on the real property of the owner. Real property taxes become a lien on the property assessed.

"Full cash value," upon which the state law decrees that assessments must be made, is determined by the local tax assessors. The assessee must be the owner of the property as of the first day in March prior to the commencement of the applicable fiscal year on July 1. *Comparable properties must be assessed at equivalent values.* Property owners may file objections shortly after July 1 to the local board of supervisors sitting as a "board of equalization." The assessment of properties is in no way based on the amount of money to be raised. The tax rate is raised or lowered depending on the expenses to be met. Inequities in assessed values are often the result of an understaffed assessor's office. An owner making an appeal for adjustment in his assessment must do it on the basis of other properties in the area comparable to his own.

Note: In 1966, the California legislature enacted a bill making it mandatory that all property on the tax rolls be assessed at 25 percent of actual cash value.

When Taxes Become a Lien. Taxes become a lien on real property the first day in March. The first installment becomes due November 1 and is delinquent if not paid by 5:00 P.M., December 10, at which time a penalty of 6 percent is added. The second installment, due February 1, becomes delinquent if not paid by 5:00 P.M., April 10. In most counties, personal property taxes must be paid in full when the tax bill is furnished, unless they are secured by real property. Personal property taxes in this event are normally paid with the first installment of the real property tax.

At the local level, many cities are levying sales and utility taxes in order to meet the mounting expenses of governmental services and to help equalize the burden of taxation, thus giving some relief to the property owner.

Tax Sale. Each year, on or before June 8, an intent to sell certain real property to the state is published, together with the date and hour of the sale. This intent to sell is published by the county tax collector and includes all those properties for which one or both tax installments are delinquent. On June 30 the property is said to be sold to the state. This date, however, is only important in that it serves to establish the date at which the statutory five-year redemption period starts. The property may be redeemed at any time during this five-year period by payment of all delinquent taxes plus any penalties.

Property Sold to the State. Five years after the first year of sale, if the property has not been redeemed, it will be deeded to the state subsequently to be sold at public auction. The property must be sold for a minimum figure representing the amount of taxes for the year in which the property was first sold to the state. For property sold after June 30, 1969 an additional penalty of 1 percent per month for the first year until redeemed, plus a redemption fee of $2 for each parcel will be assessed. For property sold to the state June 30, 1968 or prior, penalties will accrue at the rate of 1 percent per month for the first year and ½ percent per month thereafter, plus a redemption fee of $1.50 for each parcel.

Redemption. As stated above, the law provides that the owner (or his successor in interest) may redeem the tax-sold property by payment of taxes, interest, cost, and penalties. When the payment is made to the county treasurer, a controller's receipt is issued, which may then be recorded. A sale of tax-deeded property may be initiated upon application by a prospective purchaser with a minimum bid established by the board of supervisors. The purchaser receives a tax deed, which is acceptable for title insurance after one year has passed since issuance of the deed, provided the former owner is not in possession, current taxes are paid, and no serious defects show up in the title search. Title companies in over half of the state are accepting tax deeds for insurance.

Veteran's Exemption

Veterans are provided with special benefits at both state and federal levels, which affect their property ownership. A California resident who has given military service in time of war is entitled to a $1,000 exemption on the *assessed value* of his property. This exemption applies also to the widow, widowed mother, or a pensioned father or mother of a deceased veteran. If the veteran, or others entitled to the exemption, owns property worth $5,000 or more, he ceases to become eligible.

Homeowner's Property-Tax Exemption

On November 5, 1968 legislation was enacted providing the homeowner with certain tax exemptions as follows:

1. An exemption of $750 on the assessed value of a residence will be allowed provided the dwelling is occupied by the owner as his principal place of residence.
2. All household furnishings and personal effects of a householder are exempt.
3. The standard income-tax deduction is increased to $1,000 for single persons and to $2,000 for married couples.

The claim for exemption must be filed prior to April 15 each year. The application form to be filed states in effect that:

1. The claimant either holds title to the property or is buying it under a contract of sale, and that he is occupying the property as his principal place of residence.
2. The building does not contain more than two units.
3. The claimant has not filed a claim for homeowner's exemption on any other property in California.
4. During the current fiscal year, neither the claimant nor anyone with whom the claimant shares ownership received or expects to receive from the state, county, or city any assistance (other than senior citizen's property-tax assistance) containing an allowance for property tax on the described building.

Special Assessments

These are assessments levied for the cost of specific local improvements, such as streets, sewers, sidewalks, irrigation, and drainage. There is no uniform method of spreading the cost; some cities spread the cost over a period of years, whereas others require payment the first few years. Because the assessment is levied for public improvement and, as such, is presumed to add to the property value, it is not allowed as a deduction under federal income-tax laws. In some cases, special assessments are periodically levied by improvement districts, or the city or county may levy assessments for particular improvements.

Normally, the district issues its own bonds. To repay the funds borrowed, the districts have the power to assess all lands in the district on an ad valorem basis. These assessments constitute a lien on the land until paid and (1) can be foreclosed by sale and (2) are prior to private property interests.

Tax-Exempt Property

The main categories of tax-exempt properties are: (1) government properties and (2) religious, charitable, and educational institutions.

Properties owned by local, state, or federal governments are not subject to taxation. Cities that are capitals of states naturally are particularly affected by government holdings, owing to the need to provide space for government activities.

The tax exemption of religious, charitable, or educational institutions is based on their contribution to the cultural and religious needs of the communities. Also, it is assumed that tax exemption should be granted them because, owing to their nonprofit character, they are supposedly unable to pay taxes. Although it is true that the services performed by the exempt institutions probably could not be provided were the organizations required to pay taxes, the question arises as to whether this exemption forces property owners to carry a disproportionate tax burden.

Taxes on Transfers of Property

The owner of property, whether it is real estate, stocks, bonds, or other property in any form, naturally wishes to pass on to his dependents an estate free of debt. Whether the estate is passed under will or by gifts or trusts during his lifetime, there will be certain taxes payable to the state and federal governments in cash. To secure payment, taxing authorities claim liens against the estate. These taxes are usually the largest single item of expense in the estate.

State Taxes

California Inheritance Tax[1]

This tax applies to:

1. Property acquired by the survivor under a joint tenancy.
2. Property transferred by deed, assignment, or gift made without adequate consideration in contemplation of death of the grantor.
3. Property passing through probate.
4. Life or accident insurance payable on account of the death of the insured.
5. Property passing under the homestead laws.
6. Property subject to power of appointment.

Certain exemptions from the tax apply as follows:
(1) Specific exemption:
Relation to decedent:

Class A. Wife, husband, lineal issue, lineal ancestor, adopted or mutually acknowledged child.
Exemption to each recipient:
Minor child $12,000
Wife 5,000
Husband 5,000
Others 5,000
Class B. Brother, sister, or descendant of either, wife or widow of a son, husband of a daugther. $2,000
Class C. Uncle, aunt, or descendant of either. $300

California Gift Tax. A tax upon gifts is also imposed by the state of California. The amount of this tax depends not only on the value of the property transferred but also on the relationship that the recipient bears to the person making the gift.

[1] For full treatment of this law, information may be obtained by writing the California State Inheritance Tax Department (State Comptroller).

In addition to certain specific exemptions, there is an annual exclusion that permits gifts totaling $3,000 to be made by one donor to each of any number of donees in any calendar year free of tax. This annual exclusion, however, does not apply if the transfer is of a future interest. Any person making gifts with a value in excess of the annual exclusion referred to is required to make a gift-tax return prior to April 15 of the following year.

The tax on gifts for a calendar year is computed by determining the aggregate sum of the total net gifts for such calendar year, the net gifts for each of the preceding calendar years, and the specific exemption, excepting therefrom such portion of the specific exemption as was used in the preceding calendar years.

In California, gifts by husband and wife, or from one to the other, should be discussed with an attorney. California, for example, does not permit the "gift-splitting" of the donor's separate property, permitted under the federal gift tax, the one who gives the property being the sole donor. Gifts of their community property to third persons, however, are, as in the federal law, considered to be made one-half by each spouse. One-half the value of community property given by one spouse to the other is exempt from tax. "Quasi-community property" transferred to a person other than one of the spouses is subject, on the election of both spouses, to such splitting. Transfers of "quasi-community property" to community or tenancy in common or joint tenancy of the spouses are also subject to special rules and, as with all gifts that might be subject to tax, should be first discussed with an attorney.

Miscellaneous Taxes

Unsecured personal-property taxes are due on March 1 and become delinquent after August 31. *Secured* personal-property taxes are normally due at the same time as the first installment of real-property taxes. A penalty of 6 percent is levied September 1 on all unsecured personal-property taxes unpaid at that date. Beginning January 1 of the following year there is an additional 1 percent a month penalty. Unsecured personal-property taxes do not constitute a lien on the real property.

Sales and Use Tax

The state of California imposes a *state sales tax* upon retailers who sell tangible personal property at retail. *The state use tax* applies where tangible personal property purchased from a retailer is stored, used, or otherwise consumed. This tax becomes the liability of the purchaser, whose obligation it is to pay it to the state or to a retailer authorized to collect the tax. The rate is 5 percent—4 percent of which goes to the state, and 1 percent to the local government.

The tax applies to the transfer of buildings, if pursuant to the contract of sale the buildings are to be severed by the seller. It does not apply if the sales contract provides that the buildings are to be severed by the purchaser.

In the sale of a retail business, the purchaser may be liable as a successor for tax owed by the seller. (See about successor's liability Chapter 16.)

Unemployment-Insurance Tax

Any employer paying wages in excess of $100 in a calendar quarter to employees in the subject employment is liable for contributions to the national system of unemployment insurance and to the state program of disability and hospital insurance for non-work-connected disabilities. *Licensed real estate salesmen and brokers whose compensation is solely by commissions are not covered.*

California Workmen's Compensation Law

This is an insurance payable by an employer and providing for weekly benefit payments to employees injured on the job, and who are unable to work as a result of these injuries or illness. Included also is payment of all medical and hospital costs applicable to the injury.[2]

Federal Taxes

Federal Estate Tax. The federal estate tax is a tax imposed on the transfer of property at the death of the owner. It is based on the net value of the estate without regard to the amount of the distributve shares or the relationship of the beneficiaries. The net value of the estate is determined by deducting from the total estate, debts, funeral and administration expenses, certain other items, and an exemption amounting, in the case of a citizen or resident of the United States, to $60,000. Property is valued as of the date of death, or under certain limitations, the executor may elect to value it as of one year after the decedent's death, except that sale or transfer of property during the year fixes the date of valuation.

[2] Further information on the California Workman's Compensation Law may be obtained from any insurance carrier or from the State Compensation Insurance Fund, Sacramento.

All proceeds of insurance on the life of the decedent payable to his estate must be included in the gross estate, as must also all such insurance payable to named beneficiaries if, at the time of death, the decedent retained certain rights incident to ownership. The present law does not provide any exemption of life insurance as such.

Property held in joint tenancy and transferred upon the death of the owner is included in the gross estate to the extent of the contribution by the decedent to such joint-tenancy property.

Only one-half of the community property is subject to tax on the death of the first to die. However, community property acquired before July 29, 1927 is considered separate property and is subject to tax.

The federal estate tax provides for the allowance of a marital deduction (with certain limitations) for estate-tax purposes, as to separate property passing to the decedent's surviving spouse, not exceeding one-half of the decedent's adjusted gross estate. Married persons owning separate property may now arrange their estates so that the marital deduction can be used to effect substantial estate-tax reduction.

A limited credit is allowed for state inheritance taxes paid in the case of net taxable estates over $100,000.

Under California law, unless the decedent directs otherwise, the federal estate tax must be equitably prorated among the persons taking a taxable share of the estate in proportion to their interests.

Federal Gift Tax

The federal government imposes a tax on gifts payable by the donor in the year following that in which the gifts are made. If not so paid, the taxing authority will claim a lien against the property transferred.

A specific exemption of $30,000 is allowed to citizens or residents. This is not an annual exemption, but it is the total specific exemption allowed a donor during his lifetime on the aggregate value of all gifts. The donor has the option of taking the entire exemption in one year or spreading it over any number of years, but once the exemptions taken total $30,000, no further specific exemption is deductible.

Following the same principles applicable to the federal estate tax, a donor spouse is permitted a deduction of one-half of the value of a gift to his spouse, the interest transferred may be considered as made one-half by each if the spouses so elect. Gifts of community property are considered made one-half by each spouse. The gift tax is cumulative; that is, it must be computed each year on the aggregate value of all gifts. From the tax as figured on all such gifts, a credit may be taken for gifts previously reported.

In addition to the $30,000 specific exemption, the donor may deduct gifts for charitable purposes as well as the first $3,000 given to each of any number of donees in any calendar year. The $3,000 exclusions do not apply to gifts of future interests in property. However, since 1954, gifts in trust for minors will not, if such trusts conform to the particular requirements of the Code, lose the $3,000 annual exclusion.[3]

Federal Income Tax

Real estate is one of the most versatile vehicles for planning a sound financial future, and it is an ideal tax shelter against inflation. Although the basic concept behind the federal income tax is that all income is to be taxed regardless of how derived, certain tax benefits are accorded to ownership of real estate:

1. The deduction for depreciation permits a tax-free recovery of capital, even though the value of the property increases at a faster rate than its physical depreciation.
2. Real estate is one of the few types of assets that may be disposed of in a "tax-free" exchange. Thus the character of one's real estate investment may be changed at any time without incurring a tax on the exchange.
3. Certain lease arrangements allow the tenant to pay for improvements and additions to the property without subjecting the landlord to tax.
4. Selling real estate on the installment or deferred-payment plan spreads the tax on the profit realized into small amounts over the installment period.
5. The profit made when investment real estate is sold is taxed as a capital gain. The loss is subject to the usual capital loss rules. But Section 1231 property is accorded special treatment.[4]

This includes:

a. Property used in trade or business, subject to depreciation, and held for more than six months.
b. Real property used in trade or business and held for more than six months.

[3] The subject of taxation is one of great complexity and constantly subject to change. Real estate practitioners are cautioned against giving tax advice without consulting certified public accountants or tax experts.

[4] Individual long-term capital losses could formerly be used to offset $1,000 of ordinary income, with a carryforward of unused capital loss credits. Under the 1969 Tax Reform Act, the benefit of such loss was substantially cut—in half—so that $2,000 of long-term capital loss is required to offset an annual maximum of $1,000 of ordinary income.

c. Leases held for an indefinite period, such as certain oil and gas leases that are considered as real property.
d. Trade or business property involuntarily converted, or other capital assets involuntarily converted and held for more than six months. ("Involuntary conversion" relates to property destroyed or condemned for public use, and for which money or other property is received.)

For tax purposes all real estate falls into five categories:

1. That used as one's residence.
2. That used in one's business.
3. That used for income purposes.
4. That held for sale ("dealer" property).
5. That held as an investment.

Taxes on Property Transfers

Real estate brokers are constantly being asked to assume the role of investment counselors and estate planners for their clients. Familiarity with the tax laws as well as with the tax position of the client is basic to any counseling; however, interpretation of the tax laws as they apply to real estate investments should be attempted only with the aid of tax experts. Two basic precepts should be made clear:

1. The purchase price of a property may not be as important as the client's tax position after the acquisition and sale.
2. Tax consciousness should start *before* acquisition of the property.

As we have mentioned above, the law accords many tax benefits to real estate ownership. Included in these benefits are:

1. Deduction for depreciation.
2. Spreading tax on installment sales.
3. Capital gain treatment on investment-property sales.
4. "Tax-free" treatment on certain property exchanges.

Depreciation and capital gain are the keys to real estate tax savings. A *sale* is generally a transfer of property in return for money only. It is not always easy to determine whether a transaction is a sale, for example, sale versus lease. It is important to distinguish a lease from a conditional sales contract.

Familiarity with some of the common terms applying to the income-tax field is necessary because of the close relation of this tax to most real estate transactions.

Capital Assets

Everything owned by a person is a capital asset except:

1. *Property held primarily for sale to customers* or that will become physically a part of merchandise intended for sale to customers.
2. *Accounts or notes receivable* acquired in the ordinary course of a trade or business for services rendered, or from the sale of any of the properties described in (1) above.
3. *Depreciable property* used in trade or business (even though fully depreciated).
4. *Real property* used in trade or business.
5. *A copyright on a literary, musical, or artistic composition.*
6. *Certain short-term discount obligations* issued by federal, state, or municipal governments.

Whether property is held primarily for sale to customers in the ordinary course of business is a question of fact to be determined in each case. Among the factors to be considered in making this determination are: (1) the purpose for which the property is acquired; (2) the development of the property between the time of acquisition and the time of sale; (3) the number and frequency of sales; and (4) the length of time the property is held before it is sold.

Property held for personal use is a capital asset. Gain from a sale or exchange of such property is a capital gain. *Losses from sales and exchanges of such property are never deductible.*

Investment property is a capital asset and *a gain or loss* from a sale or exchange thereof is capital gain or loss.

Rental property. Gain or loss from the sale or exchange of rental property is determined from the length of time the property has been held.

Business property of the type described in (3) and (4) under "Capital Assets" above is not a capital asset, but it may be treated as such under certain circumstances.

Discounted notes. If the evidence of indebtness, which is purchased at a discount, was issued by an individual, its retirement will generally not be given capital-gains treatment. But if the discounted obligation is sold to someone other than the maker (original borrower), the gain is a capital gain. In determining the adjusted basis in the note, the original basis is not reduced by the portion of the principal payment received that is discount income, taxable as interest income.

Example. A second-trust deed was purchased (from an individual) on which $10,000 was still owed. Principal payments totaling $4,000 were made. The note was then sold for $3,800. Because only 60 percent ($6,000/$10,000) of the $4,000 received represents a return of the investment and the balance is discount income (interest), the cost is reduced by only $2,400 ($4,000 × 60 percent) in determining the adjusted basis. The capital gain is $200, computed as follows:

Selling price of note		$3,800
Less: Cost of note	$6,000	
Return on investment	2,400	
Adjusted basis of note		3,600
Capital gain		$200

Options to Buy or Sell. Gain or loss from the sale or exchange of an option (or privilege) to buy or sell property, which is, or if it is acquired would be, a capital asset is considered as gain or loss from the sale or exchange of a capital asset. Gain or loss from the sale or exchange of an option to buy or sell property that is not, or would not be, a capital asset, is ordinary gain or loss. Under certain circumstances, such gain or loss may be treated as a capital gain or loss.

Capital Gain

Gains and losses are either long term or short term. If the capital asset is held for six months or less, any gain or loss is *short term.* If it is held for more than six months, the gain or loss is *long term.* Short-term gain is taxed as ordinary income. *Short-term capital gains and losses* are merged with each other by adding the gains and the losses separately and subtracting one total from the other to obtain the net short-term capital gain or loss. Long-term capital gains and losses are merged with each other to obtain the net long-term capital gain or loss.

Holding Period. To determine if property has been held over six months, the count is begun on the day following the day the property was acquired. This same day of each succeeding month is the beginning of a new month, regardless of the number of days in the preceding month. In the computation the day on which the property was disposed of is included.

Example: An asset is purchased on January 4. The count is started on January 5 and the fifth of each succeeding month is the beginning of a new month. Thus, if the property is sold on July 4, the holding period would not be over six months. If the property is sold on July 5, the holding period would be over six months.

Nontaxable Exchange. If the asset is acquired in an exchange for another asset and the basis for the new asset is determined, in whole or in part, by reference to the basis in the old property, then the first day of the holding period of the new property is the day following the date the old property was acquired.

Real Property Purchased. To determine how long real property that is the subject of an unconditional contract of sale has been held, counting begins on the day following that on which title passes, or on the day following that on which delivery of possession is made and the burdens and privileges of ownership are assumed by the purchaser, whichever occurs first. Delivery of possession of real property under an option agreement is without significance until a contract of sale comes into being through exercise of the option. The holding period of the seller cannot end before the date the option is exercised.

Capital-Gain Deduction

A noncorporate taxpayer whose net long-term capital gain exceeds his short-term capital loss, may claim a deduction equal to 50 percent of such excess. If he has no short-term capital loss, the capital gain deduction is 50 percent of the net long-term capital gain.

Example:

During the year, an individual had the following transactions:

Long-term capital gain	$5,400
Long-term capital loss	(1,750)
Net long-term capital gain	$3,650
Short-term capital gain	$2,600
Short-term capital loss	(3,790)
Net short-term capital loss	(1,190)
Excess of net long-term capital gain over net short-term capital loss	$2,460

Although the net gain of $2,460 is included in gross income, only 50 percent, or $1,230, is actually taxed because the taxpayer may deduct 50 percent of the excess of the net long-term capital gain over the net short-term capital loss. Note: *Corporations* are not permitted this deduction.

Alternative Capital-Gains Rate. Formerly 25 percent was applicable only to the taxpayer beyond the 50 percent bracket. For the noncorporate taxpayer the 25 percent alternative capital gain continues to apply, but only to the first $50,000 of capital gains or $25,000 in the case of married taxpayers filing separate returns. One-half of the balance over $50,000 will be added to the taxpayer's gross income and will be taxable at ordinary rates. This limitation on the alternative capital-gains rate is phased in over a three-year period, with certain options available to the taxpayer.

Rehabilitation Expenditures. Under the new

law, capital improvements made on residential buildings for low- and moderate-income families (as defined by the secretary of Housing and Urban Development) on or after July 25, 1969 may be written off on a sixty-month basis. The write-offs in reality are depreciation deductions and are subject to the same recapture provisions that generally apply to residential construction under the new law.

Any excess over straight line recaptured at the time of sale is taxable as ordinary income if the building rehabilitated is disposed of within 100 months. Beginning the 101st month, the percentage of the excess over the straight line that would be subject to taxation at ordinary rates would begin to decline by 1 percent a month. The maximum capital improvement subject to the first write-off is $15,000 per unit. The sum of the capital expenditures over any two-year period would have to be more than $3,000 per unit. (This special provision is scheduled to expire on December 31, 1974, unless it is extended by Congress.)[5]

Individual Long-Term Capital Losses. Under the 1969 Tax Reform Law these losses, which could formerly be used to offset $1,000 of ordinary income (with a carry-forward of unused capital loss credits), must now be increased to $2,000 of long-term capital loss to offset an annual maximum of $1,000 of ordinary income.

Depreciation and Investment Credit

New residential-income improvements remain eligible for accelerated depreciation as under the former law (that is, 200 percent declining balance, sum-of-the-year's digits, and so on).[6]

New nonresidential-income improvements. 150 percent declining-balance method or less-rapid methods of accelerated depreciation are permitted.

Used residential-rental improvements. 125 percent declining-balance method if the useful life at date of acquisition is twenty years of more.

All other used income property is limited to the straight-line method of depreciation.

Recapture of Depreciation

Under the new law, tougher recapture rules apply to that portion of depreciation in excess of straight line.

Sales within One Year of Acquisition. This rule is unchanged. Gain is taxed as ordinary income to the extent of any depreciation taken.

Residential Property Held 12 to 100 Months. The gain is ordinary income to the extent that depreciation taken is in excess of straightline.

Residential Property Held 100 to 200 Months. That portion of the gain subject to ordinary income treatment because of the depreciation taken beyond straight line is reduced 1 percent for each month beyond 100 months, becoming fully eligible for long-term capital-gains treatment after 200 months of holding.

Exception. New "subsidized" residential property [financed under FHA 221d (3) and 235, and so on] is still subject to the former recapture rules, reducing the amount subject to recapture at ordinary rates by 1 percent for each month of holding beyond 20 months, becoming fully eligible for long-term capital-gains treatment after 120 months of holding.

Limitation on Deduction of Investment Interest

Buyers or owners of "investment property" (such as land that produces little or no current income) pay substantial amounts in interest, which is deductible against other income. The 1969 act limits the deductibility of such interest by noncorporate taxpayers and corporate taxpayers electing to be taxed as individuals, beginning 1972. Prior to 1972, investment interest was treated as "tax-preference income" subject to a 10 percent additional tax (under certain conditions). The new law disallows 50 percent of the net investment-interest expense beyond aggregate of $25,000 (or $12,500 if the taxpayer is married and is filing a separate return), plus the excess of long-term capital gain over net short-term capital loss, plus net investment income. Disallowed investment interest may be carried over to subsequent years, but is limited each year to one-half of the excess of net investment income plus $25,000 exemption over the greater of $25,000 or the investment interest paid in the succeeding year.

Time for Replacing Property Involuntarily Converted

Where property has been condemned, or destroyed by casualty, or otherwise converted involuntarily, the time within which the taxpayer may replace the

[5] Parts of the above were taken from "Explanations of Provisions in Tax Law," *Realtor's Headlines,* January 12, 1970.

[6] Residential-income property is defined as property receiving 80 percent of its gross income from nontransient dwelling units.

property has been extended by one year to "within two taxable years after the close of the first taxable year in which any part of the gain was realized."[7]

Cost Basis. This is one of the most important factors to be considered in computing gain or loss on a real estate transaction. The cost basis is interpreted as the purchase price paid for the property on its original acquisition. It is also used in computing depreciation. Although the term *cost* is used, it is applicable to other types of acquisition; for example, by inheritance, where the cost basis is the market value as of a given date (usually the date of the death of the owner). The basis for property acquired by *gift* is the donor's cost for computing the gain, and the lower of donor's cost or fair market value at date of gift for computing the loss.

Adjusted Cost Basis. The "cost basis," with certain additions or deductions applied to it, constitutes the adjusted cost basis. Cost of improvements would be considered a plus and depreciation a minus factor in calculating the adjusted cost basis. All expenses of acquisition, brokerage commissions, escrow, or other costs of sale may be added to the cost basis.

Tax-Free Exchange. Exchange of property of a like kind if held for productive use in trade or business or as an investment is known as a tax-free exchange, although tax deferment more aptly describes the situation created, because only the death of the taxpayer can create a truly tax-free situation. In the tax-free exchange, the taxpayer's old cost basis is transferred to the property taken in exchange. *Unless another tax-free exchange is effected, the entire tax will become due upon the sale of the acquired property.* To qualify as a "tax-free" exchange, the properties involved must be vacant land held for investment, or a rental or business site.

Boot. In the tax-free exchange, complications may arise if the transaction involves cash or other assets. These assets constitute "boot," and, although loss is not recognized, gain becomes taxable at the time of the exchange to the extent of the value of the boot. *Relief from mortgage* is also interpreted as boot. If *one* of the properties in the exchange is mortgaged, tax is due on any gain at the time of the exchange to the extent of the taxpayer's relief from such liability. If both properties are mortgaged, the difference between the mortgages is taxable to the extent of the actual gain.

[7] The above information on the changes brought about by the 1969 Tax Reform Law were excerpted from *CID LETTER,* No. 13, March, 1970, National Association of Real Estate Boards.

Gain from Sale or Exchange of Residence

Generally, gain is recognized on the sale or exchange of a residence. But a special rule for nonrecognition of gain applies if property used by the taxpayer as his principal residence is sold by him and

1. the taxpayer purchases a new residence and uses it as his principal residence within one year before or after he sells his old residence, or
2. he starts the construction of the new residence within the year before or after he sells the old residence and uses the new property as his principal residence within eighteen months after he sells his old residence.

If the taxpayer fits the above tests, gain on the transaction is recognized only to the extent that the adjusted sales price of the old residence exceeds the cost of the new residence.[8]

Tax-Free Sales of Home. A taxpayer sixty-five years of age or over who sells his home for more than he paid for it *does not have to pay any tax on the gain* if his adjusted sales price is $20,000 or less. If his adjusted sales price is more than $20,000, a pro rata part of the gain is tax free—in the ratio that $20,000 bears to the actual *adjusted* sales price.

Adjusted sales price is the total selling price reduced by (1) broker's commissions and similar expenses and (2) fixing-up expenses.

To illustrate:

> *Example 1.* Ten years ago, Jones bought his residence for $10,000. In June, 1972, he sells it for $22,000. Assume that the broker's commission is $1,000 and fixing-up expenses amount to $1,000. RESULT. Gain is $11,000 ($22,000 minus $1,000 broker's commission minus $10,000 basis). Nevertheless, because the *adjusted* sales price [see (2) above] does not exceed $20,000, Jones's entire gain is tax free.
>
> *Example 2.* Assume the facts of Example 1, except that the selling price is now $32,000. Now the gain, assuming that the broker's commission and fixing-up expenses remain the same, is $21,000 and the adjusted sales price is $30,000. RESULT. The tax-free gain is now $14,000 ($20,000/$30,000 × $21,000 gain).[9]

The taxpayer must have reached the age of sixty-five *before* the sale and must elect to use the tax benefit. One tax-free sale in a lifetime is all a taxpayer can ever get, but the election can be made

[8] "7 Federal Tax Angles that Create Enormous Real Estate Business," *Real Estate Opportunities,* (Englewood Cliffs, N.J. Prentice-Hall, Inc.) Section 3, August 6, 1963, p. 29.

[9] "What the Giant New Tax Law Means to You", *Real Estate Opportunities* (Englewood Cliffs, N.J. Prentice-Hall, Inc.) Section 3, March 3, 1964.

or revoked within three years of the year of sale. He must have used the property as his principal residence for at least five of the eight years before the sale. If the property is part-residence, part-business, he can still get tax-free treatment on the part of the gain attributable to the residence. If man and wife own the property jointly and file a joint return, they get tax-free treatment if either is sixty-five or over. A surviving spouse qualifies if he or she is sixty-five or over and the deceased spouse had met the holding-period and use tests.

This new break extends to owners of co-op apartments and, presumably, condominiums.

Acquisition of Real Estate

Persons planning to purchase real property should be aware of the various methods of acquisition and their consequences on the later tax liabilities. The *method of taking title may constitute* an important factor in computing the amount of tax due upon sale of the property. Title may be taken individually, in joint tenancy with another, or as a corporation. Individual ownership may later be transferred to tax-free corporate ownership. Under *corporate ownership,* dealers may segregate their investment property from their stock in trade and establish for tax purposes the true nature of each type of property. Under joint tenancy, ownership cannot be controlled by will; and, upon death of one joint tenant one-half of the property *cost basis* is retroactive to acquisition.

Disposition of Real Estate

A "sale" of real estate is construed to have occurred when either a deed or possession is delivered to the buyer. The sale as a taxable event may be postponed as long as the seller withholds either the delivery of deed or possession (in the event of a contract of sale). Several optional methods of postponing the tax payment are available, the installment sale being one. Under this method the buyer pays not more than 30 percent of the purchase price *in the year of sale* in cash or other property. This method of paying tax is also known as *a deferred-payment sale,* and the taxpayer is permitted to report his taxable gain over a period of years. When reporting income, the seller has the advantage of not having to pay tax on income that he has not received but rather he includes in his gross income only that portion of each payment received that constitutes profit.

Lease. Property may be disposed of by lease. In most cases, rent received by the lessor is taxed as ordinary income; and if it applies to business property, rent paid by the lessee may be deducted as a business expense. In the event of advance rent, the lessor must report this in the year received, and the lessee must deduct it in the year paid. On the other hand, security deposits remain the property of the lessee until default and are not deductible by the lessee nor are they reportable by the lesssor until forfeited.

QUESTIONS

1. What is meant by the statement: "Tax consciousness should take place *before* acquisition of property"?
2. Distinguish between cost basis and adjusted cost basis.
3. In 1960 Smith buys a home for $12,000. At this time he is fifty-eight years of age. In 1970 he decides to sell his home and move to an apartment. He lists his home with a broker, who sells it in December of that year for $27,000. Smith spent $2,000 on repairs on the home to make it more salable. He paid the broker a 6 percent commission on the sales price. Does Smith owe income tax on the sale? (Disregard any outside income he may have for that year.)

SUGGESTED REFERENCES

"Explanations of Provisions in Tax Law," *California Real Estate Magazine.* Los Angeles: California Real Estate Association, February, 1970.

Document No. 5048 (12–65), *Sales and Exchanges of Assets.* U.S. Treasury Department, Internal Revenue Service. Washington, D.C.: Government Printing Office.

Document No. 5108 (12–65), *Installment and Deferred-Payment Sales.* U.S. Treasury Department, Internal Revenue Service. Washington, D.C.: Government Printing Office.

Document No. 5383 (12–65), *How the Federal Income Tax Applies to Condemnations of Private Property for Public Use.* U.S. Treasury Department, Internal Revenue Service. Washington, D.C.: Government Printing Office.

Document No. 5516 (12–65), *Cost or Other Basis of Assets.* U.S. Treasury Department, Internal Revenue Service. Washington, D.C.: Government Printing Office.

Reference Book, 1971 ed. Sacramento: Department of Real Estate.

13

Exchanges

Theory of Real Estate Exchanges

Although the exchanging of properties is fundamentally simple, definite techniques are required in the actual procedures. Today's broker who is lacking in knowledge of real estate exchanging is missing out on one of the most lucrative aspects of his business. Reduced to basic fundamentals, real estate exchanging constitutes the old-time barter and trade system. The value of exchanging was recognized by George Washington as far back as 1778, as is evidenced by his letter to his stepson, J. P. Custis, on October 12 of that year. In part, he states:

> By parting from your lands you give a certainty for an uncertainty, because it is not a nominal price—it is not ten, fifteen or twenty pounds an acre—but the relative value of this sum to specie (coin) or something of substantial worth, that is to constitute a good price. The advice I give is that you do not convert the lands you now hold into cash faster than a certain prospect of vesting it in other lands more convenient requires of you.
>
> This will, in effect, exchange land for land, for it is a matter of moonshine to you, considered in that point of view simply, how much the money depreciates, if you can discharge one point with another, and get land of value to that you sell.

It is obvious that even then two facts were recognized: (1) depreciation of stored-up money and (2) the value of real estate ownership as a hedge against inflation.

Reasons for an Exchange. There are numerous reasons why it might be an advantage to a property owner to make an exchange rather than to sell outright. In some cases, an exchange is the only solution to the owner's problem of disposing of his property. In cases where the buyer's only working capital is the equity in his property, exchanging can eliminate the hazard of buying on the contingency of his property selling within the escrow period. In times of tightening money, with the resultant drop in sales volumes of real estate, exchanging often provides the catalyst that energizes the market.

Many brokers are inexperienced in the technique of trading, even to the point of not recognizing the nucleus of an exchange when it presents itself. By the same token, most property owners are unfamiliar with the advantages of and the methods utilized in making exchanges until they have worked with a broker skilled in trading techniques. Through the advertising of these brokers, the public is becoming exchange-conscious; and in cases where a tax problem is involved, property owners have found the "tax-free" exchange the only solution to disposition of their real estate holdings.

Advantages of an Exchange

To the Property Owner. As was mentioned above, one logical exchange client is the homeowner with only the equity in his present home with which to work. Exchanging homes, however, is one of the most difficult types of trades. Unless all conditions are favorable, it is difficult to work with the uninitiated homeowner. Brokers experienced in the field recognize that exchanges are made *between people.* With the many human emotions involved in home ownership, it is difficult for the principals to be objective about the transaction.

The man with a grown family may find his large home no longer fits his requirements but that he is still burdened with tax and maintenance costs. He may be the professional man or the business executive in a high-income bracket. A logical exchange for him might be the luxury-type apartment complex. The equity in his home can be exchanged for that of the income-producing property, providing him not only with the advantage of being able to maintain his same standard of living (by occupying one of the apartments) but affording him a tax write-off in terms of depreciation, maintenance costs, and building repairs.

Builders of speculative homes or residential-income properties are good exchange prospects for the unencumbered smaller home. The older property in a good area can be modernized by the builder to make it more salable. He is also provided an opportunity to generate needed cash by placing a mortgage on the property taken in trade. Provided he is not classified as a dealer, he may want to rent out the property for a period of time to give it an "investment" status.

Land is the builder's stock in trade. Acreage, in large or small parcels, or the vacant lot can usually be traded to him for his speculative building or trust deeds.

Other fields of exchange include:

1. *Tax-conscious owners.*
2. *Egotistical owners.* They have bought a "white elephant" and refuse to sell at a loss. (If the broker talks difference in *value* rather than *price* he can sometimes generate a trade.)
3. *Speculators.* They are interested only in making a profit.
4. *Unrealistic or uninformed owners.* An exchange may be the best way to acquaint them with true market value.
5. *Climatic conditions.* Homeowners may need to move to a different climate for health reasons.

It is most important for the exchange broker to determine exactly *why* the parties want to exchange. All properties in the exchange should be submitted at fair market value, and the owner who is stubbornly unrealistic in his price should be passed up for the more realistic and thus better-qualified exchange client. *Exchanges are made between people, rather than between properties.* For this reason, the well-motivated property owner is more important to the transaction than the best-qualified property. This concept is vitally important when reappraising a client's exchange position at a later date. The property has remained the same in most cases, but the client's situation may have altered considerably. In the case of investment property, he may have depreciated it out, and he may need to trade for another property to start his depreciation schedule over again. Many such situations may require a completely new evaluation of the client's present position.

To the Broker. Once the broker becomes trade-conscious and exchanging has become an integral part of his business, every prospect and every property with which he comes in contact is viewed in the light of a possible exchange. Once having established a reputation as an expert exchanger and one capable of assisting with a client's real estate problem, the broker is established in business. Whereas, in the selling field, the broker is required to make two sales to make two commissions, as an exchanger he is entitled to a commission from each party to the exchange.

The large, pretentious office is not essential to successful trading. Many flourishing exchange businesses are being conducted from one-man offices in multistory office buildings. Advertising costs, which constitute one of the major expense items in the average brokerage office, can be all but eliminated. One well-written, well-placed exchange advertisement will bring more replies than can be serviced readily. The problem then becomes one of selectivity. Many replies come from those who are not really exchange prospects. Unless the exchange is one that will benefit the property owner, it should not be undertaken. The old "horse-trading" theory, whereby one party to the trade must of necessity gain an advantage over the other, is not applicable to modern-day exchanging.

Finding Exchange Clients

As was stated above, one well-placed ad will bring a wealth of clients to the exchange broker. In addition, every prospect inquiring about property generally may be an exchange possibility. Each listing should be analyzed for its exchange potential. Discussions on exchanging should be included in the agenda of all office sales meetings. The problem property listed by one salesman may be exchanged for that of another salesman.

Many boards of realtors have weekly trading-post sessions where members discuss their exchange problems. The California Real Estate Association's Exchange Committee has a division known as Certified Property Exchangers, whose members must have qualified for membership by education, examination, and experience. Selected members of this professional exchange group conduct exchange seminars on the principles of exchange and taxation and outline the mechanics of exchanging, such as listing, financing, negotiating, contract writing, and escrowing. The advanced seminars give instruction and allow for actual practice in putting together exchanges. Completion of both the basic and advanced seminars are prerequisites for membership in the Certified Property Exchangers and for the designation of CPE.

The International Traders Club of the National Institute of Real Estate Brokers is a national clearinghouse for its members. Organized in 1953, its primary purpose is to provide a listing service on an information basis for its realtor members, whose exchanges may involve properties in any state in the Union as well as Canada.

In no other phase of the real estate business is cooperation more important. Because the loner is at a distinct disadvantage in the field of exchanging, most exchanges are made on a cooperative basis. The true exchanger recognizes his need for a cooperative attitude toward his fellow broker, whose assistance may be needed especially in the area of appraisal. In addition, the broker acting as agent for only one party to the exchange is in a better position to view the exchange objectively, without the danger of a conflict of interest.

How to Start an Exchange Program

Taxes as related to exchanges assume a more important role as profits realized from cash sales are penalized by the tax laws. With specialization becoming the order of the day, many brokerage offices are departmentalizing their operations. Property management, insurance, loans, escrow, and income properties are complex real estate areas requiring specialized knowledge. But it is only recently that brokerage firms have felt the need of setting up an exchange department, headed by trained specialists skilled in tax and accounting fields. Too often the uninitiated broker has attempted to negotiate exchanges for clients without full knowledge of the complexity of the transaction or the tax implications.

To the neophyte in the field of exchanging, the natural question is, "How do I begin?" Certainly the key to the success of the transaction, once the client is persuaded to make an exchange, is the knowledge of exactly how to start. As in dancing, the best way to learn to become an exchanger is to practice the steps. The complete transaction must be visualized, step by step, and certain fundamental rules should be observed: (1) Most important of all, a verbal exchange should never be attempted; (2) The broker should have a long-term exclusive listing on at least one of the properties; (3) All properties in the exchange should be listed at fair market value, and (4) Only *one* price should be quoted. Cash price and trading price should be the same.

The first step is for the broker to familiarize himself with the exchange agreement. Under no circumstances should the broker write up an exchange on the ordinary sales agreement-form or deposit-receipt form. The California Real Estate Association Standard Exchange Agreement is the one in general use throughout the state.[1] For practice, the broker should draw up several hypothetical exchanges, using the exchange-agreement form until he is completely familiar with the terms and conditions of the problem. It is not necessary to have more than one party interested in exchanging. The agreement can be drawn from the terms submitted by the first party and presented to the second party for approval, much as is done in any sales transaction. The broker should anticipate any points that may be unacceptable and be prepared to "give ground" if necessary. Several agreements may have to be drawn before there is a meeting of the minds.

Types of Exchanges

Exchange of "Like" Property. Tax aspects of this type of exchange have been touched on in the previous chapter. Such an exchange provides the owners with certain tax advantages that are not available in the outright sale of a property. Under the Internal Revenue Code, Section 1031, gain or loss is not recognized if property held for *productive use in trade or business or for investment* is exchanged for a property of *like kind to be held for the same purpose.* Like kind is not intended to imply the same *grade* or *quality* of property. The taxpayer cannot have acquired the property for resale. Likewise, dealer property (that held primarily for resale) or the taxpayer's *personal* residence are not included. The property exchanged must be in actual existence (not a building to be constructed). Examples of like-kind property exchanges are: farm or ranch for an apartment building; vacant land held for investment for a business site; fee interest for a lease of thirty years or more.

Boot. As was explained in the previous chapter, boot constitutes any nonqualified property, such as stocks, cash, or other assets, or *relief from mortgage* received in a tax-free exchange.

Exchange of Mortgages. Much misunderstanding arises from the relief-from mortgage interpretation of boot. If an existing mortgage indebtedness is *assumed* by one of the parties to the exchange, the other party being thereby relieved of all or part of the liability, boot is recognized to the extent of the relief.

If one of the properties to an exchange is mortgaged, the owner will have his gain recognized to the extent of the indebtedness transferred. This is

[1] See the sample form on p. 188.

true whether the encumbrance is *assumed* by the other party or the property is transferred *"subject to."* The interpretation is that the original owner of the property has gained relief from his liability.

Example 1. Taxpayer Green owns an apartment house that is unencumbered and for which he paid $90,000. (The basis.) It now has an appreciated fair market value of $100,000. He exchanges it for Brown's apartment house that has a fair market value of $250,000, encumbered with a mortgage in the amount of $110,000 and a basis of $175,000. Green pays Brown $40,000 cash to adjust the equities. Green has a basis for his newly acquired apartment of $90,000,[2] plus the assumed indebtedness of $110,000.

BROWN'S POSITION

Value of Green's apartment	$100,000.00
Mortgage assumed in the exchange	110,000.00
Total consideration received	$210,000.00
Less adjusted basis of Brown's property	$175,000.00
Brown's gain realized on the exchange	$ 35,000.00
Amount of boot received (mortgage relief in transferred indebtedness)	$110,000.00
Taxable gain recognized	$35,000.00

If both properties are mortgaged, the *net* reduction in any outstanding mortgages of either party is treated as a *cash equivalent* received, and any gain will be taxed to that extent. (Expenses, such as brokerage, escrow, and so forth, are deducted to arrive at the *net.*)

Example 2 (using the same exchangers as in Example 1 with different properties):

	Green Property	*Brown Property*
Basis	$60,000.00	$40,000.00
Fair market value	80,000.00	60,000.00
Mortgage	30,000.00	20,000.00
Equity	$50,000.00	$40,000.00

In this example, Green's equity is $10,000 greater than Brown's equity. In the exchange, Brown may be required to pay Green $10,000 in cash. In addition, Green has obtained a net reduction in indebtedness of $10,000. His total taxable gain is limited to $10,000.

Example 3

	Green Property	*Brown Property*
Basis	$40,000.00	$70,000.00
Fair market value	80,000.00	80,000.00
Mortgage	30,000.00	50,000.00
Equity	$50,000.00	$30,000.00

In this examiple, Green has assomed a larger mortgage in the amount of $20,000. This is a difference in equities of $20,000. Assume that Brown pays Green $20,000 cash to adjust this difference. In addition, Green is relieved of a $300,000 mortgage but has assumed a mortgage of $50,000, a net increase in mortgages of $20,000. Green may not use this increase in indebtedness to offset the $20,000 cash received from Brown. He therefore has a taxable gain in the amount of $20,000 cash received.

The Trade-In Program

Automobile distributors have long been engaged in the automobile trade-in program. Appliance dealers are taking trade-ins every day on new merchandise. This aspect of the business world is accepted without question today as a means of energizing a sluggish market. The real estate industry has been the laggard in the field, and only in the past 18 years has the real estate trade-in program begun to be accepted as a modern way to merchandise property.

It must be understood that there is a distinct difference between *trade-ins* and *exchanges* as they are known in the real estate business. *Exchanging* is basically the transferring of ownership of one property to that of another. There may be an agent acting as negotiator, but he is not customarily a principal to the transaction. The principal feature of the *trade-in* is the introduction of an agent or dealer into the transaction as a third party to provide the capital, time, and knowledge as principal to the transaction. "Trade-ins are confined almost entirely to the residential sales field, since they are designed to meet the problems of the housing market and not the needs of sophisticated investors able to 'trade' large holdings by the 'exchange' method."[3]

The broker who develops a trade-in plan in his office can provide a valuable service, particularly to industry personnel who are subject to transfer and faced with the problem of disposing of a home in a relatively short time. Some companies have even set up their own trade-in programs for their employees, to handle the homes involved. The homebuilder has an interest in the plan, because it can provide him with (1) extra business, (2) larger down payments (from the equity in the purchaser's home), (3) elimination of the contingent sale, and (4) opportunity to make a profit from the new-home sale without considering a profit on the used home.

The *speculator* is always on the alert for good

[2] No depreciation factor is taken into consideration in these examples, nor is either party to the exchange considered a dealer.

[3] David Stone, *How to Operate a Real Estate Trade-in Program,* (Englewood Cliffs, N.J.: Prentice-Hall, Inc., 1962), p. 2.

buys. He is usually willing to do some renovating or to make certain improvements to increase his margin of profit. His interest in the trade-in plan is not one of altruism but strictly one of profit making. He will be interested in (1) properties that will return him 15 to 25 percent on his investment, (2) trades that will be of help in reducing his capital-tax problems, and (3) a profit on his investment, over and above all trading costs. He can usually be sold on any property where the margin is great enough to warrant his capital outlay and where he feels that the risk is justified.

Investors are often interested in trade-in programs. Those wth a small amount of capital may be interested in syndicate programs if they can be assured of a 10 to 25 percent return on their investment. The investor who is not classed as a "dealer" has the added advantage of a tax-shelter potential. For the small investor, participation in a well-managed real estate company's operating "trading fund" can be of greatest benefit.

The primary lender has a special interest in the residential trade-in plan. Increased business generated as a direct result of cooperating with trading organizations can work to the lender's advantage. Benefits apply to savings and loan associations, mortgage bankers, insurance companies, and commercial banks.

The broker, among all those sharing an interest in the trade-in program, has the most to gain. He is in the field of merchandising houses already, and in close touch with his local estate market. His success is dependent on his ability as an expert appraiser, because careful appraising is a requisite to the success of any trade-in program. The forward-looking broker who has built his future on the referred business he develops has the strongest motivation to build a trade-in program. On the other hand, the office with no interest in a business built on customer service will probably have no interest in the program, which is primarily one of long-range potential. The trade-in program can provide, among others, the following advantages to the broker: (1) attraction of more buyers and sellers to his office; (2) a steady flow of salable listings through the office; (3) the advantage of working with builders in the area; (4) a steady source of referrals from cooperating brokers; and (5) an excellent merchandising tool, providing a definite lead over his competitors in the field.

Starting the Trade-In Program

David Stone, San Jose realtor, in his book, *How to Operate a Real Estate Trade-in Program,* has the following suggestions: (1) start small; (2) analyze the market potential; (3) analyze your organization and personnel; and (4) determine your source of capital.[4]

Obtaining adequate capital to operate is basic to the program. No fixed amount can be stipulated, because it is dependent upon the size of the operation. The smaller operation will, of course, have smaller capital requirements; however, experienced traders have found that the ratio between the capital required and the number of trades handled need not be large. Capital may be obtained from a number of sources, including (1) syndicate of employees or salesmen, (2) trust account at a savings and loan company, (3) outside investors, (4) line of credit with a bank, or (5) the *FHA trade-in plan.* Whereas, under the old law, a borrower who did not occupy the property was not permitted to obtain a maximum insured loan, since 1959 duplicate closing costs in the trade-in procedure have been eliminated. The broker is permitted to obtain a loan on the same terms available to an owner-occupant, the only provision being that 15 percent of the loan funds be held in escrow until the home is sold to an owner-occupant. Under this ruling, the broker or builder is able to obtain maximum financing on the house taken in trade. The house also can be sold without having to be refinanced, thus saving the owner the expense of duplicate sets of closing costs. The broker or builder (nonoccupant borrower) is allowed eighteen months in which to find a buyer qualified to assume the loan. In the event that a buyer is not found, that portion (15 percent) of the original principal mortgage held in escrow is applied to reduce the loan. In order to receive the commitment, the trade-in broker (or builder) is required to furnish the FHA district office a detailed accounting of his actual acquisition costs before he can receive the commitment and the release of the funds in escrow. Each application must be accompanied by FHA form No. 314, (escrow-commitment certificate).[5]

With expert appraising, (the foundation on which the trade-in program succeeds or fails), the prudent broker accepts properties only in areas with which he is completely familiar or else seeks the services of a reliable outside appraiser. The use of a consulting appraiser is wise policy also if the trade-in property is a difficult one to evaluate. The trade-in home must be considered as though it were actually being *bought* by the broker for resale, and careful estimates must

[4] Stone, *Real Estate Trade-in Program.*

[5] See copy of form in Appendix, p.

Exchange Agreement

CALIFORNIA REAL ESTATE ASSOCIATION STANDARD FORM

Willard D. Starr and Gladys M. Starr

hereinafter called first party, hereby offers to exchange the following described property, situated in City of New Town, County of Los Angeles, California:

Lot 48 in Tract 227 also known as 123 Fourth Street.

Subject to:

1. General and special taxes 1971-72
2. Conditions, covenants, restrictions, reservations, rights, rights of way and easements of record, if any.
3. Note secured by deed of trust of record payable $520 per month including principal and interest at 7.2% per annum. Present balance approximately $58,000.00

For the following described property of David L. Swift and Charlotte T. Swift

hereinafter called second party, situated in City of Old Town, County of Riverside, California:

Lot 17, of Tract 722.

Subject to:

1. General and special taxes 1971-72
2. Conditions, covenants, restrictions, reservations, rights, rights of way and easements of record, if any
3. Note secured by deed of trust of record payable $1,725 per month including principal and interest at 7.2% per annum. Present balance of approximately $170,000

Terms and Conditions of Exchange:

1. First party to exchange his property as described above for property of second party plus first party to add $6,900.00
2. Each party to submit rental statement on his property within 2 days after acceptance of this offer with tenant's names and vacancy where indicated showing scheduled monthly income of not less than : 1st property: $2,300 - 2nd property $3,460.
3. Each party to furnish at his expense a report from a licensed pest controloperator covering termites, dry rot and fungus in accessible areas on his property. If such report shows active infestation or resultant damage then such party will eliminate such infestation and repair damage at his expense. Any treatment to be made to guard against future infestation shall be at the option and expense of person receiving said property.
4. Any advancements, deposits on leases, cleaning or breakage to be adjusted in escrow to the new owner.
5. If at the close of escrow the loans of record are more or less than the amounts shown herein, then any differences shall be adjusted in cash.
6. Each party to have right to approve all units of the property they are acquiring within 3 days after acceptance of this offer. Said approval to be assumed unless broker is notified to the contrary in writing within 3 days.

The parties hereto shall execute and deliver, within 10 days from the date this offer is accepted, all instruments, in writing, necessary to transfer title to said properties and complete and consummate this exchange. Each party shall supply Preliminary Title Reports for their respective properties. Evidences of title shall be California Land Title Association standard coverage form policies of title insurance showing titles to be merchantable and free of all liens and encumbrances, except taxes and those liens and encumbrances as otherwise set forth herein. Each party shall pay for the policies of Title Insurance for the property to be acquired ☐ conveyed ☒.

If either party is unable to convey a marketable title, except as herein provided, within three months after acceptance hereof by second party, or if the improvements on any of the herein named properties be destroyed or materially damaged prior to transfer of title or delivery of agreement of sale, then this agreement shall be of no further effect, except as to payment of commissions and expenses incurred in connection with examination of title, unless the party acquiring the property so affected elects to accept the title the other party can convey or subject to the conditions of the improvements.

Taxes, insurance premiums (if policies be satisfactory to party acquiring the property affected thereby), rents interest and other expenses of said properties shall be pro-rated as of the date of transfer of title or delivery of agreement of sale, unless otherwise provided herein.

David L. Brown of New Town Calif. 446-8531
Broker Address Phone No.

is hereby authorized to act as broker for all parties hereto and may accept commission therefrom. Should second party accept this offer, first party agrees to pay said broker commission for services rendered as follows:-

($6,250.00) Six thousand two hundred fifty dollars

Should second party be unable to convey a marketable title to his property then first party shall be released from payment of any commission, unless he elects to accept the property subject thereto. First party agrees that broker may cooperate with other brokers and divide commissions in any manner satisfactory to them.

This offer shall be deemed revoked unless accepted in writing within 30 days after date hereof, and such acceptance is communicated to first party within said period. Broker is hereby given the exclusive and irrevocable right to obtain acceptance of second party within said period.

Time is the essence of this contract, but Broker may, without notice, extend for a period of not to exceed one month the time for the performance of any act hereunder, except the time for the acceptance hereof by second party.

All words used herein in the singular shall include the plural and the present tense shall include the future and the masculine gender shall include the feminine and neuter.

Willard D. Starr

Gladys M. Starr

Dated October 30 19 71

ACCEPTANCE

Second party hereby accepts the foregoing offer upon the terms and conditions stated and agrees to pay commission for services rendered, to:-

Robert S. Elliott of Old Town Calif. 572-7735
Broker Address Phone No.

as follows:- ($12,560) Twelve thousand, five hundred sixty dollars

Second party agrees that broker may act as broker for all parties hereto and may accept commission therefrom, and may co-operate with other brokers and divide commissions in any manner satisfactory to them.

Should first party be unable to convey a marketable title to his property then second party shall be released from payment of any commission, unless he elects to accept the property of first party subject thereto.

David L. Swift

Charlotte T. Swift

Dated October 31, 19 71

For these forms address California Real Estate Association
117 W. 9th St., Los Angeles 15 (Revision approved 10/7/57)

be made of all acquisition costs as well as of the expense of fixing up and commissions to be paid.

The Conditional Trade-In Plan. Under this plan, an agreement is made to sell the buyer a particular home, provided that the buyer can sell his own home within a specified time. No obligation is involved on the broker's part to purchase the home in the event it does not sell in the time specified, nor is either party obligated to complete the sale.

The Guaranteed Trade-In Plan. This plan differs from the conditional trade-in plan basically because it is based on the broker or builder's underwriting the customer's equity. He guarantees performance if the property is not sold in the specified time, the guarantee being based on a minimum equity, which is the lowest amount the owner can receive. The broker expends all his efforts to sell the property within the time limit. If he is not successful, he is obligated to purchase the property at the predetermined guaranteed figure.

Slightly different procedures are used by the various operators of guaranteed trade-in plans. Some companies, after appraising the house to be traded to determine its market value, either guarantee the client 95 percent of the market value less a $750 trading fee, or 90 percent of the FHA-appraised value. The company takes an exclusive listing on the traded property and advances the down payment for the new-home purchase. The deed to the traded house is then placed in escrow. If the property sells before the end of the guarantee period (usually 90 to 120 days), the broker takes his commission. If, however, the house is not sold within the specified time, the company purchases it at the agreed-upon figure.

The entire trade-in program is one of many complexities. Brokers planning to enter the field should consult with those in the industry who are experienced in the program. Many fine publications are also available for research. Dave Stone has covered the subject in great detail in his *How to Operate a Trade-in Program.*[6]

Exchange Escrows

Because an exchange is in reality an equity transaction, the exchange agreement often does not mention price. Unlike the seller in the case of a straight sale, the first party in an exchange is only interested in the amount of cash or boot he is to put into the transaction. The second party is interested in how much he is to receive in addition to his equity. (An example of an exchange agreement where no price is mentioned may be found on pages 188 and 189.)

Tax considerations are more often than not the main reason for an exchange. When a sale is made of property being held for investment or one held for use in trade or business, any profit made is taxable. If the seller is not classed as a dealer, the profit normally would be considered capital gain. Unlike the situation involving the sale of a residence, the tax on the capital gain is payable in the year of sale, regardless of whether the funds are reinvested in another property in a concurrent escrow or in the purchase of another piece of property. If the property owner is to qualify under Section 1031 of the Internal Revenue Code, he must make an actual exchange, *with the title passing directly to the party owning the property he is acquiring, and vice versa.*

If the property owner *receives any cash, net amount of mortgage relief or boot* in the transaction, the exchange may not be considered completely tax free. He may however *pay cash, assume a larger mortgage than that of which he is being relieved, and/or give boot.* For the above reasons the broker must use extreme care in drawing the original exchange agreement (as must the escrow officer when drawing escrow instructions,) if the parties are to receive the tax-free benefits provided under the law.

Any cash paid at the close of escrow to the party interested in obtaining the tax benefit would be taxable. For this reason care must be taken to have any sales expenses estimated as accurately as possible, to avoid any cash refunds. One solution might be the insertion of a clause in the exchange agreement and in the escrow instructions providing for any cash due after expenses to be credited against the note and trust deed drawn in favor of the other party to the exchange. (Trust deeds and notes might be drawn just prior to close of escrow for the exact amount.)

[6] See also "Suggested References" p. 191.

QUESTIONS

1. List three advantages to a property owner in exchanging his home rather than making an outright sale.
2. List three advantages to the realtor in including an exchange program in his office in addition to his regular brokerage operations.
3. What is your understanding of a tax-free exchange? What are the qualifications of the property to be exchanged under this category?
4. What is meant by cost basis? What by adjusted cost basis?

SUGGESTED REFERENCES

RENO, RICHARD, *Profitable Real Estate Exchanging.* Englewood Cliffs, N.J.: Prentice-Hall, Inc., 1956.

———, *How to Operate a Trade-in Program.* Englewood Cliffs, N.J.: Prentice-Hall, Inc., 1962.

STRAUB, DON, "Apartment Buildings—When to Sell and When to Exchange," *Advanced Real Estate Sales.* Los Angeles: California Real Estate Association, 1968.

14

Income Property

Common Types of Income Property

The basic reasons for investors in buying income-producing properties are cash flow and tax shelter. Because competitive investments in the form of stocks, bonds, savings accounts, and life insurance are always under consideration by investors, the broker-counselor must be in a position to analyze these investments in order to defend the merits of real estate as a preferred investment.

Investments are measured by their (1) liquidity, (2) stability, (3) appreciation, (4) yield, (5) spendable cash, and (6) tax shelter.

The safest type of investment, measured in terms of liquidity, is a government bond, which may be taken to any bank and converted into cash. Blue-chip stocks or triple-A leases are generally characterized as stable investments. Carefully selected growth stocks or strategically located real estate are examples of investment appreciation. The investor seeking the best *yield* turns to the stock showing the most consistent record of dividend payment, the discounted trust deed or income property with the highest *net spendable* income.

The investor in a high income bracket will be interested in the property that will give him the greatest tax benefit in the form of depreciation.

Residential-Income Property

This is the type of real estate most commonly bought for investment and applies more particularly to the apartment house. (The purchase of a single-family residence strictly as an investment is not considered economically sound.) Other types of residential income appeal to certain types of buyers, however, and must be considered in any discussion of real estate investment. A different appraisal and a different sales approach are indicated in each case.

Duplexes and Triplexes. Duplex and triplex buyers generally fall into four classifications:

1. Those making the purchase primarily for a home.

   Being home-conscious, these buyers usually are interested only if the property is located in a home-environment neighborhood.
2. Those wishing to build an equity.

   Because they are not considering the duplex or triplex as a permanent home but, rather, as a short-term purchase, they are less concerned with the neighborhood environment. They may, however, be interested in property in a newer area where there is a strong possibility of their equity growth. They expect the income from the rental to provide its share of the fixed expenses.
3. Those considering a high-return, owner-manager type of investment.

   They consider the duplex or triplex a true income property with themselves as managers. The sedentary worker is usually in this buyer classification. The activity connected with managing and maintaining the property supplies a a diversion from his confining duties. Often, the relative liquidity of the investment appeals to him, because the duplex or triplex is probably more readily marketable than the single-family residence.
4. Those wishing a moderate return with a minimum amount of care—usually retired or semi-retired people.

   For example, the widow living alone often purchases a duplex for the personal as well as financial security it affords. The additional income from the rental unit serves to supplement retirement or other income while at the same time providing her a "rent-free" home. The low-maintenance property with a limited amount of yard care appeals to her. For this reason, well-constructed buildings in good areas are best suited to this type of buyer.

Apartment Houses. The building, selling, and management of apartment buildings is one of the fast-growing segments of the real estate business in California. These multiple-dwelling units range in size from four-family buildings to the very large structures, including the luxurious apartment hotels.

The risk (the stability factor) in purchasing an apartment house is one of the major considerations from the investor's standpoint. Because people make values, a market analysis of the supply-and-demand factors is vital. In other words, an apartment house must have a *reason* to exist. California's population is expected to reach 22,100,000 by 1975. This represents an overall gain of 2,224,000 people or 11.3 percent since 1969. At the same time southern California's population is projected as 13,200,000. (The greatest concentration of population in the state is in the five-county area of Los Angeles.) Availability of land is shrinking rapidly. To quote James C. Downs, the nationally known real estate researcher, "God made all the land he is going to make the day he made the earth, but he is still making people." The movement of people from east to west has been called the greatest mass migration in history. With the migration continuing and with available land areas shrinking, the only solution to the problem of meeting the housing needs of our increasing population is higher land density, a problem confronting not only the large cities but the rural communities as well.

Another factor in the demand for apartment buildings is the advent of the war babies into the market who are becoming the apartment renters while accumulating the necessary funds for purchase of a home.

Older persons whose families are grown and who no longer wish to maintain a large home, with its attendant high maintenance costs, make up the larger group of the luxury-apartment tenants. Divorced persons and widows constitute an important segment of the group of tenants for the one-bedroom apartments.

Overbuilding can be a factor affecting the stability or risk of apartment-house investment. Directly attributive is the high vacancy factor that constitutes a major consideration in most California cities, necessitating careful investment selectivity based on an intelligent market survey.

Because the apartment house cannot be classified as a trouble-free investment (as are stocks, bonds, and mortgages), the buyer will demand a higher return from this type of investment. This return will include certain tax advantages. In considering apartment-house ownership over other forms of investment, three major points must be considered:

1. The *yield* on a carefully selected apartment house is more than twice the net return on stocks.
2. *Depreciation* allowed under the federal income-tax laws permits much of the income to be tax-free.
3. *Leverage* is the method whereby the owner may borrow the purchase money at one rate and invest it for a higher yield. The investor also has the benefits of equity appreciation and a depreciation write-off. From this standpoint, income-property owner-ship is unique in the investment field. Leverage is not necessarily advantageous for every investor. Because high returns are predicated on risk, leverage should not be employed by the older investor who is dependent on his investment for all, or as a supplement, to his retirement income. This type of buyer should have a minimum of a 50 percent equity in any purchase. Conversely, the younger man in the high-income bracket is the ideal type of investor to benefit most from the leverage factor.

Apartment Investment Analysis

James D. Glenn, realtor, lists nine major factors to give a critical analysis of a prospective apartment investment.[1]

1. *Area analysis.* The area or location of a property can be the actual cause for the success or failure of a venture. This means convenience to shopping and transportation as well as accessibility to schools, libraries, churches, and recreational facilities. Area analysis also should include surveying the area from an *economic* standpoint. (Is the area on the upgrade or is it regressing? What outside influences may be affecting it for good or for bad?)
2. *People analysis.* Highly important in making a critical analysis of an apartment house is studying the type of people who will occupy it. Is this type available in the area? The potential occupants may be divided into four groups:
   a. Middle-aged and older people.
   b. Unmarried employed people.
   c. Young married people.
   d. Normal family units.
3. *Asset-growth and yield analysis.* A sound apartment house investment should show both growth and yield. The *growth* is the increase in value in value in dollars after deduction of the cash spendable, whereas the *yield* represents the cash

[1] James D. Glenn, "Apartment House Investment," *Developing, Selling, and Syndicating Real Estate Investment Property* (Los Angeles: California Real Estate Association, 1964).

funds generated by the asset after deducting all expenses and payments.

4. *Rental analysis.* Rents should be analyzed properly *before* the purchase is made. A good criterion of the ability of the renter to qualify for any given unit is a monthly rental of 20 percent of his take-home pay. Having to lower rents to keep the apartment building fully occupied can result in a lowered value and thus loss to the owner at the time he decides to sell.
5. *Tax analysis.* Investors today are interested in what the apartment house will do for them taxwise. The progressive tax rate means that the higher the income is the greater the tax will be. Income-producing real estate can offer many desirable tax benefits. *Depreciation* (defined as the *theoretical* loss that results in an asset over its normal life) is the key to the tax analysis of an apartment investment.
6. *Management analysis.* Because of the time and effort required to maintain an apartment building, sound management practice is a critical factor in the analysis of the desirability of the investment. Management analysis is therefore a *must*: it is basic to setting up the property management function.
7. *Equity analysis.* The total loan payment on a real estate investment is made up of principal (equity) and interest. Thus, the equity purchase is related directly to the interest charged on the loans on the property. Available loans and the costs of each at any given time must be analyzed carefully. Interest rates and other terms and conditions of the loan fluctuate from time to time, adding or subtracting from the desirability of the investment.
8. *Negative factor analysis.* Advantages or disadvantages of an apartment-building investment will be based upon the above factors. Any of these might prove to be a negative influence and should not be overlooked in the total analysis of the investment. Each is tied in with the other and totaled should answer the question as to whether the investment will produce an adequate return.
9. *True net.* This is not to be confused with what is termed "broker's net".[2] The *true net* is made up of cash spendable income plus the equity purchase. To obtain the cash spendable *all* loan payments must be subtracted from the gross income.

Terms Used in Real Estate Investments

No discussion of income as related to real estate investments can be understood without a knowledge of certain technical terms. These include the following more commonly used:

Gross Scheduled Income. The income that is the maximum amount that can reasonably be expected when the property is fully occupied and utilized to its highest and best use.

Gross Operating Income. The gross scheduled income less a reasonable allowance for vacancy and rent loss, or the actual income that has been produced over a reasonable experience period under competent management.

Net Operating Income. The gross operating income less all operating costs, including such fixed costs as taxes, insurance, management, services, and utilities, in addition to maintenance, repairs, labor, advertising, fees, supplies, and replacements (or a reasonable allowance estimated to pay these expenses when they occur).

Taxable Income. The net operating income less interest on encumbrance and allowable depreciation, if any.

Spendable Income. The net operating income less principal and interest payments and the income tax on the taxable income.

Equity Income (return or yield on the cash investment). Spendable income plus the principal payments on the loans.

Depreciation Methods

In the sense applied in this section, we are concerned with the *theoretical* or age–life methods, as opposed to the *observed* or structural-analysis method of depreciation. It is related to the income or capitalization approach to appraising, based on the remaining economic or useful life during which time provision is made for the recapture of the cost of the improvements. These methods were devised for accounting purposes and are used for periodic write-offs of property investments for business and income tax purposes. They are also referred to as "book depreciation."

Theoretical depreciation methods commonly used are:

1. Straight-Line Method. This is the most widely used, owing to its simplicity of application and its general acceptance by the Internal Revenue Burean for income-tax determination. It involves dividing the total economic life of the property into 100 percent of value. The annual rate derived is then multiplied by the *effective age*[3] to give the percent of depreciation.

[2] "Broker's net" is a net figure that does not include such items as maintenance, management, and vacancy allowance.

[3] Effective age is determined by subtracting from the total *economic* life of the building the appraiser's estimate of remaining *productive* life.

CALIFORNIA REAL ESTATE ASSOCIATION STANDARD FORM

Income Property Statement

PRESENTED BY John Jones Realtor

IMPROVEMENT: 6-unit Apartment House
ADDRESS: 465 N. Cypress
CITY Homeland, California
( ) BLOCKS N-S OF
( ) BLOCKS E-W OF
SALES REPRESENTATIVE:
TELEPHONE (Circle One)
SHOWING INSTRUCTIONS: OWNER - MANAGER - TENANT
TELEPHONE KEY

(Picture of property or business card may be placed in above space)

SPECIAL FEATURES:

Tenants pay gas and electricity - Court style units

Units recently painted

GENERAL INFORMATION:

LOT SIZE ZONE AGE CONST. ELEVATOR STYLE
LEGAL PARKING STORIES SEWER HEAT AIR COND.

EXISTING FINANCING: NO. YEARS
FIRST LOAN 30,000 PYMT. 2,796 INT. 7 ORIG. TO GO
LENDER LOCKED IN YES NO
SECOND LOAN PYMT. INT. DUE ACCEL.
LENDER
OTHER LOANS PYMT. INT. DUE ACCEL.

INVESTMENT INFORMATION BASED ON:
FIRST LOAN 39,000 PAYMENT 3,927 INTEREST 9 NO. YEARS
LENDER COST $
SECOND LOAN 10,000 PAYMENT 1,000 INTEREST 9 DUE
LENDER
SELLER WILL CARRY: PAYMENT INTEREST DUE

SCHEDULED INCOME:

#	DESC.	RENT	#	DESC.	RENT
1	1 Br	$120			$
2	1 Br	$120			$
3	1 Br	$120			$
4	1 Br	$120			$
5	1 Br	$120			$
6	1 Br	$120			$
		$			$
		$			$
		$			$
		$			$
		$			$
		$			$
		$			$
		$			$
		$			$
		$			$
		$			$
		$			$

TOTAL MONTHLY INCOME $

OPERATING EXPENSES:

Taxes	$1,200
Insurance F&L	$ 200
License & Fee	$ 20
Utilities:	
Water	$ 330
Electricity	$
Gas	$
Management	$ 360
	$
Trash	$ 75
Gardener	$
Pool	$
Maintenance (Est.) %	$ 420
Other	$ 75
TOTAL	$2,680

INVESTMENT INFORMATION:

Price	$60,000
Loan ( )	$49,000
Down Payment	$11,000
Scheduled Income	$ 8,640
Vacancy Factor (Est.) %	$ 260
Gross Operating Income	$ 8,300
Operating Expenses	$ 2,680
Net Operating Income	$ 5,620
Loan Payments	$ 4,927
Gross Spendable	$ 693
Furniture Reserve (Est.)	$ —
Carpet Reserve (Est.)	$ —
Adjusted Gross Spendable	$ 693
Paid on Principal	$ 739
Total Return	$1,432

Earns 9.3 % on Sale Price
Spendable of 6.3 % on Down Payment
Earns 13 % on Down Payment
Purchase Price is 6.9 Times Gross

ASSESSED VALUE:

	Amount	Per Cent
Land	$17,100	30 %
Improvement	$37,050	65 %
Pers. Prop.	$ 2,850	5 %
TOTAL	$57,000	100%

Above information is from sources believed reliable but not guaranteed. FORM # IPS-11

For these forms address California Real Estate Association, 520 So. Grand Ave., Los Angeles 90017.

The replacement cost new of the building improvements is then multiplied by the *percent* of depreciation to arrive at the total *dollar amount* of the accrued depreciation.

To illustrate: Let us assume an effective age of twenty-five years, a total economic life of fifty years, and a replacement cost new of $30,000. To compute the amount of accrued depreciation, the following steps should be followed:

1. 100% ÷ 50 (total economic life)
 = 2% per year
2. 2% per year × 25 (effective age)
 = 50%, accrued depreciation
3. 50% × $30,000 (replacement cost new)
 = $15,000, accrued depreciation

2. Sum-of-the-Digits Method. Under this method, the cost or other basis, less salvage, is depreciated in accordance with the number of digits contained within the elapsed years of age, as compared with the total number of years allocated to the property when in new condition.

For example: A property has an economic life of fifty years. The sum of the digits (1 + 2 + 3 + 4 + 5 + . . . 50) = 1,275. The remaining economic life is twenty years. The sum of the digits remaining (1 + 2 + 3 + 4 + 5 + . . . 20) = 210. The digit years applied as depreciation = 1,275 − 210, or 1,065. By dividing 1,275 into 1,065 the percentage of accrued depreciation is arrived at: in this case, 83.5 percent. It can be seen that, under this method, the building is depreciated at a steadily diminishing rate per annum.

3. Declining-Balance Method. Here no salvage value is deducted. The first year's depreciation is deducted from the basis used. The following year, the rate is applied to the new base. This amount may be accelerated up to 150 percent in the event of a *first user.*[4]

To illustrate: The basis for depreciation is $50,000. Using a rate of 4 percent per annum, the first year's depreciation is $2,000. Subtracting this amount from the base, we have $48,000. This figure is now used for the base for the next year's depreciation. 4% × $48,000 = $1,920. If this amount is accelerated to 150 percent, we have a figure for the first year of $50,000 × 6% = $3,000.

[4] *First user* is a term for the investor who first rents out the units. In the event that a builder permits a tenant to take possession of a unit, the buyer may not be considered a *first user.* By holding any prepaid rents in escrow until the buyer's deed is recorded, he may be ruled a first user by the Internal Revenue Service.

Depreciation is a protection against inflation and taxes and can be considered the same as *additional income.* It cannot be claimed on property sold in the same year in which it was purchased. The 1969 tax law made certain changes relating to depreciation. The tax law formerly applicable to all depreciable real property permitted developers (first owners) of buildings all three methods of accelerated depreciation. Second and subsequent owners were allowed depreciation at the rate of 150 percent of straight line on the declining balance.

Under the 1969 law affecting owners of residential income properties (those generating at least 80 percent of their gross rental income from the leasing of rental space) there is no change for developers (first owners). But for second and subsequent owners of residential construction, the depreciation rate depends upon the remaining useful life of the structure. If the remaining life is *less* than twenty years, the owner will be limited to the straight-line method. If the remaining life is *more* than twenty years, the owner is permitted to depreciate the building at the rate of 125 percent of straight line on the declining balance.

When Applicable. Changes in depreciation rates apply generally to buildings *acquired after July 24, 1969.*

Recapture of Depreciation. "Recapture" is a term used to describe depreciation allowances that are recovered in the sale price. If a building, exclusive of land, cost $300,000 and was depreciated by $30,000, the cost basis of the building is reduced to $270,000. If it is sold subsequently for $500,000 there is a gain of $200,000, but $30,000 of this represents recaptured depreciation.

New provisions under the 1969 tax law concern the holding period of a property. For owners of residential construction the holding period during which all excess depreciation recaptured at the time of sale is taxed as ordinary income is increased from 20 to 100 months. Then the percentage of the excess over straight line that is taxable as ordinary income begins to decline by 1 percent per month. Full capital gains treatment is not available until 16-2/3 years of ownership, if accelerated methods of depreciation have been used.

It is not the intent of this text to explore income tax in depth. It is, however, important that the broker counseling his client on investment property or on estate building be aware of the impact of the tax laws and of the necessity of working with the client's tax adviser.

Capitalization of Income

This approach to appraising is based on the *present worth of future benefits* of a property. Although it is not used as the *only* approach to appraising, it generally carries the most weight in the appraisal of income-producing property. It is concerned with the *net* income that an informed buyer can expect property to produce during its remaining useful life. (The gross income is normally used in the appraisal of one- or two-family income properties where the appraisal is based on the *gross-multiplier* method.) The capitalization approach involves the following three steps:

1. *Establishing the net annual income* by deducting the expenses from the gross income. Figures from a period of several years should be used, and *future trends* of income and expenses should be considered.
2. *Selecting the capitalization rate.* This is the most important step of the three. From this selection is derived the *present worth* of the property. Generally speaking, the greater the anticipated risk, the higher the rate. The *comparison* method is the one most commonly used for selection of the capitalization rate. It involves a study of the ratio between the net earned income and the sales price of comparable properties, or a comparison of other types of investments with comparable risks.
3. After determining the net income and the capitalization rate, the third step is to *capitalize the income.*
   If the income is to be calculated as perpetual ("in perpetuity"), it is divided by the capitalization rate to arrive at the capitalized value of the property. This value can undergo a substantial change if the capitalization rate is changed by even as much as 1 percent. Assume that the net return on an apartment house is $42,000. With a capitalization rate of 6 percent, the capitalized value of the property would be $700,000. With a rate of 7 percent, the resultant value would be $600,000. It can be seen that the capitalized value changes in inverse ratio to the *rate.*

Valuation of Vacant Land

The highest and best use of land can be determined by the capitalization approach to the value of vacant land; but, to be most effective, the technique known as the "land residual process" should be used only by skilled appraisers. It is accomplished by calculating the probable resultant income from the property developed for different purposes. It is based on the theory that the value of land depends on its utilization in combination with labor and capital investment. This approach is used either for land that is vacant and available for development to its highest and best use, or for land improved with a new building that constitutes the highest and best use of the property.[5]

Commercial Property

Retail Stores. According to realtor Charles E. Street, Jr., specialist in commercial properties, the following essentials for a well-selected retail-store investment require careful analysis by the investor:

> There are at least seven basic essentials in a well-selected investment that require careful analysis before a decision to purchase should be made. These essentials are:
>
> First and foremost, *location,* which is the true index to rental value and generally represents the deciding factor in the success or failure of the investment.
>
> Second, *rental value,* which is the basis for determining land value.
>
> Third, *tenancy,* which furnishes stability and dependability, provided that it is of high quality and established financial strength.
>
> Fourth, *leases,* which supply the terms and agreements between the owner and the tenant and may make or break an investment which is otherwise most desirable.
>
> Fifth, the *improvements,* which are the housing of the investment, which brings up the question: How should improvements be evaluated?
>
> Sixth, *market value* as compared and reconciled with *intrinsic value.*
>
> Seventh, *financing.* An investment that embodies all six of the essentials above may produce a loss or necessitate selling at a consequent loss of investment position solely because of unwise or unsound financing.[6]

Location. What constitutes a good location? For the answer to this, the commercial-property investor seeking a good location should make a study of the growth trends of the city and, more particularly, the business area under consideration. A complete survey would include studies of its beginnings and the direction in which it is growing. Because land values are based on rental values, it is important to know the going rental per square foot in the area. The value of any retail store is based on the potential purchasing power from which it can draw, together with such important factors as the amount of traffic, the number of shoppers, and the ease of shopping. Suburban shopping centers built on the "one-stop" service con-

[5] For further information on the residual techniques of capitalization as they apply to land valuation, see Alfred A. Ring, *The Valuation of Real Estate* (Englewood Cliffs, N.J.: Prentice-Hall, Inc., 1970), Chap. 19.

[6] Charles E. Street, Jr., "Retail Store Properties," *Commercial and Investment Properties, a Series of Lectures,* Handbook No. 1 (Berkeley: University of California, 1955), pp. 3–4.

cept have proved the value of shopping convenience by making the stores easily accessible to a large segment of the shopping public. This has been done by selection of areas near freeways and providing adequate parking for large numbers of cars.

Rental Value. In simple terms, it can be stated that the tenant who produces the largest volume of sales can afford the highest rent. Choice sites are known as *100 percent* locations and are usually occupied by "key tenants" with long-term leases. They are referred to as being "anchored" to the location. Thus, rental and land values are maintained over the period of these long-term leases.

Tenancy. The type of tenant is a strong factor in the value of the retail-store investment, the responsible tenant tending to stabilize the business district, contributing more or less to the rental value. Careful investigation should be made of his financial strength and responsibility. These can be determined from several sources. State sales-tax figures provide a check on his sales volume. The quantity and quality of the fixtures may be a good stability index. His financial rating can be readily checked through a local credit bureau or Dun & Bradstreet.

Improvements. In evaluating the site improvements, market value rather than intrinsic value is generally given the most weight. Certain factors, however, must be considered. For example, is the lot over- or underimproved? Is the area declining? Is a future rise in taxes indicated? How adequate are the parking facilities? A change of tenancy may render the building inadequate or create a need for "face lifting." In the case of the older building, the cost of modernization is a very important factor. Will zoning and fire ordinances permit remodeling? If so, will the same type of structure be permitted? Is the building being utilized under a nonconforming use? What physical and functional depreciation factors must be considered? Obsolescence of electrical wiring, plumbing and lighting fixtures, and heating and air-conditioning equipment can prove very costly. Before making his decision to purchase, the investor should obtain cost estimates on any items needing replacement. In the final analysis, what is the maximum net return that the property can produce?

Leases. All existing leases should be examined for possible objectionable clauses that may have an effect on the value of the investment. What improvements are the responsibility of the tenant? What is the length of the lease? Is there an escalator clause based on cost-of-living index? A tax clause? A percentage clause? Does the tenant have an option to renew the lease; and, if so, on what terms? Does he have an option to purchase? If so, is he willing to sell his option, and, if so, at what figure? As in any investment, the quality dictates the yield. The lease on any retail-store building is the index to the quality or worth of the investment.

Financing. Long-term financing is one of the keys to a sound investment in commercial properties. The leverage provided by the high yield on a comparatively small investment with low financing is one of the principal attractions to the investor. With fixed monthly payments, an investment plan can be established. New capital can be created out of the income. This capital may be used to build the equity by accelerating the debt. Finally, more desirable and higher-priced properties can be purchased with long-term financing. Any short-term loan that is to be assumed should be carefully scrutinized for renewability at maturity. Because the short-term loan carries heavier monthly payments, allowance may not have been made for an adequate cushion against loss of income, and foreclosure could result.

Office Buildings. The trend today is toward the small outlying office building, prirncipally because it can be built at lower cost away from restrictive fire and zoning regulations. Unfortunately, this has led to an increase in vacancies in office buildings in many of the larger cities. From an investor's standpoint, the questionable vacancy factor and the cost of providing utilities and services, added to loan payments, usually leaves a small return on the investment. However, by analysis of the financial statements, the trained building manager (or appraiser or financial expert) can arrive at the greatest possible net return to be anticipated from a given building.

For the interested investor, a further analysis would be required involving a market survey to determine the going rate of the best office space in the area. By analyzing such data as building type, location and transportation, district, office interiors, parking, tenants, and management, each building can be compared with the other; and, from a correlation of this information, a fair rental rate for the subject building can be established.

As was true of the retail-store investment, tenants of the office building can create a reputation, good or bad, for the property. Location or appearance can never overcome the disadvantages of a building filled with undesirable tenants. Good management dictates care in tenant selection for two reasons: (1) financially stable and responsible tenants will not lease in the same building with tenants of questionable nature; (2) leases made with undesirable tenants often will force the good tenant to leave.

Depreciation. Under the 1969 tax law, changes in the depreciation allowances for owners of nonresidential (commercial, industrial, and all other depreciable buildings) mean that developers (first owners) are now limited to the 150 percent method of depreciation. The 200 percent double-declining balance and sum-of-the-years digits methods are no longer available. Second and subsequent owners are no longer entitled to any form of accelerated depreciation. The straight-line method of depreciation must be used by these owners.

Recapture Provisions. All depreciation in excess of straight line recaptured at the time of sale is now taxable as ordinary income regardless of the time of sale. This applies only to original owners, second and subsequent owners being limited to straight-line depreciation. Taxpayers using the straight-line method of depreciation were not affected by the 1969 law.

Hotels and Motels

Although this is a highly specialized field of real estate, some mention of data relating to this type of income property might be in order here. For the first twelve centuries hotels were primarily of the "inn" type, providing only the basics in food and lodging. Two general types of hotel operation are in effect today: the European plan and the American plan. The European plan, under which most American hotels operate, does not include food and drink in the price of the room. The American plan, which paradoxically is popular in Europe, bulks food with housing accommodations under one fixed price per day.

Hotel operation generally can be broken down into six categories, each with its own characteristics:

1. Small hotels of from ten to twenty rooms. Normally, only 20 to 50 percent of these rooms have private baths. This very limited type of operation would not provide a living for more than one individual.
2. Hotels with twenty to forty rooms. These are suitable for the husband-and-wife type of operation, where the maintenance and managerial duties can be performed with little additional help.
3. Hotels with forty to sixty rooms. Additional labor, with its attendant cost, is required for this type of operation.
4. Hotels with 60 to 100 rooms. These require sales personnel, as well as maintenance and housekeeping crews. This type of operation demands careful appraisal because of the high labor costs, particularly where this group of workers is completely unionized.
5. Hotels with 100 to 150 rooms. Because it can be operated with a minimum front staff with maximum benefit, this is considered an economically sound operation. Maximum efficiency can also be obtained from the housekeeping and maintenance staffs.
6. Hotels of 150 rooms or more. This calls for multiple crews. Customers for this type of operation require a better caliber of service, which, in turn, commands higher rates for the hotel. It is the most popular type of hotel for investment by the large hotel chains.

The motel industry, although relatively new, is one of the fastest growing types of activities in the entire country. From the crude, one-night cabin stand of thirty years ago, the motel industry has reached a high level, in some cases surpassing the finest accommodations in the better hotels. As a service to the traveling public, the motel is rapidly developing into a major consideration in the area of travel and accommodations.

Various types of motels are in operation today: The transient-tourist type, the most prevalent, has from 10 to 100 units incorporating all the modern conveniences and, in the larger deluxe type, provides the tourist not only with room accommodations but with fine restaurants, swimming pools, and other attractions. The tourist-type motor courts are seasonal types of activity except in the warmer climates of California, Florida, and Arizona, where year-round operation is in effect.

The permanent-type motel caters to travelers staying for prolonged periods of time. They usually include kitchens and cooking facilities and are rented by the week or by the month.

The smallest-sized motel adequately suited to operation by an individual or a couple is the one with from ten to twenty units. It can be operated by a couple without outside help. The twenty-to-forty-unit motel is the most popular size to build, because it can be operated effectively by a husband and wife with the addition of a maid.

The larger size, comprising forty units or more, is coming more into prominence. By providing more luxury and added attractions, a higher return is possible for the dollar invested in high-cost construction. This type of motel is becoming popular as the small-convention center. Situated on large parcels of ground just outside the city limits, in addition to the usual attractions, it may provide high-class nightclub entertainment, featuring headline stars. Some of the larger and more attractive motels that are springing up throughout the state in some cases provide service and accommodations surpassing those in many of the large hotels.

The Travelodge is an innovation in the type of motel development where the developer, as a corporation, assists in the planning and building of the motel. A lease-purchase agreement is made with the operator. Primarily, it is the individual's operation. The Travelodge leases the ground on a long-term lease, builds the building, then sells one-half interest to the operator on payment of an agreed sum. As such, he is still the individual operator of the units.

In the smaller cities where motels exist, the traveler prefers them to hotel accommodations. This is due to various things. Approach is easy (because motels are usually located near a freeway), dress requirements are more casual, there is no tipping, and there is direct contact with the traveling car.

Motel investments must be carefully scrutinized. In appraising motels, it is necessary to consider their actual value, plus any premium on the actual earning capacities at the time of sale. This condenses the appraisal to the value of the building, plus the value of the lot and a small profit accorded the seller.

It must be remembered that merchandising of hotels and motels is a highly specialized field involving thorough understanding of the operation, the competition, and the other hazards involved. Motels, particularly, are expensive to build. Rates are highly competitive and, as fluctuations occur in the supply and demand, the investor must study more carefully the financing, the fixed expenses, and the increase in labor costs.

Investment Brief

Although real estate meets today's three major investment considerations: high rate of return, security, and growth with inflation, it has not been accepted generally by many potential investors, principally because of poor merchandising practices. If real estate is to be merchandised to anywhere near it potential, adoption of proven, professional methods must be employed.

Real estate investments are in direct competition with all other forms of investment—stocks, bonds, insurance annuities, savings accounts, and so forth. Today's investor is an intelligent, shrewd individual who demands detailed facts and figures on his potential investments. One telephone call to his stockbroker will bring him the necessary information on any particular stock or bond; his insurance salesman presents a personalized insurance brief showing all the facts and figures of various types of programs. Buyers of real estate investment property require detailed facts and figures on their prospective investments. Realtors also need to develop an "investment brief" to serve as the "cutting edge" of their sales tool.

What Is a Brief? The real estate investment brief simply involves putting down on paper a sales presentation with facts and figures of why a prospective investor should buy a particular piece of property. Naturally, the brief for a duplex will not contain details that will be contained in a brief for a twenty-five-unit apartment house. Besides providing the prospective investor with the facts and figures on a particular piece of property in a professional manner, the brief has some other advantages: (1) it forces the salesman to know his product thoroughly; (2) the written word has many advantages when used in conjunction with an oral presentation; (3) it provides an accurate and convenient way of doing silent selling when the salesman is not there; and (4) psychologists point out that the printed word is much more convincing than the spoken word.

How to Make a Brief. A professional brief should have an attractive, eye-catching cover, a title page, the body of facts and figures, and a concluding summarizing paragraph pointing out the advantages of owning this particular piece of property, how to see it, and who is handling it.

An attractive cover is a "must." The Duo-Tang folder, which includes fasteners designed to hold standard 8½ by 11-inch paper, is an inexpensive cover that does an effective job. Equally important is the next page, which should contain the psychological appeal of personal effort especially for a particular client and incidentally the name of the salesman and his firm, bringing this brief to his attention as something prepared especially for his needs.

One page of the brief should be devoted to an analysis of income and expense relating to the investment property. The amount and rate of return on the total investment, and also the amount and rate of return on the equity investment (the down payment), should be shown. For instance, a $100,000 property which nets $10,000 per year offers a 10 percent return on the total. But if the property requires $40,000 cash and a $60,000 loan at 6 percent, the net return on the actual amount initially invested would be 16 percent. The breakdown can be presented in the brief like this:

Property	$100,000.00	
Loan @ 6 percent	$ 60,000.00	
Cash or equity	$ 40,000.00	
Net income		$10,000.00
Less 6 percent interest on $60,000.00		3,600.00
Net income after interest requirement		$ 6,400.00
16 percent return on equity or actual amount invested		

One of the greatest selling points in merchandising real estate investment properties, as has been mentioned above, is the tax write-off through depreciation. To use the brief to its greatest advantage as a selling tool, the investor's tax advantages should be shown.

Some Extra Hints. A picture of the property and a site-location map will add a professional touch to the brief. It may also be possible to compile and duplicate an investor's guide for a particular location. This would include background statistics and information that might interest an investor.

Across the bottom of each sheet, an error-protection clause should be imprinted, such as, "This information has been obtained from reliable sources, and although we do not guarantee it, we believe it to be correct."

Progress in all forms of endeavor is made possible by putting into effective use the new techniques, methods, and tools that are being developed. Those who are selling investment real estate in our dynamic American economy must be constantly progressing. By standing still, we fall behind. The adoption of these new methods that other professional selling agencies have tried and proven is a must if real estate investments are going to be merchandised to anywhere near their potential.

The brief will help do a selling job by telling:

1. Location: street number and city
2. Legal description: lot and block
3. Size of plot: in feet
4. Tax code area: obtained from County Assessor
5. Assessed valuation, present tax rate, and present taxes
6. Type of property: apartment, office, etc.
7. Direction which the property faces
8. Zoning: Be exact, give number and type.
9. Community attributes: Briefly tell why this is a good community to invest in, its potentials, etc.
10. Location advantages: factors making it a good location.
11. Description of improvements: Describe the type of construction, room sizes, over-all square feet, roof, equipment type, and capacity.
12. Income: Give present income and tell how it can be improved. *Don't overstate.*
13. Expenses: Give upkeep allowance, depreciation, vacancy allowance, insurance, management, and utilities figures. *Don't understate.*
14. Net profit: a simple estimated statement showing rate of return on total investment and also in equity
15. Income tax considerations
16. Price and terms
17. Inspection: how to see the property, your name, and phone[7]

CASE STUDY

David Jaquith purchases a commercial building from a developer for $100,000 cash. A retail clothing store holds a fifteen-year lease on the building at an annual rental of $24,000. All expenses other than taxes and insurance are paid by the tenant. The total annual payments on the taxes and insurance premiums amount to $3,150.

1. What is Jaquith's annual *net* income from the building?
2. What is his *rate* of return?
3. As a *first owner,* what tax advantage does Jaquith have?

Now assume that Jaquith mortgages the property for $75,000 at 8 percent for twenty-five years, this being the going rate for this type of loan. Figuring his average mortgage payments at $12,500 annually:

1. What is his net return on his *equity?*
2. What is his *rate* of return?
3. In your opinion, is Jaquith justified in accepting this rate of return on his investment? Why, or why not?
4. If Jaquith is looking for a tax shelter, which of the above two situations would best meet his requirements? Explain.

SUGGESTED REFERENCES

CASE, FREDERICK E., *Real Estate.* Boston: Allyn & Bacon, Inc., 1962.

——— *Apartment Houses.* Los Angeles: California Real Estate Association, 1968.

——— *Developing, Selling, and Syndicating Real Estate Investment Property.* Los Angeles: California Real Estate Association, 1965.

——— *Real Estate Investment. Los Angeles:* California Real Estate Association, 1963.

——— *Real Estate Investment Opportunities.* Los Angeles: California Real Estate Association, 1965.

——— *Reference Book.* Sacramento: State Department of Real Estate, current issue.

[7] From William T. Leonard, *Selling Real Estate the "Brief" Way* (Richmond, Calif.: West Contra Costa Board of Realtors).

A Real Estate Investment

Prepared Especially For

By

SELLING REAL ESTATE THE "BRIEF" WAY
BY
WILLIAM T. LEONARD
Executive Secretary, West Contra Costa Board of Realtors

Professionalization in the Real Estate Industry is one of the goals of organized real estate that you and your Board have been striving toward. We and our counterparts in organized real estate must make use of the new methods, ideas, and techniques that are being used in other areas of professional selling. This project is one suggestion that can be used to help you sell income or investment property. Briefs have gained prominence in other fields of professional selling. The days are fast drawing to a close when we can expect to sell real estate for investment purposes with a few figures on a piece of scratch paper. For years, successful REALTORS have carefully prepared a comprehensive Brief for major real estate transactions.

Our potential investors in real estate are also potential investors in Stocks, Bonds, Insurance annuities, and other investments. The Insurance companies have Insurance Briefs that carefully show their advantages graphically with facts and figures that can be adapted for each individual and each policy. The preparation of facts and figures into a Brief for a real estate investment is a more difficult task because each parcel of real estate is unique. But just because it is more difficult does not mean that it CANNOT and SHOULD NOT be done for each piece of INVESTMENT TYPE REAL ESTATE. Naturally, the Brief for a duplex will not contain the detail that a Brief for a 25-unit apartment house will contain.

The BRIEF for a real estate investment is simply the putting down on paper the sales presentation with facts and figures of why a prospective investor should buy your particular piece of property. The written word has many advantages when used in conjunction with an oral presentation. It doubles the number of our senses that can absorb the presentation...both the eyes and the ears. It provides an accurate and convenient way of doing "silent selling" when we are not there. The printed word is much more convincing than is just the spoken word. This Brief project by the West Contra Costa Board of Realtors is designed to make it easy for you to prepare a Brief that will do a professional job for you with a minimum of effort and expense.

Your Real Estate Brief will do a better job for you if it contains the following information:

1. Location -- Street number and city.
2. Legal -- lot and block.
3. Size plot -- in feet.
4. Tax Code Area -- obtain from County Assessor, then exact information can be easily assembled.
5. Type -- What kind of property is it--Apartment house, commercial, etc.
6. Face -- Direction the property faces: North, etc.
7. Zoned -- Be exact, give number and type. Example: C-2--general commercial.
8. Community Attributes -- A paragraph telling what factors make it a good location.
9. Location advantages -- paragraph telling why this particular community is a good one to invest in, what are its potentials, etc.
10. Description of Improvements -- Describe type of construction, room sizes, overall square feet, roof, equipment type and capacity (not just a 'hoist' but a 5-ton Elliot overhead hoist).
11. Income -- What is its present income, can it be improved, how? Don't overstate!
12. Expenses -- Taxes, city and county, up-keep allowance, depreciation, vacancy allowance, insurance, management, utilities? Don't understate!
13. Net profit -- Make a simple estimated statement showing Rate of Return on total investment and also in equity (down payment).
14. Income tax considerations.
15. Price and terms.
16. Inspection -- how to see the property--your name and phone.

Look over the sample Brief and then try one yourself. New income can be yours by just an hour's preparation -- and think how much better a salesman you'll be -- because you'll really know your property! Just a final note -- make sure the real estate investment is better than your Brief represents it to be.

COMMERCIAL BUILDING LEASED TO MONTGOMERY WARD

LOCATION:	4411 Macdonald Ave., Richmond, Calif.	TYPE: Commercial Bldg. plus off-street parking
LEGAL:	Lots 4, 5, and 6; block 7, Richmond Pullman Townsite, Richmond, California	FACES: South
SIZE PLOT:	75' x 100'	ZONED: C-2 (general commercial)

TAX CODE AREA: 801

LOCATION ADVANTAGES: Main offramp of freeway (Highway 40) to Richmond joins Macdonald Avenue 300' east of the property. One block to new $260,000 Bank of America, Mira Vista Branch, and intersection of Macdonald and San Pablo Avenue Shopping area. Bus to Oakland and San Francisco goes by door. Daily traffic count on Macdonald Avenue is 12,500. Macdonald is a growing commercial street (5 new buildings last 2 years) connecting the center of Richmond to upper income residential district plus connector avenue of Freeway and San Pablo Avenue to center of Richmond Downtown and Industrial Area. 20 acre parcel directly across street that has excellent Shopping Center potential.

COMMUNITY ATTRIBUTES: A Growing Diversified Industrial base of peace-time originated industries employing 38,000. Supports a growing population of 75,000. New Freeways 95% completed. Bring auto travel time to San Francisco to 25 minutes. Oakland, 15 minutes.

DESCRIPTION OF IMPROVEMENTS: Modern concrete block building, 5 years old, 30 x 90 (2700 sq.ft.). Divided into glassed store or show room 20 x 30.
Plus 6 stalls, 30 x 8, and 2 rest rooms.
Radiant heat, thermostatically controlled.
Hamilton Gas fired boiler, 4" concreted floors, tar and gravel roof.
Garwood Hydraulic auto. life. A Doual Compressor.
550 gal. underground gasoline tank. 45' x 100' (4,500 sq.ft.)
Macadamized parking area; 25 ft. driveway.

INCOME: Now leased to Montgomery Ward at $300 per month. Annual income $3,600. 3 years to go on lease with option to renew for 5 years at $325 per month.

EXPENSES: Taxes only -- Taxes, City and County, currently are $579.00
Tenant pays all upkeep and maintenance on property except roof.

NET PROFIT: Should be, after all expenses $3,000 per year
8.5% return on Total Investment

PRICE: $34,750.00 $10,000 down and owner will carry a first deed of trust for the $24,750 at 6% for 20 years.

This information has been obtained from reliable sources, and while we do not guarantee it, we believe it to be correct.

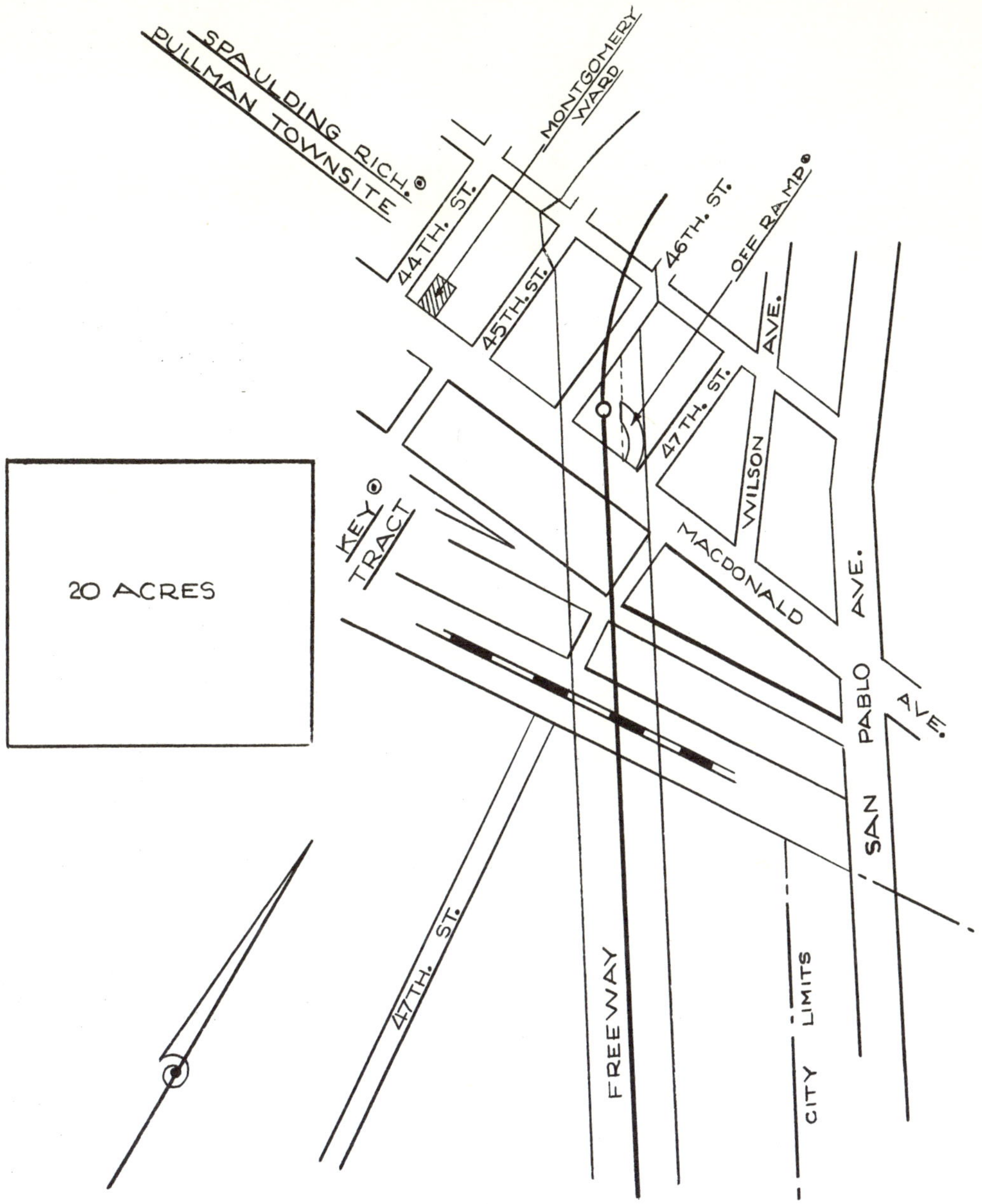

This information has been obtained from reliable sources, and while we do not guarantee it, we believe it to be correct.

INCOME

INVESTMENT AND TAX CONSIDERATION

		Now	When tenant renews lease 3 years hence
Annual Gross Income		$3600	$4000
Annual Expenses			
Taxes	$ 579.00		
Roof-15 year life $2 sq. ft. replacement fund	$ 125.00		
Total Expenses	$ 704.00	$ 704.00	$ 704.00
NET INCOME		$2996.00	$3296.00
NET INCOME SHOWS a return of on the total investment of $34,750		8.5%	9.5%

or

INVESTMENT	$34,750.00
Mortgage	24,750.00
Return of investment	2,996.00
Interest requirement	1,484.00
Net after Interest (before depreciation allowance)	1,512.00
Percentage return on equity	15%

INCOME TAX CONSIDERATION

For income tax purposes. depreciation can be charged as an annual operation expense. Under Bulletin F of Internal Revenue Service. a building five years old can be depreciated in 25-30 years. 25 years or 4% on a straight line basis has been used in this consideration. (Under the 1964 tax laws there is no recapture at all on buildings held over one year if a straight line depreciation is used.)

Net after interest but before depreciations from above		$ 1,512.00
Building, $25,000 value Land, $9,350	4% per year	$ 1,000.00
Taxable Net Income		$ 512.00

This information has been obtained from reliable sources, and while we do not guarantee it, we believe it to be correct.

BUYING

PRICE: asking $34,750

TERMS: $10,000 down, balance to be carried by seller on 1st Deed of Trust @ 6%, 20 years. $24.750 @ 6%, 20 years is $177.29 per month or $2,128.48 per year including principal and interest.

CLOSING COST would be approximately $350.00 and would consist of proration of taxes, and Title Insurance policy.

This real estate investment shows a yearly net of approximately $2,996, which is an 8.5% return on the total investment of $34,750. The roof is the only part of the building that is the responsibility of the new buyer. The tenants take care of all other maintenance.

With $10,000 down, this property would pay for itself in 20 years plus earning for you an extra cash income of $858 per year during this period. Yet the income tax would only apply on approximately $512 per year, due to interest, depreciation, property tax deductions. After the property has paid for itself in 20 years, the spendable net income would be $3,000 per year.

INSPECTION: Call John Doe, Realtor
4216 Macdonald Avenue, Richmond
BEacon 3-1152
for appointment to inspect.

This information has been obtained from reliable sources, and while we do not guarantee it, we believe it to be correct.

APARTMENT-BUILDING INVESTMENT OPPORTUNITY

THIRTY-SIX UNITS

816 S. JACKSON PLACE

BIGTOWN, CALIFORNIA

Prepared by:

ROBERT E. ELLIOTT
2121 North Peacock Lane
Anaheim, California

DAVID L. LUNDBERG
30 East Santa Anita
Arcadia, California

January 13, 1972

An investment opportunity is being offered for the purchase of a thirty-six unit apartment-house complex in Bigtown, California. This property is considered an excellent investment for the following reasons:

1. Purchase price is <u>six</u> times scheduled gross.
2. Projected spendable income is equal to 11 percent of down payment.
3. A shortage of apartments is developing in prime southern California areas.
4. The present rents are under the market.
5. The property is located in an area that should experience substantial rental increases within one year.
6. The property is functionally and aesthetically designed superior to competition in the area.
7. Location is in central Bigtown. Property is eight miles northeast of downtown Los Angeles. Rapid transit, buses, and freeways provide easy access to downtown Los Angeles and Bigtown.

PROPERTY INFORMATION

LOCATION:

816 South Jackson Place, Bigtown, California. Approximately two blocks north of Mountain Boulevard, one-half block south of Pueblo Street, and two blocks west of Pacific Boulevard.

PURCHASE PRICE:

$355,000 (or 6.1 x gross).

TERMS:

$ 90,000 cash or submit

$265,000 loan commitment - 7¼ percent - 25 years - $1,917 per month.

IMPROVEMENTS:

thirty-six-unit apartment building. Constructed 1960. Property unusually well maintained with minimum deferred maintenance (estimated $4,000).

LOT AREA:

36,360 square feet (.9 acre) with 100 feet of frontage on Jackson Place and 200 feet on Christina Lane (to rear).

NEIGHBORHOOD AND COMMUNITY:

The apartment is located in the central portion of Bigtown, eight miles from the Los Angeles Civic Center (fifteen minutes by freeway). Public transportation is available with bus service to the north, south, east, and west within three blocks. Shopping facilities are located at Pacific and Mountain boulevards. All leading church denominations are represented in the city.

Bigtown is noted as a convenient place to live and work, with 200 diversified industrial firms engaged in manufacturing, processing, and engineering. Bigtown also serves as a "bedroom" community for the downtown Los Angeles work force.

CONSTRUCTION:

A well-constructed, two-story frame and stucco building with adequate, easily accessible carports for thirty-six automobiles.

The complex contains the following units:

fourteen	one-bedroom	unfurnished
seven	one-bedroom	furnished
eight	two-bedroom	unfurnished
seven	two-bedroom	furnished

Each unit has one bath with shower and tub, and kitchen with built in range-oven, hooded fan, and garbage disposal. All units have new draperies, wall-to-wall carpeting, well-mounted air conditioners, and thermostatically controlled gas wall furnace for heat.

The grounds are beautifully landscaped with heated pool, badminton court, barbecue, and attractive lanai.

The laundry room and major portions of the automobile parking area are located at the rear of the building, conveniently adjacent to Christina Lane.

PROPERTY SETUP

(Based on owner's information)

SCHEDULED INCOME:			MONTHLY	ANNUALLY	
14	One-bedroom unfurnished	@ 110.00	$1,540.00		
7	One-bedroom furnished	@ 130.00	910.00		
8	Two-bedroom unfurnished	@ 125.00	1,000.00		
7	Two-bedroom furnished	@ 150.00	1,050.00		
			$4,500.00	$54,000.00	
36	Units				
	Cleaning fees and laundry income			804.00	
				$54,804.00	
*	Less vacancy – 2 percent			1,100.00	
	Adjusted gross				$53,700.00

EXPENSES:		
Resident manager	$ 150.00	
Telephone	8.00	
License	6.00	
Advertising	32.00	
Trash service	40.00	
Gas (utility rooms)	20.00	
Electricity	56.00	
Water	41.00	
Cleaning supplies	9.00	
Interior repairs	41.00	
Interior painting	85.00	
Furniture repair	57.00	
Carpet cleaning	24.00	
Drapery cleaning	16.00	
Gardening	100.00	
Exterior repairs	42.00	
Pool maintenance	45.00	
Gas (pool heater)	25.00	
Insurance	57.00	
Property taxes	608.00	
Miscellaneous	25.00	
	$1,487.00	$17,844.00
Net income before loan		35,856.00
First trust deed payment		23,000.00
Spendable income		12,856.00

Annual return on down payment – 14 percent

(12,856 90,000)

* Actual 1970

REVISED PROPERTY SETUP

(Based on current comparative rent study
and suggested expense budget)

Gross expectancy – 1972

21 One-bedroom @ 120.00				
15 Two-bedroom @ 135.00				
Total unfurnished basis	$4,545.00			
15 Furnished @ 20.00 extra	300.00			
Cleaning and laundry	70.00			
Total monthly	$4,915.00			
Total annually			$58,940.00	
Less vacancy – 5 percent			2,947.00	
Adjusted gross				$55,993.00
Budgeted expenses:				
Taxes		$7,300.00		
Resident manager		3,450.00		
Property management		2,800.00		
Insurance		700.00		
Pool maintenance		540.00		
Gardening		1,200.00		
Reserves – furniture replacement		3,600.00		
Maintenance and miscellaneous		3,403.00		$22,993.00
Net income				33,000.00
Mortgage payment				23,000.00
Spendable income				$ 10,000.00

Return on down payment – 11 percent

10,000 90,000

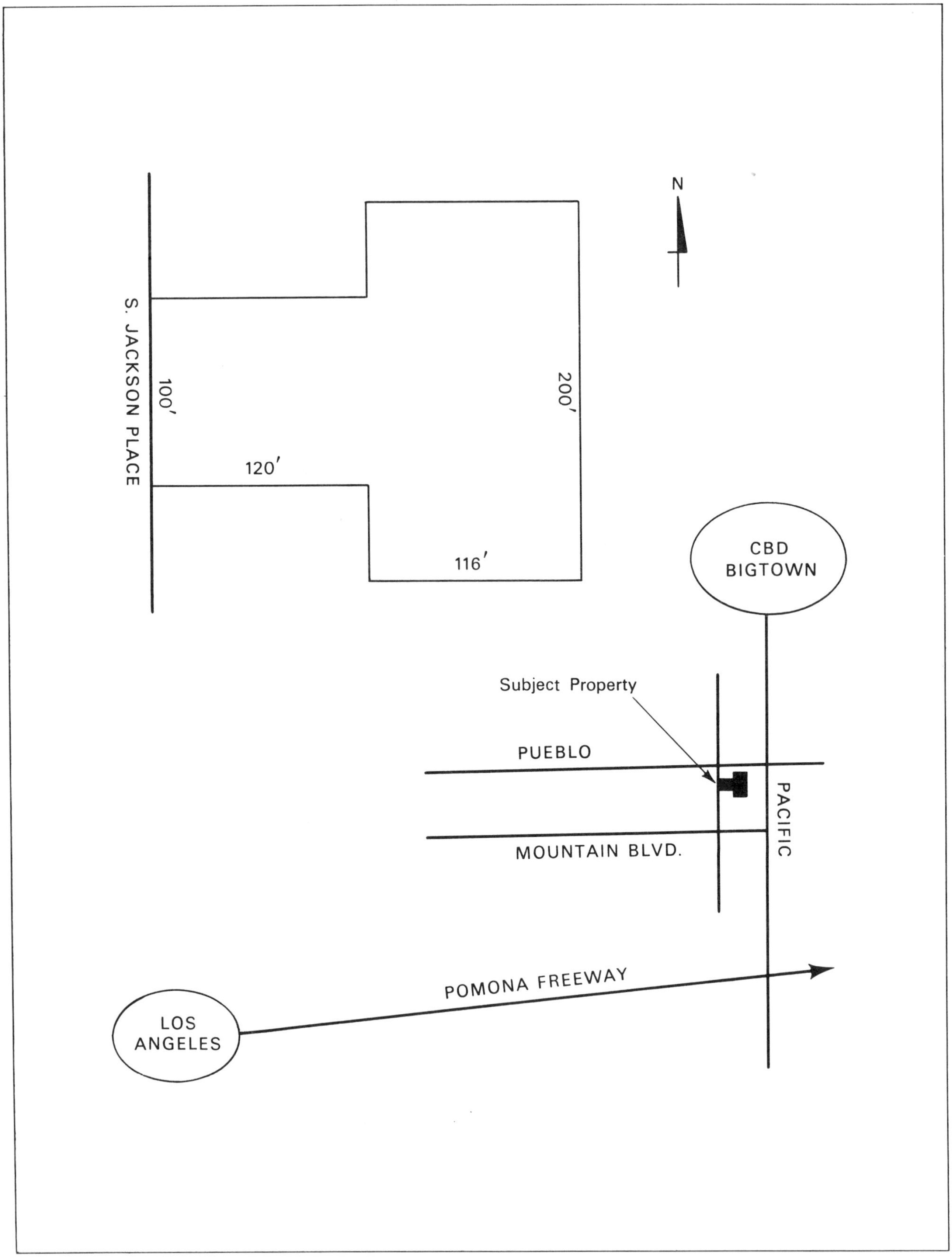
N
S. JACKSON PLACE
100′
120′
200′
116′
CBD
BIGTOWN
Subject Property
PUEBLO
MOUNTAIN BLVD.
PACIFIC
POMONA FREEWAY
LOS
ANGELES

15

Property Management and Leasing

Most brokerage offices participate to a greater or lesser degree in some type of management of property, being concerned primarily with the single-family residence, the duplex, the triplex, or the small apartment house. However, property management as a separate department of the brokerage office has enjoyed a steady growth. Organized property management is a relatively recent field. It had its origin in 1933 in the founding of the Institute of Real Estate Management, composed of individual professional property managers and sponsored by the National Association of Real Estate Boards. It is a professional society that, by certifying the character and ability of its members, recognizes it responsibility to the building-owning public. The Institute of Real Estate Management sets up certain standards of firm operation under which these organizations may be accredited, much the same as certain educational associations rate the standing of schools and universities. The number of universities that have added courses in real estate management to their curriculum denotes the growing public recognition of real estate management as a needed service.

Real estate management, *as it is known today,* received its impetus from three factors:

1. Urbanization. Beginning in the early 1940s, urbanization led to a high concentration of population in strategic areas where employment was high. At this time, because of the scarcity of rental space, there was no need for property managers, because the demand for space far exceeded the supply.

2. Development of Steel-Frame Buildings and Elevators. No longer were buildings limited to one-story structures. The office skyscraper and high-rise apartment building came into being, bringing with them the problems of servicing large developments. Adequate service meant large maintenance crews and technicians, with their attendant supervisors. Property owners found that the complexity of their problems necessitated the hiring of property managers.

3. Absentee Ownership. Inflationary trends following World War II led to an increase in the use of real estate as an investment. This inflation, coupled with the attraction of tax advantages, made the purchase of income property a profitable venture. The same conditions that brought about the increase in investment property also caused a rapid increase in the number of persons engaged in property management. These persons were primarily rent collectors and bookkeepers operating in the guise of "property managers," principally as a service to their sales customers. Professional property management, as such, had not come into existence, and it was only when the real estate agent realized the potential profit in this relatively new field that management of property as it is known today came into being.

During the depression, insurance companies, banks, and trust companies, finding themselves the owners of income properties as a result of foreclosures, had set up their own property-management departments concerned primarily with collection of rents and building maintenance. The need for adequate market analysis, scientific, administrative, and executive functions was ignored, for the most part. Following the depression, these building were purchased by syndicates or wealthy individuals who retained property managers charged with producing the highest net return to the owners. With no experience data upon which to draw, many of these managers proved grossly inefficient.

The Institute of Real Estate Management was organized by a group of Realtors principally for the purpose of providing experience data to its members, which included a group of private firms. These firms adopted certain ethical standards of trade practice, and this was the first step taken by property managers to establish fixed principles of qualification. Membership in the institute charged each firm with:

1. Setting up separate bank accounts for its own funds and for funds of its clients, with no commingling of these funds;
2. Carrying a satisfactory fidelity bond on all its employees whose duties involved the handling of funds; and
3. Refraining from taking discounts or commissions or otherwise profiting from purchases, contracts, or other expenditures of clients' funds without full disclosure to the property owner, and then only with his full consent.

Professional Designations

In 1938, some of the original organizers of the institute recognized that, although they had taken a long step in the direction of setting up certain principles of responsibility, they had failed to provide a background of professionalism for member firms. It was generally recognized that a firm or corporation as such could not be certified as having the prime qualities needed for management. These qualifications of "ability," it was agreed, could be possessed only by the executive who headed the management organization, and thus only he could be certified as a *qualified property manager.* As an outgrowth of this premise, the Institute of Real Estate Management was reorganized along professional lines. The membership was restricted to individual members "specializing in the management of real estate."[1]

Certified property manager (CPM). This title is conferred upon only those *individuals* who have demonstrated their experience, skill, and integrity to the satisfaction of the admissions committee and the governing council of the institute. Any firm, partnership, or corporation with the required experience, skill, and integrity, and which agrees to certain standard ethical and operating requirements as set forth by the institute, may be designated an *accredited management organization* (AMO). Ability, experience, and integrity are the prime requisites for membership AMO designation. The principal distinction between the CPM and the AMO designations is in the *individual* professional designation (CPM) as against the *firm* designation (AMO). To qualify as a CPM, the candidate must have (a) demonstrated his ability to manage real estate; (b) been actively engaged in a responsible position in the real estate management business for a minimum of three years; (c) met the minimum educational requirements; (d) given evidence of integrity beyond reproach; (e) subscribed to the institute bylaws and upheld the professional pledge; and (f) been a member of the local real estate board or the National Association of Real Estate Boards.

In addition, two written examinations are required of the candidate, which may be waived if (1) he has successfully passed the examinations in the institute's lecture courses I and II or (2) he has had fifteen years of active management experience, in which case arrangements may be made for him to take a single special examination. Upon acceptance by the institute, the individual is privileged to display the official certificate designating him a CPM and to wear the gold key engraved with his name and certificate number.

Types of Real Estate Managers

These can be broken down into three categories: (1) the property manager; (2) the individual property manager; and (3) the building superintendent or resident manager.

The *property manager* is a member of a real estate agency that manages a number of properties for various owners. He may be in business for himself as a managing agent; he may be one of a number of managers in a real estate firm; or he may be an individual member of the firm and devote his time entirely to property management.

The *individual manager* may be employed directly by the owner or by the property manager. More generally than not, he is employed on a salary basis.

The *resident manager* is employed by a real estate agency or a managing agent and lives on the property. He is usually qualified for such work by previous management experience or by special training. A *building superintendent* is the representative of a real estate agency who employs him in a supervisory capacity. His chief duties are those of overseeing maintenance and operation. He is also responsible for the hiring of janitors, elevator operators, maintenance men, and scrubwomen.

Functions of a Property Manager

The responsibility of the property manager is dual in nature. He acts as administrator for the owner, who is primarily interested in (1) the highest return

[1] For further study, consult James C. Downs, Jr., *Principles of Real Estate Management* (Chicago: Institute of Real Management, 1964).

from the property commensurate with its highest and best use and (2) the enhancement of the physical value of the property. Property management must not be confused with rental agency, whose functions are limited to the selection of tenants and the collection of rents. Under the rental-agency contract, the owner retains the rights and responsibilities of maintenance and operation of the property, as well as of dictating all policies in connection with management. Under property management, total executive functions are assumed by the manager. The owner is relieved of all details connected with the operation or physical upkeep of the property.

The social and civic obligations of the property manager are coming to assume greater proportions. It is his responsibility to be informed on current zoning and building restrictions, in addition to assuming a role in the general welfare and growth of his community. The principal functions of management in the broad sense include:

1. Marketing of space, advertising, and securing desirable tenants at the best rates obtainable.
2. The collection of rents.
3. Physical care of the premises and attendance to tenant complaints.
4. Purchase of supplies and equipment and expenditure for repairs.
5. Hiring of employees and maintaining good public relations.
6. Keeping proper accounts and rendering periodic reports.[2]

Establishing the rental schedule is the most important step in the marketing of space. Although, in theory, rents (price of space) are based on the fixed expenses and operating costs with a fair rate of return to the owner, in actual practice supply and demand govern the rental figure. To establish the rental schedule, a skilled and thorough neighborhood analysis must be made. Full knowledge of his own building and the ability to compare it objectively with other similar properties in the neighborhood are the marks of a good manager. The analysis should incorporate:

1. The character of the neighborhood.
2. Economic level and family size.
3. Domestic status and trends.
4. Availability of transportation, recreation, shopping, churches, and schools.
5. Physical aspects as well as lot coverage.[3]
6. The breadth and growth of local industries.
7. Population-growth trends.
8. Personal-income range, financial capacity, and stability of income.
9. Growth and expansion of the community.
10. Condition of the housing market in terms of inventory on the market, sales-price range, new construction, and vacancy.

Neighborhood Analysis. First, "neighborhood" should be defined. According to Webster, a neighborhood is a community, district or area especially with regard to some characteristic or point of reference. From the property manager's standpoint, the area involved in the analysis of the neighborhood might range from three to four blocks to many square miles, but it should be one in which there are common characteristics of population and land use. In making the neighborhood analysis, the first consideration should be the fixing of boundaries. To assist in the establishment of these neighborhood limits, data from the U.S. census, newspapers, or city libraries are usually readily available. What criteria are used to make the analysis? Among the more important items to consider are: (1) population trends, (2) economic level of population, (3) average family size, (4) domestic status (number of married, single, and divorced persons), (5) composition of the population (ages and number of senior citizens, "war babies," and young marrieds), (6) movement or change in the population makeup.[4]

Market Analysis. This may be termed "appraising rental value." In making this type of appraisal, it must be recognized that there are differing markets even within the residential-property field. For example, among the major classifications are to be found those of single-family residences, duplexes and triplexes, small four- to six-unit apartments, and the multistory apartments. These are then further classified as to quality features and size (one, two, or three bedrooms). Each of these markets varies as to rent schedule, expenses, supply, and demand. A careful correlation and analysis of all available statistics should provide the information necessary to produce a comparable rental schedule.

The Rental Schedule. The scheduled rents must, of necessity, be only estimates of true rental figures, because they are based on an individual's appraisal of available data. Occupancy records and public reaction in the final analysis are the only accurate gauges of the correctness of the rent schedule. In the final analysis, the objective of good property management

[2] Philip A. Benson, L. North, and Alfred A. Ring, *Real Estate Principles and Practices* (Englewood Cliffs, N.J.: Prentice-Hall, Inc., 1960), p. 296.

[3] *Reference Book* (Sacramento: Department of Real Estate).

[4] Further exploration of this topic may be found in James C. Downs, Jr., *Principles of Real Estate Management* (Chicago: Institute of Real Estate Management, 1964).

is to attain as near 100 percent occupancy as possible without having to underprice the space. Even with the proper rent schedule, careful space merchandising, and efficient collection policies all contributing to the owner's maximum gross return, the property manager has failed in his duty if he cannot show a proper *net* profit for his client. This situation may be attributable to the manager's inability to make an accurate survey of the probable current as well as the deferred maintenance of the building.

The property manager is also charged with supervising all purchasing operations. He must set up operating policies that provide the tenants with the best possible accommodation commensurate with adequate dollar return to the owner. The manager is also an employer, in the sense that he is responsible for the supervision of the maintenance and housekeeping crews and for maintaining the schedule of each.

Finally, the property manager's duties include setting up and maintaining adequate records and making periodic reports to the owner. A detailed annual statement for the purpose of cost accounting is vital for an analysis of the variations in income and expenses on which to base future rental schedules.

Tenant Selection. Because the economic value of any building is established by its income, the reliability of each tenant responsible for rental income is vital to the stability of the investment. Although the rent-paying ability of a tenant cannot be discounted, other criteria enter into the total picture of tenant qualification. For example, the long-term tenant is of more financial value to the apartment owner than the one who, although he may make prompt payment of his rent, moves constantly from place to place. Because of the added maintenance cost, the *stability* of a tenant thus becomes a major factor in the net return.

Consider also the tenant's housekeeping ability. Obviously, less maintenance expense is involved where good housekeeping is practiced. A building reflects the tenant characteristics. When the building is maintained in a neat and orderly manner, a better class of tenant is attracted, rent schedules are more easily maintained, and the level of tenant morale is naturally higher.

Should families with children be accepted? It is generally agreed that there should not be a mixed pattern of childless couples and those with children in the same building. Some property owners have a general policy of never accepting children in their apartments. This rigid policy may, however, work to the disadvantage of the owner, because he may be overlooking the desirable quality of stability in the tenant. Generally speaking, tenants with children tend to stay longer and to live better-ordered lives. In this area, the problem of tenant selection is a difficult one. How is the property manager to determine whether the applicant exercises reasonable child discipline? The family of well-disciplined children could make ideal tenants. On the other hand, the undisciplined child can be a destructive force. Personal investigation is probably the only sure way of determining the desirability of the applicant. This can be done by a visit to his present home, or, if this is impossible, references from previous landlords should be requested and checked.

In the multiunit apartment house, because of the close proximity of the units, living habits become of extreme importance. The person who plays his radio, hi-fi, or television too loud is certainly undesirable in the opinion of his fellow tenants. Any manner of living that deviates from the accepted pattern may infringe on the rights of others. Because of the difficulty of evicting this type of tenant, more emphasis should be placed on this phase of selection. Again, the only sure way correctly to prejudge this type of tenant is through personal investigation.

Earnings. Property-management agencies customarily operate on a percentage of the gross rents collected. These percentages may vary from 1 percent on large properties to as high as 10 percent on single-family residences or on those of two to six units.

The Management Agreement. Although the management agreement will vary with each operation, it is imperative that it be in writing and that it cover certain basic points, including:

1. Complete description of the property to be managed.
2. Complete and exact names of the owner and the manager.
3. Term of the contract, including beginning and termination dates.
4. Statement of responsibility and authority of the agent, as well as any limitations restricting his operation of the property.
5. Compensation clause, stipulating the rate of compensation to be paid for management service, as well as agreement to reimburse the manager if collections are not sufficient to meet operating costs.
6. Provision for manager accounting and submission of monthly statements of receipts, expenses, and charges.
7. A "save harmless" clause, wherein the agent shall be held harmless from damage suits or from liability from injury suffered by any employee.[5]

[5] See the management-contract form on pp. 221–222.

MANAGEMENT AGREEMENT

PARTIES

In consideration of the covenants herein contained ____________________

(hereinafter called "Owner"), and ____________________

(hereinafter called "Agent"), agree as follows:

EXCLUSIVE AGENCY

1. The Owner hereby employs the Agent exclusively to rent, lease, operate and manage the property known as ____________________

upon the terms hereinafter set forth for the period of ________ beginning on the ________

RENEWAL

day of ____________ 19______, and ending on the ____________ day of ____________, 19______, and thereafter for annual periods unless on or before sixty (60) days prior to the date last above mentioned, or on or before thirty (30) days prior to the expiration of any such renewal period, either party hereto shall notify the other in writing of an intention to terminate this agreement in which case this agreement may be terminated prior to the last mentioned date. Either party may terminate this agreement upon thirty (30) days written notice after the expiration of ______ months of the original term.

TERMINATION

RENTING OF PREMISES AGENT TO NEGOTIATE LEASE

2. The Agent accepts the employment and agrees:

a) To use due diligence in the management of the premises for the period and upon the terms herein provided, and agrees to furnish the services of his/its organization for the renting, leasing, operating and managing of the herein described premises.

MONTHLY STATEMENTS

b) To render monthly statements of receipts, expenses and charges and to remit to Owner receipts less disbursements. In the event the disbursements shall be in excess of the rents collected by the Agent, the Owner hereby agrees to pay such excess promptly upon demand of the Agent.

SEPARATE OWNERS' FUNDS

c) To deposit all receipts collected for Owner (less any sums properly deducted or otherwise provided herein) in a Trust account in a national or state institution qualified to engage in the banking or trust business, separate from Agent's personal account. However, Agent will not be held liable in event of bankruptcy or failure of a depository.

BONDED EMPLOYEES

d) Agent's employees who handle or are responsible for Owner's monies shall be bonded by a fidelity bond in adequate amount.

AGENT'S AUTHORITY

3. The owner hereby gives to the Agent the following authority and powers and agrees to assume the expenses in connection herewith:

a) To advertise the availability for rental of the herein described premises or any thereof, and to display "for rent" signs thereon; to sign, renew and/or cancel leases for the premises or any part thereof; to collect rents due or to become due and give receipts therefor; to terminate tenancies and to sign and serve in the name of the Owner such notices as are appropriate; to institute and prosecute actions; to evict tenants and to recover possession of said premises; to sue for in the name of the Owner and recover rents and other sums due; and when expedient, to settle, compromise, and release such actions or suits or reinstate such tenancies. Any lease executed for the Owner by the agent shall not exceed ________ years.

REPAIRS

b) To make or cause to be made and supervise repairs and alterations, and to do decorating on said premises; to purchase supplies and pay all bills therefor. The Agent agrees to secure the prior approval of the Owner on all expenditures in excess of $________ for any one item, except monthly or recurring operating charges and/or emergency repairs in excess of the maximum, if in the opinion of the Agent such repairs are necessary to protect the property from damage or to maintain services to the tenants as called for in their leases.

EMPLOYEES

c) To hire, discharge and supervise all labor and employees required for the operation and maintenance of the premises; it being agreed that all employees shall be deemed employees of the Owner and not the Agent, and that the Agent may perform any of its duties through Owner's attorneys, agents or employees and shall not be responsible for their acts, defaults or negligence if reasonable care has been exercised in their appointment and retention.

SERVICE CONTRACTS

d) To make contracts for electricity, gas, fuel, water, telephone, window cleaning, ash or rubbish hauling and other services or such of them as the Agent shall deem advisable; the Owner to assume the obligation of any contract so entered into at the termination of this agreement.

4. The Owner further agrees:

SAVE HARMLESS

a) To save the Agent harmless from all damage suits in connection with the management of the herein described property and from liability from injury suffered by any employee or other person whomsoever, and to carry, at his own expense, necessary public liability and workmen's compensation insurance adequate to protect the interests of the parties hereto, which policies shall be so written as to protect the Agent in the same manner and to the same extent they protect the Owner, and will name the Agent as co-insured. The Agent also shall not be liable for any error of judgment or for any mistake of fact of law, or for anything which it may do or refrain from doing hereinafter, except in cases of willful misconduct or gross negligence.

b) The agent is hereby instructed and authorized to pay mortgage indebtedness, property and employee taxes, special assessments, and to place fire, liability, steam boiler, pressure vessel, or any other insurance required, and the agent is hereby directed to accrue and pay for same from the Owner's funds, with the following exceptions: ____________________

____

c) Upon and after the termination of this agreement pursuant to the method described in Paragraph 1 hereof, Owner shall recognize Agent as the broker in any pending negotiations of said premises, or any part thereof, and in the event of the consummation thereof Owner shall pay to Agent a commission therefor at the rate prescribed on Paragraph 4 d) hereof.

d) To pay the Agent:

(1) For Management ____________________

(2) For Leasing ____________________

(3) For Modernization ____________________

(4) For Refinancing ____________________

(5) For Sale ____________________

(6) For Fire Restoration ____________________

(7) Other ____________________

e) Other Items of Mutual Agreement. ____________________

This Agreement shall be binding upon the successors and assigns of the Agent, and the heirs, administrators, executors, successors and assigns of the Owner.

IN WITNESS WHEREOF the parties hereto have affixed or caused to be affixed their respective signatures this ________ day of ____________ 19______.

WITNESS:

____________________ Owner

____________________ Agent

(This is a STANDARD FORM OF THE INSTITUTE OF REAL ESTATE MANAGEMENT of the National Association of Real Estate Boards, 36 South Wabash Avenue, Chicago 3. When placing your order specify FORM PM-7)

MANAGEMENT AGREEMENT

between

Owner ____________________

and

Agent ____________________

For property located at ____________________

Beginning ____________ 19____

Ending ____________ 19____

The Lease. *Rent* is the consideration for the use of the property. The *lease* is commonly defined as a contract by which one conveys real estate for life, for a term of years, or at will, and usually for a specified rent. Under California law, leases for one year or less need not be in writing. However, the prime purpose of a written lease is to establish a *written record of a contract* between a lessor and a lessee. From the tenant's standpoint, a written lease provides him the *security of possession* for the term of the lease. For the landlord, on the other hand, the lease assures him of the *tenant's occupancy and obligation to pay rent* over a given period. There are advantages and disadvantages to the signed lease. In a rising market, the landlord is bound by a fixed rental. In a falling market, the tenant is held to a rental above the going rates for comparable space. In order to create a leasehold, the lease must include the names of the parties, description of the property, the amount of the rental payment, and the term of the lease. California law provides that if the lease is in writing, it must be signed by the lessor, but delivery to and acceptance of the lease by the lessee is sufficient, *even though he has not signed.* Courts have held that the terms of the lease may be construed as having been accepted by the lessee if he takes possession of the premises and is paying rent.

The lease should cover certain specific situations, such as the extent and amount of the service to be supplied by the landlord and responsibility for decorating or minor repairs. May the tenant make alterations or do any decorating without consent of the lessor? There should be some provision for a guarantee by the tenant that he will leave the premises in as good a condition as it was as the time of possession. If a cleaning deposit is required, the lease should contain a specific agreement as to the conditions under which it may be retained by the lessor. *Use* of the premises should be spelled out, as well as a stipulation as to the number of occupants permitted. (Residential leases normally require that immediate members of the family only may occupy the premises.)[6]

The Percentage Lease. This type of lease applies to the rental of commercial space. It was originated primarily to equalize the inequities in fixed rentals resulting from fluctuations in market trends; thus, in a long-term lease, no market advantage is given to either lessor or lessee. Under the terms of the percentage lease, the relationship between the volume of business being done by the tenant and the fair rental of the space is expressed by a percentage figure. From the standpoint of the tenant, it can be argued that such a clause incorporated into the lease is not an equitable one, because any increase in the business being done is due to the business acumen of the tenant rather than the value of the occupied space. Conversely, the landlord may justifiably contend that the long-term lease (the only type justifying the percentage lease) protects the tenant from eviction at

[6] See the lease form on pp. 224 and 225.

SEPARATE RECORD FOR EACH PROPERTY MANAGED

Owner	Fridolph Gazze	Deposit	
Address		Monthly Rent	$355.00
Property	Morgan Arms Apts.	Commission:	
Tenant's Name	Marsh #1, Hacker #2	Leases	
Units		Collection	10%
Remarks		Management	Included

Date	Received From or Paid To	Description	Receipt or Check No.	Amount Received	Date Deposited	Amount Disbursed	Balance
4-8-69	Troy Marsh	April Rent Apt. #1	Rcpt. #2	175.00	4-8-69		$175.00
4-8-69	Mildred Hacker	April Rent Apt. #2	Rcpt. #3	180.00	4-8-69		$355.00
4-9-69	City Water Co.	3/69 Water Bill				$25.00	$330.00
4-10-69	Paul Hill	Collection & Mgmt. Fee	CK #2			$35.50	$294.50
4-10-69	Fridolph Gazze	Apt. Rental Proceeds	CK #3			$294.50	—0—

LEASE

(RESIDENTIAL)

CALIFORNIA REAL ESTATE ASSOCIATION STANDARD FORM

THIS IS INTENDED TO BE A LEGALLY BINDING AGREEMENT—READ IT CAREFULLY

Lakeview City, California

January 10 1972

Alfred A. Graham, Landlord,

and Leonard and Sonja Morris, husband and wife, Tenant, agree as follows:

1. Landlord leases to Tenant and Tenant hires from Landlord those premises described as: 4582 Oleander Drive (a single family residence)

together with the following furniture and fixtures: 1 nine-foot General Electric refrigerator 1 Westinghouse four burner electric range (yellow in color)

(Insert "as shown on Exhibit A attached hereto" and attach the exhibit if the list is extensive.)

2. The term of this lease shall be twelve months **
(years/months)
commencing January 15 1972 and terminating January 14 1973.

3. Tenant is to pay rent as follows: $ 400.00 upon signing of this lease, such sum representing the first and twelfth months' rent.

The rent shall be paid at the office of the landlord, 165 West Railroad Avenue, Lakeview City or at any address designated by the Landlord in writing.

4. Tenant agrees to pay upon execution of this lease, in addition to rent, a [X] refundable [ ] non-refundable cleaning charge of $ 100.00 **********. If refundable, such charge shall be refunded only if the premises are left thoroughly clean by Tenant upon termination of occupancy.

Tenant also agrees to pay upon execution of this lease, in addition to rent, a security deposit of $______. Said deposit will be returned to Tenant by Landlord or his successors upon full performance of the terms of this lease.

5. Tenant agrees to pay for all utilities except water. Landlord also agrees to pay for rubbish and trash removal service. which shall be paid for by Landlord.

Gardening and general yard maintenance *************************** to be at the expense of the tenants.

6. Tenant has examined the premises and all furniture and fixtures contained therein, and accepts the same as being clean and in good order, condition and repair, with the following exceptions: Carpeting in rear bedroom is stained near the west window.

7. The premises are rented for use only as a residence for a single family and for not more than two adults and two children.

No animal or pet except one miniature schnauzer dog ************************************ shall be kept on the premises without Landlord's prior written consent.

8. Tenant shall not disturb, annoy, endanger or inconvenience other tenants of the building or neighbors, nor use the premises for any immoral or unlawful purposes, nor violate any law or ordinance, nor commit waste or nuisance upon or about the premises.

9. Tenant shall obey the Rules and Regulations for the property attached hereto.

10. Tenant shall keep the premises rented for his exclusive use in good order and condition and pay for any repairs caused by his negligence or misuse or that of his invitees. Landlord shall maintain any other parts of the property and pay for repairs not caused by Tenant's negligence or misuse or that of his invitees.

11. Tenant shall not paint nor make alterations of the property without Landlord's prior written consent.

12. This lease will terminate if the premises become uninhabitable because of dilapidation, condemnation, fire or other casualty for more than 30 days. Rent will be reduced proportionately if the premises are uninhabitable for any shorter period.

13. With Tenant's permission, which shall not unreasonably be withheld, Landlord or his agent shall be permitted to enter to make repairs, and to show the premises to prospective tenants or purchasers. In an emergency, Landlord or his agent may enter the premises without securing prior permission from Tenant, but shall give Tenant notice of such entry immediately thereafter.

14. Tenant shall not let or sublet all or any part of the premises nor assign this lease or any interest in it without the prior written consent of Landlord.

15. If Tenant abandons or vacates the premises, Landlord may at his option terminate this lease, re-enter the premises and remove all property.

16. The prevailing party may recover from the other party his costs and attorney fees of any action brought by either party to enforce any terms of this lease or recover possession of the premises.

17. Either party may terminate this lease in the event of a violation of any provision of this lease by the other party.

18. Time is of the essence. The waiver by Landlord of any breach shall not be construed to be a continuing waiver of any subsequent breach.

Alfred A. Graham
Landlord

Leonard Morris
Tenant

____
Landlord

Sonja Morris
Tenant

FORM LR-14

CITIZEN PRINT SHOP

CREDIT APPLICATION FOR LEASE

Property Address: 4582 Oleander Drive, Lakeview City, California Apt. No.

Name(s) of Applicant(s): Leonard Morris Married? Yes

Name of Spouse: Sonja Morris No. of Children: 2 Ages (boys): 6 (girls): 4

Other occupants (Number & Relationship): None ****************************

Pets (Number & Type): One miniature schnauzer dog

Present Address: 2538 First Avenue Apt. # 38 Lakeview City, California

How long? one year Reason for leaving: Children need yard in which to play

Name of Owner or Owner's Agent: Richard T. Higgins

Previous Address: 356 North Camellia Avenue, Casa Blanca, California

How long? two years Reason for leaving: Street was too noisy

Name of Owner or Owner's Agent: Blaine R. Lampe

Employment Social Sec. No. 533-28-9369 Drivers License No. Z938406

Present Employer: Zenith T V Repair Shop How long? 10 years

Address: 754 North Railroad Avenue, Montrose, Ca. Telephone: 426-3338

Employed as: Reapirman Salary: $ 650.00 per month

Employment (spouse) Social Sec. No. 625-38-4825 Drivers License No. Z827456

Present Employer: Lakeview City School District How long? 2 years

Address: 256 East Highland Ave. Lakeview City, Ca. Telephone: 446-8131

Employed as: Typist-secretary Salary: $ 600.00 per month

Other Income: $ none Bank Accounts: Savings: $ 4,000.00 Checking: $200.00

Credit References (3): Roberts Dept. Store, Lakeview City

Lakeview City National Bank, Lakeview City

Standard Oil of California

Automobile License No. HKW 195 State of Registry: California

Make & Model: Ford four-door Fairlane Year: 1970 Color: white

Name of Closest Relative: Robert M. Morris Relationship: Father

Address: 2865 West Brightview Avenue, Lakeview City, Ca Telephone: 447-2228

Have you ever filed a petition in bankruptcy? No

Have you ever been evicted from any tenancy? no Have you ever wilfully and intentionally refused to pay any rent when due? no

I DECLARE THE FOREGOING TO BE TRUE UNDER PENALTY OF PERJURY.

I agree that Landlord may terminate any agreement entered into in reliance on any misstatement made above.

Date January 10 19 72 Applicant: Leonard Morris

Telephone No. 446-3862 Applicant: Sonja Morris

RECEIPT FOR DEPOSIT

The undersigned acknowledges receipt of $100.00 ********* in the form of ☐ Cash, ☒ personal check or ☐ ********************************** payable to Brian M. Working, Realtor to be applied in accordance with the foregoing lease if accepted by Landlord.

Brian M. Working

Agent

LEASE
(RESIDENTIAL)

TO

Dated

RESIDENTIAL RENTAL AGREEMENT

CALIFORNIA REAL ESTATE ASSOCIATION STANDARD FORM

THIS IS INTENDED TO BE A LEGALLY BINDING AGREEMENT—READ IT CAREFULLY

_______________, California

_______________ 19 ____

1. _______________, Landlord

agrees to rent to _______________, Tenant,

the premises described as: _______________

____

together with the following furniture and fixtures: _______________

____

____

(Insert "as shown on Exhibit A attached hereto" and attach the exhibit if the list is extensive.)

2. The rental shall commence on _______________, 19 ____, and shall continue from month to month unless otherwise stated here: _______________

____

This rental may be terminated at any time by either party by giving written notice 30 days in advance unless a longer or shorter period of advance notice (not less than 7 days) is specified here: _______________

Tenant agrees to pay $ _______________ per month on the _______________

day of each month _______________ at _______________

____

3. Tenant agrees to pay upon execution of this agreement, in addition to rent, a ☐ refundable, ☐ nonrefundable cleaning charge of $ ________ If refundable, such charge shall be refunded only if the premises are left thoroughly clean by Tenant upon termination of occupancy.

4. Tenant agrees to pay all utilities except _______________ which shall be paid for by Landlord.

5. Tenant has examined the premises and all furniture and fixtures contained therein, and accepts the same as being clean and in good order, condition and repair, with the following exceptions: _______________

____

6. The premises are rented for use only as a residence for a single family and for not more than _______________

adults and ____________ children.

No animal or pet except _______________ shall be kept on the premises without Landlord's prior written consent.

7. Tenant shall not disturb, annoy, endanger or inconvenience other tenants of the building or neighbors, nor use the premises for any immoral or unlawful purposes, nor violate any law or ordinance, not commit waste or nuisance upon or about the premises.

8. Tenant shall obey the Rules and Regulations for the property attached hereto.

9. Tenant shall keep the premises rented for his exclusive use in good order and condition and pay for any repairs caused by his negligence or misuse or that of his invitees. Landlord shall maintain any other parts of the property and pay for repairs not caused by Tenant's negligence or misuse or that of his invitees.

10. Tenant shall neither paint nor make alterations of the property without Landlord's prior written consent.

11. With Tenant's permission, which shall not unreasonably be withheld, Landlord or his agent shall be permitted to enter to inspect, to make repairs, and to show the premises to prospective tenants or purchasers. In an emergency, Landlord or his agent may enter the premises without securing prior permission from Tenant, but shall give Tenant notice of such entry immediately thereafter.

12. Tenant shall not let or sublet all or any part of the premises nor assign this agreement or any interest in it without the prior written consent of Landlord.

13. If Tenant abandons or vacates the premises, Landlord may at his option terminate this agreement, re-enter the premises and remove all property.

14. The prevailing party may recover from the other party his costs and attorney fees of any action brought by either party to enforce any terms of this agreement or recover possession of the premises.

15. Either party may terminate this agreement in the event of a violation of any provision of this agreement by the other party.

16. Time is of the essence. The waiver by Landlord of any breach shall not be construed to be a continuing waiver of any subsequent breach.

_______________ Landlord   _______________ Tenant

_______________ Landlord   _______________ Tenant

CREDIT APPLICATION FOR RENTAL

Property Address: ______________________________ Apt. No. ______

Name(s) of Applicant(s): ______________________________ Married? ______

Name of Spouse: ____________ No. of Children: ______ Ages (boys): ______ (girls): ______

Other occupants (Number & Relationship): ______________________________

Pets (Number & Type): ______________________________

Present Address: ______________________________

How long? ____________ Reason for leaving: ______________________________

Name of Owner or Owner's Agent: ______________________________

Previous Address: ______________________________

How long? ____________ Reason for leaving: ______________________________

Name of Owner or Owner's Agent: ______________________________

Employment: ________ Social Sec. No. ____________ Drivers License No. ____________

Present Employer: ______________________________ How long? ______

Address: ______________________________ Telephone: ____________

Employed as: ______________________________ Salary: $ ________ per ______

Employment (spouse) Social Sec. No. ____________ Drivers License No. ____________

Present Employer: ______________________________ How long? ______

Address: ______________________________ Telephone: ____________

Employed as: ______________________________ Salary: $ ________ per ______

Other Income: $ ____________ Bank Account Savings:: $ ________ Checking: $ ________

Credit References (3); ______________________________

____

____

Automobile License No. ______________________________ State of Registry: ____________

Make & Model: ____________ Year: ________ Color: ________

Name of Closest Relative: ______________________________ Relationship: ________

Address: ______________________________ Telephone: ________

Have you ever filed a petition in bankruptcy? ______________________________

Have you ever been evicted from any tenancy? ________ Have you ever wilfully and intentionally refused to pay any rent when due? ____________

I DECLARE THE FOREGOING TO BE TRUE UNDER PENALTY OF PERJURY.

I agree that Landlord may terminate any agreement entered into in reliance on any misstatement made above.

Date ____________ 19 ____ Applicant: ______________________________

Telephone No. ____________ Applicant: ______________________________

RECEIPT FOR DEPOSIT

The undersigned acknowledges receipt of $ ____________ in the form of ☐ Cash, ☐ personal check or ____________ payable to ____________ to be applied in accordance with the foregoing rental agreement if accepted by Landlord.

____

Agent

____

RENTAL AGREEMENT
RESIDENTIAL

TO

Dated ____________

the whim of the lessor. Thus, the tenant has a form of protection, and, in the event of future neighborhood enhancement, any increased trade will contribute to his business profit.

Security Deposits. The 1970 California State Legislature enacted into law Assembly Bill 1189, which added Section 1951 to the Civil Code, relating to regulation of payments or deposits of money given primarily to secure performance of rental agreements.

The landlord holds the deposits in trust for his tenant, who has a lien upon such portion as is not lawfully claimed by the landlord. The landlord may now claim only such amounts as are reasonably necessary to remedy any default in the rent, to repair damages, or to clean the premises at the termination of the tenancy. He must return any unearned deposit within two weeks after termination of the tenancy.

Willful retention of an unearned deposit is a misdemeanor, punishable by a maximum fine of $200.

Accounting Records

The selection and maintenance of an adequate trust-fund accounting system is necessary in property management due to the fiduciary nature of the business. As we have seen in Chapter 11, a record must be kept of all trust funds passing through the broker's hands. Entries from the "trust cash receipts and disbursement journal" require more information for property-management accounting than the basic "record of all trust funds received" required of the sales broker. An example of a "separate record for each property managed" will be found on p. 238.

California-Fair Housing Act

More commonly known as the Rumford Act, this legislation became effective September 20, 1963. It is a law prohibiting discrimination in housing and states that discrimination in supplying housing accommodations because of race, color, religion, national origin, or ancestry is against public policy in California. It forbids such discrimination in the sale, rental, lease, or financing of housing and establishes methods of preventing and remedying violations. The basic change from existing laws made by the Rumford Act is the assignment to the California Fair Employment Practice Commission of responsibility for administration and enforcement of the act. The Rumford Act does not put any *additional restraints* on the real estate broker acting as agent for an owner. Since 1959, the broker, because he is considered to be operating a business establishment, has been excluded from discriminatory practices in any properties handled by him. The act applies to all owners of property specified by law. An owner is defined as including a *lessee, sublessee, assignee, managing agent,* or *any person having right of ownership or possession.* It specifically includes real estate brokers and salesmen. Included also are persons, banks, mortgage companies, or other financial institutions making home loans for construction or purchase.

Housing Covered by the Rumford Act. Included in the housing specifically covered by the provisions of the law are public and redevelopment housing; publicly assisted, owner-occupied, single-unit homes; publicly assisted apartments in structures of three or more units; *any* apartment rentals in structures of five or more units. (Courts have ruled that, under the Unruh Act as regards brokers and salesmen, *three* or more units are covered.)

Any person claiming to have been wrongfully denied housing accommodations because of his race, color, national origin, or ancestry may file a complaint with the FEPC. The complaint must be filed within *sixty* days after the alleged violation. In the event he does not learn of the alleged violation until the sixty days have elapsed, he is allowed another sixty days in which to file.

On November 3, 1964 legislation was enacted by initiative providing an amendment to the California State Constitution that nullified certain portions of the Rumford Act. The amendment reserved to the owner (see above) freedom of choice in the sale, rental, or lease of property. The amendment was later declared unconstitutional, so that the Rumford Act again became law.

The Unruh Act. This act bans any discriminatory practices by business establishments. The act became effective in 1959 and covers all real estate brokers because they operate business establishments.

Fair Employment Practice Commission. This is the commission charged with the enforcement of the Fair-Housing Act. If a complainant elects FEPC enforcement, he waives court action under the Unruh Act. If the FEPC finds that discrimination has indeed been practiced—and if all attempts at conciliation fail—it may take the following actions:

1. Order the sale or rental to the complainant if the housing accommodation is still available.
2. Order the sale or rental of a like accommodation if one is available, or the next vacancy in a like accommodation.
3. Order the payment of damages not to exceed $500 if neither remedy (1) nor (2) is practical.

The commission may ask a superior court to enforce the order should it be violated, with the violator subject to contempt-of-court action. All commission orders are appealable to the courts.

Federal Open-Housing Law (Fair-Housing Law).[7] Enacted on April 11, 1968, this bill became effective in three steps:

1. *Effective immediately.* A ban on discrimination in the sale or rental of housing insured or guaranteed by the federal government or located in a federally assisted urban-renewal or slum-clearance project (subject to exception for certain single-family and one-to-four-family homes). The ban applied to all such housing backed by the government after November 20, 1962, unless payment was made in full before the date of enactment. Also covered were dwellings owned or operated by the federal government and dwellings built with the aid of loans, advances, grants, or contributions made by the federal government.
2. *Effective January 1, 1969.* All dwelling units, regardless of how financed, came under the ban, with the exception of (1) single-family homes whose owner did not own more than three single-family homes at one time (if the owner was a nonoccupant of a single-family home that he sold, he was exempted for only one sale wtihin a twenty-four-month period); (2) one-to-four-family dwellings if the owner occupied one of the units.

Lending institutions were barred from discrimination in making loans on apartment buildings or homes, whether the loan was to be made for purchase, repairs, or construction.

Real estate organizations and multiple-listing services were not permitted to discriminate in their membership rules.

3. *Effective January 1, 1970.* Single-family homes were no longer exempted if they were sold or rented through a real estate broker or his salesman. The owner could still discriminate against a buyer if he sold or rented his home himself. He was not permitted to employ any discriminatory words or references in any advertising of his home for sale or for rent. Sales of vacant lands were covered if the property advertised for sale or lease was for the construction of a dwelling.

   Note: The law was not clear on cooperative apartments and condominiums. Such units often have the characteristics of both apartment units and single-family homes.

Enforcement of the Law. A written complaint must be filed with the Department of Housing and Urban Development (HUD) by any person who believes he has been discriminated against. If the matter cannot be settled by conciliation and persuasion, the person filing the complaint may file suit in a federal court, subject to the following exception:

> If a state or local fair-housing law is substantially equal to the federal law, HUD must release the case to the local enforcement officials. In such cases the person who complains may not sue in the federal courts.[8]

Forms of Relief. Any or all of the following forms of relief may be granted by the courts: (a) permanent or temporary injunction; (b) temporary restraining order; (c) actual damages; (d) punitive damages up to $1,000 and court costs. If the court finds that the plaintiff is financially unable to assume reasonable attorney fees, the fees may be awarded to the winning plaintiff.

1968 Supreme Court Ruling. On June 17, 1968, the U.S. Supreme Court in *Jones* v. *Mayer* ruled that an 1866 Act of Congress (now 42 U.S. Code Sec. 1982) had banned racial discrimination in renting and selling all houses. The Court cited the constitutional authority of the Thirteenth Amendment barring slavery and granting to Congress the power to enforce the ban "by appropriate legislation." Today, with this new Supreme Court ruling and Title VIII of the Civil Rights Act of 1968, there is an *all-encompassing* set of rules that prohibits discrimination on the part of property owners and their agents. *Wherever federal law is applicable it is paramount,* and it even applies to local transactions. All prohibitions of the Unruh and Rumford acts remain in effect. In addition, any area of discrimination not covered by them is now covered by federal law. *There are no exceptions.* No one may refuse to sell, lease, or rent to another because of race or color, and no real estate licensee may do so because of his principal's directions. *If a principal should seek to restrict a listing according to race or color, the licensee must refuse to accept the listing.* Moreover the licensee may not make, print, or publish any notice, statement, or advertisement with respect to the sale or rental of a dwelling that suggests discrimination because of race, color, religion, or national origin.[9]

CASE STUDY

Mr. *A* owns three apartment buildings located side by side. Each contains twelve two-bedroom units. The

[7] Title VIII of the Civil Rights Act of 1968.

[8] California is one of many states that have passed fair-housing laws.

[9] For further clarification of the state and federal laws covering discrimination as it applies to the real estate broker, see *Reference Book.*

buildings were built in 1958 and have had no modernization program. The units rent for $100 to $150 monthly. The suburban city where the apartments are located is known as a "bedroom" town. The residents are mostly upper-middle-class people who work in the metropolitan area. They are in the $12,000- to $20,000-income bracket.

The tenants in the buildings are mostly retired people whose families have grown, but some are younger people with growing children.

Mr. *A* hires a resident manager who has had little experience in management but has been recommended for his honesty and his pleasant personality. The resident manager uses no scientific tenant selection, believing it most important to have full occupancy. However, he has had a large turnover of tenants because of apparent incompatibility.

The area surrounding the units is one of older homes but is zoned for multiple dwellings. Developers have had little success in the past in securing any of the property for development, the elderly owners preferring to live out their lives in "familiar surroundings." Recently, however, several lots have been purchased, and a builder is constructing a large, garden-type apartment house of sixty units. It will have the most modern appointments, with two- and three-bedroom units, each with two baths. The rents are scheduled at $175 and $250 a month.

1. Do you believe that Mr. *A* should place his property in the hands of a professional manager? Assuming that you are a CPM, what arguments would you use to persuade him to employ you as property manager?
2. Do you feel Mr. *A*'s apartments, as presently being operated, will suffer from the competition of the new development?
3. What would you suggest as the most important item to be considered if a general modernization program were to be undertaken by Mr. *A*?

SUGGESTED REFERENCES

BENSON, PHILIP A., NELSON L. NORTH, and ALFRED A. RING, *Real Estate Principles and Practices.* Englewood Cliffs, N.J.: Prentice-Hall, Inc., 1960.

CASE, FREDERICK E., *Real Estate.* Boston: Allyn & Bacon, Inc., 1962.

DOWNS, JAMES C., JR., *Principles of Real Estate Management.* Chicago: Institute of Real Estate Management, 1964.

Reference Book, Sacramento: California Department of Real Estate.

16

Business-Opportunity Brokerage

Effective January 2, 1966 business-opportunity licenses in the state of California were phased out, so that today there is no special license classification for negotiating the sale of business opportunities. Any real estate licensee may now legally negotiate the sale of a business opportunity and the commissioner expects of the licensee that his general real estate knowledge includes terminology, laws, and practices relative to the sale of businesses or business opportunities.

What is a Business Opportunity? The real estate law defines "business opportunity" as meaning a business, a business opportunity, and good will of an existing business, or a combination thereof. Typical business-opportunity sales would include restaurants, dry-cleaning establishments, laundromats, clothing stores, camera shops, and so on. The sale normally includes the inventory, fixtures, and good will of the business. Transfer of any leases involved are also part of the business transfer. Business licenses, permits, sales tax, and certain legal requirements inherent in a business-opportunity transaction make up the technicalities encountered. The broker involved in the sale is expected to be well informed about all of these.

Listing the Business Opportunity. The broker is responsible for the accuracy of the information appearing on the listing agreement. This includes particularly the owner's motive for selling, and he should point out to the seller that nondisclosure of material facts may constitute fraud.

There are many types of business-opportunity listing forms in use. It is important that an "exclusive authorization to sell business opportunity" form be used. (See sample form on p. 000.) If certain figures relating to the business cannot be verified by the broker, the form should read, "not verified by agent." The broker also must inform the seller that he will need to certify that all equipment used in the operation of the business will be in working condition on the day the buyer takes possession.

Clearances. The broker has to take care that all clearances from government agencies required for legal transfer of the business are secured. He must also advise the seller that any sale will be subject to receipt of all required licenses and/or permits by the buyer.

Form BT 471. If sales and/or Social Security and unemployment taxes are involved in business opportunities, the broker must remind the seller that no funds will be released to him from escrow until such time as he has furnished escrow with the clearances from the State Board of Equalization (Form BT 471) and the Department of Employment. The importance hereof is exemplified in the term "successor's liability." This simply means that the buyer can be held responsible for unpaid taxes of his predecessor *up to the amount of the purchase price.* The sales tax that must be paid on the transfer of furniture and fixtures of the business is the responsibility of the seller as far as the state is concerned. The buyer pays the tax to the seller, who in turn pays the state, which looks to the seller for collection of the tax.

As is true in the sale of investment properties, the sale of a business opportunity is usually made contingent upon inspection and approval by the buyer of the seller's records.

Lease of the Premises. The broker is responsible for careful examination of any existing lease on a business for which he is acting as agent. Certain items particularly should be given his attention. Can the lease be assigned? If so, under what terms and conditions? Can the lease be renewed, and if so, will the

CERTIFIED BUSINESS OPPORTUNITY
EXCLUSIVE LISTING AGREEMENT,

Business Name ______ Kind ______
Owner ______ Bus. Phone ______
Owner ______ Bus. Phone ______
Address ______ Zone ______
Price ______ Includes ______
Plus Stock ______ Priced @ ______
TOTAL ______ Pro Rates ______ Lease Deposit ______
Down ______ Balance $ ______ @ $ ______ per Mo. incl. Int. @ ______
LEASE: $ ______ per Mo. ______ Yrs. to go. Option ______ See At ______
Net Profit $ ______ Including owners wages, before depreciation, of ______
Gross Sales $ ______ Gross Profits $ ______ Total Expenses ______
Outstanding Obligations ______ Accounts Receivable ______
See Books At ______ Checks Cashed ______
Number of Employees ______ Wages ______ Owner Works ______
Size of Store ______ Parking ______
Store Hours ______ Deliveries? ______
Date Business Started ______ Present Owner Since ______
Reason for Sale ______
Road Changes Expected ______ Competition ______
Possession Date ______ Can Be Seen ______
Trade for ______
Seller will not compete within ______ miles for ______ years

GROSS MONTHLY SALES			EXPENSES
Year ______	Year ______	Year ______	Rent ______
Jan. ______	______	______	Utilities ______
Feb. ______	______	______	Insurance ______
Mar. ______	______	______	Advt. ______
Apr. ______	______	______	Acct. ______
May ______	______	______	Supplies ______
June ______	______	______	Telephone ______
July ______	______	______	Taxes ______
Aug. ______	______	______	License ______
Sept. ______	______	______	Equip. Rental ______
Oct. ______	______	______	Repairs ______
Nov. ______	______	______	Wages ______
Dec. ______	______	______	______
			______
Total ______	______	______	Total ______

Keys or Show ______
Owner (Print) ______ Phone ______
Address ______ City ______
Occupied By ______ Phone ______

CERTIFIED BUSINESS OPPORTUNITY
Exclusive Listing Agreement

For and in consideration of the services to be performed by the undersigned Realtor, I hereby grant said Realtor the exclusive right to sell or exchange for me and accept a deposit thereon for the herein described business situated within the County of .... State of California, effective .... 19 ....
for a price of $ .... and on terms set forth herein, or upon any other price and terms acceptable to me. This employment and authority to sell shall be irrevocable until 12:00 midnight on .... 19 ....

In the event a purchaser is secured by said Realtor, his agent, or cooperating Realtors, brokers and agents, or anyone, including myself, during the period of this agreement, or the subsequent 90 days; to persons with whom Realtor has negotiated during this agreement, or offered or presented my property, or who has inspected my property during the term of this listing; I hereby agree to pay said listing Realtor .... per cent of the selling price, as commission, for professional services rendered. If action be instituted on this agreement to collect said commission, owner agrees to pay such sums as the Court may fix as reasonable attorneys' fees.

Permission is hereby given Realtor to represent all parties and collect commissions from all parties to any exchange.

It is understood that said Realtor is a participant in .... of the .... and it is further agreed that said Realtor shall refer this listing to said Service to be by it referred as it may deem advisable, to such of its participants, subscribers or any members of any Realty Board with which it has a Reciprocal listing service agreement, and that such persons may act as sub-brokers in procuring or attempting to procure a purchaser in accordance with this agreement. In the event a sale or exchange shall be made through any sub-brokers, all of the terms of this agreement shall apply to such transaction.

I hereby agree to permit a For Sale sign and/or Lok-Box to be placed upon my property by the undersigned Realtor.

Receipt of a copy of this agreement is hereby acknowledged.

To Show, See Owner, Mgr., Tenant .... Phone ....

....
PRINT REALTOR ADDRESS

by: ....
SIGN TELEPHONE

Dated: ....
OWNER

.... 196 ....
OWNER

....
OWNER'S ADDRESS

....
CITY AND STATE PHONE

DO NOT CLOSE A SALE WITHOUT FIRST CONSULTING THE ABOVE NAMED REALTOR.

Realtor shall deliver this listing to the .... within 48 hours.

FORM EL11CBO

terms be the same? If the lessor will require a bonus for a new lease, who is to be responsible for payment of it? If the lease has a percentage clause, how is it to be paid? Is there any prepaid rent on the lease? What about a security deposit? If any of these conditions exist, it is the responsibility of the buyer to reimburse the seller for them. If a lease is to be transferred, the buyer should read the terms and indicate by initialing the document that he has read and that he understands all the terms.

Appraisal. A number of items enter into the appraisal of a business opportunity, including the length of time the business has been in operation, the age and condition of the fixtures, the physical appearance of the property, the location of the building, the terms of the lease, and the business reputation in the community. Certain businesses have rules-of-thumb guides, which can be ascertained from trade journals. As in a real property transaction, market data, if available, should be given considerable weight. Market prices will vary considerably based on some of the above factors. If the broker is unfamiliar with the type of business he is listing, or if the business is a large one, involving a great many details of operation, he would be well advised to suggest to the owner that a specialist in the field be called in to make an appraisal.

Good Will. This is defined as "the expectation of continued public patronage." Establishing the value of good will (if any) is based on many factors, such as:

1. How long has the business been established in its present location?
2. Can the business be increased, or has it reached its potential?
3. What is the present or future situation regarding competition?
4. Is the business name to be included as part of the transaction?
5. Will the seller agree not to compete (within the limits of the law)?
6. What are the characteristics of the business with reference to:
   a. Customer traffic.
   b. Foot traffic, automobile traffic, or both.
   c. Repeat business.
   d. Personality and ability of the owner and/or key personnel—what effect will their absence have on the business.
   e. General reputation of the business in the community.[1]

[1] In transfers of on-sale general or off-sale general liquor licenses *originally issued on or after June 1, 1961,* the maximum amount attributable to good will is one-twelfth the amount of the gross sales of alcoholic beverages in any period of twelve consecutive months.

Bulk Sales and Uniform Commercial Code

Under Division 6 of the Uniform Commercial Code sellers and buyers must observe the laws designed to warn transferor's creditors of the impending transfer so that they may obtain payment of their claims *before* the assets of the business are disposed of or encumbered. The law requires that *public notice* be given by:

1. *Recordation of a notice* in the office of the county recorder (of the county or counties in which the property to be transferred is located) at least ten days before the bulk transfer is to be consummated, or the sale, if by auction, is to commence; and
2. *Publication of the notice at least once* in a newspaper of general circulation published in the judicial district in which the property is located, or, if there is none, then in a newspaper of general circulation in the county in which the business is located.

Notice is to be given at least five days before the bulk transfer is to be consummated and must contain the following information:

1. Information that a bulk transfer is to be made.
2. Names and business addresses of the transferor, and all other business names and addresses used by the transferor within the past three years as far as is known to the transferee.
3. Location and general description of the property to be transferred.
4. Place and date on or after which the bulk transfer is to be consummated.

Escrows. If an escrow is provided for under a bulk-sales notice, subject to the requirements of Division 6 of the Uniform Commercial Code the transferee (buyer) is required to deposit *the full purchase price* with the escrow holder. If at the time for closing the escrow the amount of money deposited is insufficient to pay in full all the creditors' claims, the escrow holder is required to delay the closing and give notice to the creditors of the deficiency. The law prohibits payments from the escrow of fees and commissions prior to close of escrow.

Effect of Noncompliance. When compliance with Division 6 is necessary but the legal filing and publication requirements are not met, the transfer is rendered fraudulent and void against those creditors of the transferor (seller) who hold claims based on transactions or events occurring before the bulk transfer. (In an auction sale, the auctioneer is responsible for giving the statutory notice.) Certain transactions are exempt from the provisions of Division 6. These include transfers made to create a security interest in durable goods having a retail value of over $500 or in a motor vehicle, trailer, house trailer, semi-trailer, farm and construction machinery (and repairs for them), or aircraft.

Division 9. Entitled "Secured Transactions," sale of accounts, contract rights, and chattel paper establishes

> a unified and comprehensive scheme for regulation of security transactions in *personal property* and supersedes existing laws on chattel mortgages, conditional sales, trust receipts, assignments of accounts receivable, etc.
> Covered are transactions in any form which are intended to create such a security interest in goods, documents, installments, chattel paper, accounts, or contract rights.[2]

California Sales- and Use-Tax Provisions

Knowledge of this tax is most important in connection with transactions involving sales of businesses when sales of tangible personal property at retail are made, particularly in connection with:

1. The necessity of taking out a "seller's permit" when engaging in business.
2. The posting of security.
3. The obtaining of a "clearance receipt" that covers the 4 percent sales tax and the 1 percent municipality or county tax. This protects the buyer against "successor's liability" (see above, under Form BT 471).

Alcoholic Beverage Control Act

The licensee who is interested in engaging in business-opportunity transactions should be familiar with the legal controls imposed upon the sale and distribution of alcoholic beverages, particularly as they apply to the methods governing the issuance of licenses and permits.

1. *General policies.* The Department of Alcoholic Beverage Control is charged with the administration of the Alcoholic Beverage Control Act, and the issuance of licenses thereunder. Local officials and the department are in charge of enforcing the law.
2. *Licenses.* Alcoholic-beverage licenses are issued to qualified adult persons, partnerships, fiduciaries, and corporations for use at particular premises that have been approved by the department. The applicant must be of good moral character.
   a. The department may deny the license if there is any attempt to conceal an arrest record. A complete background disclosure and fingerprinting is required of each applicant and corporation official.
   b. The premises may be disapproved if they are in the immediate vicinity of a school, a church, a public playground, or other consideration point and the premises may interfere with the operation of any of the above. They may also be disapproved for such reasons as:
      (1) An overconcentration of alcoholic-beverage licenses in the area.
      (2) The creation of a police problem.
      (3) Delinquent tax payments on the part of the transferor.
   c. On-sale general and off-sale general licenses are limited in numbers by law. Distilled-spirits wholesalers and distillers licenses are limited by department rule.
   d. Before filing for a transfer application with the department for a retail license limited in number, or for an on-sale general license for seasonal business, the applicant and licensee must file a notice of intended transfer with the county recorder and establish an escrow.
      (1) No consideration may be paid out of the escrow before approval of the transfer.
      (2) Transfer of title to the licensed business must coincide with the transfer of the license.
      (3) No licensee may enter into an agreement pledging the transfer of his license as security for a loan or for the fulfillment of any agreement. Each transfer application must be accompanied by a mutually verified statement to this effect.
      (3) The purchase price that may be paid by a transferee or received by a transferor of an on-sale general license or off-sale general license *originally issued on or after June 1, 1961* may not exceed $6,000.
      (4) Each applicant and transfer is subject to protest by local officials and private parties. A license may not be issued while a valid protest is pending or on appeal.
      (5) The department may decline to transfer a license while disciplinary action is pending against the transferor.
      (6) A license issued for a specific location must be placed in use within thirty days of the date of issuance.

Beverage Law and Business Regulations

No employee of the department is authorized to give any applicant any assurance that a license will be granted, nor does any applicant require any outside influence to obtain a license.[3]

[2] For complete information on this Division, a booklet entitled "Procedure and Forms for Filing under Divisions 9 and 10 of the Uniform Commercial Code" may be obtained from the office of the secretary of state, Sacramento. Sample copies of the standard forms may also be obtained from this office.

[3] A copy of the Alcoholic Beverage Control Act may be obtained from the nearest office of the Department of Alcoholic Beverage Control. Licensees dealing in transactions involving the transfer of licenses under the act would be well advised to obtain a copy of the act for study.

Speculation in licenses is condemned by the department, and a complaint may be filed against a broker who participates in such speculation or violation of the law in connection with the transfer of a license; or any licensee who participates in the sale of a license against which disciplinary action is pending, if he should fail to determine such fact and to advise the purchaser of the fact.

Licenses may not be purchased by a broker at a bankruptcy or trustee's sale with the expectation of a transfer to a nominee. The only person who may legally hold an interest in an alcoholic-beverage license is the person who is operating or who intends to operate the licensed premises.

Original On-Sale and Off-Sale Fee. (Payable with the application for the license).[4]

For on-sale general license	$6,000.
For on-sale general license (seasonal business)	$4,500.
For on-sale beer and wine	$ 300.
For on-sale beer license	$ 200.
For off-sale beer-and-wine license	$ 50.
Original off-sale general license	$6,000.

Person and Location—Use within Thirty Days. A license must be issued to a specific person and to a specific location (excepting licenses issued for the sale of alcoholic beverages on trains or boats, or the serving of alcoholic beverages on airplanes). Any license issued for a specific location must be placed in use at that location within thirty days of the date of issuance.

Premises under Construction. Licenses may be issued for the retail sale of alcoholic beverages for or transferred to premises to be constructed or that are in the process of construction. No alcoholic beverages may be sold pursuant to the license until the premises have been completed.

Person to Person—Premises to Premises—Intercounty. Each license may be transferred, upon the approval of the department, from the licensee to another person, and from one premise to another premise.

On-Sale License from Person to Person. On-sale licenses issued for a bona fide public-eating place may be transferred to another person, for use in a bona fide public-eating place, or for public premises. (See paragraph above.)

Surviving Spouse—Corporations—Fiduciaries. The license of the spouse may be transferred to the other spouse under certain conditions. (See State Department of Real Estate *Reference Book,* business opportunities, excerpts from Alcoholic Beverage Control Act, Section 24071.)

Transfer Fees. For transfer of a license other than a retail license from a licensee to another person the fee is equal to 70 percent of the annual fee for a license, except as provided in Section 24071.

For a retail license from a licensee to another person the fee is equal to 50 percent of the original fee for the license but may not exceed $1,250 (if no original fee is provided by law, then the fee is $100). For a license transferred from one premise to another, the fee is $100. An off-sale general license transferred from one county to another county has a fee of $3,000.

License Transfer—Seasonal Business. No numerically limited retail license, or on-sale general license for seasonal business may be transferred without the prior filing of a notice of intention with the county recorder of the county in which the transferee's premises are located.

Escrow

Before filing a transfer application with the department, if a purchase price or consideration is involved, the licensee and the intended licensee must establish an escrow. *The full amount of the purchase price must be deposited with the escrow holder.* An agreement between the licensee (seller) and the transferee (buyer) is then deposited in escrow, directing the escrow holder to:

1. Pay out of the purchase price all claims of bona fide creditors of the licensee who file their claims prior to the department's notification of its approval of the transfer of the license.
2. Distribute claims in the following order (if the purchase price or consideration is insufficient to pay all claims in full):
   a. Claims for wages, salaries, or fringe benefits of employees of the seller or transferor, earned or accruing within ninety days prior to the sale, transfer, or opening of an escrow for sale.
   b. Claims of secured creditors to the extent of the proceeds arising from the sale of the security.
   c. Claims of the United States based on income or withholding taxes, and thereafter based on any tax other than taxes (1) arising in full or in part out of the exercise of an alcoholic-beverage license and (2) due under the following:
      Alcoholic Beverage Tax Law.
      Sales and Use Tax Law.
      Personal Income Tax Law.
      Bank and Corporation Tax Law.

[4] These fees do not include licenses issued upon renewal or transfer of a license.

Tax on unsecured property as defined in Section 134 of the Revenue and Taxation Code. Any amount due under the Unemployment Insurance Code, when such liability arises out of the conduct of a business licensed by the Department of Alcoholic Beverage Control.

d. Claims on mechanics' liens.
e. Escrow fees, claims for prevailing brokerage fees for services rendered, and claims for reasonable attorney's fees for services rendered.
f. Claims for goods sold and delivered to the transferor for resale at his licensed premises and claims for services rendered, performed or supplied in connection with the operation of the licensed business.
g. All other claims.

Note: If the Alcoholic Beverage Control Board has approved transfer of the license subject to payment of state-tax claims, these claims must be considered priod to all other claims, including federal-tax claims. These claims are to be paid in full from proceeds of the sale of the license after approval of the transfer of the license (subject only to the condition that the tax claims be paid), and upon written instructions from the transferor and the transferee to do so.

If the transferor licensee disputes any claim, the amount or pro rata amount thereof must be retained by the escrow holder for a period of twenty-five days and if not attached must be paid to the transferor licensee.

Purchase Price. The purchase price that may be paid by a transferee or received by a transferer of an on-sale or an off-sale general license issued on or after June 1, 1961 may not exceed $6,000.

Regulations Applicable to Fiduciaries and Brokers

1. Applications and Contracts to Transfer. No licensee holding a license limited in numbers or other person acting in the capacity of executor, administrator, guardian, conservator, trustee, or assignee for the benefit of creditors may sell, assign, or otherwise hypothecate an alcoholic-beverage license or any interest therein unless the department has first notified such licensee or fiduciary in writing that it has approved the qualifications of the proposed transferee and the proposed premises.

2. License Limitations. The aggregate number of rectifiers and distilled spirits wholesalers' licenses issued in any county is limited to 1 for each 100 on-sale and off-sale general licenses in the aggregate issued in the county in which the rectifier's or distilled spirits wholesaler's premises are located.

Except when an applicant can show that substantial public demand cannot otherwise be satisfied, no *original* on-sale beer-and-wine license may be issued and no on-sale beer-and-wine license may be transferred premise to premise unless the premises to be licensed qualify and operate as a bona fide public-eating place.

Transfer of General Licenses

1. No on-sale general license or off-sale general license originally issued on or after June 1, 1961, is transferable to other premises for a period of two years from the date of the original issuance, unless the department should rule that such transfer is necessary to prevent undue hardship.

2. All applications for the transfer of on-sale or off-sale general licenses must be accompanied by an affidavit declaring the total purchase price to be paid and the true purchase for each asset to be transferred, including but not limited to the following items:

a. Transfer of the license.
b. Good will.
c. Realty or interest therein.
d. Fixtures.
e. Inventory.

3. In transfer of on-sale or off-sale licenses originally issued on or after June 1, 1961, the maximum value of *good will* of a business shall be presumed to be an amount equal to the gross sale of alcoholic beverages under such license for the average month of any twelve consecutive months. If only the license is being transferred, without the sale of a going business, the entire consideration shall be attributable to the license and no part of the consideration may be allotted to good will.

4. In the transfer of an on-sale or an off-sale general license originally issued on or after June 1, 1961, any consideration in excess of the fair market value of the realty or interest therein, the fixtures, inventory, and the maximum value of good will as prescribed in (3) above is presumed to be consideration for the transfer of the license.

QUESTIONS FOR STUDY

1. As a broker representing a buyer of a business opportunity, do you consider your responsibility to him any greater than to a buyer of a residential property? Why or why not?
2. What is meant by "successor's liability"? Under what circumstances might this term apply in the sale of a business opportunity?
3. Included in the sale of a business opportunity is

an on-sale liquor license, issued originally in November, 1963. What is the maximum amount that may be charged for the license? How would the maximum amount to be charged for good will in this sale be computed?

SUGGESTED REFERENCES

BERSTON, HYMAN MAXWELL, *California Real Estate Practice*. Homewood, Ill.: Richard D. Irwin, Inc., 1968, Chap. 15.

Reference Book. Sacramento: Department of Real Estate.

SEPARATE RECORD FOR EACH PROPERTY MANAGED

CALIFORNIA REAL ESTATE ASSOCIATION STANDARD FORM

Owner	Deposit
Address	Monthly Rent
Property	Commission:
Tenant's Name	Leases
Units	Collection
Remarks	Management

Date	Received From or Paid To	Description	Receipt or Check No.	Amount Received	Date Deposited	Amount Disbursed	Balance

Reprinted from Advanced Real Estate Sales,
Book No. 17 Published 1968 by:
California Real Estate Association
520 South Grand Avenue
Los Angeles, California 90017

Form TF-11-3

For these forms, address
California Real Estate Association
520 South Grand Avenue, Los Angeles 90017

17

Land Utilization

Land Investment

Supply and demand and highest and best use, although they are familiar terms in the real estate industry, apply more accurately to land development. The law of supply and demand, simply stated, means that, as the pressure of *demand* increases on a fixed *supply,* the value of the supply goes up. Because land is one commodity whose supply is definitely fixed, smart investors base their selection first on supply-and-demand factors. Their second concern is the highest and best use for the land, as the term is defined: "that use most likely to produce the highest net return over a given period of time."

According to the Los Angeles land investment firm, Property Research Corporation (whose function, as stated by them, is "to serve as a catalyst between buyers and sellers of land"), the investor who shifts from stocks or income property to land does so because it is "good economic sense." This is based on three important qualities inherent in land: (1) it is relatively secure; (2) it is emotionally satisfying; and (3) its earning record is excellent. However, the corporation is careful to point out certain details that are involved in the purchase terms that can either turn the investment into a booby trap or greatly enhance its value. These details include:

1. Leverage. Leverage is the ratio of *carrying charges to growth rate.* As applied to land purchase, it is that principal that allows the investor to purchase a piece of land with a minimum amount invested.

> ...Let's take an example of leverage (without principal payments the first three years after the down payment):

Buy in 1964

Purchase price	$100,000
Cash down payment	25,000
Ist trust deed @ 6%	$ 75,000
Sell in 1967	
Net sales price	$140,000
Trust deed transferred	75,000
	$ 65,000
Less interest & other expenses	15,000
	$ 50,000
Less capital investment	25,000
Gain	$ 25,000

The example illustrates that if you buy a $100,000 parcel with $25,000 down, and it appreciates 40% in three years, you double your money. That is, you put in $40,000 including about $15,000 interest, property taxes, etc., and sell for $140,000 If, however, the appreciation period extends over nine years, instead of three, you *lose* money, with the same leverage. Your carrying cost on the unpaid balance adds up to more than you gain.

Buy in 1964

Net purchase price	$100,000
Cash	25,000
Trust deed @ 6%	$ 75,000
Sell in 1973	
Net sales price	$140,000
Trust deed transferred	75,000
	$ 65,000
Less interest & other expenses	45,000
	$ 20,000
Less capital invested	25,000
	$(5,000)

When the income tax advantages of leverage are considered, the picture brightens. In the above example with the $5,000 loss, an investor in an average 35% tax bracket would have an after-tax gain. This is because of the ordinary income deduction vs. the capital gain. The higher the tax bracket, the higher the gain. Because leverage is one of the attractive things about land investment, buyers are sometimes tempted to use it where it does not apply. They overlook one "detail"—carrying charges vs. growth rate. . . .[1]

2. Mineral Rights. These do not necessarily come with the title. It is important for the investor to know who holds the mineral rights, what kind of rights they are, and how they are likely to affect his plans for the land. FHA normally will not make loans where surface rights above 550 feet have been reserved. There are many kinds of mineral rights in existence, some of which can be quitclaimed from the third-party interests for small sums. Some cannot be purchased for any dollar amount. It is highly important that the land investor uninitiated in these matters seek professional advice.

3. Interest-only Payments. This detail is important when making any type of short-term investment in bare land. Even with no buildings to depreciate, there may be several reasons why the seller insists on a substantial down payment rather than prepaid interest: (1) he may want to consume (or invest) his principal; (2) he may be unfamiliar with the interest-only payments type of purchase, (3) he may realize that the purchaser is not getting value for the money expended; or (4) there may be tax disadvantages. This last, however, is usually offset by a higher purchase price. It can be advantageous from the investor's standpoint (depending on his tax bracket), because he will be increasing his earnings on his investment.

4. Easements. The existence of an easement on land contemplated for purchase constitutes another detail. There are many and varied types of easements, some unrecorded. In the case of the unrecorded easement, sometimes only physical inspection of the property will reveal the interests of another in the property.

5. Resale. The wise land investor thinks about resale before he buys. As in any investment, the tax aspects must be considered *before* the purchase. Methods of financing the purchase are of prime importance. Flexible financing can greatly widen the market at the time of resale.

The above are only a few of the details that, if overlooked, can turn an otherwise profitable venture into a loss for the investor. From this also can be seen the responsibility of the broker acting as investment counselor. He should appreciate the inherent rights of all Americans to acquire, improve, and develop their landholdings for their own personal profit or collective gain, but should realize that, in any investment, the greater the potential margin of profit, the greater the risk. The wise investor is aware of the hazards associated with marginal lands but is dependent many times on the facts presented by the broker.[2]

Market Research

Market research is vitally necessary before the acquisition and development of any parcel of land to determine the environmental factors affecting the area. The research should include an analysis of such factors as employment, population trends, present housing needs, and availability of financing. This involves a great amount of time and effort on the part of the broker but is an essential part of his professional service to his client. Few land investors or developers have the time or the resources to make a thorough market survey. Such work is normally relegated to the investment broker or professional researcher, who then submits his findings to the developer. Based on this analysis, the developer must make a careful selection of the properties under consideration. To be of value, the results of the research and analysis must be presented in a concise, factual, easily understood form, with supporting information in the way of maps, charts, and figures.

Investors in raw land are particularly interested in its *accessibility, utility,* and *availability.* By *accessibility* is meant that the land must have access roads with public rights of way and must be easily accessible for sewers, water, and electricity. Although the investor may be thinking only in terms of conventional uses, such as subdivisions or shopping centers, the broker offering the land must view it from all investment angles to arrive at its highest and best use. He will not overlook any development possibility that could produce the greatest net return to his client.

The *availability* of the property could cover a wide field of speculation as to price, financing, or condition of the title. These should be checked out first, because any problems in these areas must be resolved before the accessibility and utility features take on significance.

Land Use

The use to which land can be put is dependent on many legal and legislative controls, many of which are restrictive in nature and affect the value of the

[1] *Advice to Landholders, Present and Future* (Los Angeles: Property Research Corporation), June, 1964, pp. 1–2.

[2] From information contained in *Advice to Landholders.*

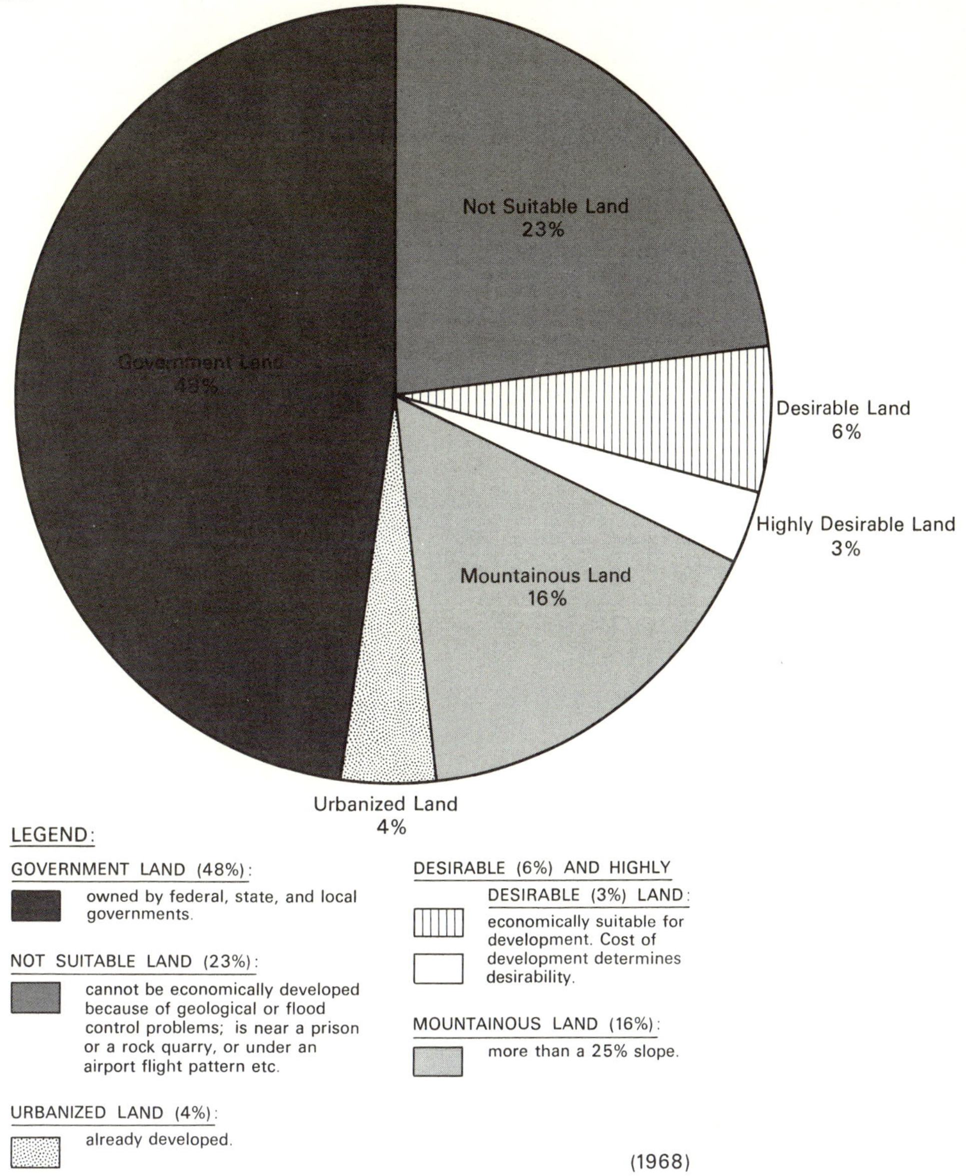

land by controlling the income that may be derived from its development. These regulations are numerous, including those affecting ownership, deed transfers, and financing. Local zoning laws, building codes, and taxing policies all serve to restrict land usage. The nature of these restrictions, particularly where the legal arrangement interferes with the most efficient use of the property, can have an adverse effect on the value.

Subdivision and Land Development. The man who subdivides and develops land is a manufacturer in the true sense of the word: he is not different from any other manufacturer who develops a product from raw material. He must supply the capital and take all the characteristic business risks coincident with any manufacturing process, the only difference being in the basic material, which, in the developer's case, constitutes raw land. His success or failure is dependent on how imaginative he is and how efficient in his planning. As Donald Stone, president of Stone and Schulte, Inc., San Jose realtors, puts it, "Investment capital is returned at a high yield when it has served a valuable function in acquiring, developing, improving, or filling the needs of others as regards the use of land."[3]

California has long been the leader in the field of regulation of the real estate industry. Included in these regulations for the protection of the buying public are those laws governing the subdiving of land.

[3] Donald Stone, "Lot and Land Development Investment," *Real Estate Investment* (Los Angeles: California Real Estate Association, 1963), p. 120.

SUMMARY OF ZONING REGULATIONS
CITY OF LOS ANGELES

CLASSIFICATION	ZONE	USE	MAXIMUM HEIGHT: STORIES	MAXIMUM HEIGHT: FEET	REQUIRED YARDS: FRONT	REQUIRED YARDS: SIDE	REQUIRED YARDS: REAR	MINIMUM AREA PER LOT AND UNIT	MINIMUM LOT WIDTH	LOADING SPACE	PARKING SPACE	EAGLE PRISMACOLOR PENCIL CHART
COMMERCIAL	CR	LIMITED COMMERCIAL MOST R5 USES - OFFICE BUILDINGS BANKS - BUSINESS SCHOOLS NO MERCHANDISE DISPLAY OR SALE	6	75 FT. *	10 FEET INTERIOR LOT, EXCEPT ON MAJOR HIGHWAY	5' TO 10' - CORNER LOT ONLY RESIDENTIAL USES - SAME AS IN R4 ZONE	15' PLUS 1' EACH STORY ABOVE 3RD	SAME AS R5 FOR DWELLINGS. OTHERWISE NONE	50 FEET FOR RESIDENCE USE		ONE SPACE FOR EACH 500 SQUARE FEET OF FLOOR AREA	939 FLESH
	C1	LIMITED COMMERCIAL R3 USES - LOCAL RETAIL STORES, OFFICE OR BUSINESS	UNLIMITED *		ONLY IF PART OF BLOCK IN DWELLING ZONE	NONE UNLESS LOT ADJOINS DWELLING ZONE	NONE UNLESS ABUTTING "A" OR "R" ZONE OR IN RESIDENTIAL USE	SAME AS R3 FOR DWELLINGS EXCEPT 5,000 SQ. FT. PER UNIT IN C1-H. OTHERWISE NONE	50 FEET FOR RESIDENCE USE	WHERE LOT ABUTS ALLEY ▼ MINIMUM LOADING SPACE 400 SQUARE FEET ADDITIONAL SPACE REQUIRED FOR BUILDINGS CONTAINING MORE THAN 50,000 SQUARE FEET OF FLOOR AREA NONE REQUIRED FOR APARTMENT BUILDING 20 UNITS OR LESS	ONE SPACE FOR EACH 500 SQUARE FEET OF FLOOR AREA IN BUILDINGS CONTAINING 5,000 OR MORE SQUARE FEET MUST BE LOCATED WITHIN 750 FEET OF BUILDING	929 PINK
	C2	COMMERCIAL C1 AND R5 USES - RETAIL BUSINESS WITH LIMITED MANUFACTURING	UNLIMITED *		NONE	NONE FOR COMM'L. BLDGS. RESIDENTIAL USES - SAME AS IN R4 ZONE	NONE FOR COMM'L. BLDGS. RESIDENTIAL USES - SAME AS IN R4 ZONE	SAME AS R4 FOR DWELLINGS. OTHERWISE NONE	50 FEET FOR RESIDENCE USE			922 SCARLET RED
	C4	COMMERCIAL C2 USES (WITH EXCEPTIONS)	UNLIMITED *		NONE	NONE FOR COMM'L. BLDGS. RESIDENTIAL USES - SAME AS IN R4 ZONE	NONE FOR COMM'L. BLDGS. RESIDENTIAL USES - SAME AS IN R4 ZONE	SAME AS R5 FOR DWELLINGS. OTHERWISE NONE	50 FEET FOR RESIDENCE USE			924 CRIMSON RED
	C5	COMMERCIAL C2 USES - LIMITED FLOOR AREAS FOR LIGHT MANUFACTURING	UNLIMITED *		NONE	NONE FOR COMM'L. BLDGS. RESIDENTIAL USES - SAME AS IN R4 ZONE	NONE FOR COMM'L. BLDGS. RESIDENTIAL USES - SAME AS IN R4 ZONE	SAME AS R5 FOR DWELLINGS. OTHERWISE NONE	50 FEET FOR RESIDENCE USE			925 CRIMSON LAKE
INDUSTRIAL	CM	COMM'L. MANUFACTURING C2 USES - WHOLESALE BUSINESS STORAGE BUILDINGS LIMITED MANUFACTURING	UNLIMITED *		NONE	NONE FOR INDUSTRIAL OR COMM'L BLDGS. RESIDENTIAL USES - SAME AS IN R4 ZONE	NONE FOR INDUSTRIAL OR COMM'L BLDGS. RESIDENTIAL USES - SAME AS IN R4 ZONE	SAME AS R5 FOR DWELLINGS. OTHERWISE NONE	50 FEET FOR RESIDENCE USE			905 AQUA-MARINE
	M1	LIMITED INDUSTRIAL CM USES - LIMITED INDUSTRIAL AND MANUFACTURING USES NO "R" ZONE USES	UNLIMITED *		NONE	NONE	NONE	-NOTE- "R" ZONE USES PROHIBITED	NONE			904 LIGHT BLUE
	M2	LIGHT INDUSTRIAL M1 USES - ADDITIONAL INDUSTRIAL USES STORAGE YARDS OF ALL KINDS NO "R" ZONE USES	UNLIMITED *		NONE	NONE	NONE	-NOTE- "R" ZONE USES PROHIBITED	NONE			902 ULTRA MARINE
	M3	HEAVY INDUSTRIAL M2 USES - ANY INDUSTRIAL USES NUISANCE TYPE 500 FEET FROM ANY OTHER ZONE - NO "R" ZONE USES	UNLIMITED *		NONE	NONE	NONE	-NOTE- "R" ZONE USES	NONE			931 PURPLE
PARKING	P	AUTOMOBILE PARKING - SURFACE & UNDERGROUND PROPERTY IN A P ZONE MAY ALSO BE IN AN "A" OR "R" ZONE PARKING PERMITTED IN LIEU OF RESIDENTIAL OR AGRICULTURAL USES						NONE UNLESS ALSO IN AN "A" OR "R" ZONE	NONE UNLESS ALSO IN AN "A" OR "R" ZONE	—	—	967 COLD GREY LIGHT
	PB	PARKING BUILDING AUTOMOBILE PARKING WITHIN OR WITHOUT A BUILDING	**	—	0', 5' OR 10' DEPENDING ON ZONING IN BLOCK	5' TO 16' IF ABUTTING "A" OR "R" ZONE	5' TO 16' IF ABUTTING "A" OR "R" ZONE	NONE	NONE	—	—	936 SLATE GREY
SPECIAL	SL	SUBMERGED LAND ZONE COMMERCIAL SHIPPING NAVIGATION FISHING RECREATION										919 SKY BLUE
	(T)	TENTATIVE CLASSIFICATION USED IN COMBINATION WITH ZONE CHANGE ONLY - DELAYS ISSUANCE OF BUILDING PERMIT UNTIL SUBDIVISION RECORDED										
	(F)	FUNDED IMPROVEMENT CLASSIFICATION AN ALTERNATE MEANS OF EFFECTING ZONE CHANGES AND SECURING IMPROVEMENTS (WHEN NO SUBDIVISION OR DEDICATIONS ARE INVOLVED)										

SUPPLEMENTAL USE DISTRICTS (ESTABLISHED IN CONJUNCTION WITH ZONES): G ROCK AND GRAVEL • O OIL DRILLING • S ANIMAL SLAUGHTERING • K HORSE-KEEPING

* HEIGHT DISTRICT	
Nº 1	FLOOR AREA OF MAIN BUILDING MAY NOT EXCEED THREE TIMES THE BUILDING AREA OF THE LOT
Nº 1L	SAME AS Nº 1 AND MAXIMUM HEIGHT - 6 STORIES OR 75 FT.
Nº 2	FLOOR AREA OF MAIN BUILDING MAY NOT EXCEED SIX TIMES THE BUILDABLE AREA OF THE LOT.
Nº 3	FLOOR AREA OF MAIN BUILDING MAY NOT EXCEED TEN TIMES THE BUILDABLE AREA OF THE LOT.
Nº 4	FLOOR AREA OF MAIN BUILDING MAY NOT EXCEED THIRTEEN TIMES THE BUILDABLE AREA OF THE LOT.

** PB ZONE HEIGHT DISTRICT	
Nº 1	2 STORIES AND ROOF
Nº 2	6 STORIES
Nº 3	10 STORIES
Nº 4	13 STORIES

NOTE: ALL IMFORMATION GENERAL. FOR SPECIFIC DETAILS CHECK WITH DEPARTMENT OF BUILDING AND SAFTY

SHEET 2 OF 2

PREPARED BY CITY PLANNING DEPARTMENT — JUNE 1969

SUMMARY OF ZONING REGULATIONS
CITY OF LOS ANGELES

CLASSIFICATION	ZONE	USE	MAXIMUM HEIGHT STORIES	MAXIMUM HEIGHT FEET	REQUIRED YARDS FRONT	REQUIRED YARDS SIDE	REQUIRED YARDS REAR	MINIMUM AREA PER LOT	MINIMUM AREA PER DWELLING UNIT	MINIMUM LOT WIDTH	PARKING SPACE	EAGLE PRISMACOLOR PENCIL CHART
AGRICULTURAL	A1	AGRICULTURAL ONE-FAMILY DWELLINGS - PARKS - PLAY-GROUNDS - COMMUNITY CENTERS GOLF COURSES - TRUCK GARDENING - EX-TENSIVE AGRICULTURAL USES	3	45 FT.	25 FT.	25 FT. MAXIMUM 10% LOT WIDTH 3 FT. MINIMUM	25 FT.	5 ACRES	2½ ACRES	300 FT.	TWO SPACES PER DWELLING UNIT	909 GRASS GREEN
	A2	AGRICULTURAL A1 USES	3	45 FT.	25 FT.	25 FT. MAXIMUM 10% LOT WIDTH 3 FT. MINIMUM	25 FT.	2 ACRES	1 ACRE	150 FT.	TWO SPACES PER DWELLING UNIT	912 APPLE GREEN
	RA	SUBURBAN LIMITED AGRICULTURAL USES	3	45 FT.	25 FT.	10'-1 & 2 STORIES 11'-3 STORIES	25 FT.	17,500 SQ. FT. *	17,500 SQ. FT. *	70 FT. *	TWO GARAGE SPACES PER DWELLING UNIT	910 TRUE GREEN
ONE FAMILY RESIDENTIAL	RE40	RESIDENTIAL ESTATE ONE-FAMILY DWELLINGS PARKS PLAYGROUNDS COMMUNITY CENTERS TRUCK GARDENING	3	45 FT.	25 FT.	10 FT.	25 FT.	40,000 SQ. FT. *	40,000 SQ. FT. *	80 FT. *	TWO GARAGE SPACES PER DWELLING UNIT	950 GOLD
	RE20				25 FT.	10 FT.	25 FT.	20,000 SQ. FT. *	20,000 SQ. FT. *	80 FT. *		
	RE15				25 FT.	10 FT. MAXIMUM 10% LOT WIDTH 5 FT. MINIMUM	25 FT.	15,000 SQ. FT. *	15,000 SQ. FT. *	80 FT. *		
	RE11				25 FT.	5'-1 & 2 STORIES 6'-3 STORIES	25 FT.	11,000 SQ. FT. *	11,000 SQ. FT. *	70 FT. *		
	RE9				25 FT.	5 FT. MAXIMUM 10% LOT WIDTH 3 FT. MINIMUM	25 FT.	9,000 SQ. FT. *	9,000 SQ. FT. *	65 FT. *		
	RS	SUBURBAN ONE-FAMILY DWELLINGS - PARKS PLAYGROUNDS - TRUCK GARDENING	3	45 FT.	25 FT.	5'-1 & 2 STORIES 6'-3 STORIES	20 FT.	7,500 SQ. FT.	7,500 SQ. FT.	60 FT.	TWO GARAGE SPACES PER DWELLING UNIT	911 OLIVE GREEN
	R1	ONE-FAMILY DWELLING RS USES	3	45 FT.	20 FT.	5'-1 & 2 STORIES 6'-3 STORIES	15 FT.	5,000 SQ. FT.	5,000 SQ. FT.	50 FT.	TWO GARAGE SPACES PER DWELLING UNIT	916 CANARY YELLOW
	RW1	ONE-FAMILY RESIDENTIAL WATERWAYS ZONE	3	45 FT.	10 FT.	● 4' PLUS 1' EACH STORY ABOVE 2ND 10% LOT WIDTH	15 FT.	2,300 SQ. FT.	2,300 SQ. FT.	28 FT.	TWO GARAGE SPACES PER DWELLING UNIT	914 CREAM
MULTIPLE RESIDENTIAL	RW2	TWO-FAMILY RESIDENTIAL WATERWAYS ZONE							1,150 SQ. FT.			
	R2	TWO-FAMILY DWELLING R1 USES TWO-FAMILY DWELLINGS	3	45 FT.	20 FT.	5'-1 & 2 STORIES 6'-3 STORIES	15 FT.	5,000 SQ. FT.	2,500 SQ. FT.	50 FT.	TWO SPACES ONE IN A GARAGE	917 YELLOW ORANGE
	RD1.5	RESTRICTED DENSITY MULTIPLE DWELLING ZONE TWO-FAMILY DWELLING APARTMENT HOUSES MULTIPLE DWELLINGS	HEIGHT DISTRICT NO. 1 3 STORIES 45 FT. HEIGHT DISTRICT NOS. 2, 3 OR 4 6 STORIES 75 FT.		20 FT.	6 FT.	20 FT.	6,000 SQ. FT.	1,500 SQ. FT.	60 FT.	ONE SPACE EACH DWELLING UNIT OF LESS THAN THREE ROOMS ONE AND ONE HALF SPACES EACH DWELLING UNIT OF THREE ROOMS TWO SPACES EACH DWELLING UNIT OF MORE THEN THREE ROOMS ONE SPACE EACH GUEST ROOM (FIRST THIRTY)	940 SAND
	RD2				20 FT.	10 FT.	25 FT.	8,000 SQ. FT.	2,000 SQ. FT.	60 FT.		
	RD3							12,000 SQ. FT.	3,000 SQ. FT.	70 FT.		
	RD4								4,000 SQ. FT.			
	RD5								5,000 SQ. FT.			
	RD6								6,000 SQ. FT.			
	R3	MULTIPLE DWELLING R2 USES APARTMENT HOUSES MULTIPLE DWELLINGS			15 FT.	5'-1 & 2 STORIE 6'-3 STORIES	15 FT.	5,000 SQ. FT.	800 TO 1,200 SQ. FT.	50 FT.		918 ORANGE
	R4	MULTIPLE DWELLING R3 USES CHURCHES HOTELS - SCHOOLS	UNLIMITED *		15 FT.	5' PLUS 1' EACH STORY ABOVE 2ND 16 FT. MAX.	15' PLUS 1' EACH STORY ABOVE 3RD 20 FT. MAX.	5,000 SQ. FT.	400 TO 800 SQ. FT.	50 FT.		943 BURNT OCHRE
	R5	MULTIPLE DWELLING R4 USES CLUBS - HOSPITALS LODGES - SANITARIUMS	UNLIMITED *		15 FT.	5' PLUS 1' EACH STORY ABOVE 2ND 16 FT. MAX.	15' PLUS 1' EACH STORY ABOVE 3RD 20 FT. MAX.	5,000 SQ. FT.	200 TO 400 SQ. FT.	50 FT.		946 DARK BROWN

* SEE HEIGHT DISTRICTS AT THE BOTTOM OF PAGE 2

● FOR TWO OR MORE LOTS THE INTERIOR SIDE YARDS MAY BE ELIMINATED, BUT 4 FT. IS REQUIRED ON EACH SIDE OF THE GROUPED LOTS.

* "H" HILLSIDE OR MOUNTAINOUS AREA DESIGNATION MAY ALTER THESE REQUIREMENTS IN THE RA-H OR RE-H ZONES, SUBDIVISIONS MAY BE APPROVED WITH SMALLER LOTS, PROVIDING LARGER LOTS ARE ALSO INCLUDED. EACH LOT MAY BE USED FOR ONLY ONE SINGLE-FAMILY DWELLING. SEE MINIMUM WIDTH & AREA REQUIREMENTS BELOW.

ZONE COMBINATION	MINIMUM TO WHICH NET AREA MAY BE REDUCED	MINIMUM TO WHICH LOT WIDTH MAY BE REDUCED
RA-H	14,000 SQ. FT.	63 FT.
RE20-H	10,000 SQ. FT.	60 FT.
RE15-H, RE11-H	7,500 SQ. FT.	60 FT.
RE40-H	20,000 SQ. FT.	NO REDUCTION

SHEET 1 OF 2

CP FORM 10

PREPARED BY CITY PLANNING DEPARTMENT

JUNE 1969

With the official population forecast for Greater Los Angeles alone being 22,000,000 by 1980, it can be seen that not only is land shrinking rapidly, but that controls on its usage are becoming more urgent.

Subdivision and *land development,* although not synonymous, are often confused in the mind of the public. The subdivider is a manufacturer of raw land; the developer is the builder who adds the house or other type of building to the subdivided lot. As was mentioned above, the acquisition, subdividing, and development of the land are subject to many regulatory factors, all of which must be carefully considered in the light of their contribution to the cost and future enhancement of the finished product.

The subdivision and development of the city lot are regulated by local bodies as to size, setback lines, land use, and street improvement. Private deed restrictions may be placed on the property by the owner or developer that further regulate its use.

Types of Zoning. Land use typically established by zoning regulations describes which land areas may be used for (1) residential (normally single-family, duplex, or multifamily dwellings), (2) commercial, or (3) industrial purposes. In some areas, special-use buildings, such as churches, schools, and hospitals, are placed in a separate zoning category. Zoning ordinances usually cover two areas of control: (1) blanket zoning and (2) "spot" variances. In cases where the property owner feels that the blanket zoning is affecting his property adversely, he may make application for a zone change or a "spot" variance (a "petition for exception to use") to cover his particular property. In some areas, land density is controlled by zoning laws, through regulation of the number of units per square foot which may be built on a given lot, or through the requirement of a certain percentage of the lot to be used for parking.

Building restrictions are additional regulatory measures designed to protect the investment of the buyer and to assure that any development planned will not be at variance with the city's master plan. These restrictions may involve regulation of building materials used and the architecture and height of the structure, as well as the front and side setback lines.

Deed Restrictions. Owners or developers may put additional restrictions on the use of land by recording private deed restrictions. This is done by inserting a covering provision into the deed by which the property is transferred. Deed restrictions may control such items as type of building materials to be used, architecture, building design, size, and property maintenance. Land *use* may also be covered (as, "No sheep are to be grazed on the land"). As restrictive devices, they normally add value to the property by giving it an exclusiveness that sets it apart from the ordinary development. Deed restrictions may run with the land or for a given period of time (twenty to fifty years). Occasionally, a "reverter" clause is inserted providing that the property reverts to the seller in the event of a claimed and proven violation.

Successful developers generally are very neighborhood-conscious. Strong public and private property restrictions rigidly enforced are important to the marketability of their finished product. They are therefore acutely aware that the demand for their homes is dependent upon the neighborhood characteristics, the income level of the residents, and the condition of the existing homes, yards, and streets.

City Development

High-grade city areas tend to follow a definite pattern. Generally speaking, the growth is toward high ground, where the higher-priced properties are usually to be found. This is due in part to the higher cost of development of hillside lots, but demand is also a factor. As the center of cities declines, the trend is toward the suburban areas, particularly toward those of natural beauty (rivers, lakes, or seashore). Promoters have taken advantage of this flight to the suburbs and, to some extent, have *inclined* the trend toward certain areas by planned developments in shopping centers, high-class housing tracts, and industrial centers with housing for future employees.

Redevelopment. With decentralization an established fact today, evidenced by the number of outlying shopping centers and industrial communities, the city has become in danger of decay at the core. A growing lack of downtown parking facilities and easy access to outlying areas by means of networks of freeways have driven workers to the suburbs, where they are employed in the many branch industries that have taken advantage of lower land costs and ease of access to locate away from the city center.

City planners have undertaken to save the city's central areas by urban renewal or redevelopment plans. Stricter conformance with health and building codes is called for as a measure to maintain declining neighborhoods. Redevelopment by private means has proved more difficult than was anticipated, owing to the difficulty of obtaining the necessary land plottage. It has become necessary in some cases for public bodies to exercise eminent domain rights to demolish older structures and permit the cities to begin a program of redevelopment. In 1949, the Federal Housing Act recognized slums as a national menace. Under Title I of this act, federal loans and grants are made available to clear certain types of blighted areas for redevelopment. When the areas are cleared, they may be sold or leased to private or public investors who will improve the land in keeping with the original master plan. Recognition of the lack of adequate parking facilities as one of the main causes of downtown district blight in U.S. cities has been the principal contributory factor to rehabilitation of the metropolitan areas.

It is interesting to note, however, that some cities have been successful in creating outstanding mall-type developments almost entirely from private funds, Pomona being an outstanding example of this mall-type development. Dedicated entirely to pedestrian traffic, an elaborate off-street parking system has been devised.

> The Pomona Plan, apart from its private enterprise initiative and funding, is unique among urban development projects because the city is fighting to retain its strong identity in an area dominated by the giant megalopolis of Los Angeles. To do so, it is determined to retain downtown Pomona as the heart of the entire Pomona Valley expansion. The effort is being watched with interest by literally hundreds of other communities with somewhat similar problems in the United States.[4]

Condominiums. While on the topic of subdivisions, this new type of upright subdivision should be considered. Section 783 of the Civil Code defines a *condominium* as "an estate in real property consisting of an undivided interest in common in a portion of a parcel of real estate together with a separate interest in space in a residential, industrial or commercial building on such real property, such as an apartment, office or store. A condominium may include, in addition, a separate interest in other protions of such property."

It can be seen from this that the person buying a condominium owns the *air space* in which his particular unit is located. He owns a fee interest in it—a deed to it—and is assessed and pays taxes on it. Any title insurance company will issue a policy on it; and, as the owner, he may transfer his interest as he would with any other property (subject to the approval of the association). He also owns a certain undivided interest in common in certain other defined areas.

Because the word *condominium* had never appeared in California law prior to 1963, no precedent has been established to aid in solving the legal problems that arose concerning the construction, financing, and sale of this new vertical-type development.

When A. B. 600 was passed by the California Legislature in 1963, defining *condominium,* it added certain provisions to the Civil Code, the Business and Professions Code, and the Revenue and Taxation Code pertaining to its regulations. The real estate commissioner requires a subdivision public report containing all the statutory and regulatory provisions binding on any other type of subdivision. Added to this is the requirement that a permit to sell securities must be obtained from the corporations commissioner before any condominium may be *sold* in California.

Section 2792.6 of the commissioner's regulations specifies certain documents that must be submitted when filing a condominium report with the commissioner, and Section 2792.7 requires a detailed statement of maintenance and operating costs to be filed with the subdivision questionnaire. Incorporated in the statement is certain required information relating to (1) fixed charges, (2) operating expenses, and (3) reserve for replacements. A declaration of restrictions, bylaws, and any other agreements relating to the management and control of the condominium must also be approved by the commissioner. These provisions, among others, cover such items as (1) management policy, (2) voting rights, (3) rights of the management body, (4) contracts for insurance and maintenance of the property, (5) payment of taxes and special assesments, and (6) provision for reconstruction in case of damage from any cause.[5]

The skyrocketing price of land convenient to the metropolitan area has been one of the basic reasons for the enthusiasm over the condominium style of apartments. Some experts have termed them "the greatest single thing to come our way since the amortized mortgage." In spite of the fact that many forecasters hold with the idea of all city residents wanting a home in the country, thousands of families have voluntarily chosen apartment living. These people are principally in the middle-income group, families who want the luxuries of a medium-priced home with built-ins and other modern features.

Mortgage lenders are looking with favor on this new type of apartment. In the event of default, they have the protection offered in an individual rather than a blanket trust deed. Finally, the land scarcity is forcing the metropolitan areas to grow "up" rather than "out." The condominium would appear to be the only solution to a growing problem of high cost of single-family residences on land selling as high as

[4] "Urban Renewal by Private Enterprise in Pomona Features Pedestrian Mall," *California Real Estate Magazine* (Los Angeles: California Real Estate Association), Vol. 42, No. 10 (August, 1962), 11.

[5] For full text on regulations governing condominiums, see *Reference Book* (Sacramento: Department of Real Estate, 1971).

Title Insurance and Trust Company Presents Some Comments on–

LAND

Since the beginning of man, land has been a most important item in his life. On it he built a cave he called home...planted the seed that gave him food. In it he mined the minerals that made him rich. Land contained the water that he drank and land caused the wars he constantly fought. When land was neglected, man had famine. When land flourished, man flourished. Time has changed little of this.

It wasn't until Thomas Jefferson announced the Louisiana Purchase, however, that the real value in terms of land began to be realized. For the first time in history, land assumed value in terms of money. In fact, the Purchase caused a nationwide uproar because of the devout feeling that a young nation had been cheated and swindled by shrewd financial wizards of the Old World. No one could visualize that the Louisiana Territory would be worth many, many times the 15 million dollars that it cost.

The Louisiana Purchase was followed by the Alaska Purchase in 1867. This was referred to as Seward's Folly... "A stupid purchase of worthless, frozen wasteland." "A waste of money." During an interview in 1960, Anastas Mikoyan, then first deputy premier of the U.S.S.R., offered to pay the United States 1000 per cent profit if we would sell Alaska back to Russia.

Yes, land is still the most important item in man's life.

WHY IS IT VALUABLE?

Land has made more people rich, happy, secure and healthy than any other commodity in the world, yet there is much misunderstanding about land values.

You will hear someone say, "That isn't worth what they are asking. It is too far away." And they are right, except that our problem of population is growing so fast and transportation is becoming so advanced that no land is too far away.

You will hear someone say, "That property is no good–it is all desert." And they are right, except that someone will bring water to it. Isn't that what happened to Imperial Valley, Coachella Valley, Palmdale, Lancaster, Palm Springs...and to Los Angeles and Apple Valley?

There is no one thing that makes land valuable. It is more a series of things. First, of course, there is only so much of it and no more. We cannot manufacture land like we manufacture automobiles and refrigerators. This fact alone increases land values, and if we are talking about land near water then we can multiply this factor by a hundred, because there is less land near water than any other kind. Farm land, for instance, that would ordinarily bring $1500 or $2000 an acre in Riverside County would be valued at $60,000 to $90,000 per lot if that land were located near water...say in Malibu, Newport or Lido Isle.

Second is the use to which the land is put. Will it be suitable for an apartment, homesite, or motel...or a recreation area...a business site for a store or arcade?

Third is the location of the land. Is it near a city, good transportation, schools, shopping, a lake or resort area? Is it a new area that is just starting to grow so that it will gain in value faster than normal? What are the restrictions on the use of the property and the adjacent properties?

All of these factors determine the true value of land. And finally, if your investment is in a new community where there is a good pattern of growth, your land increases in value because you are buying at the start of a rise and not in the middle or near the top.

LAND INVESTMENT

Every day millions of Americans are investing unknowingly in land. The money that is placed for safekeeping in the savings and loan associations, banks, and insurance companies is, to a large degree, invested in real estate. Profits from these investments are the backbone for the dividends paid to the policy or bank book holders. If these companies can do it for you, why can't you do it for yourself? You can. All you have to do is start. Let's look at it this way: Land is a money savings investment–a sort of forced savings with a growing dollar value. The sooner you start, the more money you will make. Select good property with a potential and **START.** This simple philosophy of investment is the keynote to success and has been the foundation of many a millionaire's bank roll.

HOW TO MAKE A PROFIT

Land increases in value because of what happens in surrounding communities. Values depend upon progress, the use to which the land is put and the general activity of the area, population-wise. Since there is only so much land, as we increase our population, we automatically increase the value of the land. If it is a healthful climate, has recreational facilities, and is near enough to industry or agricultural center which provide population expansion, then it will increase in value rapidly. People would rather live in clean suburbs, at the seashore or in the mountains because they like to fish, hike, camp, go boating, or play golf. Of course, as these events take place other people come into the area to provide the services needed for them–the stores to buy in and the motels in which to live. When 1500 families move to a new area, we need 320 doctors, dentists and lawyers. We need 22 school rooms and 18 teachers. We need 320 cars (this includes family cars, delivery trucks and the accompanying services). We need 33 stores and these stores will do a gross business of over ½ million dollars per year. It is this cycle that makes real estate a secure and profitable investment. Unlike the automobile or typewriter, land does not lose its value from the start of the purchase; in fact, the rule of the thumb is that it increases in value from the start. Land appreciates–an automobile depreciates.

If you understand this difference, then the following facts will fall into place logically and easily for you:

Land increases in value by growth in the area, better accessibility to adjacent areas because of new roads or transportation, new pleasure outlets and the need for healthful climate, free from smog, where a person can relax and enjoy life. If you buy in the path of growth, this means that profits can be accrued right from the start and every activity in the development will help your land increase in value. This means that every carload of goods shipped into the adjacent areas or the goods shipped out of the adjacent areas automatically adds value to your property.....This is activity.....this is growth.....this is progress. This means that every building built on or near your property adds to your profit. The improvement a developer makes, the streets he puts in, the water lines and the electricity he contracts for–all add to the value of your property immediately. It means that the original buyers of the development have thousands of other people working for them to make their property increase in value. We all know someone who has sold a house or lot for more than he paid for it in spite of the fact he did nothing to improve his own property. This seems to be the inevitable course that all good real estate investments follow.

The important factor of profit in land investment is time. It does not happen in a day or a month's time–it does happen often in just a few years. This time factor determines how great the profit will be. What is a 25 per cent profit in three years could very well become 50 per cent profit in the fourth year. Once land begins to appreciate, it increases in value each year. The reason for this is that the whole area is increasing in value and not just a single isolated portion. Once the area gains momentum a good profit is inevitable–time is the element that makes it so.

COMMON SENSE

Look for good planning in the development you are interested in. Has it been laid out with a thought for the future? Does it have proper zoning and restrictions so each piece of property will gain full value in the minimum amount of time? Are the streets being paved? Will sewers and water mains be installed? Are telephones and power available? See the development with the understanding that time is the important profit ingredient. Remember that the earlier you come into the project, the greater the profit will be–but your waiting time will be a little longer. Remember that land is a money savings investment. Treat your investment like any other security and allow it to mature, let it mellow with time and you will get your reward. Remember when you opened your savings account? You were in no hurry to make a profit...you were merely "Salting it away for a rainy day." Be as patient with your land investment. Others have made money in real estate and.....**SO CAN YOU**!!!!!!!!!!!!

POPULATION GROWTH

The next ten years will go down in history as the greatest boom this country has ever known. This entire boom will have more effect on land than on any other commodity. Why? Because millions more people will be added to these United States and because land is limited in quanity. This statement, startling in its simplicity, is profound in its meaning. It is the fundamental reason why land will increase in value and become the best investment that you can make.

As the tremendous forces of birth rate, increased business and giant industry move in an avalanche on the limited supply of land, the full meaning of this observation becomes more obvious. Our population is exploding. A greater and greater demand is being made and will continue to be made on that precious commodity–land.

It is unique that the supply of land was fixed when the earth took shape and it is an inevitable consequence of the law of supply and demand that as greater calls are put upon the supply, its value will go up. This plain reasoning should throw considerable light upon the part that real estate will play in the boom ahead.

As we look at this nationwide picture, we begin to wonder where California will fit into the scheme of things. In 1964, California became the largest state in the Union. New residents are coming into California at the rate of 1,000 per day. Every Monday morning when we wake up, there will be 23,700 more cars on the highways than there were the Monday before. Economists predict a solid city 250 miles long and 90 miles wide reaching from the Mexican border to Santa Barbara, and it will be termed "San–San."

The Board of Equalization figures show that California property increases in value at about $400.00 per second. In other words, in the time it took you to read this short paragraph, the value of California property increased a little over $2,000.00.

Real Estate has always been our greatest source of security and profit. The greatest profit seems to occur in the areas where there is the greatest influx of families and there is no greater area in the world in this respect than Southern California.

Now let us look into **YOUR FUTURE** and see where you fit into this prosperity picture. Every important person owns property. Possession of real estate is the basis of credit in banks, department stores, and loan associations. That is why a property owner is considered important–he automatically becomes a somebody because he has good credit. The most important person in your neighborhood is **YOU**–and you are on the threshold of the greatest opportunity of your life to profit by the tremendous boom that lies just ahead. What are you going to do about it? Are you going to be better off financially as the result of good thinking and planning, or are you going to stand on the sidelines and watch the parade go by?

Under similar economic conditions when people stand face to face with opportunity, they usually divide themselves into three psychological groups:

First are those who step in at the very beginning and become wealthy. They see the opportunity, have confidence in what they see and invest what they can afford. It may not be much, but they have taken a step in the right direction, and they know it. Their investment pyramids from there on. These are the doers.

When a parcel of land is deeded to you and you walk on it and call it your own, it seems as if you had joined into partnership with the original proprietor of the Earth. Nothing gives a person more confidence than owning land.

The second is the more conservative type. They usually wait a few years "just to see how things are going"–and come into the picture in the middle of rising real estate values and pay somebody else a profit that should have been theirs. These are the procrastinators.

The third group will pass up the opportunity altogether. They prefer to "go home and think it over." For the next ten years they dream about it and offer thin-skinned alibis to themselves–and to anyone who will listen to them–to hide their own shortcomings: "If I were ten years younger"..."If I just had the Money"...if...if...IF. Money does not buy real estate....vision does.

This "think it over" routine has become a thought-habit with them, and they go through life passing up one opportunity after another. At the end of ten years, they are no better off financially than they are today. These people rarely acquire anything in life but a membership in the "I Coulda Club." They see the opportunity as well as you do, but they lack the intestinal fortitude to do anything about it.

This is not for you. Join the first group...you'll be better off. Remember the successful person didn't start at the top. Usually, all he had in the beginning was an idea and very little capital. His idea turned into a plan...he put his plan into action. He did something about it. He let nothing interfere with his plan. What little capital he had, he invested in his plan. As the plan grew...he grew. As he grew...the plan became big...he became big. The one dominating feature of his very existence was that he had a plan and put it into action. This simple reasoning is the basis of every successful career. In other words, out of an idea came a **PLAN** and **ACTION**. With these ingredients, he created his own destiny. Every successful investor in real estate has followed this same pattern. **YOU** can do it, too.

12-10-68

TI

BUYING REAL ESTATE
IS THE SAFEST WAY OF INVESTING MONEY

THEODORE ROOSEVELT said: *"Every person who invests in well selected real estate in a growing section of a prosperous community adopts the surest and safest method of becoming independent, for real estate is the basis of wealth."*

MARSHALL FIELD said: *"Buying real estate is not only the best way, the quickest way, and the safest way, but the only way to become wealthy."*

HETTY GREEN said: *"Real estate is an imperishable asset, increasing in value. It is the most solid security that human ingenuity has devised. It is the collateral to be preferred above all others, and the safest means of investing money."*

ANDREW CARNEGIE said: *"Ninety per cent of all millionaires become so through owning real estate. More money has been made in real estate than in all industrial investments. The wise young man or wage earner of today invests his money in real estate."*

BRUCE BARTON said: *"There was a vacant lot opposite my home which could have been bought for five thousand dollars. A month ago, a man bought it for twenty-eight thousand, and two weeks later, it sold for sixty thousand. I take off my hat to him. He saw it was a gold mine! It didn't look to me like anything more than a vacant lot."*

$18,000 an acre. In addition, the builder or developer cannot hope that rents can be continually pushed up to provide the necessary margin of profit. Competition from other multifamily projects in the area will provide a leveling factor that will inevitably increase his vacancy rate.

Cooperative Apartments. These differ from the condominium-type development principally in the type of ownership involved. Under the cooperative-type development, a corporation is formed by the developer. He sells shares to the individual purchaser, who is given a "proprietary" lease on the unit of his choice. Under his lease agreement, the purchaser is responsible for payment of his share of taxes and mortgage installments. In addition, he must pay his portion of the maintenance and repair of common halls, as well as of the building exterior and grounds. *Under the cooperative plan, the purchaser does not receive fee title to his apartment.* Also, usually he cannot purchase his unit free and clear because the building quite often is encumbered by a maximum construction loan. In the event that one of the purchasers is delinquent in his payments, a situation may arise where all the tenants share in the liability. The corporation usually has the right, however, to sell or lease the apartment.

An additional advantage in the condominium type of apartment is the purchaser's ability to obtain individual financing of his own choosing. He receives an individual tax bill covering his share of an easement interest in the common halls, swimming pool, grounds, and any recreational facilities.

Shopping Centers

The term *shopping center* has been loosely applied to a grouping of retail stores ranging from three or four units to the large development involving as much as forty acres. The determining factor in size and location selection of the shopping center is its proximity to competitive developments and the buying power of the area from which the center hopes to draw. Two major factors, the automobile and the freeway, have contributed to the advent and the success of the outlying shopping centers. Following closely on these two, and both contributing to and dependent upon them, is today's increasing trend toward suburban living. Today, any available tract of land comprising five acres or more is a potential site for the neighborhood shopping center. There is some evidence that this type of development may be overdone in California. There are also concerns that some of the bigger developments are located without the basic surveys necessary to determine whether a need for the shopping center in the area actually exists. Large department stores wishing to locate in a given area customarily acquire the necessary acreage, then contact a developer to build a shopping center, with the department store as a nucleus. There may be a valid need for the department store, but the purchasing power to support the smaller retail stores planned to complete the center may not be present.

Experts in shopping-center planning concur in the necessity for a detailed survey and analysis of the buying potential in the contemplated development area. The success or failure of the venture probably is in direct ratio to the depth and accuracy of such a survey.

Agricultural Lands

Of the 65,000 acres absorbed annually by California's mushrooming population, by far the largest share is being diverted from agricultural uses. This diversion has contributed to a steady rise in farmland values. Even in areas where urban prices are holding firm, rural prices continue to rise. In the northern parts of the state, where fishing and hunting are available, small ranch sites are particularly in demand. The subsistence farm is popular today as a result of the back-to-the-land trend of many city-dwellers, particularly those with large families. The desire to rear children in a country atmosphere away from the temptations and hazards of heavily congested areas has created a competitive market for the small (five- to twenty-acre) ranch where a cow, a pet horse, and an orchard or a vegetable garden may make its contribution to the family togetherness and security.

How to Make More Profitable Land Investments

Land profits may be made three times:

1. At time of purchase.
2. During the holding period.
3. At time of sale.

1. *Profit at time of purchase*
   a. Selection of parcel:
      (1) Have a plan in mind (three-, four-, five-year holding period).
      (2) Review the county master plan.
      (3) Research the economics of the area.
      (4) Look for predeveloped land.
      (5) Check soil, geology, and flood conditions.
      (6) Secure a preliminary title report.

   b. *Financing the parcel*
      (1) Leverage.
      (2) Interest-only payments.

(3) Multiple-trust deeds.
(4) Acreage-release clauses (release with down payment).
(5) Profits—cash or paper.

c. *Pitfalls to watch*
(1) Mineral rights.
(2) Easements—recorded and unrecorded—prescriptive rights, rights of adverse possion.
(3) Deed restrictions.
(4) Purchase contracts (alienation clauses, and so on).

2. *Profit during holding period*
a. Aesthetics.
(1) Planting trees and shrubs.
(2) Brushing.
(3) Bulldozing roads.
b. Easements:
(1) Shifting existing easements.
(2) Increasing access (appurtenance easements).
c. Change of zoning.
d. Increasing frontage.
e. Peripheral zoning.

3. *Profit at time of sale*
a. Determine buyer.
b. Do not shop—qualify the buyer.
c. Leave some profit.
d. Subdivision problems (capital gains).
e. Partial sale.

QUESTION

1. Assume that you are a developer planning a shopping center. What steps would you take to acquire the necessary plottage?
2. Outline the steps you would take to determine the need for a shopping center in the area.
3. Mrs. Brown's husband dies, leaving her $50,000 tax-free. She is in her early sixties, with no dependent children. She lives in a $25,000 condominium apartment, which she owns free and clear. She owns no stocks or bonds, nor has she any other assets. She comes to you, as a real estate investment broker, for your advice on investing the money. Would you advise her to invest in:
   (a) Bare land?
   (b) Income property?
   (c) Well-secured second-trust deeds?
4. Assume that you list a ten-acre parcel of unencumbered, unimproved land in a rapidly developing area where the taxes are relatively low. The acreage can be bought for $3,000 an acre, which is under the market price. The owner prefers a low down payment to cash because of his tax bracket. He will carry the balance on a land contract. Would you advise your client, Mrs. Brown, to purchase this property? Give your reasons.

SUGGESTED REFERENCES

CASE, FREDERICK, E., *Real Estate.* Boston: Allyn & Bacon, Inc., 1962.

CLARK, WM. DENNISON, JR., "What Leverage Means to the Investor," *Real Estate Today,* Vol. 4, No. 2 (National Association of Real Estate Boards, April, 1971).

Community Builder's Handbook. Washington, D.C.: Urban Land Institute, 1968.

Real Estate Syndication Workbook. Los Angeles: California Real Estate Association, 1970.

Subdivision Manual. Sacramento: State Department of Real Estate, current issue.

WEIMER, ARTHUR M., and HOMER HOYT, *Real Estate,* 5th ed. New York: The Ronald Press Company, 1966, Chap. 15.

Appendix

Glossary of Building Terms

Acoustical tile Blocks of fiber, mineral, or metal, with small holes or rough-textured surface to absorb sound, used as covering for interior walls and ceilings.

Attic exhaust fan Large, quiet fan installed in attic or upper story of a house, to be turned on when windows are opened in the evening to draw in cool outside air.

Awning-type windows Windows with horizontal panes, hinged at the top or on a pivot.

Baseboard A wood member carried around the walls of a room and touching the floor.

Base mold Molding applied at top of baseboard.

Base shoe Molding applied at junction of baseboard and floor.

Batten A narrow strip of wood attached to a wall to cover a joint between two pieces of siding; used both for weathertightness and decorative effect.

Breezeway A covered porch or passage, open on two sides, connecting house and garage or two parts of the house.

Bridging Wood members used to brace floor joists.

Building paper Heavy waterproofed paper used over wall sheathing to provide insulation.

Built-in Any wardrobe, kitchen cabinet, or similar feature built as part of the house.

Casement A window frame hinged at the side that swings outward; usually operated by a small crank.

Circuit breaker A device in the electrical system to interrupt the circuit when an overload occurs; an automatic switch, which can be reset, is used instead of a fuse to protect each circuit.

Circulating fireplace Fireplace built around a metal form, with air ducts to distribute heat by convection.

Clapboard Siding of narrow boards, thicker at one edge, used as exterior finish for frame houses.

Combed (striated) plywood Popular building material in modern homes, particularly for interior finish. The exposed surface is "combed" in parallel grooves.

Combination door Permanent door with screen panel for summer use and glass panel to be installed in winter.

Cross bridging Cross bracing between floor joists to provide rigidity.

Deck An open second-story porch, usually on the roof of a ground-floor porch or wing.

Dutch door A door divided horizontally in the middle, so that the bottom half remains closed while the top is opened.

Expansible house Home planned for practical and economical additions in the future.

Facade The principal face of a house.

Finish floor Finish floor strips are applied over wood joists, deadening felt, and diagonal subflooring before finish floor is installed; finish floor is the final covering on the floor: wood, linoleum, cork, tile, or carpet.

Flashing Metal used in waterproofing the joint between chimney and roof, or used similarly in roof valleys and hips.

Flush door A door that is smooth on both sides, with no panels; it may be solid or hollow.

Furring strips Wood strips nailed onto masonry walls, to which lath and plaster are applied.

Gable, gabled roof A gable is a triangular wall at the end of a house, outlined by the edges of the gabled roof.

Gambrel roof A curb roof, having a steep lower slope and a flatter one above, as seen in Dutch colonial architecture.

Girder A heavy wood or steel structural member supporting beams, joists, and partitions.

Hip roof A roof with sloping sides and ends.

Insulating glass Double glass with dead air in sealed space between two panes.

Jalousie A slatted blind or shutter, like a Venetian blind but used on the exterior to protect against rain as well as to control sunlight.

Joists Horizontal wood structural members, to which the boards of a floor and the laths of a ceiling are nailed.

Load-bearing wall An integral part of the house, which helps to support the floors or roof and cannot be moved readily if at all, as distinguished from a partition that carries no load and can be removed.

Load center Electrical distribution center for a house, either the main center or a branch distribution point, equipped with circuit breakers instead of a main switch and fuse box.

Louver A single louver board, or an opening fitted with louvers, which are slats set at an angle to provide ventilation without admitting rain or direct light.

Mercury switch Wall switch that makes contact through mercury and works silently.

Overhang The part of a roof that extends beyond the walls of a house to cover walks and shade windows from summer sun.

Parquet floor Hardwood flooring laid in squares or patterns, not strip flooring.

Party wall A dividing wall erected upon and over a line separating two adjoining properties and in which the owners of the respective parcels have common rights to its use.

Perimeter heating Baseboard heating, or any system in which registers or radiators are located along the outside walls of a room, particularly under the windows.

Picture window A large window, usually a fixed pane of plate or insulating glass, with ventilation provided by smaller windows alongside; sometimes divided into small panes; it should command an interesting view.

Plywood Laminated wood made up in panels; several thicknesses of wood glued together with grain at different angles for strength.

Radiant heat A method of heating that carries hot water or air through ducts embedded in walls, ceiling, or floors; panel heating.

Rafters The sloping wood members of a roof.

Riser The upright board at the back of each step of a stairway. In heating, a riser is a duct slanted upward to carry hot air from the furnace to the room above.

Roman brick Thin brick of slimmer proportions than standard building brick.

Rooftree The ridgeboard supporting the rafters at the peak; also called ridgepiece, ridge plate, and ridgepole.

Sash The wood or metal frames in which window panes are set; the movable part of the window.

Septic tank An underground tank in which sewage from the house is reduced to liquid by bacterial action and drained off.

Shakes Long shingles split from logs.

Sheathing Covering of wood or other material applied to the walls of a house outside the studs and under waterproof building paper and the exterior finish.

Shed roof A one-pitch roof sloping from front to back or back to front.

Shutters Movable screens or blinds for windows, usually louvered; though commonly used for decorative effect, well-designed shutters are adequate to cover the windows and usable as a practical means of storm protection.

Sill The board or stone at the foot of a door, or the woodwork or masonry on which a window frame stands.

Soffit The underside of a cornice, eaves, or overhanging roof; exterior soffits of overhanging roofs correspond to interior ceilings.

Solar window A large window, properly placed in a correctly oriented building, designed to take advantage of winter sunshine for heat as well as light.

Studs Vertical structural timbers in the walls of a house.

Termite shield A metal protective shield applied on top of the foundation wall to prevent subterranean termites from attacking the structural wood members supporting the building.

Traverse rod Arrangement for hanging draperies or window curtains on a rod fitted with slides, pulleys, and cords by means of which draperies may be drawn.

Treads Horizontal boards of a stairway.

U-shaped kitchen Kitchen with range, refrigerator, sink, cupboards and other fixtures on three sides.

Utility room Ground-floor room in a basementless house containing heating equipment and other fixtures.

Veneer A layer of material covering a base of another substance, such as walnut veneer on other less-valuable wood, or brick exterior finish over wood framing or a concrete block wall.

Wainscoting Wood lining of an interior wall; also the lower part of a wall when finished differently from the wall above.

X-bracing Cross bracing in a partition.

Glossary of Real Estate Terms

Abstract of title Condensed history of the title; summarizes various links in chain of title, together with statement of all liens, charges, or encumbrances. Purpose is to show that ownership of property is uncontested and clear up to the current owner.

Acre A measure of land, 4,840 square yards; 43,560 square feet.

Ad valorem A tax according to value.

Affidavit A declaration in writing sworn or affirmed to before one who has authority to administer an oath or affirmation.

Agent One who has power to transact business for another.

Agreement of sale A written agreement whereby the purchaser agrees to buy certain real estate, and the seller agrees to sell according to the terms stated.

Amortization The payment of a debt on an installment basis. The more you pay off, the more the loan is amortized.

Appraisal An estimate of quantity, quality, or value. FHA and VA both send you a copy of their appraisals. When you get a conventional mortgage, make sure you ask to see it. An appraisal is mainly a market evaluation: what the house would sell for in case of foreclosure.

Assessed valuation A value placed on property by a unit of government for taxation purposes.

Assessment Charge against real estate to cover the proportionate cost of an improvement, such as streets, and so on.

Binder An agreement to cover a down payment for the purchase of real estate as evidence of good faith on the part of the purchaser.

Blanket mortgage A single mortgage covering several pieces of real estate.

Bona fide In good faith, without fraud.

British thermal unit (Btu) Unit of measure of quantity of heat required to raise temperature of one pound of water one degree Fahrenheit.

Building code Regulation concerning the construction of buildings within a city or town.

Building line Line defined by law or agreement, usually parallel to property line, beyond which a structure may not extend. Generally does not apply to uncovered entrance platforms, terraces, steps.

Certificate of title This paper proves ownership of a house and contains a legal description of both house and land.

Closing costs Various expenses involved in the transaction of selling a house, changing title, procuring and processing a mortgage. All these are paid over and above the price of the house and lot.

Closing statement An accounting of funds in a real estate sale made by a broker to the seller and buyer. In areas where transactions are closed in escrow, settlement sheets are prepared by the escrow officer for buyer and seller.

Cloud on the title An encumbrance that, if valid, would affect or impair the owner's title.

Community property Property accumulated through joint efforts of husband and wife living together.

Contract A legally enforceable agreement between two or more parties to do certain things for a consideration.

Conveyance The means or medium by which title to real estate is transferred.

Deed An instrument, in writing, duly executed and delivered, in which real estate is conveyed or transferred.

Deed of trust Used instead of a mortgage in some states; they are generally in use in California. The deed is held by a third party, not the mortgage holder, until it has been paid or defaulted.

Default The nonperformance of a duty, whether arising under a contract or otherwise; failure to meet an obligation when due.

Deficiency judgment The difference between the amount owed and the amount for which a property is sold under foreclosure.

Depreciation Loss in value brought about by deterioration through ordinary wear and tear. The usual rate is from 2 percent to 3 percent of total price each year.

Easement Vested or acquired right to use land other than as tenant for specific purpose; such right being held by someone other than owner who holds title to the land.

Easement rights A neighbor may have the legal right to use part of your property (such as a driveway) because a previous owner gave him the right to this specific limited use of the land.

Eminent Domain The right of the people or government to take private property for public use upon payment of compensation.

Encroachment An obstruction or building that impairs the free passage or use of the property of another person.

Encumbrance A claim, lien, charge, or liability attached to and binding upon real property that reduces the fee value but does not prevent conveyance of the fee by the owner.

Equity The interest or value that an owner has in real estate in excess of the mortgage. When your mortgage is fully paid up, you have 100 percent equity in your house.

Erosion The wearing away of land through processes of nature, as by streams and winds.

Escrow Money or papers delivered to a third person to hold until all conditions in a contract are fulfilled.

Estate The amount of interest that a person has in real property he owns.

Exclusive agency The appointment of one real estate broker as sole agent for the sale of a property for a designated period of time.

Floor area Total area of all stories or floors finished as living accommodations. Does not include space in garages, carports, attics. Measurements are taken to outside of exterior walls.

Floor plan Drawing of a house, as though seen from above with roof off, showing rooms, partitions, windows, doors, stairs.

Foreclosure Mandatory transfer of property ownership by order of court in satisfaction of an unpaid debt.

Front foot A standard of measurement, 1 foot wide, extending from street line for a depth, generally conceded to be 100 feet on commercial property and 150 feet on residential.

Grantee A person to whom real estate is conveyed; the buyer.

Grantor A person who conveys real estate by deed; the seller.

Installment contract Purchase of real estate upon an installment basis; upon default, payments are forfeited.

Joint tenancy Property held by two or more persons together with the distinct character of survivorship.

Junior mortgage A mortgage that is secondary to the lien of a prior mortgage.

Land contract A contract for the purchase of real estate upon an installment basis; upon payment of last installment, deed is delivered to purchaser.

Legal description A description recognized by law that is sufficient to locate and identify the property within oral testimony.

Lien A charge against property whereby the property is made security for the payment of a debt.

Lot line Line bounding lot as described in the title to the property.

Marketable title Such a title as a court would compel a purchaser to accept; it is free from any encumbrances or clouds.

Market value The highest price that a buyer willing but not compelled to buy would pay, and the lowest a seller willing but not compelled to sell would accept.

Mechanic's lien A charge against property by those who provide labor or materials for improvement whereby the property is security for payment.

Mortgage An instrument that pledges certain real property as security for a debt.

Mortgagee A person to whom property is pledged until an indebtedness is liquidated.

Mortgagor An owner who conveys his property as security for a loan.

Open listing A nonexclusive listing of real estate for sale or rent.

Option The right to purchase or lease a property at a certain price for a certain designated period, for which right a consideration is paid.

Platte Map, plan, or chart of city, town, section, or subdivision; indicates location and boundaries of properties.

Platte book A public record of various recorded plans in a stated area.

Plot Parcel of land consisting of one or more lots or portions thereof; usually described by reference to a recorded platte.

Principal note The promissory note that is secured by the mortgage or trust deed.

Property line Recorded boundary of a plot.

Purchase money mortgage A mortgage executed by the purchaser as part of the purchase price.

Quiet title A court action brought to establish title and to remove a cloud on the title.

Quitclaim deed Deed of conveyance whereby whatever interest the grantor has in the property described in the deed is conveyed to the grantee without warranty.

Release The relinquishment of some right or benefit to a person who already has some interest in the property.

Release of lien The discharge of certain property from the lien of judgment, mortgage, or claim.

Restriction A device in a deed for controlling the use of land for the benefit of the land.

Restriction covenant A clause in a deed limiting the use of the property conveyed for a certain period of time.

Right of way An easement over another's land; also used to describe a strip of land used as a roadbed by a railroad or other public utility for a public purpose.

Setback The distance from curb or other established line within which no building may be erected.

Severalty ownership Real property owned by one person only; sole ownership.

Subordination clause A clause in a mortgage or lease stating the rights of the holder shall be secondary or subordinate to subsequent encumbrances.

Survey The measurement of a piece of land to determine its area.

Tax deed A deed issued for property that has been sold for nonpayment of taxes.

Title The sum of all the evidence that constitutes proof of ownership.

Title by adverse possession Acquired by occupation and recognized as against the paper title owner.

Title insurance An insurance policy that indemnifies the holder for any loss sustained by a defective title.

Title search Examining and checking ownership papers on file at courthouse or statehouse to make sure there are no liens against the house. Title search is usually mandatory before a house is sold.

Trust deed A conveyance of real estate to a third person (trustee) that states his authority and conditions binding upon him in dealing with the property held in trust.

Waiver The renunciation or surrender of claims, rights, privileges.

Warranty deed An instrument in writing that guarantees that the grantor will protect the grantee against any claimant.

Zoning ordinance The regulation of the character and use of property in prescribed areas through the legitimate application of police power.

FHA FORM NO. 314

FEDERAL HOUSING ADMINISTRATION

ESCROW COMMITMENT CERTIFICATE

MORTGAGOR'S CERTIFICATE

Date..

To: FEDERAL HOUSING ADMINISTRATION

The undersigned, in order to induce the Federal Housing Commissioner to issue an Escrow Commitment to insure a mortgage loan on the property described in the application, certifies to the Federal Housing Commissioner and agrees that:

(1) Check Applicable Box

- ☐ (a) The undersigned is or will be the builder of the dwelling.
- ☐ (b) The undersigned proposes to acquire the dwelling as a trade-in house in connection with the sale of another dwelling. Copy of purchase contract attached.
- ☐ (c) The undersigned proposes to purchase the dwelling from a person who intends to use the sale proceeds to purchase another dwelling. Copy of purchase contract attached.
- ☐ (d) The undersigned is the owner of the property and intends to use the proceeds of the loan to purchase another house for his occupancy.

(2) The undersigned will not rent for a rental term of less than thirty (30) days or more than sixty (60) days, sell (except where the insured mortgage is paid in full as an incident of the sale), or occupy the property prior to the 18th amortization payment of the mortgage except with the prior written approval of the Federal Housing Commissioner. (An owner occupant who has checked (d) of Item (1) above need not obtain the approval of the Commissioner to occupy the property.)

(3) An amount not less than 15 percent of the original principal of the mortgage has been or will be deposited in an escrow, trust, or special account. If the property is not sold prior to the due date of the 18th amortization payment of the mortgage to a purchaser acceptable to the Federal Housing Commissioner who will occupy the property, assume, and agree to pay the mortgage indebtedness, the amount held in escrow, trust, or special account will be applied in reduction of the outstanding principal amount of the mortgage as of the due date of the 18th amortization payment of the mortgage.

(4) The application of the escrow will be mandatory, prepayment will not affect the monthly payments to be made by the mortgagor as required by the mortgage, and will not be used as a "riding" prepayment.

....
Mortgagor

....
Mortgagor

MORTGAGEE'S CERTIFICATE

Date..

To: FEDERAL HOUSING ADMINISTRATION

The undersigned, in order to induce the Federal Housing Commissioner to issue an Escrow Commitment to insure a mortgage loan on the property described in the application, certifies to the Federal Housing Commissoner and agrees that:

(1) An amount not less than 15 percent of the original principal of the mortgage proceeds has been or will be deposited in an escrow, trust, or special account.

(2) If the mortaged property is not sold prior to the due date of the 18th amortization payment of the mortgage to a purchaser acceptable to the Federal Housing Commissioner who will occupy the property, assume and agree to pay the mortgage indebtedness, the amount held in escrow, trust, or special account will be applied in reduction of the outstanding principal amount of the mortgage as a mandatory prepayment as of the due date of the 18th amortization payment of the mortgage.

(3) If the property is not sold by the due date of the 18th amortization payment, the Mortgagor will not be permitted to "ride" the prepayment by being relieved of the obligation of paying future monthly installments of escrow, principal and interest, and that the mandatory prepayment will serve solely to accelerate the maturity of the mortgage.

(4) Any portion of the fund held in escrow, trust, or special account, not applied to the mortgage in accordance with the applicable Regulations of the Federal Housing Commissioner shall be deducted from the amount of debentures to which the Mortgagee would otherwise be entitled if a claim for debentures is filed.

....
Mortgagee

By:..
(Signature and Title of Officer)

INSTRUCTIONS FOR USE

Each Example demonstrates a different use of the table

EXAMPLE 1: What constant monthly payment is required to amortize in full, a $20,000 loan; 6% interest; 15 years?

ANSWER: Locate factor in tables (6%, 15 years) .844; Multiply ($20,000 × .844) = $16,880. Move decimal 2 places to left = $168.80 per month.

EXAMPLE 2: What is the balance due on the loan (in Example 1) after making constant monthly payments for 5 years?

ANSWER: Locate factor in tables (6%, 10 years) 1.110. Divide factor into monthly payment ($168.80 ÷ 1.110) = $152.07, move decimal 2 places to right $15,207 is balance due. In this example, 6% for 10 years is used because it is the interest rate and amount of time left to retire the loan.

EXAMPLE 3: How much interest has been paid on the loan during the 5 year period?

ANSWER: Original loan for $20,000
Balance due on loan after
5 years (from Ex. 2) 15,207

Amount of principal paid in 5 years $ 4,793
Total payment in 5 years is $168.80 per month for 60 months (5 years) × $168.80 = 10,128
Less Principal paid 4,793

Amount of interest paid in 5 years $ 5,335

EXAMPLE 4: What principal sum is due on a Note that has terms of 6% interest, $168.80 per month and will pay out in 15 years?

ANSWER: Locate factor in table (6%, 15 years) .844. Divide factor into payment (168.80 ÷ .844 = $2,000. Move decimal 2 places to right = $20,000.

EXAMPLE 5: What interest rate is required to retire a loan for $20,000, payments to be $168.80 per month for 15 years?

ANSWER: Divide $20,000 into payment (168.80 ÷ 20,000) = .00844. Move decimal 2 places to right = .844. This is factor for 15 years. Look in table for 15 years. Follow along horizontal line and find factor .844 appears in the 6% column.

EXAMPLE 6: How many years is required to retire a loan of $20,000, payments of $168.80 per month, 6% interest?

ANSWER: Divide $20,000 into payment (168.80 ÷ 20,000) = .00844. Move decimal 2 places to right = .844 which is factor for 6%. Locate factor in 6% column, read 15 years at side of table.

REMEMBER

When multiplying move decimal point in answer 2 places to left.

When dividing move decimal point in answer 2 places to right.

SIMPLIFIED COMPUTING TABLE

INTEREST RATES

YEARS	4%	4½%	5%	5½%	6%	6½%	7%	8%	9%	10%	YEARS
1	8.515	8.538	8.561	8.584	8.607	8.630	8.653	8.699	8.764	8.792	1
2	4.343	4.365	4.387	4.410	4.432	4.455	4.477	4.523	4.569	4.615	2
3	2.952	2.975	2.997	3.020	3.042	3.065	3.088	3.134	3.180	3.227	3
4	2.258	2.280	2.303	2.326	2.349	2.372	2.395	2.441	2.489	2.537	4
5	1.842	1.864	1.887	1.910	1.933	1.957	1.980	2.028	2.076	2.125	5
6	1.565	1.587	1.611	1.634	1.657	1.681	1.705	1.753	1.803	1.853	6
7	1.367	1.390	1.413	1.437	1.461	1.485	1.509	1.559	1.609	1.661	7
8	1.219	1.242	1.266	1.290	1.314	1.339	1.363	1.414	1.466	1.518	8
9	1.104	1.128	1.152	1.176	1.201	1.226	1.251	1.302	1.355	1.408	9
10	1.012	1.036	1.061	1.085	1.110	1.136	1.161	1.213	1.267	1.322	10
11	.938	.962	.987	1.011	1.037	1.062	1.088	1.142	1.197	1.252	11
12	.876	.900	.925	.950	.976	1.002	1.028	1.083	1.139	1.196	12
13	.823	.848	.873	.899	.925	.951	.978	1.033	1.090	1.148	13
14	.778	.803	.829	.855	.881	.908	.935	.991	1.049	1.108	14
15	.740	.765	.791	.817	.844	.871	.899	.956	1.015	1.075	15
16	.706	.732	.758	.784	.811	.839	.867	.925	.985	1.046	16
17	.676	.702	.729	.756	.783	.811	.840	.898	.959	1.022	17
18	.650	.676	.703	.730	.758	.787	.816	.875	.937	1.000	18
19	.627	.653	.680	.708	.736	.765	.794	.855	.917	.982	19
20	.606	.633	.660	.688	.716	.746	.775	.837	.900	.966	20
21	.587	.614	.642	.670	.699	.728	.758	.821	.885	.951	21
22	.570	.597	.625	.654	.683	.713	.743	.806	.872	.939	22
23	.555	.582	.610	.639	.669	.699	.730	.794	.860	.928	23
24	.541	.568	.597	.626	.656	.687	.718	.782	.849	.918	24
25	.528	.556	.586	.614	.644	.675	.707	.772	.840	.909	25
26	.516	.544	.573	.603	.634	.665	.697	.763	.831	.902	26
27	.505	.534	.564	.593	.624	.656	.688	.754	.823	.896	27
28	.495	.524	.554	.584	.615	.647	.680	.747	.817	.888	28
29	.486	.515	.545	.576	.607	.639	.672	.740	.813	.883	29
30	.477	.507	.537	.568	.600	.632	.665	.734	.805	.878	30
31	.469	.499	.529	.561	.593	.626	.659	.728	.800	.873	31
32	.462	.492	.522	.554	.586	.620	.653	.723	.796	.870	32
33	.455	.485	.512	.548	.581	.614	.648	.718	.792	.866	33
34	.449	.479	.510	.542	.575	.609	.643	.714	.788	.863	34
35	.443	.473	.505	.537	.570	.604	.639	.710	.784	.860	35
36	.437	.468	.500	.532	.566	.600	.635	.707	.782	.858	36
37	.432	.463	.495	.528	.561	.596	.631	.704	.778	.855	37
38	.427	.458	.490	.523	.557	.592	.628	.701	.776	.853	38
39	.422	.454	.486	.519	.554	.589	.624	.698	.774	.852	39
40	.418	.450	.482	.516	.550	.586	.621	.695	.772	.849	40
YEARS	4%	4½%	5%	5½%	6%	6½%	7%	8%	9%	10%	YEARS

INTEREST RATES

FHA 203-B
OWNER OCCUPANT

DOWN PAYMENT

97% of First	$15,000	Maximum loan on this program is	$33,000
90% of Next	$10,000	Maximum for Duplex & Triplex is	$35.750
80% of Remainder		Maximum for Fourplex is	$41,250
		FHA loans are made in increments of	$50.00
Eligibility		Any competent adult.	

Down payment and impounds are to be paid by the buyer from his own funds.
Down payment is not to be borrowed or in the form of secondary financing.

MMI

ALL FHA LOANS INCLUDE MUTUAL MORTGAGE INSURANCE (MMI) WITH THE EXCEPTION OF THE "FHA 222 IN SERVICE LOAN."

MMI IS FHAs INSURANCE PREMIUM, collected by the mortgage company and paid to FHA on an annual basis. This premium is FHAs fee and has nothing to do with fire or mortgage insurance.

The MMI premium is ½ of 1% of the original loan amount and is paid by the borrower each month with the payment. Amortized over the full term of the loan.

APPRAISAL

FEE $40.00 SINGLE FAMILY TO FOURPLEX

Remember the most acceptable appraisal in the real estate market today is the FHA appraisal.

The FHA appraisal is good for six months and renewal for an additional six months.
THE RENEWAL FEE IS $25.00
comparables: Should be left for the appraiser at the property, or given to him.
On all FHA loans seller must provide a current termite report.

SUGGESTED DEPOSIT RECEIPT

Buyer to obtain a new maximum FHA loan, payable principal, interest, MMI, and impounds.
Balance of the purchase price to be paid in cash.
Buyer to pay 1% of loan origination fee, initial impounds and normal closing costs.
Seller to pay points as required by lender (or specify).
Seller to comply with FHA requirements.

Buyer/Seller to pay for FHA appraisal.

(The above is suggested wording only, and not necessarily correct in every case.)

March 1971

CALIFORNIA MORTGAGE SERVICE

FHA 222 IN SERVICE LOAN

DOWN PAYMENT

97% of First .... $15,000 MAXIMUM LOAN
90% of Next .... $10,000 Must be a single unit.
85% of Remainder

Eligibility .... Any person serving in the Armed Forces of the United States. who has served a minimum of two years active duty.

Down payment and impounds are to be paid by the buyer from his own funds. Down payment is not to be borrowed or in the form of secondary financing.

MMI

Mutual Mortgage Insurance in this program is paid by the department of Defense, or in the case of Coast Guard personnel, by the Treasury Department.

To figure the payment on this loan, use the V.A. chart at the current rate of interest.

At such time as the borrower is released from military service, the MMI premium payment is assumed by him.

GENERAL INFORMATION

Same appraisal as the regular FHA loan.

Veteran would also be eligible for a VA loan and Special Terms for Vetran loan (FHA VET).

This loan would be most helpful to higher income military personnel, such as officers who do not want to use their VA eligibility, but still wish to take advantage of a slightly lower payment.

SERVICEMEN MUST OBTAIN FORM DD802 FROM APPROPRIATE MILITARY AUTHORITIES PROPERLY EXECUTED IN FOUR COPIES.

SUGGESTED DEPOSIT RECEIPT

Buyer to obtain a new maximum FHA in-service loan payable principal, interest and impounds. (MMI is omitted)
Balance of the purchase price is to be paid in cash.
Buyer to pay 1% loan origination fee, initial impounds and normal closing costs.
Seller to pay points as required by lender, (or specify).
Seller to comply with FHA requirements.
Buyer/Seller to pay for FHA appraisal.

(The above is suggested wording only, and not necessarily correct in every case).

CALIFORNIA MORTGAGE SERVICE

March 1971

FHA – VA
SPECIAL TERMS FOR VETERANS

DOWN PAYMENT

* 100% on the first $15,000
90% of next $10,000
85% of remainder

* Provided the veteran buyer pays at least $200.00 for pre-paid items.

MUST BE A SINGLE UNIT

FHA loans are in increments of $50.00

EXAMPLE

Selling price	$14,000	Selling price	$20,000
Closing costs	350	Closing costs	350
Mortgage	14,350	Mortgage	19,800
Impounds;	200	Impounds	200
Total Cost To Vet	200	Totat Cost To Vet	750

Buyer paying $200.00 or more impounds pays no down payment on the first $15,000
The above examples are figured using total acquisition.

ELIGIBILITY

Active duty not less than 90 days, Discharge other than Dishonorable.
Eligibility certificate is called "Certificate of Veteran Status." Form 8261
This form, signed by the veteran is sent to the Veterans Administration along with separation papers.
The form is approved and returned to the mortgage company.
The loan is then submitted to FHA for approval.
ENTITLEMENT DOES NOT EXPIRE AS IN THE VA PROGRAMS. ELIGIBLE VETS MAY USE THESE TERMS MANY TIMES.
Veterans who served less than 90 days may still be eligible if they served under hazerdous conditions.

SUGGESTED DEPOSIT RECEIPT

Buyer to obtain a new maximum FHA VET loan payable, principal, interest,
Balance of the purchase price to be paid in cash.
Buyer to pay 1% loan origination fee, initial impounds and normal closing costs.
Seller to pay points as required by lender (or specify).
Seller to comply with FHA requirements.

Buyer/Seller to pay for FHA appraisal.

(The above is suggested wording only, and not necessarily correct in every case).

CALIFORNIA MORTGAGE SERVICE

March 1971

FHA 221 D2
LOW INCOME BUYERS

DOWN PAYMENT

NO DOWN PAYMENT ON DISPLACED PERSONS.
3% DOWN PAYMENT ON OTHERS. (Figured on total acquisition (plus impounds).

The 3% down payment is figured by taking the sales price, adding the closing costs plus the impounds. Take 97% of the sum for the loan amount. (To the nearest lowest $50.00)

This program may be used to purchase up to four units.

EXAMPLE

Sales Price	$17,500	Sales Price	$20,000
Closing Costs	300	Closing Costs	350
Total Acquisition	17,800	Total Acquisition	20,350
plus impounds	200	plus impounds	200
	18,000		20,550
	x 97%		x 97%
	*$17,460		*$19,933
Maximum loan	$17,450	Maximum	$19,900
Buyers Investment	$ 550	Buyers Investment	$ 650

*Reduce to nearest lowest $50.00 increment

MAXIMUM LOAN AMOUNTS

		Your Area
Maximum loan for any home LOW COST AREA is	$18,000	________
Maximum loan four or more bedrooms LOW COST AREA is (Five or more persons in family buying)	$21,000	________

Maximum loan amounts vary for different areas throughout Southern California

(Low Cost)		(High Cost Areas)		Your Area
Maximum loan Duplexes	$24,000	Maximum loan Duplexes	$30,000	________
Maximum loan Triplexes	$32,400	Maximum loan Triplexes	$38,000	________
Maximum loan Fourplexes	$39,600	Maximum loan Fourplexes	$45,600	________

SUGGESTED DEPOSIT RECEIPT

Buyer to obtain a new maximum 221-D2 loan, payable principal, interest MMI, and impounds.
Balance of the purchase price to be paid in cash.
Buyer to pay 1% loan origination fee, initial impounds and normal closing costs.
Seller to pay points as required by lender (or specify).

Buyer/Seller to pay for FHA appraisal.

(The above is suggested wording only, and not necessarily correct in every case.)

CALIFORNIA MORTGAGE SERVICE

March 1971

VA PROGRAM

APPRAISAL

Appraisers are FEE appraisers, appointed by the Veteran Administration.
Veteran may pay for the CRV, only if his name appears on the request.
Loans are guaranteed on existing swellings one year old or older, or new construction built under FHA specifications.
CRV expires six months from date issued.
CRV never expires when issued in the name of a specific veteran.

COSTS	
Single family	$30.00
Duplex	$40.00
Triplex	$45.00
Fourplexes	$50.00

(Cost will increase for additional structures)

ELIGIBILITY

WW2	: Active service during the period Sept. 16, 1940 to July 25, 1947.
Korea	: Active service during the period June 27, 1950 to Jan. 31, 1955.
Public Law 358 (Cold War)	: Active service any time after January 31, 1955 – 181 days active service, any part of which was after Jan. 31, 1955 – 730 days continuous service after Jan. 31, 1955, never having been discharged.

To order "Certificate of Eligibility" Veterans separation papers (DD 214) for all periods of service are needed.

Six month active duty training programs are not eligible.

MORE ON ENLISTMENT

* WW2 AND KOREA
Veteran who has served on active duty not less than 90 days, any part of which occurred between September 16, 1940 and July 25, 1947 – WW2 – June 27, 1950 and Jan. 31, 1955 –Korea
Discharged under conditions other than dishonorable
Service connected disability – less that 90 days O.K.

* Service after Jan. 31, 1955 (so called Cold War)
Veteran who has served on active duty not less than 181 days, any part of which occurred after Jan. 31, 1955. Discharged under conditions other than Dishonorable or discharged for a service connected disability or who is now on active duty and has served a minimum of two years with a break.

ENTITLEMENT MORE THAN ONE LOAN

A VETERAN MAY BE ELIGIBLE FOR MORE THAN ONE LOAN

Re-instatement
- (1) Previous home must have been sold
- (2) Previous loan has been paid in full
- (3) Relocation was due to an urgent and compelling reason, such as health, military or job transfer.
- (4) Veteran must have need for a new home

Remaining Eligibility
Use of remaining eligibility is permissable even though veteran still has a VA loan in his name.

Eligibility under more than one program
If the veteran requalifies under a new program, he may receive a new entitlement if first home is sold even though his old loan is not paid off. It is required that said loan be current

March 1971

CALIFORNIA MORTGAGE SERVICE

FIRST PAYMENT DATE	Months Impounds	IMPORTANT DATES
April 1	1	First installment taxes due Nov. 1st.
May 1	2	Delinquent December 12th.
June 1	3	
July 1	4	Second installment taxes due Feb. 1st.
Aug. 1	5	Delinquent April 10th.
Sept. 1	6	
Oct. 1	7	
Nov. 1	8	
Dec. 1	2 or 9	2 If first half paid.
Jan. 1	3 or 10	
Feb. 1	0	With full year paid.
Mar. 1	0	With full year paid.
April 1	1	With full year paid.

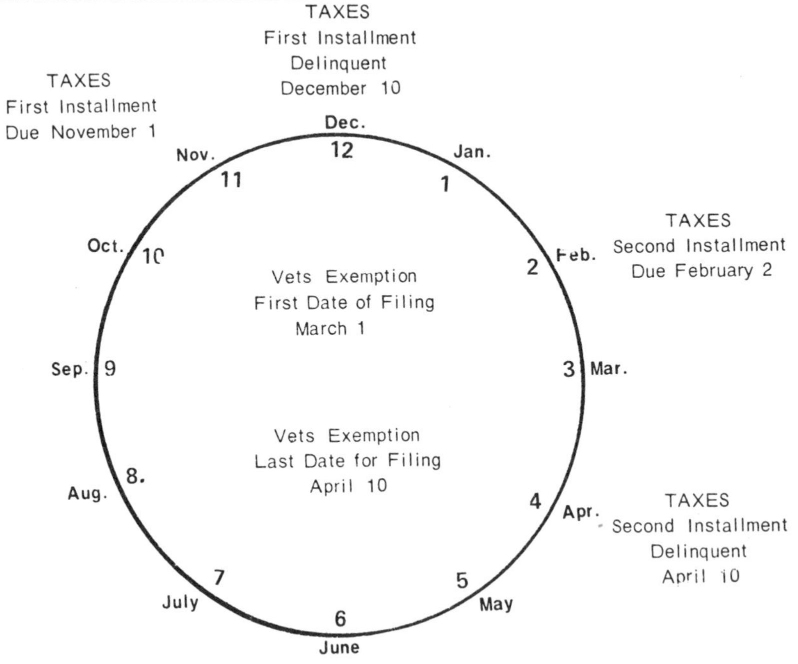

CALIFORNIA MORTGAGE SERVICE

March 1971

OTHER FHA INFORMATION

1. Any one person can own as many as seven units under FHA, but can obtain maximum loan only on the property being occupied. (25% equity requirement)
2. Prepayment penalty waived when new FHA loan is placed on home already having FHA loan.
3. Prepayment penalty clause outlaws in ten years.
4. Any Mortgagor can pay 15% in excess of required payments in any one year, without penalty, but most lenders require notification of additional payments 30 days in advance.
5. A second home can be purchased under FHA as a vacation home and the people buying such a vacation home can obtain a maximum FHA loan.
6. Anyone with sufficient equity can refinance their present home under FHA and include improvements at time of refinancing.

FEDERAL HOUSING ESTIMATED CLOSING COSTS

\$ 8,000.00 – \$11,000.00	\$200.00
\$11,000.00 – \$14,000.00	\$250.00
\$14,000.00 – \$18,000.00	\$300.00
\$18,000.00 – \$23,000.00	\$350.00
\$23,000.00 – \$28,000.00	\$ 400.00
\$28,000.00 – 34,000.00	\$450.00
\$34,000.00 – \$40,000.00	\$500.00

INTEREST RATE CHANGES

The following is a list of the interest rate changes for the FHA and VA and the effective dates of those changes:

	FHA	VA
5.25%	5/29/61	7/2/59
5.50%	2/7/66	3/3/66
5.75%	4/11/66	4/11/66
6.00%	10/3/66	10/3/66
6.75%	5/7/68	5/7/68
7.50%	1/24/69	1/24/69
8.50%	1/5/70	1/5/70
8.00%	12/2/70	12/2/70
7.50%	1/12/71	1/12/71
7.00%	2/18/71	2/18/71

Present Rate of Interest is –

CREDIT APPLICATIONS

In having buyers fill out credit applications, it is important that they be as complete as possible. Social Security numbers, account numbers of charge accounts and loans are most helpful. Military unit numbers and or military addresses of military personnel are most important. The more complete the credit application, the faster service the credit agencies are able to give.

CALIFORNIA MORTGAGE SERVICE

VA LOAN

BUYER'S COSTS

1. NO Down Payment required
2. NO more than 1% Loan Fee (based on loan amount)
3. NO Escrow Fee (must be paid by Seller)
4. Recording of Deed of Trust and Grant Deed
5. Tax Service Contract ($15.00)
6. Credit Report (not to exceed $10.00)
7. ALTA Lender's Title Policy (concurrent issue rate)
8. Tax Impounds (ours lowest available)
9. Fire Insurance and Impounds (total 14 months)
10. Prorate of Taxes
11. Adjusted Interest on New Loan
12. Appraisal Fee $30.00 if ordered by Veteran

SELLER'S COSTS

1. Discount (based on Buyer's Credit, Income and Property
2. Usual full Escrow Fee
3. Revenue Stamps ($1.10 per M)
4. Standard Owner's Title Policy
5. Pay-off of existing Encumbrances and Penalties (if any)
6. Impoundment Reserve Credit (if any)
7. Prorate of Taxes, etc. Payment of Assessments.
8. Termite Clearance and Repairs (if necessary)
9. BROKER'S COMMISSION

REMEMBER

In a VA Sale – the Seller can pay ANY or ALL of the Vet's costs listed above – absolutely NO money to Buyer.

FHA LOAN

BUYER'S COSTS

1. Down Payment (as required per FHA program used)
CALL OUR OFFICE BELOW FOR HELP IN DETERMINING
2. NO more than 1% Loan Fee (based on loan amount)
3. ½ of Escrow Fee (not to exceed $65.00)
4. Recording of Deed of Trust and Grant Deed
5. Tax Service Contract ($15.00)
6. Credit Report (not to exceed $10.00)
7. ALTA Lender's Title Policy (concurrent issue rate)
8. FHA Mortgage Insurance Premium (one month)
9. Tax Impounds (ours lowest available)
10. Fire Insurance and Impounds (total 14 months)
11. Prorate of Taxes
12. Adjusted Interest on New Loan
13. Appraisal Fee $35.00

SELLER'S COSTS

1. Discount (based on Buyer's Credit, Income and Property)
CALL OUR OFFICE BELOW TO HELP DETERMINE AMOUNT
2. Escrow Fee – all over $65.00
3. Revenue Stamps ($1.10 per M)
4. Standard Owner's Title Policy
5. Pay-off of existing Encumbrances and Penalties (if any)
6. Impoundment Reserve Credit (if any)
7. Prorate of Taxes, etc. Payment of Assessments.
8. Termite Clearance and Repairs (if necessary)
9. BROKER'S COMMISSION

HELPFUL HINTS

Buyer's cost, items two through seven, are included in FHA's appraisal. They may be financed for Buyers to reduce cash investment and paid by SELLER under any FHA program. Items eight through ten (prepaids) must be paid in cash by Buyer except the FHA 221-d-2 program. Under 221, prepaids may be added to Sales Price to reduce Buyer's cash required.

CALIFORNIA MORTGAGE SERVICE

March 1971

FHA LOAN-TO-VALUE RATIOS

1970 HOUSING LAW

	MAXIMUM LOAN			MAXIMUM LOAN	
FHA VALUE	FHA REGULAR	FHA-VETERAN	FHA VALUE	FHA REGULAR	FHA VETERAN
14,400	13,950	14,400	25,600	24,000	24,500
14,500	14,050	14,500	25,800	24,150	24,650
14,600	14,150	14,600	26,000	24,350	24,850
14,800	14,350	14,800	26,200	24,500	25,000
15,000	14,550	15,000	26,400	24,650	25,150
15,200	14,700	15,150	26,500	24,750	25,250
15,400	14,900	15,350	26,600	24,800	25,350
15,500	15,000	15,450	26,800	24,950	25,500
15,600	15,050	15,500	27,000	25,150	25,700
15,800	15,250	15,700	27,200	25,200	25,850
16,000	15,400	15,900	27,400	25,450	26,000
16,200	15,600	16,050	27,500	25,550	26,100
16,400	15,800	16,250	27,600	25,600	26,200
16,500	15,900	16,350	27,800	25,750	26,350
16,600	15,950	16,400	28,000	25,950	26,550
16,800	16,150	16,600	28,200	26,100	26,700
17,000	16,350	16,800	28,400	26,250	26,850
17,200	16,500	16,950	28,500	26,350	26,950
17,400	16,700	17,150	28,600	26,400	27,050
17,500	16,800	17,250	28,800	26,550	27,200
17,600	16,850	17,300	29,000	26,750	27,400
17,800	17,050	17,500	29,200	26,900	27,550
18,000	17,250	17,700	29,400	27,050	27,700
18,200	17,400	17,850	29,500	27,150	27,800
18,400	17,600	18,050	29,600	27,200	27,900
18,500	17,700	18,150	29,800	27,350	28,050
18,600	17,750	18,200	30,000	27,550	28,250
18,800	17,950	18,400	30,200	27,700	28,400
19,000	18,150	18,600	30,400	27,850	28,550
19,200	18,300	18,750	30,500	27,950	28,650
19,400	18,500	18,950	30,600	28,800	28,750
19,500	18,600	19,050	30,800	28,150	28,900
19,600	18,650	19,100	31,000	28,350	29,100
19,800	18,850	19,300	31,200	28,500	29,250
20,000	19,050	19,500	31,400	28,650	29,400
20,200	19,200	19,650	31,500	28,750	29,500
20,400	19,400	19,850	31,600	28,800	29,600
20,500	19,500	19,950	31,800	28,950	29.750
20,600	19,550	20,000	32,000	29,150	29,950
20,800	19,750	20,200	32,200	29,300	30,100
21,000	19,950	20,400	32,400	29,450	30,250
21,200	20,100	20,550	32,500	29,550	30,350
21,400	20,300	20,750	32,600	29,600	30,400
21,500	20,400	20,850	32,800	29,750	30,600
21,600	20,450	20,900	33,000	29,950	30,800
21,800	20,650	21,100	33,200	30,100	30,950
22,000	20,850	21,300	33,400	30,250	31,100
22,200	21,000	21,450	33,500	30,350	31,200
22,400	21,200	21,650	33,600	30,400	31,300
22,500	21,300	21,750	33,800	30,550	31,450
22,600	21,350	21,800	34,000	30,750	31,650
22,800	21,550	22,000	34,200	30,900	31,800
23,000	21,750	22,200	34,400	31,050	31,950
23,200	21,900	22,350	34,500	31,150	32,050
23,400	22,100	22,550	34,600	31,200	32,150
23,500	22,200	22,650	34,800	31,350	32,300
23,600	22,250	22,700	35,000	31,550	32,500
23,800	22,400	22,900	35,200	31,700	32,650
24,000	22,650	23,100	35,400	31,850	32,800
24,200	22,800	23,250	35,500	31,950	32,900
24,400	23,000	23,450	34,400	32,000	33,000
24,500	23,100	23,550	35,800	32,150	33,000
24,600	23,150	23,600	36,000	32,350	33,000
24,800	23,350	23,800	36,200	32,500	33,000
25,000	23,550	24,000	35,400	32,650	33,000
25,200	23,700	24,150	36,500	32,750	33,000
25,400	23,850	24,300	36,700	32,900	33,000
25,500	23,950	24,400	36,850	33,000	33,000

*If Vet invests $200 or more in impounds.
Above is for owner-occupied, proposed or over 1 year old.

March 1971

INCOME TO MONTHLY PAYMENT RATIOS

Monthly Payment Including Taxes, Ins.	Income Required At: 4 to 1	4½ to 1	5 to 1
100	400.00	450.00	500.00
105	420.00	472.00	525.00
110	440.00	495.00	550.00
115	460.00	518.00	575.00
120	480.00	540.00	600.00
125	500.00	563.00	625.00
130	520.00	585.00	650.00
135	540.00	608.00	675.00
140	560.00	630.00	700.00
145	580.00	653.00	725.00
150	600.00	675.00	750.00
155	620.00	698.00	775.00
160	640.00	720.00	800.00
165	660.00	743.00	825.00
170	680.00	765.00	850.00
175	700.00	788.00	875.00
180	720.00	810.00	900.00
185	740.00	833.00	925.00
190	760.00	855.00	950.00
195	780.00	878.00	975.00
200	800.00	900.00	1,000.00
205	820.00	923.00	1,025.00
210	840.00	945.00	1,050.00
215	860.00	968.00	1,075.00
220	880.00	990.00	1,100.00
225	900.00	1,013.00	1,125.00
230	920.00	1,035.00	1,150.00
235	940.00	1,058.00	1,175.00
240	960.00	1,080.00	1,200.00
245	980.00	1,103.00	1,225.00
250	1,000.00	1,125.00	1,250.00
255	1,020.00	1,148.00	1,275.00
260	1,040.00	1,170.00	1,300.00
265	1,060.00	1,193.00	1,325.00
270	1,080.00	1,215.00	1,350.00
275	1,100.00	1,238.00	1,375.00
280	1,120.00	1,260.00	1,400.00
285	1,140.00	1,283.00	1,425.00
290	1,160.00	1,305.00	1,450.00
295	1,180.00	1,328.00	1,475.00
300	1,200.00	1,350.00	1,500.00
305	1,220.00	1,373.00	1,525.00
310	1,240.00	1,395.00	1,550.00
315	1,260.00	1,418.00	1,575.00
320	1,280.00	1,440.00	1,600.00
325	1,300.00	1,463.00	1,625.00
330	1,320.00	1,485.00	1,650.00
335	1,340.00	1,508.00	1,675.00
340	1,360.00	1,530.00	1,700.00
345	1,380.00	1,553.00	1,725.00
350	1,400.00	1,575.00	1,750.00
355	1,420.00	1,598.00	1,775.00
360	1,440.00	1,620.00	1,800.00
365	1,460.00	1,643.00	1,825.00
370	1,480.00	1,665.00	1,850.00
375	1,500.00	1,688.00	1,875.00
380	1,520.00	1,710.00	1,900.00

TABLE OF INCOME CONVERSIONS

Per Hour	Per Week	Per Month	Per Year	Per Hour	Per Week	Per Month	Per Per Year
1.00	40.00	173.33	2,080.00	3.50	140.00	606.67	7,280.00
1.25	50.00	216.67	2,600.00	3.55	142.00	615.33	7,384.00
1.50	60.00	260.00	3,120.00	3.60	144.00	624.00	7,488.00
1.55	62.00	268.67	3,224.00	3.65	146.00	632.67	7,592.00
1.60	64.00	277.33	3,228.00	3.70	148.00	641.33	7,696.00
1.65	66.00	286.00	3,432.00	3.75	150.00	650.00	7,800.00
1.70	68.00	294.67	3,536.00	3.80	152.00	658.67	7,904.00
1.75	70.00	303.33	3,640.00	3.85	154.00	667.33	8,008.00
1.80	72.00	312.00	3,744.00	3.90	156.00	676.00	8,112.00
1.85	74.00	320.67	3,848.00	3.95	158.00	684.67	8,216.00
1.90	76.00	329.33	3,952.00	4.00	160.00	693.33	8,320.00
2.00	80.00	346.67	4,160.00	4.10	164.00	710.67	8,528.00
2.05	82.00	355.33	4,264.00	4.15	166.00	719.33	8,632.00
2.10	84.00	364.00	4,368.00	4.20	168.00	728.00	8,736.00
2.15	86.00	372.67	4,472.00	4.25	170.00	736.67	8,840.00
2.20	88.00	381.33	4,576.00	4.30	172.00	745.33	8,944.00
2.25	90.00	390.00	4,680.00	4.35	174.00	754.00	9,048.00
2.30	92.00	398.67	4,784.00	4.40	176.00	762.67	9,152.00
2.35	94.00	407.33	4,888.00	4.45	178.00	771.33	9,256.00
2.40	96.00	416.00	4,992.00	4.50	180.00	780.00	9,360.00
2.45	98.00	424.67	5,096.00	4.55	182.00	788.67	9,464.00
2.50	100.00	433.33	5,200.00	4.60	184.00	797.33	9,568.00
2.55	102.00	442.00	5,304.00	4.65	186.00	806.00	9,672,00
2.60	104.00	450.67	5,408.00	4.70	188.00	814.67	9,776.00
2.65	106.00	459.33	5,512.00	4.75	190.00	823.33	9,880.00
2.70	108.00	468.00	5,616.00	4.80	192.00	832.00	9,984.00
2.75	110.00	476.67	5,720.00	4.85	194.00	840.67	10,088.00
2.80	112.00	485.33	5,824.00	4.90	196.00	849.33	10,192.00
2.85	114.00	494.00	5,928.00	4.95	198.00	858.00	10,296.00
2.90	116.00	502.67	6,032.00	5.00	200.00	866.66	10,400.00
2.95	118.00	511.33	6,136.00	5.05	202.00	875.27	10,504.00
3.00	120.00	520.00	6,240.00	5.10	204.00	884.00	10,608.00
3.05	122.00	528.67	6,344.00	5.20	208.00	901.34	10,816.00
3.10	124.00	537.33	6,448.00	5.30	212.00	918.67	11,024.00
3.15	126.00	546.00	6,552.00	5.40	216.00	936.00	11,232.00
3.20	128.00	554.67	6,656.00	5.50	220.00	953.34	11,440.00
3.25	130.00	563.33	6,760.00	5.60	224.00	970.67	11,648.00
3.30	132.00	572.00	6,864.00	5.70	228.00	988.00	11,856.00
3.35	134.00	580.67	6,968.00	5.80	232.00	1005.34	12,064.00
3.40	136.00	589.33	7,072.00	5.90	236.00	1022.67	12,272.00
3.45	138.00	598.00	7,176.00	6.00	240.00	1040.00	12,480.00

NEW 7% INTEREST RATES

LOAN AMOUNT	ɣA P&I	FHA P&I-MMI	LOAN AMOUNT	VA P&I	FHA P&I MMI	LOAN AMOUNT	VA P&I	FHA P&I-MMI
$12,000.00	$ 80.28	$ 84.90	$20,000.00	$133.80	$141.12	$ 28,000.00	$187.32	198.10
12,100.00	80.95	85.60	20,100.00	134.47	142.21	28,100.00	187.99	198.80
12,200.00	81.62	86.31	20,200.00	135.14	142.91	28,200.00	188.66	199.51
12,300.00	82.29	87.10	20,300.00	135.81	143.62	28,300.00	189.33	200.22
12,400.00	82.95	87.72	20,400.00	136.48	144.32	28,400.00	190.00	200.93
12,500.00	83.62	88.43	20,500.00	137.15	145.03	28,500.00	190.67	201.63
12,600.00	84.29	89.55	20,600.00	137.81	145.74	28,600.00	191.33	202.34
12,700.00	84.96	89.81	20,700.00	138.48	146.44	28,700.00	192.00	203.05
12,800.00	85.63	90.56	20,800.00	139.15	147.16	28,800.00	192.67	203.76
12,900.00	86.30	91.26	20,900.00	139.82	147.86	29,000.00	193.34	204.46
13,000.00	86.97	91.97	21,000.00	140.49	148.57	28,900.00	194.01	205.17
13,100.00	87.64	92.68	21,100.00	141.16	149.28	29,100.00	194.68	205.88
13,200.00	88.30	93.38	21,200.00	141.83	149.98	29,200.00	195.35	206.59
13,300,00	88.98	94.10	21,300.00	142.50	150.69	29,300.00	196.02	207.29
13,400.00	89.65	94.80	21,400.00	143.17	151.39	29,400.00	196.69	208.00
13,500.00	90.32	95.51	21,500.00	143.84	152.11	29,500.00	197.36	208.71
13,600.00	90.98	96.22	21,600.00	144.50	152.82	29,600.00	198.02	209.42
13,700.00	91.65	96.92	21,700.00	145.17	153.52	29,700.00	198.69	210.12
13,800.00	92.32	97.62	21,800.00	145.84	154.23	29,800.00	199.36	210.83
13,900.00	92.99	98.33	21,900.00	146.51	154.93	29,900.00	200.03	211.54
14,000.00	93.66	99.05	22,000.00	147.18	155.64	30,000.00	200.70	212.25
14,100.00	94.33	99.76	22,100.00	147.85	156.35	30,100.00	201.37	212.95
14,200.00	95.00	100.46	22,200.00	148.52	157.06	30,200.00	202.04	213.66
14,300.00	95.67	101.17	22,300.00	149.19	157.77	30,300.00	202.71	214.37
14,400.00	96.34	101.87	22,400.00	149.86	158.48	30,400.00	203.38	215.08
14,500.00	97.01	102.58	22,500.00	150.53	159.18	30,500.00	204.05	215.78
14,600.00	97.67	103.29	22,600.00	151.19	159.89	30,600.00	204.71	216.49
14,700.00	98.34	104.00	22,700.00	151.86	160.60	30,700.00	205.38	217.20
14,800.00	99.01	104.71	22,800.00	152.53	161.31	30,800.00	206.05	217.91
14,900.00	99.68	105.41	22,900.00	153.20	162.01	30,900.00	206.72	218.61
15,000.00	100.35	106.12	23,000.00	153.87	162.72	31,000.00	207.39	219.32
15,100.00	101.02	106.83	23,100.00	154.54	163.43	31,100.00	208.06	220.03
15,200.00	101.69	107.53	23,200.00	155.21	164.14	31,200.00	208.73	220.74
15 300.00	102.36	108.24	23,300.00	155.88	164.84	31,300.00	209.40	221.44
15,400.00	103.03	108.95	23,400.00	156.55	165.55	31,400.00	210.07	222.15
15,500.00	103.70	109.66	23,500.00	157.22	166.26	31,500.00	210.74	222.86
15,600.00	104.36	110.37	23,600.00	157.88	166.97	31,600.00	211.40	223.57
15,700.00	105.03	111.07	23,700.00	158.55	167.67	31,700.00	212.07	224.27
15,800.00	105.70	111.78	23,800.00	159.22	168.38	31,800.00	212.74	224.98
15,900.00	106.37	112.48	23,900.00	159.89	169.09	31.900.00	213.41	225.69
16,000.00	107.04	113.20	24,000.00	160.56	169.80	32,000.00	214.08	226.40
16,100.00	107.71	113.91	24,100.00	161.23	170.50	32,100.00	214.75	227.10
16,200.00	108.38	114.61	24,200.00	161.90	171.21	32,200.00	215.42	227.81
16,300.00	109.47	115.32	24,300.00	162.57	171.92	32,300.00	216.09	228.52
16,400.00	109.72	116.02	24,400.00	163.24	172.63	32,400.00	216.76	229.23
16,500.00	110.39	116.73	24,500.00	163.91	173.33	32,500.00	217.43	229.93
16,600.00	111.05	117.44	24,600.00	164.57	174.04	32,600.00	218.09	230.64
16,700.00	111.72	118.15	24,700.00	165.24	174.75	32,700.00	218.76	231.35
16,800.00	112.39	118.86	24,800.00	165.91	175.46	32,800.00	219.43	232.06
16,900.00	113.06	119.56	24,900.00	166.58	176.16	32,900.00	220.10	232.76
17,000.00	113.73	120.27	25,000.00	167.25	176.87	33,000.00	220.77	233.47
17,100.00	114.40	120.98	25,100.00	167.92	177.58	33,100.00	221.44	234.18
17,200.00	115.07	121.68	25,200.00	168.59	178.29	33,200.00	222.11	234.89
17,300.00	115.74	122.39	25,300.00	169.26	178.99	33,300.00	222.78	235.59
17,400.00	116.41	123.10	25,400.00	169.93	179.70	33,400.00	223.45	236.30
17,500.00	117.08	123.81	25,500.00	170.60	180.41	33,500.00	224.12	237.01
17,600.00	117.74	124.52	25,600.00	171.26	181.12	33,600.00	224.78	237.72
17,700.00	118.41	125.22	25,700.00	171.93	181.82	33,700.00	225.45	238.42
17,800.00	119.08	125.93	25,800.00	172.60	182.53	33,800.00	226.12	239.13
17,900.00	119.75	126.63	25,900.00	173.27	183.24	33,900.00	226.79	239.84
18,000.00	120.42	127.34	26,000.00	173.94	183.95	34,000.00	227.46	240.55
18,100.00	121.09	128.06	26,100.00	174.61	184.65	34,100.00	228.13	241.25
18,200.00	121.76	128.76	26,200.00	175.28	185.36	34,200.00	228.80	241.96
18,300.00	122.43	129.47	26,300.00	175.95	186.07	34,300.00	229.47	242.67
18,400.00	123.10	130.17	26,400.00	176.62	186.78	34,400.00	230.14	243.38
18,500.00	123.77	130.88	26,500.00	177.29	187.48	34,500.00	230.81	244.08
18,600.00	124.43	131.59	26,600.00	177.95	188.19	34,600.00	231.47	244.79
18,700.00	125.10	132.29	26,700.00	178.62	188.90	34,700.00	232.14	245.50
18,800.00	125.77	133.01	26,800.00	179.29	189.61	34,800.00	232.81	246.21
18,900.00	126.44	133.71	26,900.00	179.96	190.31	34,900.00	233.48	246.91
19,000.00	127.11	134.42	27,000.00	180.63	191.02	35,000.00	234.15	247.62
19,100.00	127.78	135.13	27,100.00	181.30	191.73	35,100.00	234.82	248.33
19,200.00	128.45	135.83	27,200.00	181.97	192.44	35,200.00	235.49	249.04
19,300.00	129.12	136.54	27,300.00	182.64	193.14	35,300.00	236.16	249.74
19,400.00	129.79	137.24	27,400.00	183.31	193.85	35,400.00	236.83	250.45
19,500.00	130.46	137.96	27,500.00	183.98	194.56	35,500.00	237.50	251.16
19,600.00	131.12	138.67	27,600.00	184.64	195.27	35,600.00	238.16	251.87
19,700.00	131.79	139.37	27,700.00	185.31	195.97	35,700.00	238.83	252.57
19,800.00	132.46	140.08	27,800.00	185.98	196.68	35,800.00	239.50	253.28
19,900.00	133.13	140.78	27,900.00	186.65	197.39	35,900.00	240.17	253.99

FHA PAYMENTS Include Principal, Interest and Mutual Mortgage Insurance for 30 Years.

V A PAYMENTS Include Principal and Interest 29½ Years.

March 1971

Buyers Confidential Financial Status

CALIFORNIA REAL ESTATE ASSOCIATION STANDARD FORM

Down Payment $________ Date: ________
Property Address ________ Sales Price: $________
Type Loan Req: ________ Loan Amount $________ Interest________%, Years #________
P.I. Mo.: ________ Taxes: Ann (NV) $________/mo. $________, Ins.: Mo. $________, PITI± ________
Name: ________ Wife's Name: ________
Age: ________ Date Married: ________ Age: ________
Number of Dependents: ________ Ages of Dependents: ________
Present Address: ________ City: ________ St: ________ Phone: ________
Own/Rent ________ Length of Residence: ________
Former address (if not 3 years at present address): ________
Length of residence: ________ City: ________ St: ________

EMPLOYMENT: Must Cover Two Years

APPLICANT:

Employer: ________
Address: ________
Type of Business: ________
Position: ________
Supervisor: ________
Length of Employment: ________

Former Employer: ________
Address: ________
Type of Business: ________
Position: ________
Supervisor: ________
Length of Employment: ________

WIFE:

Employer: ________
Address: ________
Type of Business: ________
Position: ________
Supervisor: ________
Length of Employment: ________

Former Employer: ________
Address: ________
Type of Business: ________
Position: ________
Supervisor: ________
Length of Employment: ________

Describe Second Job If Any: ________

INCOME: (Monthly)

Base Pay (Gross) . . . .$________
Overtime (Ann. Av./mo.) . . . . ________
Second Job (Ann. Av./mo.) . . ________
Wife's Base Pay (Gross) . . . . . ________
Wife's Overtime (Ann. Av./mo.) ________
*Income from R.E. (Net) . . . . . ________
Other Income . . . . ________
Total Income Monthly . . . . . .$________
Annual: (Mo. × 12) . . . .$________

(Buyer does not complete this Section:)

Net Monthly Income $________
PITI $________ =
________ (×) Factor
2½ × Annual Income $________

ASSETS:

Cash on Hand . . . .$________
Bank Accounts . . . . ________
Savings Bonds . . . . ________
Securities . . . . ________
Other: ________ ________
TOTAL . . . .$________
Automobile: ________$________
Automobile: ________ ________
Furniture . . . . ________
Personal Property: . . . . ________
Other: ________ ________
TOTAL . . . .$________
*Real Estate Owned:
(1) Value Estimate . . . .$________
Address: ________
(2) Value Estimate . . . .$________
Address: ________
TOTAL ASSETS . . . .$________

Have you ever filed bankruptcy? ________
Do you pay child support? ________
Do you receive child support? ________

LIABILITIES:

Installment Payments:
(1) To:________Bal. $________ Mo. $________
(2) To:________Bal. $________ Mo. $________
(3) To:________Bal. $________ Mo. $________
(4) To:________Bal. $________ Mo. $________
Number of months to go on above accounts:
(1) ________ (2) ________ (3) ________ (4) ________
Automobile Loan Bal. $________ mo. $________
Automobile Loan Bal. $________ mo. $________
Liens or Judgments:
To:________ Bal. $________ mo. $________
To:________ Bal. $________ mo. $________
Total Current Monthly Payments: $________
*Mortgage Payments:
(1) Balance Owed $________ mo. pay________
(2) Balance Owed $________ mo. pay________
TOTAL LIABILITIES $________ Mo. $________

Any current suits or judgments? ________
Do you pay alimony? ________
Do you receive alimony? ________

From what source will balance of funds come from if not shown above? ________

X________ X________
(signature) **(signature)**

(Form BCFS-11) address California Real Estate Association, 520 So. Grand Ave., Los Angeles 90017.

SEPARATE RECORD FOR EACH BENEFICIARY OR TRANSACTION

CALIFORNIA REAL ESTATE ASSOCIATION STANDARD FORM

Description	Discharge of Trust Accountability For Funds Paid Out			Trust Accountability For Funds Received		Balance of Account
	Date of Check	Check No.	Amount	Date of Deposit	Amount	

Reprinted from Advanced Real Estate Sales,
Book No. 17 Published 1968 by:
California Real Estate Association
520 South Grand Avenue
Los Angeles, California 90017

Form TF-11-4

For these forms, address
California Real Estate Association
520 South Grand Avenue, Los Angeles 90017

CALIFORNIA REAL ESTATE ASSOCIATION STANDARD FORM

Record of All Trust Funds Received - Not Placed in Brokers Trust Account

TRUST FUNDS INCLUDING UNCASHED CHECKS RECEIVED			Description Property or Identification	Disposition of Uncashed Checks or Other Funds Forwarded to Escrow or Principal	Date Forwarded
Date Received	Received From	Amount			

CALIFORNIA REAL ESTATE ASSOCIATION STANDARD FORM

Columnar Record of All Trust Funds Received and Paid Out

TRUST FUND BANK ACCOUNT											
19 Date Received	From Whom Received Or To Whom Paid	Description	RECEIVED				PAID OUT				Daily Balance of Trust Bank Account
			Amount Received	Cross Ref.	Date of Deposit	xx	Amount Paid Out	Check No.	Date of Check	xx	

30-DAY RENTAL TABLE

PER MONTH

DAYS	47.00	47.50	48.00	49.00	50.00	100.00		
1	1.56	1.58	1.60	1.63	1.67	3.33		
2	3.13	3.17	3.20	3.27	3.33	6.67		
3	4.70	4.75	4.80	4.90	5.00	10.00		
4	6.26	6.33	6.40	6.53	6.67	13.33		
5	7.73	7.92	8.00	8.17	8.33	16.67		
6	9.40	9.50	9.60	9.80	10.00	20.00		
7	10.96	11.08	11.20	11.43	11.67	23.33		
8	12.53	12.67	12.80	13.07	13.33	26.67		
9	14.10	14.25	14.40	14.70	15.00	30.00		
10	15.66	15.83	16.00	16.33	16.67	33.33		
11	17.23	17.42	17.60	17.97	18.33	36.67		
12	18.80	19.00	19.20	19.60	20.00	40.00		
13	20.36	20.58	20.80	21.23	21.67	43.33		
14	21.93	22.17	22.40	22.87	23.33	46.67		
15	23.50	23.75	24.00	24.50	25.00	50.00		
16	25.06	25.33	25.60	26.13	26.67	53.33		
17	26.63	26.92	27.20	27.77	28.33	56.67		
18	28.20	28.50	28.80	29.40	30.00	60.00		
19	29.76	30.08	30.40	31.03	31.67	63.33		
20	31.33	31.67	32.00	32.67	33.33	66.67		
21	32.90	33.25	33.60	34.30	35.00	70.00		
22	34.46	34.83	35.20	35.93	36.67	73.33		
23	36.03	36.42	36.80	37.57	38.33	76.67		
24	37.60	38.00	38.40	39.20	40.00	80.00		
25	39.05	39.58	40.00	40.83	41.67	83.33		
26	40.73	41.17	41.60	42.47	43.33	86.67		
27	42.30	42.75	43.20	44.10	45.00	90.00		
28	43.86	44.33	44.80	45.73	46.67	93.33		
29	45.43	45.92	46.40	47.37	48.33	96.67		

SECURITY TITLE
INSURANCE COMPANY

TAX ADJUSTMENT TABLE

DAY	JAN. JULY	FEB. AUG.	MAR. SEPT.	APR. OCT.	MAY NOV.	JUNE DEC.
1	.0000	.1667	.3333	.5000	.6667	.8333
2	.0056	.1722	.3389	.5056	.6722	.8389
3	.0111	.1778	.3444	.5111	.6778	.8444
4	.0167	.1833	.3500	.5167	.6833	.8500
5	.0222	.1889	.3556	.5222	.6889	.8556
6	.0278	.1944	.3611	.5278	.6944	.8611
7	.0333	.2000	.3667	.5333	.7000	.8667
8	.0389	.2056	.3722	.5389	.7056	.8722
9	.0444	.2111	.3778	.5444	.7111	.8778
10	.0500	.2167	.3833	.5500	.7167	.8833
11	.0556	.2222	.3889	.5556	.7222	.8889
12	.0611	.2278	.3944	.5611	.7278	.8944
13	.0667	.2333	.4000	.5667	.7333	.9000
14	.0722	.2389	.4056	.5722	.7389	.9056
15	.0778	.2444	.4111	.5778	.7444	.9111
16	.0833	.2500	.4167	.5833	.7500	.9167
17	.0889	.2556	.4222	.5889	.7556	.9222
18	.0944	.2611	.4278	.5944	.7611	.9278
19	.1000	.2667	.4333	.6000	.7667	.9333
20	.1056	.2722	.4389	.6056	.7722	.9389
21	.1111	.2778	.4444	.6111	.7778	.9444
22	.1167	.2833	.4500	.6167	.7833	.9500
23	.1222	.2889	.4556	.6222	.7889	.9556
24	.1278	.2944	.4611	.6278	.7945	.9611
25	.1333	.3000	.4667	.6333	.8000	.9667
26	.1389	.3056	.4722	.6389	.8056	.9722
27	.1444	.3111	.4778	.6444	.8111	.9778
28	.1500	.3167	.4833	.6500	.8167	.9833
29	.1556	.3222	.4889	.6556	.8222	.9889
30	.1611	.3278	.4944	.6611	.8278	.9944

SECURITY TITLE
INSURANCE COMPANY

HOW TO USE YOUR PERCENTAGE TABLES

TAX ADJUSTMENT TABLE

Multiply tax amount by percentage figure shown in table on pro-ration date. Example: Second half taxes $140 not paid; documents recorded March 15. Multiply $140 by .4111 = $57.55. Debit seller and credit buyer. (Also see Tax Pro-Ration on Page 37.)

INSURANCE TABLES
(Pages 28 to 31)

Multiply **paid-up** policy premium by percentage figure shown in table. Example: Premium $80; on pro-ration date, policy has 15 months, 10 days to run. Multiply $80 by .4259 = $34.07. Credit seller and debit buyer.

(Note: Insurance Tables on Pages 28-31 apply to 36-month policies only. For 39-month policies, follow same procedure and multiply result by .9231.)

5-YEAR INSURANCE TABLE

Add percentage figures in each column and multiply **paid** policy premium by total. Example: On established pro-ration date, policy has 2 years, 7 months, 19 days to run; paid premium is $80. Add .4000, .1167, and .0106; total .5273. Multiply paid premium of $80 by .5273 = $42.18. Credit seller and debit buyer.

MONTHLY PERCENTAGE TABLE

DAY	MONTHS 30 DAYS	31 DAYS
1	.0333	.0323
2	.0667	.0645
3	.1000	.0968
4	.1333	.1290
5	.1667	.1613
6	.2000	.1935
7	.2333	.2258
8	.2667	.2581
9	.3000	.2903
10	.3333	.3226
11	.3667	.3543
12	.4000	.3871
13	.4333	.4194
14	.4667	.4516
15	.5000	.4839
16	.5333	.5161
17	.5667	.5484
18	.6000	.5806
19	.6333	.6129
20	.6667	.6452
21	.7000	.6774
22	.7333	.7097
23	.7667	.7419
24	.8000	.7742
25	.8333	.8065
26	.8667	.8387
27	.9000	.8710
28	.9333	.9032
29	.9667	.9355
30		.9677

5 YEAR INSURANCE TABLE

	FIVE YEARS		
	YEARS	MONTHS	DAYS
1	.2000	.0167	.0006
2	.4000	.0333	.0011
3	.6000	.0500	.0017
4	.8000	.0667	.0022
5	1.0000	.0833	.0028
6		.1000	.0033
7		.1167	.0039
8		.1333	.0044
9		.1500	.0050
10		.1667	.0056
11		.1833	.0061
12		.2000	.0067
13			.0072
14			.0078
15			.0083
16			.0089
17			.0094
18			.0100
19			.0106
20			.0111
21			.0117
22			.0122
23			.0128
24			.0133
25			.0139
26			.0144
27			.0150
28			.0156
29			.0161
30			.0167

SECURITY TITLE
INSURANCE COMPANY

30-DAY RENTAL TABLE
PER MONTH

DAYS	40.00	41.00	42.00	42.50	43.00	44.00	45.00	46.00	DAYS
1	1.33	1.36	1.40	1.42	1.43	1.46	1.50	1.53	1
2	2.67	2.73	2.80	2.83	2.87	2.93	3.00	3.07	2
3	4.00	4.10	4.20	4.25	4.30	4.40	4.50	4.60	3
4	5.33	5.46	5.60	5.67	5.73	5.86	6.00	6.13	4
5	6.67	6.84	7.00	7.08	7.17	7.33	7.50	7.67	5
6	8.00	8.20	8.40	8.50	8.60	8.80	9.00	9.20	6
7	9.33	9.56	9.80	9.92	10.03	10.26	10.50	10.73	7
8	10.67	10.93	11.20	11.33	11.47	11.73	12.00	12.27	8
9	12.00	12.30	12.60	12.75	12.90	13.20	13.50	13.80	9
10	13.33	13.66	14.00	14.17	14.33	14.66	15.00	15.33	10
11	14.67	15.03	15.40	15.58	15.77	16.13	16.50	16.87	11
12	16.00	16.40	16.80	17.00	17.20	17.60	18.00	18.40	12
13	17.33	17.76	18.20	18.42	18.63	19.06	19.50	19.93	13
14	18.67	19.13	19.60	19.83	20.07	20.53	21.00	21.47	14
15	20.00	20.50	21.00	21.25	21.50	22.00	22.50	23.00	15
16	21.33	21.86	22.40	22.67	22.93	23.46	24.00	24.53	16
17	22.67	23.23	23.80	24.08	24.37	24.93	25.50	26.07	17
18	24.00	24.60	25.20	25.50	25.80	26.40	27.00	27.60	18
19	25.33	25.96	26.60	26.92	27.23	27.86	28.50	29.13	19
20	26.67	27.33	28.00	28.33	28.67	29.33	30.00	30.67	20
21	28.00	28.70	29.40	29.75	30.10	30.80	31.50	32.20	21
22	29.33	30.06	30.80	31.17	31.53	32.26	33.00	33.73	22
23	30.67	31.43	32.20	32.58	32.97	33.63	34.50	35.27	23
24	32.00	32.80	33.60	34.00	34.40	35.20	36.00	36.80	24
25	33.33	34.16	35.00	35.42	35.83	36.66	37.50	38.33	25
26	34.67	35.54	36.40	36.83	37.27	38.13	39.00	39.87	26
27	36.00	36.90	37.80	38.25	38.70	39.60	40.50	41.40	27
28	37.33	38.26	39.20	39.67	40.13	41.06	42.00	42.93	28
29	38.67	39.43	40.60	41.08	41.57	42.53	43.50	44.47	29

SECURITY TITLE
INSURANCE COMPANY

30-DAY RENTAL TABLE

PER MONTH

DAYS	33.00	34.00	35.00	36.00	37.00	37.50	38.00	39.00	DAYS
1	1.10	1.13	1.17	1.20	1.23	1.25	1.27	1.30	1
2	2.20	2.27	2.33	2.40	2.47	2.50	2.53	2.60	2
3	3.30	3.40	3.50	3.60	3.70	3.75	3.80	3.90	3
4	4.40	4.53	4.67	4.80	4.93	5.00	5.07	5.20	4
5	5.50	5.67	5.83	6.00	6.17	6.25	6.34	6.50	5
6	6.60	6.80	7.00	7.20	7.40	7.50	7.60	7.80	6
7	7.70	7.93	8.17	8.40	8.63	8.75	8.87	9.10	7
8	8.80	9.07	9.33	9.60	9.87	10.00	10.13	10.40	8
9	9.90	10.20	10.50	10.80	11.10	11.25	11.40	11.70	9
10	11.00	11.33	11.67	12.00	12.33	12.50	12.66	13.00	10
11	12.10	12.47	12.83	13.20	13.57	13.75	13.93	14.30	11
12	13.20	13.60	14.00	14.40	14.80	15.00	15.20	15.60	12
13	14.30	14.73	15.17	15.60	16.03	16.25	16.46	16.90	13
14	15.40	15.87	16.33	16.80	17.27	17.50	17.73	18.20	14
15	16.50	17.00	17.50	18.00	18.50	18.75	19.00	19.50	15
16	17.60	18.13	18.67	19.20	19.73	20.00	20.26	20.80	16
17	18.70	19.27	19.83	20.40	20.97	21.25	21.53	22.10	17
18	19.80	20.40	21.00	21.60	22.20	22.50	22.80	23.40	18
19	20.90	21.53	22.17	22.80	23.43	23.75	24.06	24.70	19
20	22.00	22.67	23.33	24.00	24.67	25.00	25.33	26.00	20
21	23.10	23.80	24.50	25.20	25.90	26.25	26.60	27.30	21
22	24.20	24.93	25.67	26.40	27.13	27.50	27.86	28.60	22
23	25.30	26 07	26.83	27.60	28.37	28.75	29.13	29.90	23
24	26.40	27.20	28.00	28.80	29.60	30.00	30.40	31.20	24
25	27.50	28.33	29.17	30.00	30.83	31.25	31.66	32.50	25
26	28.60	29.47	30.33	31.20	32.07	32.50	32.93	33.80	26
27	29.70	30.60	31.50	32.40	33.30	33.75	34.20	35.10	27
28	30.80	31.73	32.67	33.60	34.53	35.00	35.46	36.40	28
29	31.90	32.87	33.83	34.80	35.77	36.25	36.73	37.70	29

SECURITY TITLE

INSURANCE COMPANY

INSURANCE TABLE

0 to 8 Months

(3-YEAR POLICIES)

DAYS	0	1	2	3	4	5	6	7	8
0	.0000	.0278	.0556	.0833	.1111	.1389	.1667	.1944	.2222
1	.0009	.0287	.0565	.0843	.1120	.1398	.1676	.1954	.2231
2	.0019	.0296	.0574	.0852	.1130	.1407	.1685	.1963	.2241
3	.0028	.0306	.0583	.0861	.1139	.1417	.1694	.1972	.2250
4	.0037	.0315	.0593	.0870	.1148	.1426	.1704	.1981	2259
5	.0046	.0324	.0602	.0880	.1157	.1435	.1713	.1991	.2269
6	.0056	.0333	.0611	.0889	.1167	.1444	.1722	.2000	.2278
7	.0065	.0343	.0620	.0898	.1176	.1454	.1731	.2009	.2287
8	.0074	.0352	.0630	.0907	.1185	.1463	.1741	.2019	.2296
9	.0083	.0361	.0639	.0917	.1194	.1472	.1750	.2028	.2306
10	.0093	.0370	.0648	.0926	.1204	.1481	.1759	.2037	.2315
11	.0102	.0380	.0657	.0935	.1213	.1491	.1769	.2046	.2324
12	.0111	.0389	.0667	.0944	.1222	.1500	.1778	.2056	.2333
13	.0120	.0398	.0676	.0954	.1231	.1509	.1787	.2065	.2343
14	.0130	.0407	.0685	.0963	.1241	.1519	.1796	.2074	.2352
15	.0139	.0417	.0694	.0972	.1250	.1528	.1806	.2083	.2361
16	.0148	.0426	.0704	.0981	.1259	.1537	.1815	.2093	.2370
17	.0157	.0435	.0713	.0991	.1269	.1546	.1824	.2102	.2380
18	.0167	.0444	.0722	.1000	.1278	.1556	.1833	.2111	.2389
19	.0176	.0454	.0731	.1009	.1287	.1565	.1843	.2120	.2398
20	.0185	.0463	.0741	.1019	.1296	.1574	.1852	.2130	.2407
21	.0194	.0472	.0750	.1028	.1306	.1583	.1861	.2139	.2417
22	.0204	.0481	.0759	.1037	.1315	.1593	.1870	.2148	.2426
23	.0213	.0491	.0769	.1046	.1324	.1602	.1880	.2157	.2435
24	.0222	.0500	.0778	.1056	.1333	.1611	.1889	.2167	.2444
25	.0231	.0509	.0787	.1065	.1343	.1620	.1898	.2176	.2454
26	.0241	.0519	.0796	.1074	.1352	.1630	.1907	.2185	.2463
27	.0250	.0528	.0806	.1083	.1361	.1639	.1917	.2194	.2472
28	.0259	.0537	.0815	.1093	.1370	.1648	.1926	.2204	.2481
29	.0269	.0546	.0824	.1102	.1380	.1657	.1935	.2213	.2491

SECURITY TITLE

INSURANCE COMPANY

INSURANCE TABLE

9 to 17 Months (3-YEAR POLICIES)

DAYS	9	10	11	12	13	14	15	16	17
0	.2500	.2778	.3056	.3333	.3611	.3889	.4167	.4444	.4722
1	.2509	.2787	.3065	.3343	.3620	.3898	.4176	.4454	.4731
2	.2519	.2796	.3074	.3352	.3630	.3907	.4185	.4463	.4741
3	.2528	.2806	.3083	.3361	.3639	.3917	.4194	.4472	.4750
4	.2537	.2815	.3093	.3370	.3648	.3926	.4204	.4481	.4759
5	.2546	.2824	.3102	.3380	.3657	.3935	.4213	.4491	.4769
6	.2556	.2833	.3111	.3389	.3667	.3944	.4222	.4500	.4778
7	.2565	.2843	.3120	.3399	.3676	.3954	.4231	.4509	.4787
8	.2574	.2852	.3130	.3407	.3685	.3963	.4241	.4519	.4796
9	.2583	.2861	.3139	.3417	.3694	.3972	.4250	.4528	.4806
10	.2593	.2870	.3148	.3426	.3704	.3981	.4259	.4537	.4815
11	.2602	.2880	.3157	.3435	.3713	.3991	.4269	.4546	.4824
12	.2611	.2889	.3167	.3444	.3722	.4000	.4278	.4556	.4833
13	.2620	.2898	.3176	.3454	.3731	.4009	.4287	.4565	.4843
14	.2630	.2907	.3185	.3463	.3741	.4019	.4296	.4574	.4852
15	.2639	.2917	.3194	.3472	.3750	.4028	.4306	.4583	.4861
16	.2648	.2926	.3204	.3481	.3759	.4037	.4315	.4593	.4870
17	.2657	.2935	.3213	.3491	.3769	.4046	.4324	.4602	.4880
18	.2667	.2944	.3222	.3500	.3778	.4056	.4333	.4611	.4889
19	.2676	.2954	.3231	.3509	.3787	.4065	.4343	.4620	.4898
20	.2685	.2963	.3241	.3519	.3796	.4074	.4352	.4630	.4907
21	.2694	.2972	.3250	.3528	.3806	.4083	.4361	.4639	.4917
22	.2704	.2981	.3259	.3537	.3815	.4093	.4370	.4648	.4926
23	.2713	.2991	.3269	.3546	.3824	.4102	.4380	.4657	.4935
24	.2722	.3000	.3278	.3556	.3833	.4111	.4389	.4667	.4944
25	.2731	.3009	.3287	.3565	.3843	.4120	.4398	.4676	.4954
26	.2741	.3019	.3296	.3574	.3852	.4130	.4407	.4685	.4963
27	.2750	.3028	.3306	.3583	.3861	.4139	.4417	.4694	.4972
28	.2759	.3037	.3315	.3593	.3870	.4148	.4426	.4704	.4981
29	.2769	.3046	.3324	.3602	.3880	.4158	.4435	.4713	.4991

30-DAY RENTAL TABLE

PER MONTH

DAYS	27.00	27.50	28.00	29.00	30.00	31.00	32.00	32.50	DAYS
1	.90	.92	.93	.97	1.00	1.03	1.07	1.08	1
2	1.80	1.83	1.87	1.93	2.00	2.07	2.13	2.17	2
3	2.70	2.75	2.80	2.90	3.00	3.10	3.20	3.25	3
4	3.60	3.67	3.73	3.87	4.00	4.13	4.27	4.33	4
5	4.50	4.58	4.67	4.83	5.00	5.17	5.33	5.42	5
6	5.40	5.50	5.60	5.80	6.00	6.20	6.40	6.50	6
7	6.30	6.42	6.53	6.77	7.00	7.23	7.47	7.58	7
8	7.20	7.33	7.47	7.73	8.00	8.27	8.53	8.67	8
9	8.10	8.25	8.40	8.70	9.00	9.30	9.60	9.75	9
10	9.00	9.17	9.33	9.67	10.00	10.33	10.67	10.83	10
11	9.90	10.08	10.27	10.63	11.00	11.37	11.73	11.92	11
12	10.80	11.00	11.20	11.60	12.00	12.40	12.80	13.00	12
13	11.70	11.92	12.13	12.57	13.00	13.43	13.87	14.08	13
14	12.60	12.83	13.07	13.53	14.00	14.47	14.93	15.17	14
15	13.50	13.75	14.00	14.50	15.00	15.50	16.00	16.25	15
16	14.40	14.67	14.93	15.47	16.00	16.53	17.07	17.33	16
17	15.30	15.58	15.87	16.43	17.00	17.57	18.13	18.42	17
18	16.20	16.50	16.80	17.40	18.00	18.60	19.20	19.50	18
19	17.10	17.42	17.73	18.37	19.00	19.63	20.27	20.58	19
20	18.00	18.33	18.67	19.33	20.00	20.67	21.33	21.67	20
21	18.90	19.25	19.60	20.30	21.00	21.70	22.40	22.75	21
22	19.80	20.17	20.53	21.27	22.00	22.73	23.47	23.83	22
23	20.70	21.08	21.47	22.23	23.00	23.77	24.53	24.92	23
24	21.60	22.00	22.40	23.20	24.00	24.80	25.60	26.00	24
25	22.50	22.92	23.33	24.17	25.00	25.83	26.67	27.08	25
26	23.40	23.83	24.27	25.17	26.00	26.87	27.73	28.17	26
27	24.30	24.75	25.20	26.10	27.00	27.90	28.80	29.25	27
28	25.20	25.67	26.13	27.07	28.00	28.93	29.87	30.33	28
29	26.10	26.58	27.07	28.03	29.00	29.97	30.93	31.42	29

30-DAY RENTAL TABLE

PER MONTH

DAYS	20.00	21.00	22.00	22.50	23.00	24.00	25.00	26.00	DAYS
1	.67	.70	.73	.74	.77	.80	.83	.87	1
2	1.33	1.40	1.47	1.50	1.53	1.60	1.63	1.73	2
3	2.00	2.10	2.20	2.25	2.30	2.40	2.50	2.60	3
4	2.67	2.80	2.93	3.00	3.06	3.20	3.33	3.47	4
5	3.33	3.50	3.67	3.75	3.83	4.00	4.17	4.33	5
6	4.00	4.20	4.40	4.50	4.60	4.80	5.00	5.20	6
7	4.67	4.90	5.13	5.25	5.37	5.60	5.83	6.07	7
8	5.33	5.60	5.87	6.00	6.13	6.40	6.66	6.93	8
9	6.00	6.30	6.60	6.75	6.90	7.20	7.50	7.80	9
10	6.67	7.00	7.33	7.50	7.67	8.00	8.33	8.67	10
11	7.33	7.70	8.07	8.25	8.43	8.80	9.17	9.53	11
12	8.00	8.40	8.80	9.00	9.20	9.60	10.00	10.40	12
13	8.67	9.10	9.53	9.75	9.97	10.40	10.83	11.27	13
14	9.33	9.80	10.27	10.50	10.73	11.20	11.67	12.13	14
15	10.00	10.50	11.00	11.25	11.50	12.00	12.50	13.00	15
16	10.67	11.20	11.73	12.00	12.27	12.80	13.33	13.87	16
17	11.33	11.90	12.47	12.75	13.03	13.60	14.17	14.73	17
18	12.00	12.60	13.20	13.50	13.80	14.40	15.00	15.60	18
19	12.67	13.30	13.93	14.25	14.57	15.20	15.83	16.47	19
20	13.33	14.00	14.67	15.00	15.33	16.00	16.67	17.33	20
21	14.00	14.70	15.40	15.75	16.10	16.80	17.50	18.20	21
22	14.67	15.40	16.13	16.50	16.87	17.60	18.33	19.07	22
23	15.33	16.10	16.87	17.25	17.64	18.40	19.17	19.93	23
24	16.00	16.80	17.60	18.00	18.40	19.20	20.00	20.80	24
25	16.67	17.50	18.33	18.75	19.17	20.00	20.83	21.67	25
26	17.33	18.20	19.07	19.50	19.93	20.80	21.67	22.53	26
27	18.00	18.90	19.80	20.25	20.70	21.60	22.50	23.40	27
28	18.67	19.60	20.53	21.00	21.47	22.40	23.33	24.27	28
29	19.33	20.30	21.27	21.75	22.23	23.20	24.17	25.13	29

SECURITY TITLE

INSURANCE COMPANY

INSURANCE TABLE

18 to 26 Months (3-YEAR POLICIES)

DAYS	18	19	20	21	22	23	24	25	26
0	.5000	.5278	.5556	.5833	.6111	.6389	.6667	.6944	.7222
1	.5009	.5287	.5565	.5843	.6120	.6398	.6676	.6953	.7231
2	.5019	.5296	.5574	.5852	.6130	.6407	.6685	.6963	.7241
3	.5028	.5306	.5583	.5861	.6139	.6417	.6694	.6972	.7250
4	.5037	.5315	.5593	.5870	.6148	.6426	.6704	.6981	.7259
5	.5046	.5324	.5602	.5880	.6157	.6435	.6713	.6991	.7269
6	.5056	.5333	.5611	.5889	.6167	.6444	.6722	7000	.7278
7	.5065	.5343	.5620	.5898	.6176	.6454	.6731	.7009	.7287
8	.5074	.5352	.5630	.5907	.6185	.6463	.6741	.7019	.7296
9	.5083	.5361	.5639	.5917	.6194	.6472	.6750	.7028	.7306
10	.5093	.5370	.5648	.5926	.6204	.6481	.6759	.7037	.7315
11	.5102	.5380	.5657	.5935	.6213	.6491	.6769	.7046	.7324
12	.5111	.5389	.5667	.5944	.6222	.6500	.6778	.7056	.7333
13	.5120	.5398	.5676	.5954	.6231	.6509	.6787	.7065	.7343
14	.5130	.5407	.5685	.5963	.6241	.6519	.6796	.7074	.7352
15	.5139	.5417	.5694	.5972	.6250	.6528	.6806	.7083	.7361
16	.5146	.5426	.5704	.5981	.6259	.6537	.6815	.7093	.7370
17	.5157	.5435	.5713	.5991	.6269	.6546	.6824	.7102	.7380
18	.5167	.5444	.5722	.6000	.6278	.6556	.6833	.7111	.7389
19	.5176	.5454	.5731	.6009	.6287	.6565	.6843	.7120	.7398
20	.5185	.5463	.5741	.6019	.6296	.6574	.6852	.7130	.7407
21	.5194	.5472	.5750	.6028	.6306	.6583	.6861	.7139	.7417
22	.5204	.5481	.5759	.6037	.6315	.6593	.6870	.7148	.7426
23	.5213	.5491	.5769	.6046	.6324	.6602	.6880	.7157	.7435
24	.5222	.5500	.5778	.6056	.6333	.6611	.6889	.7167	.7444
25	.5231	.5509	.5787	.6065	.6343	.6620	.6898	.7176	.7454
26	.5241	.5519	.5796	.6074	.6352	.6630	.6907	.7185	.7463
27	.5250	.5528	.5806	.6083	.6361	.6639	.6917	.7194	.7472
28	.5259	.5537	.5815	.6093	.6370	.6648	.6926	.7204	.7481
29	.5269	.5546	.5824	.6102	.6380	.6657	.6935	.7213	.7491

SECURITY TITLE

INSURANCE COMPANY

INSURANCE TABLE

27 to 35 Months (3-YEAR POLICIES)

DAYS	27	28	29	30	31	32	33	34	35
0	.7500	.7778	.8056	.8333	.8611	.8889	.9167	.9444	.9722
1	.7509	.7787	.8065	.8343	.8620	.8898	.9176	.9454	.9731
2	.7519	.7796	.8074	.8352	.8630	.8907	.9185	.9463	.9741
3	.7528	.7806	.8083	.8361	.8639	.8917	.9194	.9472	.9750
4	.7537	.7815	.8093	.8370	.8648	.8926	.9204	.9481	.9759
5	.7546	.7824	.8102	.8380	.8657	.8935	.9213	.9491	.9769
6	.7556	.7833	.8111	.8389	.8667	.8944	.9222	.9500	.9778
7	.7565	.7843	.8120	.8398	.8676	.8954	.9231	.9509	.9787
8	.7574	.7852	.8130	.8407	.8685	.8963	.9241	.9519	.9796
9	.7583	.7861	.8139	.8417	.8694	.8972	.9250	.9528	.9806
10	.7593	.7870	.8148	.8426	.8704	.8981	.9259	.9537	.9815
11	.7602	.7880	.8157	.8435	.8713	.8991	.9269	.9546	.9824
12	.7611	.7889	.8167	.8444	.8722	.9000	.9278	.9556	.9833
13	.7620	.7898	.8176	.8454	.8731	.9009	.9287	.9565	.9843
14	.7630	.7907	.8185	.8463	.8741	.9019	.9296	.9574	.9852
15	.7639	.7917	.8194	.8472	.8750	.9028	.9306	.9583	.9861
16	.7648	.7926	.8204	.8481	.8759	.9037	.9315	.9593	.9870
17	.7657	.7935	.8213	.8491	.8769	.9046	.9324	.9602	.9880
18	.7667	.7944	.8222	.8500	.8778	.9056	.9333	.9611	.9889
19	.7676	.7954	.8231	.8509	.8787	.9065	.9343	.9620	.9898
20	.7685	.7963	.8241	.8519	.8796	.9074	.9352	.9630	.9907
21	.7694	.7972	.8250	.8528	.8806	.9083	.9361	.9639	.9917
22	.7704	.7981	.8259	.8537	.8815	.9093	.9370	.9648	.9926
23	.7713	.7991	.8269	.8546	.8824	.9102	.9380	.9657	.9935
24	.7722	.8000	.8278	.8556	.8833	.9111	.9389	.9667	.9944
25	.7731	.8009	.8287	.8565	.8843	.9120	.9398	.9676	.9954
26	.7741	.8019	.8296	.8574	.8852	.9130	.9407	.9685	.9963
27	.7750	.8028	.8306	.8583	.8861	.9139	.9417	.9694	.9972
28	.7759	.8037	.8315	.8593	.8870	.9148	.9426	.9704	.9981
29	.7769	.8046	.8324	.8602	.8880	.9157	.9435	.9713	.9991

SECURITY TITLE

INSURANCE COMPANY

30-DAY RENTAL TABLE

PER MONTH

DAYS	13.00	14.00	15.00	16.00	17.00	17.50	18.00	19.00	DAYS
1	.43	.47	.50	.53	.57	.58	.60	.63	1
2	.87	.94	1.00	1.06	1.13	1.17	1.19	1.27	2
3	1.30	1.40	1.50	1.60	1.70	1.75	1.80	1.90	3
4	1.73	1.87	2.00	2.13	2.27	2.33	2.40	2.53	4
5	2.17	2.34	2.50	2.66	2.83	2.92	3.00	3.17	5
6	2.60	2.80	3.00	3.20	3.40	3.50	3.60	3.80	6
7	3.03	3.27	3.50	3.73	3.97	4.08	4.20	4.43	7
8	3.46	3.74	4.00	4.26	4.54	4.67	4.80	5.07	8
9	3.90	4.20	4.50	4.80	5.10	5.25	5.40	5.70	9
10	4.33	4.67	5.00	5.33	5.67	5.83	6.00	6.33	10
11	4.76	5.14	5.50	5.87	6.23	6.42	6.60	6.97	11
12	5.20	5.60	6.00	6.40	6.80	7.00	7.20	7.60	12
13	5.63	6.07	6.50	6.93	7.37	7.58	7.80	8.23	13
14	6.06	6.54	7.00	7.47	7.93	8.16	8.40	8.87	14
15	6.50	7.00	7.50	8.00	8.50	8.75	9.00	9.50	15
16	6.93	7.47	8.00	8.53	9.07	9.33	9.60	10.13	16
17	7.36	7.94	8.50	9.07	9.63	9.92	10.20	10.77	17
18	7.80	8.40	9.00	9.60	10.20	10.50	10.80	11.40	18
18	8.25	8.87	9.50	10.13	10.77	11.08	11.40	12.03	19
20	8.67	9.34	10.00	10.67	11.34	11.67	12.00	12.67	20
21	9.09	9.80	10.50	11.20	11.90	12.25	12.60	13.30	21
22	9.53	10.27	11.00	11.73	12.47	12.83	13.20	13.93	22
23	9.96	10.74	11.50	12.27	13.03	13.42	13.80	14.57	23
24	10.39	11.20	12.00	12.80	13.60	14.00	14.40	15.20	24
25	10.83	11.67	12.50	13.33	14.17	14.58	15.00	15.83	25
26	11.26	12.14	13.00	13.87	14.73	15.17	15.60	16.47	26
27	11.69	12.60	13.50	14.40	15.30	15.75	16.20	17.10	27
28	12.12	13.07	14.00	14.93	15.87	16.33	16.80	17.73	28
29	12.57	13.53	14.50	15.47	16.43	16.92	17.40	18.37	29

SECURITY TITLE

INSURANCE COMPANY

30-DAY RENTAL TABLE

PER MONTH

DAYS	7.00	7.50	8.00	9.00	10.00	11.00	12.00	12.50	DAYS
1	.23	.25	.27	.30	.33	.37	.40	.42	1
2	.47	.50	.54	.60	.67	.74	.80	.84	2
3	.70	.75	.80	.90	1.00	1.10	1.20	1.25	3
4	.93	1.00	1.07	1.20	1.33	1.47	1.60	1.67	4
5	1.17	1.25	1.33	1.50	1.67	1.83	2.00	2.09	5
6	1.40	1.50	1.60	1.80	2.00	2.20	2.40	2.50	6
7	1.63	1.75	1.87	2.10	2.33	2.57	2.80	2.92	7
8	1.86	2.00	2.13	2.40	2.66	2.93	3.20	3.34	8
9	2.10	2.25	2.40	2.70	3.00	3.30	3.60	3.75	9
10	2.33	2.50	2.66	3.00	3.33	3.66	4.00	4.17	10
11	2.56	2.75	2.93	3.30	3.66	4.03	4.40	4.59	11
12	2.80	3.00	3.20	3.60	4.00	4.40	4.80	5.00	12
13	3.03	3.25	3.46	3.90	4.33	4.76	5.20	5.42	13
14	3.26	3.50	3.73	4.20	4.66	5.13	5.60	5.84	14
15	3.50	3.75	3.99	4.50	5.00	5.49	6.00	6.25	15
16	3.73	4.00	4.26	4.80	5.33	5.86	6.40	6.67	16
17	3.96	4.25	4.53	5.10	5.66	6.23	6.80	7.09	17
18	4.19	4.50	4.79	5.40	5.99	6.59	7.20	7.50	18
19	4.43	4.75	5.06	5.70	6.33	6.96	7.60	7.92	19
20	4.66	5.00	5.32	6.00	6.66	7.32	8.00	8.34	20
21	4.89	5.25	5.59	6.30	6.99	7.69	8.40	8.75	21
22	5.13	5.50	5.86	6.60	7.33	8.06	8.80	9.17	22
23	5.36	5.75	6.12	6.90	7.66	8.42	9.20	9.59	23
24	5.59	6.00	6.39	7.20	7.99	8.79	9.60	10.00	24
25	5.83	6.25	6.65	7.50	8.33	9.15	10.00	10.42	25
26	6.06	6.50	6.92	7.80	8.66	9.52	10.40	10.84	26
27	6.29	6.75	7.19	8.10	8.99	9.89	10.80	11.25	27
28	6.52	7.00	7.45	8.40	9.32	10.25	11.20	11.67	28
29	6.77	7.25	7.73	8.70	9.67	10.63	11.60	12.08	29

SECURITY TITLE
INSURANCE COMPANY

ONE YEAR PRORATION TABLE

(For Personal Property Tax, 1-Year Insurance Policies, etc.)

DAYS \ MOS.	0	1	2	3	4	5
0		.0833	.1667	.2500	.3333	.4167
1	.0028	.0861	.1694	.2528	.3361	.4194
2	.0056	.0889	.1722	.2556	.3389	.4222
3	.0083	.0917	.1750	.2583	.3417	.4250
4	.0111	.0944	.1778	.2611	.3444	.4278
5	.0139	.0972	.1806	.2639	.3472	.4306
6	.0167	.1000	.1833	.2667	.3500	.4333
7	.0194	.1027	.1861	.2694	.3528	.4361
8	.0222	.1055	.1889	.2722	.3556	.4389
9	.0250	.1083	.1917	.2750	.3583	.4417
10	.0278	.1111	.1944	.2778	.3611	.4444
11	.0306	.1139	.1972	.2806	.3639	.4472
12	.0333	.1167	.2000	.2833	.3667	.4500
13	.0361	.1194	.2028	.2861	.3694	.4528
14	.0389	.1222	.2056	.2889	.3722	.4556
15	.0417	.1250	.2083	.2917	.3750	.4583
16	.0444	.1278	.2111	.2944	.3778	.4611
17	.0472	.1306	.2139	.2972	.3806	.4639
18	.0500	.1333	.2167	.3000	.3833	.4667
19	.0528	.1361	.2194	.3028	.3861	.4694
20	.0556	.1389	.2222	.3056	.3889	.4722
21	.0583	.1417	.2250	.3083	.3917	.4750
22	.0611	.1444	.2278	.3111	.3944	.4778
23	.0639	.1472	.2306	.3139	.3972	.4806
24	.0667	.1500	.2333	.3167	.4000	.4833
25	.0694	.1528	.2361	.3194	.4028	.4861
26	.0722	.1556	.2389	.3222	.4056	.4889
27	.0750	.1583	.2417	.3250	.4083	.4917
28	.0778	.1611	.2444	.3278	.4111	.4944
29	.0806	.1639	.2472	.3306	.4139	.4972
30	.0833	.1667	.2500	.3333	.4167	.5000

SECURITY TITLE
INSURANCE COMPANY

ONE YEAR PRORATION TABLE

(For Personal Property Tax, 1-Year Insurance Policies, etc.)

DAYS \ MOS.	6	7	8	9	10	11
0	.5000	.5833	.6667	.7500	.8333	.9167
1	.5028	.5861	.6694	.7528	.8361	.9194
2	.5056	.5889	.6722	.7556	.8389	.9222
3	.5083	.5917	.6750	.7583	.8417	.9250
4	.5111	.5944	.6778	.7611	.8444	.9278
5	.5139	.5972	.6806	.7639	.8472	.9306
6	.5167	.6000	.6833	.7667	.8500	.9333
7	.5194	.6028	.6861	.7694	.8528	.9361
8	.5222	.6056	.6889	.7722	.8556	.9389
9	.5250	.6083	.6917	.7750	.8583	.9417
10	.5278	.6111	.6944	.7778	.8611	.9444
11	.5306	.6139	.6972	.7806	.8639	.9472
12	.5333	.6167	.7000	.7833	.8667	.9500
13	.5361	.6194	.7028	.7861	.8694	.9528
14	.5389	.6222	.7056	.7889	.8722	.9556
15	.5417	.6250	.7083	.7917	.8750	.9583
16	.5444	.6278	.7111	.7944	.8778	.9611
17	.5472	.6306	.7139	.7972	.8806	.9639
18	.5500	.6333	.7167	.8000	.8833	.9667
19	.5528	.6361	.7194	.8028	.8861	.9694
20	.5556	.6389	.7222	.8056	.8889	.9722
21	.5583	.6417	.7250	.8033	.8917	.9750
22	.5611	.6444	.7278	.8111	.8944	.9778
23	.5639	.6472	.7306	.8139	.8972	.9806
24	.5667	.6500	.7333	.8167	.9000	.9833
25	.5694	.6528	.7361	.8194	.9028	.9861
26	.5722	.6556	.7389	.8222	.9056	.9889
27	.5750	.6583	.7417	.8250	.9083	.9917
28	.5778	.6611	.7444	.8278	.9111	.9944
29	.5806	.6639	.7472	.8306	.9139	.9972
30	.5833	.6667	.7500	.8333	.9167	1.0000

SECURITY TITLE
INSURANCE COMPANY

30-DAY RENTAL TABLE

PER MONTH

DAYS	.50	1.00	2.00	2.50	3.00	4.00	5.00	6.00	DAYS
1	.02	.03	.07	.08	.10	.13	.17	.20	1
2	.03	.07	.14	.16	.20	.26	.34	.40	2
3	.05	.10	.20	.25	.30	.40	.50	.60	3
4	.07	.13	.27	.33	.40	.53	.67	.80	4
5	.08	.17	.33	.41	.50	.66	.83	1.00	5
6	.10	.20	.40	.50	.60	.80	1.00	1.20	6
7	.12	.23	.47	.58	.70	.93	1.17	1.40	7
8	.13	.26	.53	.66	.80	1.06	1.33	1.60	8
9	.15	.30	.60	.74	.90	1.19	1.50	1.80	9
10	.17	.33	.66	.83	1.00	1.33	1.66	2.00	10
11	.18	.36	.73	.91	1.10	1.46	1.83	2.20	11
12	.20	.40	.80	.99	1.20	1.59	2.00	2.40	12
13	.22	.43	.86	1.08	1.30	1.73	2.16	2.60	13
14	.23	.46	.93	1.16	1.40	1.86	2.33	2.80	14
15	.25	.50	.99	1.24	1.50	1.99	2.49	3.00	15
16	.27	.53	1.06	1.33	1.60	2.13	2.66	3.20	16
17	.28	.56	1.13	1.41	1.70	2.26	2.83	3.40	17
18	.30	.59	1.19	1.49	1.80	2.39	2.99	3.60	18
19	.32	.63	1.26	1.57	1.90	2.52	3.16	3.80	19
20	.34	.66	1.32	1.66	2.00	2.66	3.32	4.00	20
21	.35	.69	1.39	1.74	2.10	2.79	3.49	4.20	21
22	.37	.73	1.46	1.82	2.20	2.92	3.66	4.40	22
23	.38	.76	1.52	1.91	2.30	3.06	3.82	4.60	23
24	.40	.79	1.59	1.99	2.40	3.19	3.99	4.80	24
25	.42	.83	1.65	2.07	2.50	3.32	4.15	5.00	25
26	.43	.86	1.72	2.16	2.60	3.46	4.32	5.20	26
27	.45	.89	1.79	2.24	2.70	3.59	4.49	5.40	27
28	.47	.92	1.85	2.32	2.80	3.72	4.65	5.60	28
29	.48	.97	1.93	2.42	2.90	3.87	4.83	5.80	29

SECURITY TITLE
INSURANCE COMPANY

Index

A

D

I

J

K

L

S

T